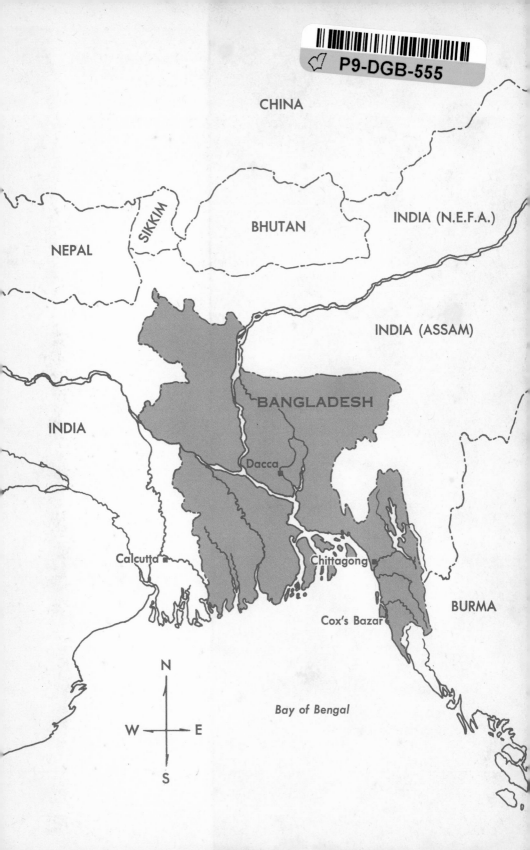

DAKTAR / DIPLOMAT
IN BANGLADESH

DAKTAR / DIPLOMAT
IN BANGLADESH

By

Viggo B. Olsen, M. D.

with

Jeanette Lockerbie

MOODY PRESS
CHICAGO

TO

my Bengali brothers and sisters who suffered so much to gain nationhood—to achieve Bangladesh! May they produce the society for which they yearn, described in their constitution as "a society in which the rule of law, fundamental human rights and freedom, equality, and justice, political, economic, and social, will be secured for all citizens."

© 1973 by

THE MOODY BIBLE INSTITUTE

OF CHICAGO

Library of Congress Catalog Card Number: 72-95021

ISBN: 0-8024-1745-0

Fifth Printing, 1974

Printed in the United States of America

CONTENTS

Introduction

Twenty years ago I first met Dr. Viggo Olsen in our church in Brooklyn, New York, where my husband was pastor. "Vic" and Joan Olsen, however, had not come to church to worship; their diabolical quest had entirely different goals and came to a startling climax during that year in New York. We became close friends of the young intern and his shiny-eyed wife.

Ten years and hundreds of surgical operations later, the Olsens transferred their lives and skills to the South Asian nation of East Pakistan, most recently reborn as Bangladesh. The account of their dedicated efforts to provide scientific, compassionate medical-surgical care to the multitudes in East Pakistan reads like a spell-binding novel. Many young men and women, including my own daughter Jeannie, willingly joined them in that herculean task. Because of this team effort, hundreds live today whose lives would have been snatched away by bullets, bayonets, cholera, malaria, and a hundred other death-dealing diseases.

Pakistan, with its east and west wings separated by eleven hundred miles of enemy territory (India), was a geographical absurdity. East Pakistanis, moreover, differed from West Pakistanis in nearly every respect: nationality, appearance, language, dress, diet, customs, and culture. Only the Islamic religion and the daily interwing flights of Pakistan International Airlines held the two disparate wings together.

East Pakistan, a subtropical, river-laced country smaller than the state of Iowa, was jampacked with 75 million citizens (twenty-five times the population of Iowa). Most East Pakistanis were Bengalis — a quick, alert, slim, volatile, poetic people. Frequently assaulted by cyclones, tidal waves, floods, and famine, they were acquainted with grief. But the Bengalis were totally unprepared for the holocaust which engulfed them in 1971 — crack West Pakistani troops pounced upon them, burning, raping, torturing, killing hundreds of thousands of men, women, and children. The Bengalis had to be

7

"put down," for they had won a national election and demanded more control over their East Pakistan affairs. With India's help, however, the jubilant Bengalis emerged victorious over the invading West Pakistan troops. The Bengali battle cry, "Joi Bangla! [Victory to Bengal!]" became a reality, and East Pakistan died a ghastly, ignominious death.

Bangladesh (Bengali nation) — the brave new country — rose from the blood-stained ashes of defunct East Pakistan. On home leave in America when the war ended in December, 1971, Dr. Olsen was quick to call and congratulate his friend, the Bangladesh ambassador to America, stationed in Washington, D.C. His first question was, "What can we do to help?" On the resultant trip to Bangladesh to confer with Prime Minister Sheikh Mujibur Rahman, he carried credentials from the Bangladesh "shadow embassy" designating him a true friend of Bangladesh. Later, Vic Olsen, by ambassadorial decree in Washington, D.C., was selected to receive visa #001 to Bangladesh — "in recognition of service to our country."

Throughout much of the uprising, the warfare and carnage that gave birth to Bangladesh, Dr. Olsen had been in action at a hospital in the southern section of the country, caring for the injured, feeding the starving, and protecting helpless Hindus from extermination. On April 10, 1971, with the civil war barely two weeks old, Bengali leaders officially declared Bangladesh the world's newest independent, sovereign nation. At that time their gesture seemed futile, for the West Pakistan war machine was already blitzing the defenseless country. Eleven days later, before units of the invading army reached them, Vic Olsen's family and team evacuated out the "back door" of stricken Bangladesh. He and colleague Dr. Donn Ketcham remained at their hospital. The next night Dr. Olsen submitted himself to the scalpel of Dr. Ketcham who repaired Vic's elbow, smashed in a strange accident. Then an unexpected message promised a night of peril for the two American surgeons who chose to remain with the Bengali people in their hour of need.

In *Daktar/Diplomat,* the doctor himself tells the exciting story of this experience, as well as the fascinating tale of his unexpected entry into the field of surgery. My own perspective comments appear in italics at various points in the book.

JEANETTE LOCKERBIE

1

Perilous Night

THE LATE AFTERNOON SUN acted wisely. It slipped through the low-lying clouds and escaped to a safer land beyond the Bay of Bengal. The time had come to face the harsh realities of night which now enveloped blood-drenched Bangladesh.

Five Bengali watchmen stood in a cluster before me on our verandah. They stood quietly. No jokes. No wisecracks. Most of their faces were impassive, but I could see the fear lurking in their eyes. I understood their fear.

"*Khawbor shunecho?* [Have you heard the news?]" I asked. All had heard something, for the "bamboo telegraph" is remarkably efficient in Bangladesh. But they wanted details; they needed to know what to expect.

I described the coming of a friend, the bearer of bad tidings, who had arrived excitedly only an hour before. "Daktar Sahib! I have terrible news for you — terrible news! The armed bandits are coming tonight to attack you and the hospital. They plan to loot all the staff houses and the hospital. Daktar Sahib, what will you do?"

A penetrating question, that. We all knew there were but two options. We could run away into the night, or we could remain and attempt to protect ourselves and our property. There were no police to call, for they were all at the battlefront fighting. The Bangladesh guerrilla army, moreover, was not available to help us. The invading West Pakistan army had not yet reached us. We were on our own.

I told the five that my colleague Dr. Donn Ketcham and I had met to plan out our defense. Our first decision? "You men have been promoted — from watchmen to guards! You will be given guns. Dr. Ketcham and his guards have gone up front to protect the hospital property. We will remain and guard the housing property." Because the hospital and housing properties were separated by nearly a half mile of forest and dense underbrush, we knew that our defense

9

Malumghat: Hospital and Housing Sites

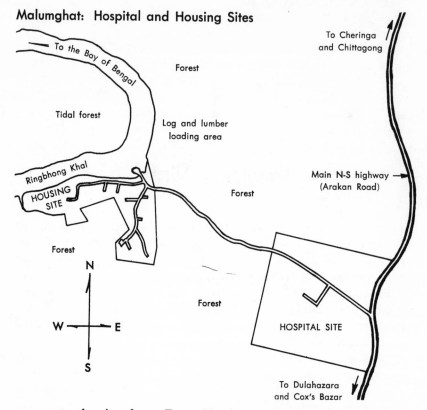

was up to the six of us. Donn Ketcham and his crew would have their own problems.

My right elbow, shattered in a freak accident, burned with post-operative pain. Donn had operated and driven a four-inch steel rod into the fragmented bone just twenty-four hours before.

I could almost read the thoughts of the five men in front of me: *Where will the bandits attack — at the hospital or here? Probably they will strike here first, for there are radios and tape recorders in the houses. They know Dr. Olsen is weak from pain and can't resist them with his broken arm useless in that hard white plaster.*

I reached for the guns. As my hand closed around the polished walnut stock of the .410-gauge shotgun, I felt uneasy. These guns had only been used to kill animals for protection or food, and now these weapons might kill a fellow human before the night concluded. This momentarily disturbing thought vanished as the name Nehemiah flitted into the front of my mind. Nehemiah, undeniably a man of God, traveled to a distant nation centuries ago to build up the wall of the holy city Jerusalem. He, too, when threatened with attack by enemies, set up armed guards over his work and workmen. Fortified by this recollection, my mind ceased debating the morality of our preparations.

Nehemiah's guards were probably more adept than mine in the use of their weapons. While some of my men had held firearms before, I didn't know whether any of them had ever fired a shot. I chose the four most responsible citizens from among them. The small .410-gauge shotgun went to the least experienced of the four. The small double-barreled gun went to the next man. The two larger 12-gauge shotguns I gave to the guards who seemed most reliable. Each man who took a gun received also several minutes of instruction in safety, loading, aiming, and firing his weapon. I assigned each man his guard point and area to be patrolled.

When I said something to them about life and about God, these Muslim men listened intently and approvingly. Then a joke. We all laughed, some a little too loud; the joke was not really that good.

They moved quickly to their respective areas and began their patrols in the garish glare of our outside lighting system. *It's a show of strength — and that's the best joke of the evening. We're all show and no strength*, I thought, as I remembered how little they knew of their weapons, and as a red-hot jolt of pain struck and stirred the embers of the fire that burned continually in that right elbow, reminding me of my weakness. *What a motley crew we are!* I reflected as I turned and retreated to the bedroom.

How does a man get himself into a fix like this? Twenty feet down the hall, in another bedroom, were two cringing, quivering men whom we were protecting from thousands of our Bengali neighbors. They represented the enemy, for they were West Pakistanis. Years earlier, they had left their homes in West Pakistan and traveled fifteen hundred miles to our area in East Pakistan to work as professional watchmen at our hospital. Now their countrymen, soldiers from the west, were driving through the East Pakistan countryside killing, torturing, raping Bengalis as they advanced. It was no wonder that our Bengali neighbors, whom we loved, hated these men. But the two West Pakistani watchmen had done nothing wrong. They had been faithful employees and had no sympathy with the acts of their own countrymen. Our duty was clear. We had to do our best to protect these two innocent men. At least three of the men in my own guard force were restless and unhappy about our intervention in this matter. But I knew my Bengali friends better than they knew themselves in those dark, impassioned days. If they were allowed to kill the two men, the day would come — a cooler, calmer, more clearheaded day — when they would regret with all their hearts the murder of two innocent men.

Will the men on my guard force who are angry about our pro-tecting the West Pakistani watchmen be loyal tonight when the at-tack comes? I wondered.

It struck me then that my five guards were all Muslims from the same village — a very homogeneous group. *Could the bandits themselves have terrorized their village and subverted my guards?* If so, the prospects for the night of April 23, 1971, were bleak indeed. But I saw no way to change the makeup of my guard force; it was too late.

I turned from my thoughts to the necessary preparations. I would have to load my small revolver (whatever good that might do — handguns are hard enough to shoot accurately with even a good right arm). My bed, immediately in front of the open window, would be directly in the line of fire. I would have to do something about that!

We would be all right until ten P.M. Our property was illuminated like a football field with outside lights. No one, seeing our guards with guns in hand, would cross the fence into that pool of white light — unless he knew, as I knew, that our guards could hardly hit a motionless haystack, let alone the small, quickly moving figure of a desperate man. Even if the bandits knew that, and even if they sus-pected, as I feared, that our inexperienced men might panic and head for the hills when the first shot was fired, they would still wait until after ten. That time was the zero hour when the electrical gen-erators thirty miles away would be shut off to conserve valuable Bangladesh diesel fuel for the war effort — when our lights would go out. We were surrounded on three sides by dense forest and on the fourth by a river. In the thick darkness, the armed robbers could silently enter our property at a hundred different points. We would be like sitting ducks! There was no way to contact that electrical station thirty miles away: it might as well have been three thousand miles distant.

How *does* a man get himself into a fix like this? There were, of course, a dozen — a hundred — steps in the process. The human mind has the astounding capacity to whittle years into seconds. Some say that the whole lifetime of a condemned man may pass before his mind's eye in that last minute before he dies. Whether that is ac-curate or not, I cannot say. But in this case, I had over an hour left to prepare and wait. And in that period, a lifetime of happenings, feelings, dreams, decisions, and experiences tumbled through my mind. In an instant of time my mind, drained by weakness and fatigue, yet lashed onward by jolts of pain and the constant stimulus of too much adrenalin, vaulted back — back —.

2

Little Guy

NOT SURPRISINGLY, I suppose, my mind catapulted to my very early days and fixed on childhood incidents containing the same ingredients as my present plight — blood, guns, and danger.

On my fifth birthday, I received the coveted pocketknife I had wanted for many weeks. But I never finished the statue I began to carve the next day. The knife slipped and embedded itself in the base of my left thumb, causing the blood to flow profusely. To this day, when filling out an application, under "identifying marks," I list "scar, base of left thumb."

"I think I cut myself kind of bad, Mom," I whispered to my sleeping mother. I must have spoken too calmly, for she was not alarmed. She sat up drowsily and slowly eased out of bed, as I headed for the kitchen. Her footsteps quickened, however, when she saw the trail of blood leading to the kitchen. Our driving time from home to hospital must have approached the current world's record. That day my doctor-uncle introduced me to the field of surgery, as he carefully sutured that cut.

At age seven, cowboys and Indians were my whole life. If only my birthday package would contain a pair of pearl-handled cap pistols with holsters and belt, I was sure I would be the happiest boy in the world. And, oh the joy as my dream came true! I could not understand why Dad and Mom smiled to each other when I tucked these new treasures under my pillow and tried to find a place to rest my head between the bumps and lumps. The next morning, up bright and early, I began practicing to develop the fastest draw in Omaha, Nebraska.

"Cowboy Olsen," age eight

In my ninth year, a second child, Jim, entered our family. We sensed his mechanical interest at age three, when he demanded "a frewdriver to frew some frews." When I was twelve, the last sibling entered the ranks, making us three sons. Enthusiastic Charles always tackled his projects "gung ho."

Dad suggested I should tackle a musical instrument. My choice (I cannot remember why) was the violin, and the agony of practice began. I never knew who found it most nerve-racking — my parents or me. They successfully hid their feelings and kept me at it. I practiced in the "opportunity room," a euphemism for the torture chamber where I agonized over the steel and catgut strings. I made progress. In a few months, I was ready for the big time — the fifth grade class musical.

At the sound of my name on performance day, I ascended the platform and looked out over the faces of my fellow students. Suddenly the vital connection between my brain and fingers parted, making my rendition a mockery of the composer's intentions. I steeled myself during the next day's postmortem of the musical and awaited the teacher's diagnosis. She pulled no punches. "Viggo, that was sour as a pickle!" As I ducked my face, the desk shook with my racking sobs. *Back to the opportunity room, Olsen,* I blubbered to myself.

When Dad fixed a basket and backboard to our garage, the neighborhood kids began flocking to the Olsens' house. Basketball, strangely enough, provided the opportunity to execute my first surgical operation. As Christmas neared, I dropped subtle hints that a basketball under the Christmas tree would please me greatly. One day, I noted with interest the mysterious square package that appeared in the closet. The box was the correct size and shape to contain a basketball; its contents rattled like a basketball. But how could a fellow be sure, unless he actually saw and felt the pebbled surface? Christmas was days away, and the folks were out for the evening. My conscience stabbed me the whole time; nevertheless, I located a razor blade and shakily made my first incision — in the brown paper wrapping. I slit with care the hidden area under the flap (standard technique in plastic surgery) and gently removed the basketball. That ball, one of the largest "tumors" I ever removed, was the only one I ever put back in.

For grade school graduation, I received a brand-new suit, two-tone shoes, and the wide-eyed adulation of two little brothers. The opportunity room had done its job, giving me more poise and skill as a violinist. As I played my solo and directed the orchestra for one

Eighth-grade graduate

number, I thought, *I wish that sour-as-a-pickle teacher could see me now!* What a cocky kid!

My father's signature read "Viggo C. Olsen." And logically enough — where else would I get a name like Viggo? Dad became an engineer-businessman who worked hard and achieved success, at last owning his own business. With his dynamic and warm personality, clubs and organizations frequently elected him president. He set a high standard for his sons. Dad has always been a wonderfully generous person and provided money for anything that would expand our minds, develop talents, or help produce maturity. Because he influenced my life for good, I think of him now with great fondness and appreciation.

Mother was a nurse and, I have no doubt, a very good one. She cared for us, not only with efficiency, but also with a never-to-be-forgotten warmth and love. Beauty may be only skin deep, but I thought it a joy to have a lovely mother. She was also a dynamic individual, and I remember her sparkling brown eyes. Despite her loving way, she did not shrink from punishing us when it became necessary. The first jig I learned to dance was animated by a switch in her hand. Mom was the motive force behind the success of the opportunity room. She, like Dad, taught us idealism, high moral standards, and doing things right. "Son, be a good boy — you'll never regret it," energized our consciences. "If it is worth doing at all, it's worth doing well," was her reminder that half-baked work is unacceptable. Mom, too, influenced my life immeasurably.

3

Swingin' Teenager

In that Bangladesh bedroom, my reverie interrupted, I rose to my feet. The clock was ticking inexorably toward my ten o'clock deadline when the lights would suddenly go out. I could not sleep in that vulnerable bed before the open window. *I'll put a decoy in the bed,* I decided. Making sure the opaque curtains were closed, I went gingerly from bedroom to bedroom, collecting pillows. Moving carelessly or too quickly brought instant reprisal from my swollen, throbbing elbow. The tender, purplish-blue swelling extended upward to my armpit and downward to the finger joints, where tight skin obstructed the further progress of oozing blood.

I was exhausted. I pitched my pillow collection into the bed and flopped into a chair. Oh-oh, that combination of weakness, pain, and adrenalin was doing it again. I could feel my heart pumping in my chest, out into that elbow, much too rapidly and forcefully.

*   *   *

That same heart, in a teenager, pounded more than once in a wild and uncontrolled way. One night, a buddy dared me to join him in climbing the grain elevator which thrust its monstrous concrete bulk high into the sky. "OK," I said, with great bravado. Flaky black paint and orange rust covered the slender steel ladder bolted to the concrete side of the elevator. Despite the brilliant moonlight, it extended up, higher than the eye could see. We grasped the first rung, out of reach eight feet above the ground, by alternately boosting and pulling each other onto the ladder. As we climbed higher and higher, the wind whined and snatched at our clothing. I reached a section with a missing rung, briefly contemplated backing down, stretched, and pressed on fifteen stories into the sky. Near the top, the wind gusted and buffeted us like a screaming banshee. I clutched the rungs as though my life depended on it — it did! Scrabbling up over the precipitous edge, I reached the solid, flat roof with a heart pounding like a jackhammer in my heaving chest. As we surveyed the treacherous edge an hour later, preparing to do down, the jackhammer resumed. The ladder stopped dead at the edge of the roof;

16

no railings arched over the top. Reaching into the blackness below, through the screaming wall of wind, which sucked at me along the perilous edge, my clutching hands and groping feet found rungs to fix upon. The jackhammer continued the full fifteen stories down and many minutes thereafter. Never again did I foolishly take a dangerous dare.

In the early morning hours of another night, a few years later, as I unsteadily opened the door of my home, the inner thumping appeared suddenly again. My mother sat in the big chair, waiting for me to come in — and I was drunk. This time, shame had pressed the jackhammer switch. "Son," she said, "where have you been?" Then she saw my condition; pain and incredulity in an instant etched themselves upon her face. Although she said no more, as I stumbled up the stairs to my room, it seemed that I could hear the echo of her voice welling up from the past, "Son, be a good boy — you'll never regret it."

I knew loneliness during my first semester in high school. My grade school pals had registered at nearby North High. Because my violin teacher conducted the orchestra there, I selected downtown Central High School. Moreover, I considered Central High academically stronger and certainly more sophisticated. Sophistication, however, provided no cure for loneliness. And the strong academic pace backfired. For the first time, I received an *F* in a course at midterm and also on the following test. Latin was the nemesis which demonstrated to me I had failed to learn in grade school the discipline of study. Until high school, subjects had required little or no study. Mortified, I wondered what I could do. Mother had the answer: "Into the opportunity room with you, Son. You have two weeks of Christmas vacation ahead of you. If you work day and night these two weeks, you'll make it." As usual, she diagnosed accurately. *A*'s in the final few daily assignments and on the final exam raised my *F*'s to a wonderful, heartwarming, incredible *B*-minus. And I remember some of those Latin roots to this day. The opportunity room had done it again! Dad provided it, Mother kept me in it, and I reaped the benefit.

One summer vacation, I worked in the lard department of a packing plant. The hard, physical work pleased me; I was eager to increase my strength and muscle power. I made a new circle of friends, many of them with Polish, Bohemian, and Slavic names. They worked hard, drank hard, and used hard language. They called me "Slim." I "made it" with them easily, for my school friends boasted similar accomplishments.

These high school friends were worldly-wise, some of them from notable families. We moved fast, attending parties and dances, frequenting bars and murky pool halls. We drank, gambled, and swore, as though these were marks of accomplishment.

My decision to attend Central had been wise, from the musical standpoint. With continuous practice, music occupied a large part of my time throughout those years.

I remembered another time when the beating heart returned — the first time I stepped onstage from the wings into the brilliant blue-white spotlight and stood, violin in hand, facing the huge Omaha Central High School Road Show audience. Theoretically, I had nothing to fear. The song I had selected was "in," calculated to please both the students and their parents. My musical skills had expanded and matured greatly over the previous two years. My accompanist was sensitive, and my tuxedo fit perfectly. Yet, as I "calmly" lifted my bow before the silent crowd, I heard only the drumbeat of my wildly pounding heart. Surely the audience must hear it too, I thought. The bow enticed from my instrument a first note which was clear, pure, and wistfully sweet; I knew then my fearful heart would not destroy the music. The runs, the staccato, the double stops — all went well. The final note, mysterious, and high as the sky, merged imperceptibly into the hushed silence. Abruptly the applause began. Engulfed by thunderous, tumultuous waves of approbation, my teenage heart began to pound again. Fear no longer impelled it; instead, it responded with inordinate pride.

Sometimes I thought deep thoughts about life, philosophy, and religion. I would lie in bed and think out into space, trying to fathom the size of the universe. I jumped my mind from my bedroom to the farthest star which I could see. Then I doubled it, projecting my mind the same distance beyond that star. I would hopscotch out into space, minute after minute, and always finish with the feeling of infinite smallness in such a huge universe. Where did it all come from? Did someone make it? Is there really a God? If so, what is He like? Are the gods of Asians and Africans the same as our American God, despite the different names? As my reason failed me in such questions, so did the church I occasionally attended. It was all right for social contacts, but the sermons and classes all missed the answers to questions that occupy a fellow's mind. Because my mother and father wanted it, I attended catechism classes and was confirmed — confirmed, it seems, in my ignorance.

Invited by a buddy one Sunday night, I attended a nearby neighborhood church. I rather enjoyed the youth group, particularly one of its blonde members, but again found the religious instruction uninteresting and irrelevant to the great questions which somehow intruded themselves into my consciousness. A number of us from this youth group attended, on one occasion, a one-week summer camp. From that week, I remember only one startling service. After sunset, the campers, each carrying a candle, walked single file down the paths to the outdoor meeting area, where they took their seats around the waiting campfire. After a rather forgettable sermon, a call was given for those to come forward who wished to volunteer their lives for the Christian ministry. Although I knew it was not for me, I remember the unexplainably powerful pull I felt to arise and go forward. I submerged the feeling with a vengeance. It was strange, though, that the feeling would be so strong.

In 1944, during World War II, I graduated from high school. Prior to graduation the Army, Navy, and Naval Air Force gave examinations and selected students for various priority programs. If I could pass the Navy V-12 examination, the US Navy would send me to college, which somehow seemed preferable to dying at a tender age on some distant battlefield.

The examination was grueling and difficult! The section on vocabulary meaning was, by all odds, the most difficult I have ever seen. Despite a respectable vocabulary, I found many words which

High school buddy with Vic Olsen, age seventeen

Premed student days

my own reading habits had never uncovered. Not only that, but also the words to be matched with the lead word were also unknowns. Frequently I was forced to dope out words from various Latin roots still vivid in my mind. Good old Latin! Good old opportunity room! I passed. The US Navy assigned me to their V-12 unit at Tulane University, New Orleans, Louisiana.

Despite Naval discipline, college in the deep South was fun. Fraternity membership opened up the way to continue the partying, dancing, drinking, and gambling of high school days. New Orleans, the great Mardi Gras city, encouraged us all into the same diversions. I lived with nine hundred roommates in the Sugar Bowl gymnasium — close fellowship, Navy style!

My decision to study medicine seemed haphazardly made. Perhaps some previous conditioning influenced me. My mother had trained as a nurse; three aunts wore white nurse's uniforms; and my Uncle Charlie was a doctor, a specialist in obstetrics and gynecology. The Navy, furthermore, offered me only three options: study to be a Navy line officer, an engineer, or a doctor. I decided quickly. A Naval career held no interest for me, nor was I greatly enamored of machines and bridges. Clearly, I preferred people to calculus and mechanics. Opting for premed, I reminded myself it was a good and idealistic thing to practice as a doctor — and the financial reward would be nothing to sneeze at. Despite the flimsy, almost frivolous, way of making such an earthshaking decision, it was certainly the correct conclusion for me.

While working with others writing a constitution for the new interfraternity council at Tulane, I discovered I had a penchant for organization. To analyze a problem, find its solution, and design a way to orchestrate the solution pleased me immensely. Perhaps for this reason I was selected as an underclassman to be an officer in this council and in my own fraternity. Any sense of reasonable humility now departed.

We attended classes year around on an accelerated program, three full semesters per year. In this way, I completed my premed requirements in the brief span of two years. Atom bombs on Nagasaki and Hiroshima brought an end to the war during that second year, allowing me to complete premed studies as a civilian. Although my extracurricular activities interfered considerably with my studies, the letter from my home state university, the University of Nebraska College of Medicine, read, "We are pleased to inform you that you have been accepted for the medical college class to begin September, 1946."

4

The Making of a Doctor

BEFORE ENTERING MEDICAL COLLEGE, I had a summer to play with. I could not foresee it would be the most important summer of my life. My father's business partner extended an invitation to join him and his son, "Sonnie" McGrath, fresh from the Marine Corps, on a fine trip to the East, complete with new scenery, big league ball games, and Times Square. I quickly agreed. Our plans changed, however, when car trouble grounded us in Fort Wayne, Indiana; and another business associate let Sonnie and me have his car and sent us off to Potawatomi Inn, a resort in Pokagon State Park. It took some persuasion before we inveigled a room at the beautiful Inn, already crowded to the rafters with honeymooners and other vacationers.

An attractive waitress named Mary Lou served us a scrumptious meal. I took her out later that evening. Then, at 10 P.M. Mary Lou and I appeared at the soda fountain, "Hiram's Barn," so-named because of its rustic furnishings. The pigtails, straw hat, and red-checkered blouse of the lovely blonde behind the counter perfectly matched the decor. This girl's name was Joan.

"I'm sorry," she said. "It's past closing time." She responded to my cajolery, saying, "All right, what can I serve you?"

We settled on two bottles of orange pop. After she brought them, she locked up the soda fountain and turned out the lights, leaving Mary Lou and me in the dark. *Thoughtful girl,* I mused, *and beautiful too, despite the pigtails and braces.*

Next day I pointed Joan out to Sonnie. He laughingly dismissed her with, "I doubt if she's a day over fourteen." (The pigtails and braces had fooled him.)

"I'll bet you a coke," I countered. He took the bet and headed toward Joan to ask her age and prove his point. I won the bet! Sonnie was chagrined to learn that she was twenty — six months older than he.

When I asked Joan for a date that day, she halfway agreed — but she stood me up! Later, I asked her for an explanation for this unsettling behavior. It sounded valid: "Mary Lou has been talking for

21

weeks about her boy friend. So when I saw you together, I assumed you were he. She's my friend, and I didn't want to cut in. Besides, we didn't make the date that definite, did we?"

As I looked into her shining blue eyes, *any* explanation would have been acceptable to me. Then, assured that I did not belong to her waitress friend, she made amends. "Tomorrow is my day off. How about a canoe trip? I can arrange a picnic from the kitchen." I agreed.

That next glorious, incredible day, I positioned Joan forward in the canoe and seated myself in the stern, and we headed for our destination seven miles across the lake. I dug my paddle in deep and hard, determined to show this slender girl how a canoe should be paddled. Later, my shoulders and arms begging for rest, I looked up to see her paddling with ease. With renewed effort, I paddled until those same muscles almost screamed for respite. Joan kept up her smooth, rythmic paddling. What a girl!

Our picnic was a grand success. After the seven-mile return trip, shower, and supper, we strolled in the moonlight then climbed the steps of the toboggan slide and, hand in hand, surveyed the moon-drenched countryside. The scene was lovely. So was the girl.

In some wonderful, extraordinary way I knew she was the one for me. The blueprint of "the girl for me," long stored in some subterranean mental vault, suddenly surfaced. She matched in every particular — and I told her so.

I left the next day, with a promise to return at the end of the summer. Love had come to us almost instantaneously. I had to return, I said, to prove that our love was more than a summer flirtation, to see if it was real.

Before the summer ended, I kept my word and returned to Potawatomi Inn. The week together did prove our love real, alive, and growing.

In the fall, Joan entered Ohio University, and I began my medical studies in Omaha at the University of Nebraska College of Medicine. Prompted by loneliness — mine and hers — Joan transferred at the semester break to the Home Economics College of the University of Nebraska, located sixty miles from my medical college. We spent time together as often as possible on weekends.

The *freshman* year at medical college is a unique experience. Because I had completed my premedical studies within the accelerated Navy program in the unusually brief span of two years, I entered as the youngest student in the class; a month earlier I had celebrated my twentieth birthday. Many of my classmates were veterans, some of them nearly twice my age.

I shall never forget the sensation on that first day we entered the anatomy laboratory. Because my family members are exceptionally long-lived, I had never seen a dead person before. In groups of four, we approached the cadavers assigned us with mingled awe, nonchalance, fear, and bravado. Very gingerly we completed our first assignments in dissection. Soon, however, our sense of awe vanished to be replaced by youthful irreverence.

Later in the freshman year, we practiced drawing blood from our bacteriology laboratory partners. I inflicted little or no damage on my partner, Joe Kovarik. Then, shaking from head to foot, Joe picked up the syringe and needle, and with an ominous look, advanced toward me. I needed no further clue to fear that it might be a case of Kovarik finishing off Olsen in the laboratory with a hypodermic needle. The jigging needle he plunged into my arm not only entered the vein but passed completely through it. Joe looked horror-stricken at the large — and growing larger — blue-purple lump in the crook of my elbow. I recovered, at least as quickly as Joe, and we pressed on together to study new mysteries.

In medical college every activity proceeded at a high tempo. We worked hard; we played hard. I joined the Phi Rho Sigma medical fraternity which soon became the focus of my social life. My gambling skills increased (dice, gin rummy, bridge, poker), and I usually managed to walk away with extra money in my pocket. Many of the group drank heavily after a big test, and I was no exception.

What strange contradictory impulses coursed through our lives: cold scientific thoughts, warm and loving feelings, irreverant attitudes, high idealism, vile language, unhealthful habits, selfish ambitions, and a desire to help suffering humanity.

Despite plenty of hard work and study, my freshman grades were only mediocre (a deficiency not totally explainable by my extracurricular activities). Somehow I would have to improve my ability to salt away huge amounts of complicated scientific matter.

The summer following my freshman year, I worked to help pay tuition and expenses. Engrossed in my own affairs, I paid little heed to the cataclysm engulfing South Asia that summer of 1947. India, far around on the other side of the globe, held no interest for me. Meanwhile, Great Britain had agreed to grant India independence. This news gratified the Indians, at least the majority who were Hindus. The minority Muslims were apprehensive, however, fearing they might be submerged by Hindu domination. So England made several districts of western India into West Pakistan, and, eleven hundred miles across India to the east, East Bengal became East Pakistan (now Bangladesh). The carving out of this new nation of

Pakistan created one of history's greatest migrations, and blood flowed freely as Muslim killed Hindu and Hindu slew Muslim.

I scarcely noticed the accounts of this tragedy. My interests were not international.

In my *sophomore* year, I encountered a subject which helped me crack the academic barrier and do well in medical college. Physiology, the science of the human body's functioning, I found so intriguing, so exciting, I simply fell in love with it. Different from anatomy, a study of the cadaveric structure of the human body, physiology teaches the living, dynamic functioning of the incredible human machine. Entranced by the subject, I studied with a new passion, making the top grades in the course.

Dog surgery, in the physiology laboratory, I found interesting but considerably less intriguing than the function and mechanisms demonstrated by the experiments. I was anxious to emerge from the nest of the science classroom and laboratory into the wide open world of the hospital.

Joan and I planned to be married after graduation, but it seemed a long time away. Without warning, one day at the conclusion of my second school year, the telephone rang. The professor of physiology said, "We have greatly appreciated your student work this year, and I want to offer you a fellowship in our department. This means you'll drop out of your current medical college class and spend a year in the department, doing teaching and research toward your master's degree. If you succeed, you will be given the opportunity to teach physiology and pharmacology to student nurses during your junior and senior years for salary. Let me know your answer as soon as possible."

Bombshell! What to do now? I consulted Joan, and we came up with a startling answer. I would accept the fellowship, and we would be married, not in two or three years but in *ten days*. Because the year would be slightly more relaxed than the regular medical college scramble, it should be a good year to begin the adjustments of married life. Joan would work, and her salary added to my stipend, would make us financially solvent.

Joan called Dad and Mom Baur in Toledo. They gasped, rallied, squared their shoulders and, responding magnificently, produced a lovely wedding in ten days. The wedding, held in a huge church, was complete with the full retinue of attendants in gossamer gowns and dignified black tuxedos. Even though the best man (Joan's brother) overslept, he and I arrived at the church just in time to see the vision in white. The minister refused to accept his fee on the grounds that the bride was so beautiful. I could only agree with his

Wedding bells for Vic and Joan

"The monster in the furnace room"

analysis — besides, I needed the money. Showered with loving best wishes and many gifts, we thoroughly enjoyed the reception. We honeymooned, of course, at Potawatomi Inn, the magic place where it all began.

Returning to Omaha, I began my fellowship work. Down rough brick stairs in the basement room of an ancient home, we built our love nest. We called it the "spackle shack," because of all the spackle, a white putty-like material we used to fill the gaps where the wall failed to meet the irregular ceiling. We used pounds of the stuff. After repairing a large hole in the concrete floor with fresh concrete, we covered the whole mess with a very inexpensive compressed hair carpet.

One room, with hideaway bed, served as bedroom, living room, dining room, and game room. The small kitchen contained a greasy stove which we scrubbed within an inch of its life. One other tiny, tiny room contained toilet facilities. Bathing required a trip through the furnace room, up the stairs to a bathroom shared with others. The monster in the furnace room daily tried my patience. Each day I had to heave enough dusty coal into its gaping, ravenous maw to keep the occupants of the huge old house warm. That job, plus shoveling the snow from the walk, gave us rent-free quarters. The stoking began at 5:00 A.M. each cold wintry day. No young man appreciated the coming of spring more than I.

Joan worked at the nearby home office of the Mutual Benefit Insurance Company (Mutual of Omaha). Her first job, filing, she found uninteresting. After plugging away several months at night school, she qualified as a stenographer, made tentative arrangements for another position, and submitted her resignation. Her superiors at Mutual, however, responded unexpectedly. Impressed by her superintendent's recommendation, they said, "We are unwilling to accept your resignation. We are offering you a new and different job which we think will interest you. We want you to be one of our claim auditors."

How ironic! For five months she had worked and studied to become a stenographer. Now she was offered a position where she would have stenographers to take *her* dictation. Joan's typing training was not wasted, however; she typed hundreds of papers and letters for me. The fine new position required her to learn volumes of material about medicine and surgery, as well as insurance policy terms. As we advanced side by side in our knowledge of medicine and surgery, we became true coparticipants in our life together.

In the physiology laboratory, I helped teach and direct the new sophomore medical students in their experiments. I loved my work. At the same time I observed that some of my fraternity brothers were quite at sea and that those who did only mediocre work could do better. The word *fraternity,* I reasoned, meant brotherhood. Why, then, could the fraternity house not be more than a center for drinking sprees, wild parties, private study, and ball games? I promptly began seminar review meetings for sophomore physiology and pharmacology students at the Phi Rho fraternity house. I learned a way to organize and summarize the material, mix it until palatable, and feed the resulting mixture into the sophomore students. The sessions were massively attended by students from my fraternity and others. Finding much satisfaction in helping others in this way, I continued in this self-given assignment for three years. Because of those sessions, some men who otherwise would have flunked out are today successful, practicing physicians and surgeons.

My own experiments involved producing a type of shock in dogs, studying and recording their response to various treatments, old and new. Often the experiments lasted well over twenty-four hours, requiring all-night vigils. Joan would bring my supper and join me watching over the dogs and the many tubes and wires connecting them to the complex recording apparatus. We took turns sleeping an hour or two, then watching an hour or two throughout the night — that's true love!

At the end of the year, I found the experimental results revealing and useful. Except for writing my thesis, I had completed the work

for my master's degree. At that point, a momentary temptation entered my life. My professors asked me to stay out of medical college, remain in the department, and complete work for a Ph.D. degree to become a professor of physiology. Having loved the year's
work, I felt sorely tempted. But upon reflection, it again came
clear that I liked people more than machines, laboratories, animals,
or "pure" science. I declined and prepared to reenter regular medical college studies in my junior year.

I eagerly approached the *junior* year of medical college. This
would be the real beginning of clinical studies, the actual care of
sick patients. We were leaving the musty halls of academic learning
for the hospital wards where we would see and begin to do. I saw
and did my first deliveries of infants. I stood by a bedside, for the
first time to see the warmth of life become the sudden chill of death.
We put on caps, masks, and gowns to observe our first surgical operation. Some found the experience distressing, and the nurse took
one of my fellow students outside the operating room doors for air.
I found myself undisturbed, but also disinterested in the possibility
of becoming a surgeon. I conceived the difference between surgery
and medicine to be like the difference between the work of a mechanic and a detective. I wanted to be a specialist in internal medicine to allow me full sway for my "detective" instincts. Let someone
else do the mechanical work of surgery.

We moved from the "spackle shack" to a more attractive apartment house in a better section of town. In return for janitorial services rendered, we received a considerable reduction in our rent. In
addition to janitor work, I held two other jobs. I sold medical-surgical equipment and taught physiology and pharmacology to students
from three schools of nursing.

I summarized, in my preliminary lectures to this huge class of
nursing students, the facts of the organic evolution of animal and
human life. One day, as an afterthought, I said, "Perhaps some of
you find some conflict between my teaching and your childhood religious teaching. If so, please see me after class and I'm sure I can
resolve your conflict."

Surprisingly, three students approached me after class, saying,
"We find it hard to agree with your teaching. What is the explanation you mentioned?"

Smiling in a faintly superior way, I responded, "Is your view
based on your religious upbringing and the Bible?"

"Yes," one of them answered.

"I think I can help you," I said. "The Bible is no doubt a good
and valuable book, but it must not be interpreted too literally. Its

stories are merely symbolic of other, greater truths." Months later, those words came back to haunt me.

I taught my students the marvelous functioning of every part of the body, including the reproductive system. My explicit lectures on the physiology of sex were enthusiastically received and considerably publicized.

As a junior medical student, I began the ritual of studying internship programs. Following graduation from medical college, an intern works in a hospital, usually for one year. Studying the appropriate journal of the American Medical Association, which cataloged all approved US internships, we listed the ten most appealing ones. At last we headed East in my father's Packard. It was the end of my junior year, and Joan had two weeks' vacation. Chicago, Cleveland, Baltimore, New York City, and Boston — we moved quickly, seeing hospital after hospital. Sometimes, near the end, we drove day and night, spelling each other during the night hours at one- or two-hour intervals. Our last stop on the circuit was Rochester, Minnesota, to visit the Mayo Clinic. There I hoped to take advanced training, following my internship, in order to qualify as a specialist in internal medicine. For the year of internship, I ultimately selected Long Island College Hospital in Brooklyn, New York.

I found my *senior* year a big and a busy year. I wrote two theses on two different aspects of shock — one for my master's degree, the other for the long-awaited M.D. Frequently, Joan pounded the typewriter on into the night.

During my quarter on the obstetrical service, Joan qualified as an obstetrical case herself. Her precarious pregnancy put her to bed for six weeks before she miscarried. At that time, life approached the intolerable level: classes, a busy obstetrical service, three jobs, cooking, caring for my bedfast wife, and finally, the grief of her miscarriage, brought me near the end of endurance. We passed through the difficult period, however, and pressed on.

Three other medical students and I formed quite an effective study group which met before examinations. We quizzed one another and generally helped each other prepare for the examinations. One day, a study partner and I stopped the car in front of the home of another medical student. Before opening the car door, my friend reminded me that this student, John, and his wife were very good, "religious" people who were preparing to become medical missionaries overseas. "Vic," said my partner, "please watch your language when we go inside." Angry, I remained in the car, refusing to go into the house with him. Analyzing my anger, I saw it was fired by guilt — my swearing had become habitual.

M.D. — at last!

First day in hospital whites

Later, John joined our study group. Coincidentally, from time to time some of the old questions about the universe, philosophy, and religion came to mind again. One night, after a study session, I decided to try some of my questions on John; after all, he was going to become a missionary. "John," I said, "now I have some questions for you about something other than orthopedic surgery. How do you know the universe was created? What proof is there? How do you know there is a God? Has anyone ever seen Him? What evidence is there for His existence? Who was Jesus? How do you really know He ever actually lived? If He did live, do you believe He did the miracles attributed to Him? Why do you think the Christian religion is any better than the beliefs of the Hindus or Confucianists or Muslims?" John, smiling an enigmatic smile, replied, "Those are pretty big questions, Vic. I'm afraid we couldn't solve all those problems at such a late hour. Maybe we'll find another time to discuss it." Having heard that John frequently talked to others about his beliefs, I was surprised at this weak response. I had opened the door for him to tell me all he knew. Later I learned the reason for his reticence: he considered reasoning with me about spiritual matters a waste of time. As he told me years later, he regarded Vic Olsen the most unlikely candidate in our class to become a Christian.

Medical college graduation climaxed seven long years of study. I was happiest for Joan who had worked so hard to help me through.

Graduation over, we purchased a big M.D. tag which I bolted to our automobile license plate. At last my wife and I were ready to drive off into the rising sun toward Long Island College Hospital, Brooklyn, New York, to begin my internship in internal medicine.

5

Spiritual Pilgrimage

AFTER A FEW MOMENTS RESTING in our Bangladesh bedroom, my heart rate returned to normal and I felt able to make the next move. Rising from my chair, I approached the dangerously located bed and stripped back the covers. From my substantial pillow collection I took the smallest pillow and tucked it where my feet should be. After one-handedly placing all the pillows in a row, I pulled the covers back over them. It had taken quite a few pillows to look like six feet four inches of me. Punching and poking, I finally modeled the covered pillows to look like the figure of a sleeping man. My feathery sculpture complete, I brought a thin mattress from another room and flopped it on the floor behind the door, away from the anticipated line of fire. This would be my bed and place of refuge after ten o'clock when the lights went out. Then I thought of loved ones half a world away in America.

What can they be thinking? I wondered.

*　　*　　*

Toledo, Ohio, Joan's home, would be our first stop on the way to New York. Heading for new adventures and appreciating nature's beauty, we drove along in a mutually happy state of mind. We looked forward expectantly to seeing Joan's folks.

Dad Baur, a capable, handsome, white-haired man, worked for the motor truck division of International Harvester Company. His great fund of good stories grew as he traveled about his territory from dealer to dealer, advising them on many complicated matters. Mom Baur, lovely, sweet, gracious, and full of fun, made life a pleasure for her family and all who came around. Many stopped in to visit and bask in the love of that home.

Only one point bothered us; we might run into a heavy barrage of religious discussion at the Baur house. After Joan left home for college, Dad and Mom Baur had some type of religious experience.

31

With sincere concern, they zealously tried to share their new beliefs with others, including us. Throughout our previous three years of marriage, nearly every letter from them had contained a pamphlet or brochure about some religious point or another. Sometimes tolerant, other times irritated, occasionally amused, and not infrequently angry, we discarded them in the circular file. Occasionally we read them, but more often we did not, for we considered church and religion unnecessary and irrelevant to our busy life.

About midnight we arrived at the Baur house and talked until four A.M. We had not been together for a long, long time. Each day our talks, sooner or later, focused upon religion. Sometimes we listened; other times we debated or argued many points. I viewed Christianity and the Bible through agnostic eyes, feeling that modern science had outmoded much of this religious sentiment. When my father-in-law spoke of flaws in evolutionary laws and other scientific dicta, I boiled inwardly.

After all, I thought, *I teach these things and have spent years studying them. I certainly know more than Joan's dad about such matters.*

We agreed, that first Sunday, to attend church with her folks. Their pastor, Rev. Reginald Matthews, not only conducted the morning church service but earlier also taught the adult Sunday school class. His teaching and preaching, arrestingly skillful, centered on the Christian Scriptures. Despite our inability to agree with all we heard, we found ourselves stimulated, even inspired, by his exposition which obviously possessed spiritual depth. At the close of the service, Rev. Matthews gave an open invitation, which we distinctly disliked, to those desiring to truly believe and receive Christ. Suddenly, it seemed very warm in the church — I felt as though "the heat was on." Never before had I walked from a church with such deep and contradictory feelings inside.

When the folks asked Joan and me if we would have an interview with their pastor, we reluctantly agreed. We appeared at his office in the Emmanuel Baptist Church, on a blazing hot Friday afternoon.

The five-hour interview exhausted us all. We discussed dozens of subjects — all the old questions which had haunted me before, plus many new ones. Many of my questions and points, of course, came from scientific fields because of my background. Because some of these fields were unknown to him, I expected Rev. Matthews would be stopped in his tracks. But, again and again, he would leaf to one section or another of the large, well-worn, black Bible in front of him — and again and again the words he read would be surprisingly pertinent. His knowledge of the Bible was remarkable. Because questions remained for discussion, we met again the next day for two and a half hours — question, answer, question, scripture passage, question, and so on. The meaning and content of the Christian's gospel were greatly clarified that day, but we continued to disagree with many points.

I believe Joan's parents were hopeful we would make some spiritual decision during the week, but our resolve remained firm. Would there be this pressure every time we visited? There must be some way to halt the endless religious dialogue and prevent inevitable family estrangement. Our last night in Toledo, at two A.M., around the kitchen table, we made a bargain with Joan's folks.

"We will study your Christian religion and Bible," I promised, "and reach our own, independent decision. With the matter settled, one way or another, we will stop these interminable religious discussions."

Dad Baur, obviously pleased, asked, "Would you also, after your arrival in Brooklyn, attend a church like ours in fellowship with the General Association of Regular Baptist Churches?"

I agreed, with the inward restriction, *But I won't say how often.* I implied that our study would be honest and objective, a sincere search for truth. But our agnostic bias made us begin the "search" in a diabolically clever way. We would prove the Bible is *not* the Word of God, that Christianity is *not* the true religion of God, and that Christ was but a man, *not* the Son of God!

"New York, here we come!" I exulted to Joan, as we departed Toledo heading East. Within a week we located an apartment in Brooklyn, Joan started her claim auditing at the Mutual of Omaha office near Times Square, and I began my work as an intern in internal medicine at the Long Island College Hospital.

The intern is the lowest doctor on the medical totem pole. Above him are first, second, third, and fourth year resident doctors; junior and senior staff physicians; section heads; and finally, the chief of the department. The intern, however, is usually the first to see the patient. He examines the sick person, takes the medical history, and orders the laboratory studies and initial treatment. The intern learns, under supervision, to suture lacerations, to perform spinal taps, proctoscopic examinations, minor operations, and numerous other procedures. He learns, painfully, to accept the death of patients whose illnesses yet defy the best-known treatment. Then he attempts to obtain permission for autopsies so medical science can advance in its relentless pursuit of new ways to help the sick and dying.

Brooklyn is a melting-pot city and seaport, receiving ships from all over the world. Because a number of our patients harbored tropical parasites and diseases, we were forced to learn more than most interns about tropical medicine. One Saturday, midday, the call came to admit a patient from the emergency room with "pneumonia." The patient — small, slim, brown, and brought from an Indian ship — could understand no English words.

Despite his labored breathing, I found that his lungs were clear, ruling out the diagnosis of pneumonia. I located his real trouble below the belt; the young man's abdomen was dangerously tender and rigid. Inserting a needle into the distended abdomen under local anesthesia, a trick learned from a very sharp staff doctor, I withdrew a syringe full of thick pus from his abdomen. One drop, under the microscope, revealed the diagnosis: parasites (amoebae) had invaded his liver, forming an abscess which had broken, exploding its pus throughout his abdomen. Powerful medicines, an oxygen tent, and finally surgery were required to snatch him back from the brink of death. His convalescence was long and difficult, but he made it. Unable because of the language barrier to voice his feelings, at the time of discharge, he clutched my hands, smiled shyly, then walked weakly down the hall toward the exit.

Internship — and more study   Long Island College Hospital

Our settling-in process complete, we started our religious studies. How could we prove the Bible a human book and Christ just another very human religious teacher? It should be simple.

"First," I said, "we will review all the agnostic arguments we heard during university and medical college years. Second, we will pick out and list the scientific mistakes in the Bible. Those mistakes in the Bible prove it to be the word of men, not the Word of some infallible Creator." With this data in hand we could honorably decide against Christianity, and silence forever the endless religious discussions with Dad and Mom Baur.

With little difficulty we assembled a number of agnostic arguments: because no man has ever seen God, there is no assurance of His existence. Man, frightened by inevitable death, merely manufactured God for his own comfort. Either God cannot prevent human suffering, in which case He is powerless; or He can prevent suffering but does not, in which case He is evil. The God of the Old Testament is "nonchristian." Immoral and contemptible incidents are recorded in the Bible. The doctrine of the Trinity is unacceptable to a rational man. No one can really be sure of the existence of God, heaven, or hell, so we must live this life with absolutely no assurance of any life to come. Well-educated higher critics, studying the Bible, have found it to be merely a collection of myths and stories. Because writing was unknown in his day, Moses could not have written the first five books of the Bible. The Bible, full of scientific errors, could not possibly be the Word of God. Jesus never claimed to be Deity, the Son of God.

These and many other arguments confirmed and strengthened our agnosticism. We were making progress. We did not call ourselves atheists, those who say "there is no God"; my studies of the incredibly intricate structure and function of the human body made me suspect at least the possibility of a Creator's existence, but I felt we could never make His acquaintance or really be 100 percent sure He is there.

One Sunday evening we visited the home of one of my professors, Dr. Milton Plotz. After supper, I explained to Dr. Plotz my theory about a new form of treatment for patients in shock from heart attacks. The theory emanated from my studies of dogs suffering another type of shock.

"If we inject fluids under pressure into the artery, rather than into the vein, we could produce an immediate blood pressure and improve the circulation to the heart," I suggested. "Then, perhaps, the heart might revive sufficiently to sustain life."

Puckering his brow thoughtfully, he finally responded, "Your principle could be correct. We have never used such a treatment before, but we should try. We will try on the next hopeless case."

Four weeks later, while visiting in that home again, Dr. Plotz picked up the ringing telephone.

"Yes. What? I'm coming! Vic, come along! One of my patients has just been admitted with a serious heart attack."

Racing to the hospital, we found the "hopeless case" barely breathing, no blood pressure, no pulse. She was nearly gone.

"This is it," I said.

"Yes, go ahead with your plan," my teacher responded.

No anesthetic was needed! Making a quick incision in the wrist, I located a quiet, blue-white structure — the artery. Normally it is pink and pulsates, dancing a jig with every heartbeat. Easing a needle into the unpromising artery, I furiously pumped fluids into the dying woman's system. Within fifteen seconds she began to stir, then to thrash about. Suddenly, with color now returning to her face, she sat bolt upright shouting, "What's going on here? My arm hurts!"

Remembering our promise to attend a church like the one in Toledo, we located the listing of churches given us by the folks. Under "New York," we found the listing for Brooklyn which contained the following entry: Bay Ridge Baptist Church; pastor, Rev. E. A. Lockerbie, with an address on Fourth Avenue.

The next free Sunday, keeping our promise, we headed for Fourth Avenue in the Bay Ridge section of Brooklyn. Upon arrival, we saw a low, flat, covered basement of an unfinished building protruding only a few feet above the ground; the small sign in front read "Bay Ridge Baptist Church." What were we getting ourselves into? We walked gingerly down the stairs into the small subterranean church. We found a seat among the worshipers. In place of the regular minister, away for the week, a theological student conducted the service and delivered the sermon. We noted, with approval, the young speaker's warmth and sincerity.

After the service, many in the congregation introduced themselves to us. We drove home, picking apart the sermon, but finally deciding to return my next Sunday off to visit these friendly people again and hear the regular minister.

During the next two weeks, we refined our agnostic arguments and added to the list. Beginning our search for scientific errors in the Bible, we found it hard going to wade through the "thees" and "thous," and words like *redemption, propitiation,* and *evil concupiscence.* It became obvious too that scientific errors did not actually abound on every page, as we had heard in college years.

The next available Sunday, we returned to the little "underground" church. Arriving a minute late, we quietly found our seats under the watchful eye of the choir and the minister — no possibility of secret entrance into a sanctuary that small! The people sang joyously until the church resounded with music. Warmly, enthusiastically, Rev. Lockerbie conducted the service. His sermon, as we expected, expounded a section of the Christian Scriptures. His earnest delivery, logic, wit, and vivid illustrations kept everyone awake, even the children in attendance.

At the close of his sermon, he gave the invitation for the kind of decision which seemed to characterize these churches. As usual, I felt discomfort and resentment rising inside me. Why did I react so strongly to these invitations? Perhaps I considered religion too private a matter for such open display. Or were my own sins and nonchristian attitudes inwardly plaguing me? Possibly the impious study we were conducting to prove Christ and Christianity untrue caused me to feel the squeeze of some unknown holy pressure. I noted with surprise and interest that some did respond to the invitation. I wondered vaguely whether we had fulfilled our promise to the folks by attending the church twice, or whether we should return. At the door, the minister greeted us with a firm handshake and, unexpectedly, an invitation for dinner that day.

Hesitantly, we agreed.

The Sunday dinner, however, marked the beginning of a long friendship between our families. Mrs. "L" shared deeply her husband's work in their church. With efficiency and a quiet, delightful sense of humor, she taught women and children, and offered warmhearted hospitality to the many who visited in their home. The Lockerbie teenagers, Bruce and Jeannie, also served their church with surprising skill. Because we seemed pleasant, I suppose, and because we did not mention our search to disprove all they held dear, the Lockerbies did not know all about the Olsens that first meeting. Only later did they learn our real intentions.

* * *

I first saw Dr. Viggo Olsen as I sat in the choir loft of our church in Bay Ridge, Brooklyn, where my husband was pastor. We invited the newcomers — the tall doctor and his wife — to come home with us. Vic's hollow-leg appetite competed with those of my teenage athletic son and slim daughter. With ease the Olsens made themselves at home.

That first Sunday dinner set the pattern for all the others. We sat around the table long after our meal was over, and the four of us talked and talked, Vic's hand automatically reaching for whatever he could munch on. The topic never varied. Always it was the Bible. They displayed an insatiable interest in discussing what the Bible said about almost everything. Questions. Questions. Questions. Vic was sober and intent, at times soaking up what was said, at times quizzical. Joan, eager as always, created a preacher's heaven: a listener who wasn't watching the clock.

Little wonder that we naturally accepted them as believers, even as highly dedicated Christians. Who else would voluntarily sit around for hours with a preacher and his wife and their Bibles!

Our church people, wonderful Scandinavians for the most part, took the Olsens to their warm hearts; and some, to their homes. The name Olsen *belonged among our Andersens and Eriksens and Johnsons. Our college students were impressed with the couple.*

In our ignorance of the situation, we had taken the doctor and his wife on appearances. That was the best thing we could have done. Had we known their true intent, or even suspected it, we undoubtedly would have felt constrained to "reach them." But we were totally unaware of their underlying quest, to disprove our basic Christian beliefs, so we were free to be ourselves. We made no secret of our gladness that they had chosen to come our way.

In our home Vic and Joan saw us just as we were, with our faults and whatever good points might have shown. We all enjoyed the Sunday dinners when Vic and Joan were our guests, sometimes crowding in with half a dozen others at our table, and rubbing elbows with a visiting missionary or a theologian. How much we might have lost if we had attacked their agnosticism! Their first visit might have been their last.

Only years later did I learn of Dr. Olsen's student achievements. Despite his fast-moving "extracurricular" life in high school, he had been elected to the National Honor Society. Only two men in his graduating class were selected for the prestigious V-12 college training program — he was one of the two.

At graduation from medical college Dr. Olsen was one of four to walk across the platform with gold braid on his shoulders signifying that his M.D. degree was granted cum laude. *Also, his M.D. thesis received special recognition. Because of his organizing and leadership skills, Vic was usually an officer in his fraternities and other student organizations. And despite his youth, medical college classmates elected him president of the student council and the student body in his senior year.*

6

Impressive Proof

OUR ATTENDANCE at the Bay Ridge Baptist Church was sporadic, but eventually the news of our agnosticism became known to some in the church family. One Sunday, as we attended another service, we sensed no inner advance warning of the high importance of the day for us. Following the service a young fellow we had met approached us with his right hand extended.

"Hi, Jack," I said, shaking his hand.

Responding with a friendly greeting, the young Christian college student handed me a book, *Modern Science and Christian Faith,*[1] written by thirteen scientists, members of the American Scientific Affiliation.

"Doc," said Jack Baldessari blithely, "I hear you are studying religion. I thought, being a scientific man, you might be interested in this book." Not one among the three of us standing there that morning could foresee any of the astonishing series of events which would come forth from Jack's simple, thoughtful act.

Jack's book opened the door into a whole new field of study previously unknown to us — Christian evidences. Although initially disinterested in reading the book, one day I picked it up and began. Boredom changed to interest, and interest became fascination, as I mentally devoured the book. The bibliography steered us to other books on the same subject. We read *The Bible and Modern Science*[2] by Henry M. Morris, Ph.D., head of the civil engineering department at Virginia Polytechnic Institute. His book summarized other valuable and exceedingly interesting material.

We discovered *A Lawyer Examines the Bible*[3] by Irwin M. Linton, a Washington lawyer, a member of the bar of the District of Columbia and of the Supreme Court of the United States. He listed a number of the older works on Christian evidences, written by such men as William Paley; Howard A. Kelley, M.D. (the outstanding Johns Hopkins surgeon); Sir Robert Anderson of Scotland Yard; and Sir William Ramsay. From many of these authors of unquestioned ability and integrity, Irwin Linton quoted provocatively in the text of his book. These and other books engaged our minds as Joan and I simultaneously sought to find error in the Christian Scriptures. Christian evidences claimed that the Christian faith is not a blind faith based on imaginary ideas but a true and living faith based on historical fact and a very large amount of valid evidence. We doubted it and fought it but kept reading.

As we studied and discussed, three paramount questions emerged:

1. Is there a *God* who created the universe?
2. If so, did God reveal Himself to the human race through the Bible or other sacred scriptures?
3. Is Jesus Christ the Son of God (deity united with a human nature), and can He help us as He claimed?

If we could answer no or "no one can know" to these three questions, we could confirm and confidently defend our agnosticism to anyone.

As we studied on, certain facts became evident about the first of these questions concerning the *existence of God*. Scientifically, we knew that the planet earth and its universe had not always existed. Once they came into existence, which meant they must have been created by some mighty force or power.

"But what proof is there that a power brought it into being?" Joan asked.

"Because," I answered, "our earth and universe are packed with power — fire power, water power, atomic energy, etc. Only a power or energy can bring into being a power-packed system."

"But was this an intelligent power or was it some undirected cosmic explosion?" we asked ourselves. After more study, the answer became clear: the very design and pattern of the universe gives testimony that the creating power, which brought it into existence, must have been an intelligent power.

At first we reacted, "But the pattern of the universe can be explained by the natural laws of the universe." Then quickly we saw that we could not have the law of gravity, the laws of thermodynamics, or any other natural laws without a lawgiver. Moreover, we could not find a design without a designer or a pattern without a pattern-maker. And there was unquestionable evidence of pattern and design in our universe and on our planet. The millions of stars and planets track their courses precisely, without collision unless some accident intervenes. The astronomer-mathematician can determine exactly how many years, months, days, hours, and seconds a heavenly body will require to travel from its present position to any given point in its course. Without fail, the earth and sun maintain their correct relationship so that we can live out our lives without being burned to a crisp or frozen into a cosmic ice cube. The marvelous design of plants and animals which fits them to their sometimes inhospitable environment is remarkable in the extreme. The human body, whose design and function I had come to know so well, possesses a million different patterns in its many organs, groups of cells, and chemical systems. By looking at a tissue slide under a microscope, I could identify the tissue as heart, lung, or brain because of the precise pattern of the cells characteristic of each organ.

At this point we found an analogy which gave us valuable perspective: suppose we take the wooden blocks from one hundred Scrabble games, each with a letter of the alphabet inscribed upon it, place the letters in a covered plastic tub, shake the letters vigorously, and throw the nine thousand wooden pieces out upon the floor. Could they naturally fall so that the letters form a story or a poem? No, we agreed, some would lie on top of others, many blocks would rest face down, other letters would fall upside down or sideways. The letters thus thrown could never form a paragraph or a poem.

Now suppose a person with fingers connected to an intelligent human mind picks up the scattered pieces, carefully forms them into words, sentences, or lines of iambic pentameter. A story or poem emerges from the heaps of wooden blocks. Power shook the tub and threw the pieces upon the floor. Another power carefully picked up the pieces and with them told the story. Then why the difference in the two results? We saw immediately that the difference lies in the types of power involved. The first power, undirected, failed to produce a pattern from the blocks; the second power, intelligent power, produced the pattern we can read as a story or poem. The analogy was obvious to us: if our planet and universe were ejected into space by some wild, explosive, undirected blast of power, the result would have been chaos and confusion, as when a high-explosive bomb detonates in the heart of a great city. Clearly, the pattern and design of our earth and our universe show us that the power which produced them was an intelligent power — that intelligent power men called God.

"But," I wondered, "can we know more of God, beyond His power and intelligence, by observation of outer space or the human race?" Based on the obvious principle that the creature cannot be greater than the creator, we discovered we could understand one more thing about God from observation and experience: Each human being, too, possesses power and intelligence. But he possesses something else, something higher and finer, called personality or soul which makes him capable of loving others. To study the needs of people and calculate how they might be helped is one thing; it is quite another thing to empathize with them, to feel their pain, to love enough to help them in their distress. And, suddenly, we were sure that God — who cannot possibly be less developed than we, His creatures — must also possess personality, be able to empathize with us, and love us in our human problems. Without recourse to formal religion or anybody's sacred scriptures, Joan and I became fully convinced that a personal creator God does exist. We had suspected it for a long time, but our studies gave us a full and settled assurance that "God is."

Our new conviction, however, did not unhinge our agnosticism, at least as far as religions and their sacred scriptures were concerned. Our persuasion about the realness of God did, however, force us to face the second great question: *did God, or did He not, reveal Himself to the human race through the Bible or other sacred scriptures?* In our search, we studied scriptures of various nonchristian religions. We failed to find among them the mark of the supernatural. We did find good ethics and good morality mixed with gross scientific error and, sometimes, disturbing and degrading precepts. The Christian Scriptures, in contrast, we found to be different and quite remarkable.

"Is it even reasonable to consider that God might reveal Himself to our race?" I asked one day at dinner.

"Well," Joan replied, "I just read something on that question. It made the point that we human beings are here, the only rational creatures in God's creation. It is unlikely that God created us whimsically, for no reason at all. And having made us, it is logical that God should reveal to us His reason for creating us. Also, if God loves us, He would want to tell us — love is like that." *That's a pretty sharp answer,* I thought to myself. We studied the teachings of Plato who stated flatly that no philosophical argument exists which upsets the possibility of divine revelation. So, we decided, revelation is logical. But, *did* God actually reveal Himself to us? Our books on Christian evidences contained mountains of material and evidence that the Christian Bible is God's instrument for revealing Himself to the human race. We found some of the data to be internal evidence, intrinsic to the book itself. Other information fit into a category called external evidence.

We spent weeks digging out these evidences. Each night Joan rode the subway home to Brooklyn from Times Square, ate, and read more on Christian evidences. When I came home, on alternate nights and weekends, we studied together, discussed, argued, shared, and analyzed. Joan would study the unresolved questions the following night to have facts ready for my next night home. Our system helped us to salt away mountains of information.

In the area of internal evidence we soon discovered the outright claim the Bible makes for itself that it is God's book for revealing Himself. The Bible asserts it is not the result of man's reaching up to manufacture a god and put words in his mouth; rather, it represents God, motivated by an eternal love, reaching down to tell us about Himself and His plans for us. Certainly such a "God's book" would claim that truth about itself. We could count on the fingers of one hand the number of books in the world which seriously made such a claim; this narrowed the field considerably. We also noted the remarkable unity and consistency evident in the Christian Scriptures. Despite its sixty-six books, written over sixteen hundred years by over forty authors (some of them peasants and fishermen; others, kings, physicians, and poets), the Bible books harmonized as though one person had written them all. We had observed that the writings of several authors of many a modern anthology hopelessly conflict even though written at the same time. Yet, in this ancient book, written by so many men over many centuries, the sense of unity was impressive.

"Who knows and comprehends all the teachings and lessons of the Bible?" we asked. No one, we learned. This inexhaustibility we recognized was notable and unique. Different from other books, the Bible's teaching is so deep and wide and high that human minds could no more contain all its facets than could a teacup contain the Pacific Ocean. Then too, there was a certain completeness of the message. Where else could we read so much about the creation of man, creation of our planet, creation of the earth and angelic beings? In this book we learned about events which occurred long before creation and other events which are to occur centuries and aeons in the future. We read about right and wrong, heaven and hell, God and Satan, and what human destiny is all about. And, we observed, the Christian Scriptures seem to have universal appeal. The Bible is believed and received, loved and followed, by men in a hundred nations and thousands of races and tribes. We had to agree it is as applicable to the West as to the Eastern world where it was written. Christianity is not a local, tribal religion.

"Let me tell you what I read about the Bible's literary superiority," I said one day. "Much of modern law can be traced back to the Old Testament, particularly its first five books. And the Bible's pages are full of adventure stories like that great spy story in the book of Joshua. The book of Proverbs is the classic example of wisdom literature. And what poetry can beat the Twenty-third Psalm?" We found that philosophy, too, fills the Bible's pages; the New Testament book of Romans, written by a philosopher-intellectual, the apostle Paul, was a classic example. And stories of romance were not lacking in the sacred page. There could be little argument about the literary excellence of the Bible.

Joan was impressed that the Holy Scriptures possess a certain time-lessness, continuing popularity, and current value beyond all other books.

"The Bible has been the best seller for decades, probably for centuries," she reminded me. The honesty of the biblical writers we found surprising and somewhat unusual. While secular authors frequently cover up their sins and faults, writers in the Bible speak openly, although repentantly, of their darkest sins and most serious failings. Nothing "fakey" about these men!

Then we studied the testimony of the four gospel records about Christ Himself. The first four books of the Bible's New Testament — Matthew, Mark, Luke, and John — are four separate records, some of them eyewitness accounts, of the life of Jesus Christ. If the records of Christ's miracles, death, and return from death are false, we mused, careful legal cross-examination of these records by an expert should show the error of these documents. Such a legal expert specializing in the laws of evidence was Simon Greenleaf. Not an ordinary lawyer, his books on evidence became the textbooks in the law schools. According to Lawyer Irwin Linton, Chief Justice Fuller of the United States Supreme Court once asserted that Greenleaf "is the highest authority cited in our courts." Linton quoted from the *London Law Journal* that Greenleaf shed more light on the laws of evidence than "all the lawyers who adorn the courts of Europe."[4]

Minutely, the eminent Greenleaf studied and cross-examined the documents written by Matthew, Mark, Luke, and John, recording his researches in a book called *Testimony of the Evangelists.* I remember how forcefully his findings struck me. He found clear evidence of no collusion between the four writers; that is to say, they did not huddle in a corner, make it all up, and foist it on an unsuspecting world. Regarding the setting, place, and time in history when the four witnesses wrote their biographies, Greenleaf stated:

> It would be difficult to select any place or period in the history of nations, for the time and scene of a fictitious history or an imposture, which would combine so many difficulties for the fabricator to surmount, so many contemporary writers to confront with him, and so many facilities for the detection of falsehood.[5]

Regarding the gospel records written by the four biographers, Greenleaf mentioned the great amount of minute detail "scattered broadcast" throughout the narratives. The details are so many and so interconnected "as to render the detection of falsehood inevitable" yet "the attributes of truth are strikingly apparent throughout the Gospel histories." He considered the "striking naturalness of the characters" an indication that real men were writing about other real, live men. He referred to "the nakedness of the narratives" and the evident consciousness shared by the biographers "that they are recording events well known to all, in their own country and times, and undoubtedly to be believed like any other matter of public history, by readers in all other countries and ages."[6]

The distinguished lawyer also investigated the character and personalities of Matthew, Mark, Luke, John, and the other apostles. He studied, too, their reaction to the adversity and persecution swirling about them. They preached Christ and Christianity "not only under the greatest discouragements, but in the face of the most appalling terrors." The laws of their countries, the attitude of their rulers, and the fashion of the world were against them. "Propagating this new faith, even in the most inoffensive and peaceful manner, they could expect nothing but contempt, opposition, revilings, bitter persecutions, stripes, imprisonments, torments, and cruel deaths. Yet this faith they zealously did propagate; and all these miseries they endured undismayed, nay, rejoicing." As one after another was put to death, their survivors kept on preaching. "It was therefore impossible that they could have persisted in offering the truths they had narrated had not Jesus actually risen from the dead, and had they not known this fact as certainly as they knew any other fact."[7]

We remembered, at this point, that Matthew, John, Peter, and Paul claimed they actually had met the risen Christ, talked with Him, and eaten with Him. From our studies we learned these facts and many more about the internal evidence for the truth and integrity of the Christian Scriptures. In addition, we learned hundreds of external evidences.

Contrary to our previous understanding, we found the Bible to be historically accurate. To the science of archeology the Bible largely owes its vindication in the matter of historical accuracy. In college days we had heard of the critics who maintained that writing was unknown in Moses' time, that the Hittites and Edomites were legendary peoples. They claimed that the Roman census which brought Joseph and Mary to the town of Bethlehem, where Jesus was born, could not be factual, for Roman censuses were unknown in that day.

We were surprised to learn that modern archeological research has shown the facts to be otherwise. Excavations have proved that writing was a known art not only in Moses' time but also in the days of his forefather Abraham and hundreds of years before that. The Hittites were discovered and recognized to be a powerful ancient nation. Edomite culture is well known; even their magnificent capital city, Petra, has been discovered and is visible for tourists to see to-

day. More current information about the Roman census, which occurred in ancient times about every thirteen years, demonstrated its
use long before the time of Christ. A statement in Dr. Henry Morris'
book startled us:

> It is significant that Dr. Nelson Glueck, probably the outstanding
> living Palestinian archaeologist said: "It may be stated categorically
> that no archaeological discovery has ever controverted a Biblical ref-
> erence. Scores of archaeological findings have been made which
> confirm in clear outline or in exact detail historical statements in the
> Bible."[8]

Then there is the remarkable scientific accuracy of the Bible. Here
was the exact target of the attack Joan and I had launched to disprove Christianity and Christ. Knowing that all ancient books contained scientific error, I felt assault at this point would bring quick
results. We encountered great difficulty, however, in finding scientific mistakes in the Bible. Again and again we were forced to cancel
out seeming mistakes because of more up-to-date evidence or information. We found this most impressive because even modern textbooks of medical science become outdated after only a few years.

"Hey, listen to this," I said to Joan one day. "I just learned the
Bible states that God hangs the earth upon nothing. That's pretty
sharp because everybody in those days thought the earth perched
on some foundation. And here's something else. Centuries before the
scientific discovery that the earth is round, Isaiah the prophet wrote
about the roundness or sphericity of the earth." We learned, moreover, that science even confirms biblical miracles such as creation,
the flood, and the long day of Joshua.

The changed lives of believers offered us further external evidence
to the claim that the Bible is a supernatural book. The original apostles — weak, cowardly, and vacillating — were so changed by talking
face to face with Jesus after his return from the dead that they became bold, powerful preachers and proclaimers of the new faith.
Although many of them were rough, uneducated men, they convinced millions; even their enemies said they "turned the world upside down." Something happened to them! Joan's folks, the Matthews, the Lockerbies, and others claimed the same thing was happening in our day. They asserted that in our modern age people
were believing in Christ, finding a new life, and living changed lives
from that time forward. Their own lives were certainly examples
which we could not deny.

Calling from the hospital one day, I said "Honey, I have come
across a whole new area of evidence — prophecy."

Little by little we learned that the literal, accurate, mathematical fulfillment of biblical prophecy was certainly one of the most powerful of the external evidences. We discovered that the Bible contains hundreds of detailed prophecies, written decades or centuries before the described events, which history acknowledges have been fulfilled in extraordinary ways. The precision of these prophetic statements and their exact fulfillments distinctly set them apart from such predictions as those of Jeanne Dixon or Nostradamus. We found that some Bible prophecies deal with sacred matters, others focus on secular events such as the fate of ancient cities: Memphis and Thebes of ancient Egypt, Babylon, Tyre, Jericho, Capernaum, etc. Countries, nations, and peoples come under prophetic purview. Prophecies regarding Israel seemed to bat one thousand. The Jews, according to prophetic insight, would suffer for disobedience and be scattered in a great worldwide dispersion, yet not be assimilated through intermarriage in the nations where they settled. Ultimately, their nation would be restored and millions would return from the lands of dispersion back to modern Israel, the Holy Land. This we were seeing fulfilled in our day!

Throughout the Old Testament we discovered numerous prophecies which related to a coming Messiah (a Christ, as the Greeks put it). His unique conception and the unusual events that surrounded His birth were foretold in detail. Among the world's millions of villages, the one village where He would be born was named seven hundred years in advance. That the Messiah would teach and heal and finally be betrayed are also detailed hundreds of years earlier. The exact price of his betrayal — thirty pieces of silver — was forecast by the prophet Zechariah. In the days of another prophetic writer, King David, nothing was known of crucifixion as a means of capital punishment. Yet David, when he spoke of the death Messiah would die, foretold that his hands and his feet would be pierced — it seemed to us a vivid description of the death of Christ at Roman hands by their means of capital punishment, crucifixion on a wooden cross.

"Did you know, Vic, on the day of the crucifixion, thirty-three great prophetic utterances were precisely fulfilled?" Joan informed me one day — and showed me the passages to prove it. The Bible even prophesied that as a nation the Jews would reject their Messiah when He appeared — obviously, that prophecy was 100 percent true.

Daniel the prophet predicted the time of "Messiah the Prince" to be 483 years from the issuing of a certain commandment and he hit the mark perfectly! Sir Robert Anderson, a notable chief of Scot-

land Yard, actually counted the days covered by the prophecy
(173,880 days). We were astonished to learn that his calculations
placed the last day of the prophecy on the first Palm Sunday, the one
day in the life of Christ that He was acclaimed by the people as the
Prince or King of the Jews.

When these facts and many others came to our attention, we were
deeply impressed. The various agnostic arguments we had collected
now seemed shallow, for we could discern fatal flaws in them. Even
our confident attack on the Christian Scriptures was bogging down.

Satisfied that God was real, suspecting against our will that the Bible
was validating its claim to be supernatural, we tackled the third
great question: *Is Jesus Christ the Son of God (deity united with a
human nature) and can He help us as He claimed?* My answer was
no! I believed Jesus to be an historical figure of ancient times. (Previously I had thought Him perhaps a myth or imaginary figure, but
our recent studies had shown that view completely untenable.)

"He was a great man," I said, "perhaps the greatest that ever
walked this earth. As for being the Son of God, that would be true
only in the sense that all of us, as members of the human race, are
sons of God. To attribute to him a supernatural birth, deity, or a part
in the creation of the universe, seems to me preposterous. No doubt
he died, as the historical records show, on a Roman cross. But who
can prove that he died for the sins of others or rose again from the
dead?" I felt he probably died as a martyr to a noble cause, and
that he "rose again," spiritually, into the lives of those who believed
and followed his great teachings.

So many conflicts, facts, proofs, ideas, and teachings tumbled end
over end down my mental corridors and collided with each other trying to scale the barriers of prejudice and unbelief I had erected at
strategic points. I found it difficult to put everything together into a
pattern that made sense. We studied on into the extraordinary life of
Christ.

The New Testament writers, we found, painted a picture of the
works and teaching of Jesus during his rather short lifetime. Matthew,
Mark, Luke, John, Peter, Paul, and James (Jesus' own brother) produced not just a picture, but, if believable, an exquisite, glowing
masterpiece. They affirmed that Jesus, before becoming man, had
existed throughout the countless ages of eternity as God. We found
ten passages which taught that, ages before He sawed and planed
wood as a carpenter of Nazareth, the Son of God was the master
Carpenter of the universe; at His Father's bidding, He constructed
the world, creating it *ex nihilo,* from nothing. Then, "when the ful-
ness of time was come, God sent forth his Son, made of a woman."

By pure miracle, the record stated, He caused a Jewish peasant girl named Mary to be the mother of the Saviour. The resulting child inherited from His mother a human body and human personality, but, as the Son of God, possessed the divine nature and attributes. He emerged into His earthly life as the God-man, Jesus Christ. And the Bible claimed He came from heaven's glory to earth's dust and distress not only to die for our sins but also to tell us what we need to know and show us, in a way that we can understand, what God is like.

"There is a certain logic to that idea," I admitted to Joan. "To communicate successfully with an ant, I would have to become one. The argument seems to be that God, to communicate effectively with us, joined us in human form." The Bible put it, "God was in Christ, reconciling the world [of men] unto himself."

The writers painted a vivid picture of His daily life. Walking rocky, sunbaked roads and eating village fare, He traveled about teaching as no man had ever taught before, loving people, enraging hypocrites, eating with ordinary folk, even sinners (I liked that), and commanding the elements. Disheveled by the surging, pawing crowds, He miraculously healed the sick by a word or a touch. Some of His patients, according to the record, incurable by the most modern medicine or surgery, responded to His quiet treatment. He seemed to possess a divine, and also a very human nature. He ate, drank, and became exhausted.

Jesus' angry enemies finally brought Him to trial and to death on a cross. Hanging there between heaven and earth, according to the Scriptures, He died not for His own sins but for our sins and the sins of the whole world. He gave His own pure and perfect life voluntarily, a sacrifice to pay the penalty for all our evil acts and impulses. But that was not all: Jesus said, before He died, "I lay down my life, that I might take it again. No man taketh it from me, but I lay it down of myself. I have power to lay it down, and I have power to take it again." As good as His word, the Bible records He did come back from the dead to walk among men and talk to them for forty days. On one occasion, over five hundred men saw Him. Many talked with Him, even touched Him. Some recorded what they saw and felt. We studied the evidence for this literal, physical resurrection of Christ and found it multifaceted, powerful, and compelling. The resurrection of Christ was to us the hinge or crux of the whole question of the deity of Christ. If He *did* rise from the dead, we would have to grant that Jesus is the Son of God, "God manifest in the flesh." And — His rising from the dead could only mean, moreover, that all Jesus ever said is true and binding. We were impressed by the evidence. We were impelled, also, by the urgency which God seemed to attach to the matter of solving the problem of evil and giving man a way to get right standing with Himself.

By then, right standing with God did not seem a trifling matter to Joan and me. We found it fascinating to work out for ourselves what was involved. According to the Bible, we unfortunately possessed wrong standing with God. We got this wrong standing by doing wrong things and thinking wrong thoughts. Our wrong and sinful acts and thoughts had separated us from God and any warm, happy relationship with Him, for God loathes evil and must punish us for our sins. The Bible put it this way: "The [penalty for] sin is [spiritual] death." That spoke to us of hell and unhappiness forever, the result of wrong standing with God. Because we mortals all did wrong, we were all in serious trouble with our Creator.

"Is there a Christian solution to this human dilemma?" we asked.

Several months earlier I would have answered, "Christianity teaches that if I do good works, live a decent life, and don't hurt anyone, these good acts will cancel out the bad, give me right standing with God, save me from hell, and someday launch me into heaven."

But I had missed it completely! My idea might square with some religions, but not the Christian religion. Passages from the Christian "handbook" showed my viewpoint naïve: *"Not by works* of righteousness which we have done, but according to his mercy he saved us"; "God, who hath saved us, and called us with an holy calling, *not according to our works,* but according to his own purpose and grace."

The biblical way of gaining salvation, of obtaining right standing with God, we had heard from Joan's parents, the Matthews, the Lockerbies, and others. Studying the New Testament passages ourselves, however, brought the true Christian teaching into more powerful focus. Succinctly, the Bible put it this way: "For God so loved the world, that he gave his only begotten Son, that whosoever believeth in him should not perish, but have everlasting life."

Because of His love for us, God sent His Son into the world to die for us. Christ loved us, too, and gave His life for us on a cross. But to gain the benefit we had to believe the record, believe on Christ as the Son of God, and receive Him into our lives as the Saviour He came to be. Salvation from sin and a place in God's family depended, the Bible said, not on our good works, as I had thought, but on our true faith in Christ. We found that the Bible explained it this way:

Believe on the Lord Jesus Christ and you will be saved.

To as many as received Christ, He gave the right to be the children of God.
Whoever shall call upon the name of the Lord shall be saved.

This act of faith, we learned, instantaneously gains the new believer the five basic "religious" benefits that most men hope or grope
for:
1. Forgiveness of sin
2. Right standing with God
3. Loving acceptance by God
4. Salvation from hell
5. Happiness forever after death

But there is more! Beyond the five basic benefits, we discovered
that a Christian's God offers at least five more startling gifts to the
new believer:
6. A spiritual rebirth within
7. A new inner life (eternal life), starting now
8. A changed life with new appetites and desires
9. A new companion and guide, God's Spirit, to live within
10. A new inner power to overcome evil, to live honorably, and to
    love and help others

Learning about all these marvelous benefits to be gained and eternity in hell to be shunned, if Christianity be true, the gravity of
the choice we were making was more deeply impressed upon us.
What a conflict! So much to gain — so much to lose!

About that time, we came across an arresting article dealing with
Pascal's wager. This famous French mathematician-scientist, living
at the time of the Pilgrims, gave much thought to this choice now
facing us in the mid-twentieth century. His conclusion was that,
even on the basis of a mere fifty-fifty chance that Christianity is true,
a thinking man would choose *for* Christianity. His reasoning:
1. In this game of life, every man must wager, that is, stake his
    life on the proposition either that Christianity is true or that it
    is not. (By refusing to wager, a man has already wagered
    that it is not.)
2. Suppose a man chooses *for* Christianity. If it is true he gains
    everything (all the benefits above and more). If it is false,
    he has lost nothing.
3. Suppose a man chooses *against* Christianity. If it is true, he
    loses everything and spends eternity in hell. If it is false he
    has gained nothing.

My gambling background had preconditioned me to follow this
argument.

"And his argument," I said to Joan, "is based on a straight fifty-fifty chance that the Christian faith is true, not even counting all the *evidence* for Christianity." Later we discovered that Blaise Pascal did say something about searching out the evidence:

> According to the doctrine of chance you ought to put yourself to the trouble of searching for the truth. For if you die without worshiping the True Creator you are lost. But, you say, if He had wished me to worship Him, He would have left me signs of His will. He has done so . . . but you neglect them. Seek them, therefore; it is well worth it.[9]

About this time I got a flash of insight about faith. I saw that millions of people consider themselves Christians, but are not truly so because their faith is dull and inadequate, not a "receiving" faith.

"Suppose," I said to Joan, "that two patients have the same fatal disease. They both believe me to be a skillful physician, feel that my diagnosis is correct, and believe that the injection I ordered will save them from dying. One patient accepts the injection and survives. The second patient, despite her faith in the doctor and the treatment, has an irrational fear of injections and refuses the treatment — she dies. What is the difference? Both patients had faith; they both believed the medicine would cure them. But faith which does not receive is inadequate faith." Similarly, no salvation or transforming miracle could happen in the life of a person possessing merely a frightened, dull, sterile "recognizing" faith. To obtain the superlative benefits of believing would require a faith that inwardly receives Christ *personally* as the Son of God and Saviour of the soul.

It sounded too good to be true. Perhaps that is one reason we continued to fight it. Admittedly, we had progressed a long way. We now believed with certainty in the God who created the universe. Furthermore our "invincible" agnostic arguments were dead or dying.

We were shaken by our failure to find scientific mistakes in the Christian Scriptures. Christian evidences, a completely new field to us, had made a deep impression.

Now we knew the facts about Jesus, what He had done, who He claimed to be, and especially His ability to cure incurable illness, raise decomposing dead bodies to life before eyewitnesses, and return Himself from the land of the dead. We were becoming captivated by this incredible person, called the Son of God, who was stronger than death.

Furthermore, we now clearly understood the "receiving faith" way of getting right standing with God and obtaining everlasting life, this vital decision that most Americans so poorly understand. But we fought on against it. Now, however, Joan seemed more quiet when I argued against Christianity and the Bible, assuming more of a listening role.

During my hospital work one day, a new anti-Christian argument struck me. Delighted with my new idea, unaware of the argument's weakness, I mentally pruned and played with it, refining the point for presentation to Joan. My day's work finished, I walked shiveringly through the sharp, late autumn air to our little apartment. I knew she would be there waiting. Bounding up the two flights of stairs, I knocked and waited with the new argument on the tip of my tongue. Joan opened the door.

"Hi, honey," I said, kissing her. *What a neat little pregnant wife I've got,* I thought as I began to unleash my new argument.

"Listen to this new idea," I began. Not even waiting to go to the living room, there in the entryway of our very plain little apartment, I carefully explained my new little argument against Christianity and the Bible. Finishing my recital, I looked down at my partner for approval. She looked back at me, with those shining blue eyes, in a way she had never looked at me before.

Softly, slowly, she said "But, Vic — haven't you really come to believe that Christ is the Son of God?" Something about her look and those words toppled the final barriers I had erected in my resisting

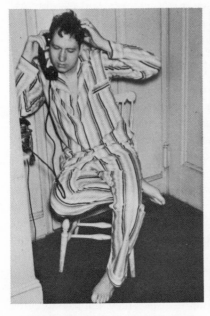

Night call received in our "crummy little apartment" in Brooklyn

My "neat little pregnant wife"

mind. Now, unimpeded by the mental obstacles, the facts learned from hundreds of hours of study, like pieces of a jigsaw puzzle come alive, scurried into their rightful places producing an instantaneous picture glowingly, beautifully complete.

Suddenly, electrifyingly, standing next to the one I loved in the entryway of that crummy little apartment in Brooklyn, I knew I also loved Another. In that unblinding flash of spiritual light I knew it was all true — Jesus *is* the Son of God — He *did die* for my sins according to the Scriptures — He *did* rise from the dead and prove it all true! In that moment I did believe, deeply, receivingly, with all my heart. Christ was not just a distant concept, some far-off Saviour of the world who died as a martyr to a great cause. He was, suddenly, my very own Saviour — warm, alive, and very near.

After a long moment, I finally replied, thoughtfully, "Yes — I really do! I know it's true! I do believe!"

Moving on to the living room, we sat down and I asked, "What about you?"

"I settled the matter several days ago," Joan admitted, "but I was afraid to tell you. All the things we studied and learned finally convinced me about the Bible, about Christ, and about my need, our need for Him. Sitting at my desk a few days ago, I knew I was completely convinced. So I prayed to God, confessed my sinfulness, and asked Christ to come into my heart to save me. And He did."

It seemed hardly possible that the great moment had come and gone for both of us. I felt all pure and good and peaceful and happy inside.

In the radiant days that followed, everything seemed different; when we found a Bible passage stating "Behold, all things become new," we understood its meaning immediately. That clean, good, happy feeling inside was great to live with, and it seemed to displace or drown out the old, compelling attitudes and appetites. Many new and important things engaged our attention.

Next Sunday the Reverend Mr. Lockerbie gave a good sermon, finishing with his usual appeal for people who wished to believe to come forward. For the first time, I sat through such an invitation not griped at the proceedings. Suddenly it seemed very reasonable that a Christian minister should preach the Christian message and imploringly challenge people to believe it and make the decision to accept Christ. Besides, the invitation no longer applied to me — I had already settled that matter. Later, when the Lockerbies and other friends in the church learned of our decision they rejoiced greatly. Joan's parents, of course, responded in exactly the same way. We learned that they all felt a part of it, for each one had prayed for us day by day, week after week, month after month. It was a strange feeling to be an answer to prayer.

Learning how to pray ourselves we found traumatic. For us, religion had always been quite a private matter, like taking a bath. Joan and I were a little hesitant and tongue-tied praying out loud, even with each other. Our friend Jack, the original book-giver, soon invited us to his home for an evening.

At the close of a delightful evening, he said "We have a lot to be thankful for; let's pray a moment before you go. We'll start with you, Edith, then each one can pray until we're finished." Gulp! The jackhammer started pounding in my chest again. Edith, obviously on close terms with God, prayed quietly and warmly. Joan, breathless and slightly quavering, prayed quite an intelligent little prayer. I croaked out a few words and Jack, with poise, finished the praying.

In the car, we held each other a minute like two frightened, shivering little children. "Wow, honey! That was tough, wasn't it?"

"It sure was," Joan agreed.

On a Sunday afternoon the pastor's son, Bruce Lockerbie, phoned to make nonchalantly an earth-shattering request.

"Dr. Olsen, in our young people's meeting this evening we are putting on a radio program and our group would like you to come and give your testimony of how you found Christ as your Saviour. Would you do it? Our meeting is 6 P.M."

"Uh. Er. Mmm. Aaah. Bruce — I'll call you some other time. I mean, I'll call you back in a few minutes. I have to think about this a minute."

Clonking down the receiver, I looked despairingly at Joan. "I can't do it. How can he expect me to do that?"

"Do what?" Joan asked.

"Bruce wants me to talk on some young people's radio program, or something. I'm not sure whether it is a radio broadcast or just some young people's stunt. Anyway, I can't do it. I don't know enough."

Joan asked the logical question: "What exactly did he ask you to do?"

"Oh, give some 'testimony,' he called it, about coming to faith in Christ. He said that coming from a doctor like me it would be a big help to the teenagers."

"Vic," she said. "It probably would mean a lot to them, and a testimony is just telling what happened to you. Besides, you have a couple of hours to prepare. Maybe your doing it would please God."

Finding her logic inescapable, I phoned Bruce, agreed to come, and learned, to my relief, that the "radio program" would not go out over the air waves. That evening, speaking from a microphone in one room to a group of teenagers gathered around a radio in another room, I shared my faith and spiritual experience with them. That first public speaking engagement, which I found thoroughly traumatic, launched me into more scary opportunities to tell other people about Jesus.

Before the winter's cold dissipated, Joan's birthday came up on the calendar. *I must make it a very special birthday celebration,* I thought. Not only were we new believers this birthday, but also we expected a new infant son or daughter to join us in three months. With reservations made at a romantic candlelight restaurant, I carefully purchased what seemed just the right presents. I even paid a professional wrapper to wrap them, rather than trust my own wrapping skills. (Taking out a gall bladder is not so difficult, but wrapping gifts beautifully is quite another matter.)

At the restaurant, we both ordered something on a flaming sword and in the candlelight talked of many things. With dessert, a Bavarian creme, I gave her the exquisitely wrapped gifts and told her of my love as though I had never done so before. It seemed a perfect night — until we stood to leave. The first hints of abdominal pain and cramping struck us both almost simultaneously; some potent germ in that Bavarian creme had attacked us even before we left the restaurant. By the time we reached our little apartment, we were both violently sick with vomiting and severe dysentery. At sunrise, tragedy struck! The explosive illness damaged the covering around the unborn infant. Despite all the medical efforts over several days, Joan went into premature labor far too early for our child to live. Finally, at the hospital, Joan delivered a tiny infant son — but he was alive! Our spirits catapulted from the depths to the heights. "Isn't it great to be Christian believers with a connection to God? God has turned the impossible into the possible for us. It must be a miracle from God!" Despite my medical knowledge and the cautioning words of colleagues, we rejoiced that God had given us our son. But — at forty hours of age he died!

Shattered, we wept together and agonized. "Oh why, God, did you take him away from us? Why didn't you keep the miracle going? Oh, Father, help us to understand!"

The door opened and a nurse entered to ask quietly, "Would you like to see your baby once again?"

I stumbled down the hall to take one last look at my son. Though he was very small, he obviously looked like me — long arms, long legs, and features like mine. I could not comprehend, that moment, all the bewildering series of events that snatched his little life from us. I only knew, that moment, that I loved my son with a love beyond the ability of human words to express. I understood in a new, deep way the meaning of Jesus' words, "The Father *loveth* the Son." If I could love an infant son who looked like me, how much the Father must have loved his Son so much like Him. My very human love focused on a tiny son I didn't even know; God's love — infinite, divine — enfolded a Son whom He "knew" for eternity. And I would have worked, struggled, and given all I possessed to snatch my son from death; yet the Father freely gave us His Son to die for us. What were those words? "For God so loved the world of men that *He gave* His only begotten Son —" My wee son was not a party to his own death — he just died. But God's Son put Himself freely into the hands of His crucifiers and died voluntarily on our behalf.

Later that intern year we learned about baptism. Because Christ said believers ought to follow Him in baptism, we decided to be baptized at the little church. Baptism would afford us, moreover, an opportunity to show and express openly our new faith. We were given opportunity, standing in the baptismal waters, briefly to share our faith and Christian experience with the congregation. We found it a moving experience to do so. Then Pastor Lockerbie placed us under the water in the age-old Christian ritual. Fortunately, we found a way to solve the one knotty technical problem — the tank, only five feet long, had to receive six feet four inches of me. I bent my knees double at just the right moment.

Somehow, our experience of having our baby taken did not make us bitter. We gained from it a deeper understanding of what it cost God to bring us into His realm and His family. We learned, too, that we would have to dig deeper into the Scriptures to learn why God allows or brings to pass such painful incidents in the lives of His people. And we learned His power to heal the hurt. But we did not really understand why this tragedy had come upon us. After all, we had given ourselves to God. Or had we? We had certainly gained an incredible treasure trove from God that day we believed. But had we given Him anything? Did He want us to give Him anything? *We must find the answers to such questions,* I thought.

7

Decisive Dedication

How quiet it is tonight, I thought, sitting there in Bangladesh. Except for the drone of insects outside my bedroom screens, silence reigned. The usual sounds — workmen singing, clattering logs — from the nearby boat landing were stilled. At the moment even the steps of my guards, pacing the far end of their beat, were inaudible.

Joan, my colleagues, and our families popped into my mind. There were thirty-four of them — four men, nine women, and twenty-one children — who had evacuated from war-torn Bangladesh. They were undoubtedly having their problems trying to travel through the guerrilla-infested jungles of northern Burma. What would they think if they knew I had to put a decoy in the bed? For a civilian, I was making some very military preparations.

*   *   *

As soon as I finished my internship, the Navy had plans for me. Because the United States Navy, through its V-12 program, had paid for two years of my college education, it now demanded two years of service in return. My first year's assignment as a Navy doctor took us to Washington, D.C., to work in a dispensary.

On arrival, we first selected an apartment in nearby Arlington and then looked for a church. None near our apartment compared with National Tabernacle, pastored by the Reverend DeLoss Scott; so we traveled eighteen miles to that church. Pastor Scott's preaching, warm and Bible-based, reminded us of that of Pastors Matthew and Lockerbie.

I enjoyed my work in Washington and found my co-workers congenial. One day at the office we viewed a training film, which came on screen with a carousing party much like those I used to help organize in medical school days. But more educational than the content of the film was my own reaction to the drunkenness in the opening scene. A sense of dislike and aversion welled up inside me. What I used to love I now found distasteful. Something powerful had happened to me in that instant of time back in the entryway of that crummy little apartment in Brooklyn. As a man turns a faucet handle to stop the flow of water abruptly and completely, so God had turned some moral "handle" inside me to stop the flow of un-Christ-like behavior and habits. Since that one life-changing moment, I never drank, gambled, or swore again.

We had a natural inclination to share with others who expressed interest in the great things we had learned and the happy change of life we had experienced. Our biblical studies strengthened this inclination. Jesus said, "You shall be my witnesses." Nancy, a stenographer in the dispensary office, drank up all we told her and attended church with us. Within a few weeks she made her decision and became an ardent follower of Christ.

Her working-for-a-living days over, Joan loved being a homemaker and putting into practice all she had learned as a home economics major. Pregnant again, she proceeded, according to the script, to threaten to miscarry at the one-month mark. Once during her first pregnancy she was bedfast, twice during her second pregnancy the same, and now for the fourth time she went to bed threatening to miscarry. *Will we ever have a child?* we wondered. We could only hope and wait and pray. As the early threat of miscarriage passed by, Joan's pregnancy continued on into the later months.

In the eighth month, our friend, another doctor's wife, did suffer a miscarriage. Home from the hospital, she was yet unable to care for her active three-year-old. With no relative or other friend to help, they turned to Joan with a request to spend every day with Donna for a week, until Keith came home from work to take over each evening. With a certain expertise, born of "long experience in the field," Joan felt sure she could help the girl emotionally and physically. With eyes wide open to the risks involved, she felt moved to spend the week with the young woman. Some heavy lifting was unavoidable. On the last day of Joan's self-given assignment, when I went to pick her up, Donna asked to hear more about the spiritual life we enjoyed. We explained.

"It's right and true," she said. "I know it is! What can I do to believe in the right way?"

To be sure she understood the way, we explained it again, and how to pray a simple prayer accepting Christ as her Saviour and Lord. She did pray, and the great transaction happened in her life.

On that last day of helping her friend, preliminary labor pains began for Joan. Although she went to bed, the process could not be completely stopped. After several days, active labor began and I took her to the hospital.

"Don't worry," she said, seeing my furrowed brow. "Even though it is six weeks early, our baby will be all right this time. I'm sure of it. It was right to help Donna despite the risk. Donna needed the help — and Donna needed Christ. When we do what's right, God will do His part."

She voiced a tremendous principle — and a prophecy. Our diminutive daughter entered the world, tiny but healthy, at seven and a half months. She weighed in at four pounds even. How exciting it was to have at last a real live daughter, our very own! We were overjoyed! Three weeks in the incubator added another pound, enough to let her come home from the hospital. We took her home to Arlington the long way around, past Washington's famed cherry blossoms. We named our new daughter Wendy, and behaved like a typical pair of proud parents. Gone was the sorrow of the year before!

Feeling that baptism should be reserved for adults or children who have taken a knowledgeable step of faith, our church did not baptize infants. Babies were, however, often dedicated at the church. After the Easter Sunday sermon, with Wendy in my arms, we walked to the front of the church. Dedicating our child to God and His safekeeping and ourselves to be godly parents made a deep impression on us.

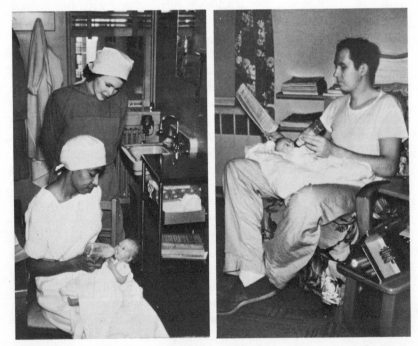

Wee Wendy's last hospital feeding   New baby, new dad

Our Bible studies revealed to us that infant-parent dedication was only a part of the overall concept of dedication. We found it to be a powerful concept! Webster's Dictionary defined dedication as "an act or rite of dedicating to a divine being or to a sacred use." We learned that from the Christian point of view, this means giving, presenting, yielding, surrendering, offering something to God. But what else did God want us to present to Him? Among other Scriptures, we saw an answer in Romans 6 and 12. The Christians in Rome were challenged to offer themselves completely to God as those who have been brought from death to life. They were encouraged to make a decisive dedication of their bodies, to present all their members and faculties as a living sacrifice.

"How logical," we remarked, "Communist leaders and other religious leaders make a similar demand upon their followers. They ask for absolute dedication and devotion to themselves and their causes. If these human, temporal leaders espousing transient, ephemeral causes, can find people to live — and even die — for them, surely God should challenge us to dedicate ourselves fully to Him and His eternal, glorious cause!"

"Now it is clear!" we said to each other. Facing us, then, was a second great decision, a second great step in the Christian life. The Bible told us that this act would put us in position to be directed into a God-guided life. Wow! God was telling us through his Word that we needed to dedicate (give, yield, surrender, offer, set apart) ourselves to God that He might take us, reshape us, direct us, and use us for good and spiritual purposes. In some hazy, unclear way, consciously or subconsciously, this point had been nagging at us since the death of our infant son. Our studies following his death had revealed to us this great truth.

Finally the day came, for each of us, when the last barrier collapsed and individually we gave ourselves back to the Lord who loved us, choosing to walk in His way for us.

Just a few weeks later came the church missionary conference. For a full week, night after night, various foreign missionaries from different lands gave addresses concerning their Christian work overseas. Although I felt it was not for me, I found their experiences, colored slides, and messages fascinating. On the final climactic Sunday night, the speaker emphasized the necessity of missions and the need for Christians to be fully dedicated to the Lord — then came the invitation. First, the speaker invited those who sensed some direction or call to be foreign missionaries to stand. Three people stood to their feet — but I remained riveted to my seat, for I sensed no such call. Then phase two of the invitation: "Friends, you may not feel called to serve as a foreign missionary, but God desires that every Christian give or dedicate his life unreservedly to Him. Perhaps you have not felt a call to missionary service, but you *are* willing to serve God however and wherever He may lead you, whether in this country or on a foreign field."

Now the time had come to make our decision public. As though our minds were one, without hesitation Joan and I stood, sealing publicly our willingness to follow God's plan for us — whatever it might turn out to be.

The Navy decided rather suddenly that I had served long enough in Washington, D.C. We were assigned to a little island in the sparkling South Pacific. Knowing we would visit our families on the way overseas, I prayed earnestly that God would assist me to help my younger brothers learn spiritual truth and believe. Sent ahead of Joan to prepare suitable housing for her coming, I arrived alone in Nebraska to visit my wonderful family.

Almost immediately I learned two things. First, my brother Jim had already gained spiritual insight and, through the influence of Inter-Varsity Christian Fellowship at his college campus, had become a Christian believer. Through Jim's experience I learned that God has ways to answer my prayers without using me directly. My youngest brother Charles did learn much those several days and professed faith in Christ.

Reluctantly departing that happy reunion, I headed overseas. Honolulu, with palm-lined boulevards, and surfers daringly riding the waves at Waikiki Beach impressed me. The last flight finally circled over a tiny green-jungled island with clean, glistening sand beaches emerging from the deep, blue Pacific. A coral reef, frosted with crashing walls of spray, etched a five-mile-long white line separating the Pacific from a smooth aquamarine lagoon. After landing I settled in and took charge of the small hospital. Within the month I cabled Joan to pick up three-month-old Wendy and come.

Joan came. But it wasn't easy! With a tiny baby in arms, and inexperienced at flying, she was hardly prepared to look out her window over the Pacific and see the propeller suddenly stop functioning. Not knowing the other three engines could maintain the plane aloft she thought, *This is it!* When the plane, at that precise moment, dipped a wing in a steep banking turn, her worst fears seemed confirmed. Then the loudspeaker crackled and barked: "Because of engine trouble we are dumping fuel. Do not be alarmed. We shall be circling and dumping fuel for ten minutes; then we will return to San Francisco for repairs." Phew! What a relief! That evening the trip resumed.

With great joy I welcomed Joan and Wendy at the end of their long journey. While the base physician's house was under construction, we were assigned to a former BOQ (Bachelor Officers' Quarters) quonset.

For the first time I practiced on my own as a physician. Hepatitis (virus infection of the liver), a scourge of overseas Americans, hit our group in epidemic form. I became expert at diagnosing hepatitis in its very earliest stages. With treatment of the cases, semiisolation, attention to base sanitation, and time, we conquered the epidemic. This experience with hepatitis would stand me in good stead years later.

A young married American woman came to the office one day complaining of very mild abdominal pain and "feeling funny." Although my examination revealed inconclusive findings, I suspected a particular illness. I told her to rest and return in two hours for another examination. Returning, she explained, "I feel the pain a little worse and now I'm slightly dizzy." Those symptoms, plus the reexamination, showed that she suffered from early internal bleeding from a pregnancy in an abnormal place, the tube alongside her uterus. That meant surgery, but the island boasted no surgeon. Although as a student I had argued against being a surgeon, I now wished I had surgical knowledge and skill for this. Fortunately, by radio we successfully arranged a mercy flight to a larger hospital on another island. The operation saved the young woman's life.

Much spiritual work needed doing on the island. Leadership of the disorganized church group soon fell on me and, with the help of Joan and several others, we kept the services going. Not infrequently, my lot was to speak in the Sunday services, still a very traumatic experience for me. Directing the church group and the base medical department gave me my first real taste of administration; I found that I liked it, possibly because it involved organizing things. With trepidation, I undertook teaching a Bible class to nationals. With the help of a superb interpreter, the teaching got across, and some of the class members made the great decision to receive Christ. I remember them now, silhouetted by the setting sun, walking into the sea to be baptized "in the name of the Father and of the Son and of the Holy Spirit." I had no notion then that these experiences were God-designed to prepare me for the future.

Weekends were adventure time. With little Wendy in a basket, we explored by jeep jungle roads and beaches. After storms or nearby typhoons, we would rise at 4 A.M., basket and baby in tow, to race for the western beaches. There we collected the blue-green glass balls, broken from Japanese fishermen's nets, which the heavy waves washed ashore. We displayed these glass balls prominently in our new, attractive base physician's home. That lovely home, with its million-dollar view of the reef and the Pacific, taught me an important lesson. Although I enjoyed the home, I learned that we were no more or less happy in it than in our former, more ordinary home. Up to that point, making big money formed an important part of my life's plan for the future. After all, Joan had worked very hard for four years to help put me through medical college and internship; to compensate for her sacrifices, I wanted to make the future plush for her. (Of course, I expected to enjoy the affluence with her.) The house episode, however, showed us that happiness and satisfaction could not be bought with money.

Our new insight into affluence did not, however, change our well-laid plans for the future. I sent in my application to the Mayo Clinic for the coveted fellowship in internal medicine. After several years of advanced study and certification as a specialist, we would establish our home in a big city in the Pacific Northwest, surrounded by recreational facilities. I would pursue private practice part-time to make money, and part-time I would do research and teach medical students and young doctors. In this way I could both earn a living and make a contribution to medical science and my profession. We would live near a strong church where we could take an active part and raise a Christian family.

As we neared the end of our tour of duty, this neat plan began to seem less pat. In Brooklyn and Washington, from time to time, Christian friends had used such expressions as "God's will for your life," "God led me to do it," etc. The implication seemed to be that God actually, in the twentieth century, can guide a person into correct decisions, and He desires to do so. The time had come to study out the facts about God's guidance. We found the study fascinating.

We learned, first of all, that God does, in fact, have a plan for each individual member of His family. That God could have a tailor-made plan for us seemed incredible, yet strangely reasonable. If God felt it wise to have a design for the universe, why shouldn't He have a design for our lives? We understood immediately that His plan would be better than our own plan; for, from His divine perspective, He knew and saw our future. And, having proved His love, we were sure He loved us even more than we loved ourselves. Moreover, He knew our weaknesses and failings, our abilities and talents more clearly and objectively than we knew them.

But we needed a way to go about determining God's plan and direction. Prayerfully, carefully, we devised a Bible-based formula*

---

*See **Appendix A. Finding God's Will and His Personal Plan.**

which has never failed us throughout these years: 1) erase and pray, 2) read and remember, 3) consider and think, 4) decide and check.

The time had come to put the formula to work, for we were nearing the end of our tour of naval duty. We had to face squarely the major question: What is God's personal plan for the life work of Vic and Joan Olsen? Setting aside two weeks, we cut our ordinary work load to the bone and spent every available minute seeking the answer to that critical question. We found our Bible-based formula an invaluable help.

First, we did, to the best of our ability, erase our own desires so that God could imprint on our "mental chalkboards" His own plan. And we prayed earnestly that He would guide our deliberations and reveal His plan to us.

Second, we did remember and study many of God's overall guiding principles pertinent to most human decisions. And we roamed far and wide through God's verbal orchard plucking many of His written truths. Many passages, we discovered, emphasize the universal, or planet-wide applicability of the gospel (good news) of Christ. Concerning this worldwideness factor a certain pattern emerged:

1. God planned a way of eternal life suitable for every single member of the human race.
2. Christ died for us all and He is able to pardon and save every one of us.
3. God's great desire is that every person hear the good news, believe it, and find everlasting life.
4. Christ commanded and commissioned His followers to go into all the world and share the good news with every person.

Well, so what? That didn't mean we would have to go overseas. After all, America is part of the world and many Americans need physical and spiritual help.

Third, we considered the actual options before us and thought through all aspects of the problem. My options were limited: some nonmedical field of work God might designate, private medical practice, medical research and teaching, military or industrial medicine, public health medicine, some combination of the above, secular medicine overseas, medical missions overseas.

The last on the list, medical missions, unpleasantly jolted us. Months before in Brooklyn, an elderly lady in the church had said, "Now that young Dr. Olsen has become a Christian believer, he'll no doubt be a missionary."

Overhearing her comment, I had inwardly curdled. *How can peo-*

ple say such things, I had thought. *My life is well planned, and I don't need any interference.*

The more we thought, meditated, and prayed about the possibilities, however, the more medical missions seemed a live option. I viewed the idea with mingled excitement and dread. Had I really erased my own plans and motives from my mind and heart? I hoped so. Was my dedication, that once-for-all offer, sincere and complete? Yes, no doubt about that. But had my self-surrender *remained* 100 percent solid, or had it slipped in an area or two making me guilty of spiritual Indian-giving?

Finally, drawing a line down a sheet of typing paper, we headed the two columns "for" and "against" medical missions. The few entries in the "against" column featured needs in America, children's education problems, and the large amount of money we could give to missions if I became a successful practicing physician. The "for" column grew longer day by day as our study and prayer brought new facts into focus. Our entries reminded us that we were young enough and healthy enough to qualify for such service. Another note, in the "for" column, stated "few are qualified." Considering the four most basic qualifications (youth, health, dedicated life, Bible training), only one in one hundred Christians, at any given moment of time, is qualified for mission service. At that given point of time, ninety-nine out of one hundred must stay home. Within the ninety-nine, however, were some (like us) who could take biblical studies and become qualified.

Another entry spoke of "the church's neglect." The professing church sends 6 percent of her workers and 4 percent of her money to the foreign field. Yet, the great mass of the world's population is "over there." Only one man in ten, in this world of ours, is a native English speaker. Nine out of ten people, the great bulk of the human race, speak some other language and live across the seas.

Our "for" column also contained the words "man's need unsatisfied." Millions around the world were not hearing the good news of God's love and forgiveness through the Lord Jesus Christ. In America any person can easily hear it, read it, or see it. In other parts of the world the situation is very different. We read the words of someone who said, "If you see ten men lifting a huge log, nine men lifting the small end and one man lifting the heavy end, and you want to help, on which end will you lift?" The logic was inescapable.

The column grew as we added pertinent points from our biblical studies. We added, "Christ's example," and were moved by the deep meaning involved. Jesus was the first foreign missionary. He was, in fact, the first foreign *medical* missionary. He brought healing to the multitudes, sight to the blind; and at His touch, the crippled leaped for joy. Christ the Lord left more than an affluent society to help us; He left behind the glories of heaven and eternal fellowship with the Father to live and work among the strange "tribe" of human beings. Twelve or thirteen thousand miles is the farthest we possibly could go for God, that is, around to the other side of the world. But Jesus came all the way from heaven, wherever it is, all the way to the pinpoint in the universe which is our planet.

We studied Christ's great tell-everybody command. When He, victorious, rose from the dead that first Easter Sunday, He returned to His disciples with an explicit command to go worldwide with His message of redemption. Jesus frightened His disciples that night when He appeared to them in person in Jerusalem. But as they looked at Him, touched Him, and ate with Him, their fears evaporated into clouds of joy. Then He addressed them in a new and different way! Jesus said, in that first back-from-the-dead sermon, "Go into all the world and preach the good news," and "As my Father has sent me, so send I you." Forty days later His last words to them were, "You shall be my witnesses in Jerusalem [the city], and in all Judea [the state], and in Samaria [the neighboring state], and to the uttermost part of the earth."

"Wow! No wonder they call it the Great Commission," I said. "Of all the religious and political figures of the world, only one, Jesus Christ, returned from the grave to give his great command." Over several days we studied more, dug deeper, reviewed the options, prayed over them, and reexamined the pros and cons of serving Christ overseas.

Point four in our outline was "decide and check" (for a sense of certainty and peace of mind). And inexorably, the day came, the day of decision. On that day, we both knew, as well as we had ever known any other fact, that God's call, His personal plan for us, was medical missionary service overseas! We had the sense of peace and certainty that we had discovered God's plan for us. And was I happy about it? No. Misery overwhelmed me.

"I can't do it, God," I agonized, resisting His sure call. I had reclaimed part of myself given months ago to God — I was a spiritual Indian-giver. Something about giving up my own carefully laid life-plans seemed unusually painful. Daily I agonized and nightly I restlessly tossed and turned. To know God's plan and reject it produces spiritual agony. Two days — four days — six days — seven days.

On the seventh day, walking alone on the beach, pressed on every side by experience, human feelings, heredity, environment, biblical teaching, God's direction, and many other forces, the crisis came. It had to come! Can the creature fight the Creator and win? No, of course not.

"God does love us," I reasoned. "I know He does. And He knows the future as well as He knows my nature and makeup. And we have learned that money and a fine house don't assure happiness. Why am I fighting this plan of His for me? How really ridiculous!"

Suddenly and surely I knew I must accept that plan. Kneeling in the white, sun-washed sand, I confessed, "Oh, Father, I've done wrong. Please forgive me for fighting You and rejecting Your plan. I had no right. You have done everything for me — for us. Oh, Lord, please forgive me. And I do agree, I do accept the plan. Please help me to follow every part of it." And, as the incoming Pacific tide advanced to cover the sands, so the vibrant, joyous deep peace of God flooded over my soul.

Returning quickly to home and Joan, I told her. She smiled, and as her eyes brimmed over, we held each other. She had waited quietly and patiently that awful seven days, waited for me to come to my senses, somehow knowing all the time that eventually I would. God wasn't the only one who knew me better than I knew myself.

Heading for the boondocks

Returning to the USA

It seemed that three conditions, or provisos, were attached to our personal plan, our call to service:

1. We must be prepared thoroughly to represent our Lord with the best medical-surgical work possible.
2. We must seek a place with a great medical need, where people die without a hospital or trained doctor to help them.
3. We must find some pioneer field with a great spiritual need, where no one has gone to share the good news.

The implications of these provisos staggered us! My long-standing plans to specialize in internal medicine were now passé, out of step with our new program. What would a specialist in internal medicine do in a pioneer area when the first surgical emergency came along? He might come apart at the seams! Obviously, I must change all the old plans and become a surgeon! Unbelievable! Me, a surgeon? After heading toward internal medicine all those years — even taking my internship only in internal medicine? There was no other way. It had to be! Not only that, but also, because broad knowledge is essential on a pioneer field, I must take a second internship, rotating through all the services of the hospital.

Three days later came the acid test in the form of a letter. The envelope's return address read: The Mayo Clinic, Rochester, Minnesota.

With slightly unsteady hands, I opened the envelope and read: "We are happy to inform you that you have been accepted for a fellowship in the Department of Internal Medicine of the Mayo Clinic."

The dream of years materialized and in my hand! I looked at Joan — she looked at me. Folding the letter, I replaced it in the envelope and laid it down. That hand must not clutch such a letter too long, for it was destined to hold a scalpel. Somehow, I did not find it difficult to write back and decline the fellowship. God's work in my heart had been done thoroughly. I was at peace.

Despite the short time left on the island, it was possible to arrange for a rotating internship back in Brooklyn's huge King's County Hospital. Then with a lump in our throats we packed up, taught our last Bible classes, turned my patients and their records over to the new doctor, received with appreciation the good wishes of our friends, boarded the plane, and headed back across the blue Pacific.

8

Shaping of a Surgeon

I DEVOTED most of the next five years, 1954 to 1959, to becoming a surgeon. During that period three more Olsen children appeared on the scene, making our family complete. To prepare ourselves spiritually for overseas service, we threw ourselves into the work of our church and carried out biblical and theological studies by means of correspondence courses. Throughout the five-year period we carefully analyzed many mission agencies and their overseas posts; when the sense of guidance came strongly, we selected our mission board and field of service.

I elected to take a second internship for three reasons. Because I had previously interned solely in internal medicine, I needed experience as a surgical intern. I required, furthermore, additional breadth of medical-surgical knowledge to serve effectively in a pioneer area of "country x." Finally, a second internship would give me time to study surgical training programs of various hospitals and gain guidance to make the correct selection. Warmly welcomed back to Brooklyn by old friends, we settled in a furnished apartment, and I began my rotating internship in one of the world's unique hospitals.

Brooklyn's Kings County Hospital was the largest general hospital in America. The ancient, massive, weather-beaten brick buildings housed over twenty-seven-hundred beds. The beds contained patients harboring some of the most difficult and challenging diseases in America. Kings County catered to the poor and underprivileged of the city. The huge wards, complex cases, the difficulty maintaining cleanliness and an adequate staff of ancillary help provided a monumental challenge to any young doctor willing to work his heart out.

I relished my months as a surgical intern on the surgical wards. Knowing I would be teaching and training surgical interns for the next four years motivated me to learn the work and understand the problems thoroughly. I worked long hard hours examining new surgical patients, incising their abscesses, splinting their fractures, and participating in their operations as a surgeon's assistant. On some occasions, during that period, the scalpel was handed to me. Whether the skin was black, white, or tan, the scalpel's razor-sharp blade always drew the same spurting red line through it. Control the bleeding — deepen the red line — control the bleeding — deepen the incision. Step by step, I followed the pattern of the operation until the tense, inflamed appendix or the bulging hernia sac appeared.

Those first operations excited me, for they represented the initial toddling steps of an infant surgeon. It was becoming quite clear that I would enjoy my life as a surgeon, despite my deprecation of surgery and surgeons during student days.

Neurosurgery, my next service, also intrigued me. Surgery of the brain, spinal cord, and nerves is difficult, usually dangerous, and sometimes disheartening. Because tumors and other surgical diseases of the brain are usually fatal if unchecked, a successful operation is thrilling. But for every success, of course, there were failures.

Sometimes hemorrhage occurs inside the skull without injury simply because a person is born with a weakness in a blood vessel. When the weak area ruptures, intracranial hemorrhage occurs. A beautiful red-headed young woman, whom I admitted, suffered from just this problem. Although the bleeding ceased, her severe headache and stiff neck lasted several days. Various members of the neurosurgical staff developed a remarkable interest in her case and hotly debated the treatment. Special X rays revealed the weak spot located in an area of the brain difficult to approach. Because sometimes a second hemorrhage never occurs, some of the doctors felt that surgery should be avoided or delayed. Others of us felt the risk of a second or third more severe hemorrhage to be greater than the risk of surgery. Finally, the neurosurgeon in charge decided that surgery should be done and scheduled the operation for the next day.

That evening I did my best to help the frightened girl emotionally and spiritually; she seemed very grateful. I could not be sure, however, that she made any step of faith or committal to God and His Son. Later the nurses cut her long red locks, shaved her scalp, and gave her a sleeping pill according to my instruction written on the order sheet. The girl never awakened. Early in the morning hours the second hemorrhage came, massively. Through the hole in that artery located deep in the brain, her heart pumped a rampaging river of blood which destroyed her brain and her life.

On weekends off we had another internship going. Pastor Lockerbie and the leaders of the church opened the way for us to receive training in a spiritual internship. Joan and I sponsored a young people's group at the Bay Ridge Baptist Church, now a new, fresh, bright, substantial structure. Joan spoke to a women's group and Sunday school classes while I gave messages at young people's and adult meetings in various churches. With trepidation I addressed a group of ministers on the subject of science and religion. I appreciated the opportunity to preach on Christ's resurrection at an Easter sunrise service in the park. Because our life would be medical missions overseas, this spiritual internship was invaluable.

We read everything we could find on various principles of medical missions. The writings of Dr. Paul Adolph, a veteran medical missionary, seemed particularly wise. Little did we suspect how intricately our lives would intertwine with his life years later. Simultaneously, we studied various mission agencies.

To become more knowledgeable about mission boards, we wrote to over twenty of them. The replies were highly educational. Some boards were denominational while others were interdenominational. Some had money in the bank to send the new appointee immediately overseas, while others required the appointee to travel about in deputation to raise his support from the churches. When two agencies sent back our typewritten letter with pencil-written answers on the same sheet, we realized that some missions were small, struggling organizations without adequate secretarial help. Other missions sent back excellent responses detailing their medical missions and explaining their urgent needs for medical personnel. Surprisingly, few agencies followed the best principles of medical missions. We read each reply with interest and carefully filed it away for future reference and study.

We also analyzed surgical training programs, called surgical residencies. After thought and prayer our criteria for the best type of program came clear. Knowing that the spectrum of patients overseas would be frighteningly extensive, I wanted an approved hospital providing very broad surgical training. To assure its scientific soundness, I wanted the program to have a medical college affiliation. The salary had to approach a living wage; we dared not go into debt, as many do, because we were not headed for a lucrative surgical practice afterward. As we had lived the last four years in the East and overseas, we hoped that a suitable program might be found in the Middle West, bringing us back into closer contact with our families.

With these criteria in mind, we obtained the appropriate journal listing all surgical residency training programs. Our criteria limited the field considerably and several letters narrowed it even further. The two outstanding choices seemed to be the Wayne County General Hospital near Detroit and the Milwaukee County Hospital.

Sensing God's personal plan usually requires gathering sufficient information. So, one cold gray winter's morning I flew to Detroit to a congenial interview with the surgical director of Wayne County General Hospital.

I flew on to Milwaukee. Most large county or city hospitals are located in the crowded urban areas of great cities. My first view of Milwaukee County Hospital, situated in a lovely residential area, provided a pleasant shock. The attractive buildings were nestled in a parklike area with green lawns, willow trees, and a duck pond. The new building under construction would be even larger, newer, and more attractive. The place was beautiful! The surgeon in charge seemed deeply interested, not only in advanced, scientific surgical treatment, but also in kind and compassionate patient care. That appealed to me. Milwaukee County Hospital, furthermore, met our criteria almost perfectly. The salary, however, was a little less than we had hoped for. Intuitively, I felt that this was it, but did not yet commit myself to the hospital authorities. After my return to Brooklyn, Joan and I discussed, studied, and prayed further; we became mutually assured that in spite of the financial sacrifice involved, the next step in our divine personal plan would be surgical training at Milwaukee County Hospital.

When our Brooklyn internship finished, we said good-bye to those dear Brooklyn friends, packed up our few belongings, and drove to Milwaukee. Unknown to us, our coming to Milwaukee coincided with the visit of two men to a country on the other side of the world called East Pakistan. Rev. C. Victor Barnard and Rev. Richard Durham were capable, dedicated men surveying the land on behalf of their mission agency, the ABWE (Association of Baptists for World Evangelism). They were to forward the survey findings to their Philadelphia headquarters where the board would decide whether or not to begin mission work in that undermissioned land.

We found an apartment with low rent and a pleasant yard. The somewhat noisy dental laboratory on the ground floor at the front of the building constituted a disadvantage. The laboratory noise, however, was nothing compared to the din and clatter of the train that passed a hundred feet away. Because the downstairs room was not large enough for company, the living room would need to be upstairs. To keep warm, we would have to feed the coal furnace, but my previous experience keeping our Omaha rooming house warm had prepared me amply for this task. We took it!

Simultaneously, we shopped around various churches in Milwaukee. We finally selected as our church home the Garfield Avenue Baptist Church. Dr. William Kuhnle had a warm and wonderful pastor's heart, and he and Mrs. Kuhnle became our life-long friends.

I admired the surgical residency system used in this country, pioneered by American surgeon Dr. William Halsted before 1900. As a surgical resident I would be given teaching and supervision, then allowed to use in practice what I learned well. Each year, as I advanced up the scale from first to fourth year resident, my instruction would become increasingly sophisticated, and I would undertake increasingly more difficult operations. This system of graded instruction and responsibility, mixed liberally with long hours of study and incredibly tense and difficult work, would make me a surgeon.

As a *first-year resident* I started in the emergency room of the Milwaukee County Emergency Hospital. After the first few days of seeing shooting, knifing, and accident cases, inebriates, addicts, and other police cases, I knew surely that this was a midwestern version of Kings County Hospital.

I liked my work and felt at home. While on this service, I wrote a paper on tetanus immunization to guide future surgeons as they worked in the emergency room. We sewed lacerations, cared for heart attack victims, treated burn cases, and attended a hundred other disabilities. It distressed me to learn that several burned children who had survived the early stage emergency room treatment ultimately died in the hospital from various complications of their burns. I began to pray, analyze, and study intently in order to be prepared later, when caring for such children in the hospital would be my responsibility.

Reading the latest surgical journals helped a great deal. Often, shortly after reading about a new technique, a patient requiring just that type of treatment would come along. I once read an article about a slick way to remove a ring seriously stuck on a swollen finger using only a simple piece of string. The next day a child came to the emergency room with a massive circle of stainless steel stuck tightly on his swollen, bluish-white finger. It would have been virtually impossible to saw safely through the heavy, hard steel. To the amazement of everyone, including myself, the string trick worked like a charm and a dangerous situation was quickly resolved.

I moved from the emergency room to a general surgical ward. Taking charge of the day-by-day operation of the ward, I felt thankful for everything I had learned on the surgical wards in Brooklyn. Each month I trained a new batch of interns and senior medical students to carry out properly their functions on the ward. Seeing the need for training materials to speed up this process, I prepared for them an orientation manual, a manual on tying surgical knots, and a paper on surgical suture material (the thread used in doing operations). I became steadily more proficient in doing appendectomies and hernia operations. I tracked down many patients needing hernia repairs in the other county institutions on the property and carried out their operations.

I worked with several other interested residents to establish a branch of the Christian Medical Society (CMS) in Milwaukee. The executive secretary of CMS, Mr. J. Raymond Knighton, came from Chicago to be the speaker at our first meeting. Our paths were destined to cross more than once in the future. We enjoyed warm fellowship with Ray who spent the night in our home. Several weeks later my name appeared in the *CMS Journal* as a new member. One of my University of Nebraska medical college classmates promptly phoned Ray long distance to complain about the grave error of including my name in the roster.

"It's a terrible mistake," he said, "The last time I saw Vic Olsen he was certainly no Christian, and of all the people I know, I would judge him about the least likely ever to follow Christ. There must be some mistake!"

Ray reassured him that our conversion was real because God's power was limitless, and that no mistake had been made.

On the genito-urinary surgery service, I learned all about catheters and how to unplug them. Most of the operations centered on the bladder and prostate gland. We saw many of the devastating effects of venereal disease. I spent time also on the orthopedic surgery service caring for broken, dislocated, and deformed bones and joints. I worked and studied hard to learn smooth plastering technique, setting common fractures, and surgically nailing broken hips.

Because our program allowed no time for Bible college or seminary studies, we determined to study more Bible and theology by correspondence. The correspondence school of the Moody Bible Institute of Chicago we found to be preeminent in this field. After completing a course in doctrine, I started the famous Scofield Bible course. Completion of the 123 lessons would give nine hours of college credit. I found the course fascinating.

Joan, too, began taking correspondence courses. She started out with surveys of the Old and New Testaments and a Sunday school teacher training course. A problem facilitated her studies. She had to live through months of another difficult, unstable pregnancy. While Wendy went to Grandma's house, Joan remained in bed for three months. My hectic schedule at that time kept me in the hospital most of the time. As Joan studied hour after hour by herself, day after day, week after week, she one day realized she was losing her voice. From that day she talked the lessons to herself, memorized Bible verses out loud, and sang songs and hymns to the walls.

When more mission board letters came in, Joan analyzed them and

put them in the file. We were shocked at the rigidity of one mission
agency which would not accept applicants with more than one child.
They expected the applicant to be willing to have his children educated in America from age six. We agreed immediately that this
approach was not for us. We felt keenly the responsibility to love,
nurture, and care for the children we hoped God would give us.

"Hi, honey," I said one night as I arrived home from the hospital.
"What are you studying tonight?"

"Oh," she responded, "I'm studying the books of Revelation and
Daniel. I feel like I have beasts and great images and little horns
whirling around in my head."

"I had a patient today with the same problem," I laughed, "only
his were on the wall."

On Christmas Eve, Lynne Christine was born, but she was not
right. The touchy pregnancy and a virus infection in the early weeks
of the pregnancy had scrambled the great blood vessels around her
heart. Often she wheezed and gasped, and crying made her turn
blue. Special X ray studies showed that an abnormal ring of blood
vessels choked her windpipe and compressed her swallowing tube.

We took Lynne home to nurse her for several months, if possible, so
she could gain a little in size before the serious life-preserving operation. We had oxygen available by her bedside at all times. When
she cried, we held her and played with her to keep the blue away. I
contacted the dean of children's chest surgeons, Dr. Willis Potts, in
Chicago. His examination confirmed the diagnosis and he agreed to
perform the surgery.

On the morning of surgery they wheeled our little Lynne down the
long corridor to the operating room. The delicate operation would
take time. We walked out the main entrance of Chicago's Children's
Memorial Hospital and made our way to the little chapel with stained
glass windows across the street.

"Gracious Father," we prayed, "we want to keep our little Lynne
— we love her so. Give the surgeons wisdom and skill to do their
part. We ask You to do Your special divine part. We pray above all
that Your will might be done because we trust You and Your love and
Your personal plan for Lynne and us. In our Saviour's name we pray.
Amen." As we prayed, a certain serenity filtered through the stress
of the moment like the sun rays which passed through the stained
glass windows making a warm glow of light in the little chapel.
We returned to the hospital to continue our vigil.

Finally the tall figure of Dr. Potts strode forth into the waiting
room.

"The diagnosis was correct," he said briskly. "It's good we didn't

Sick little Lynne at two and a half months

Operation successful! (Lynne, Vic, and Wendy)

wait longer. Her left lung was quite collapsed. We successfully divided the ring of vessels. If she gets through the postoperative period, she should be all right, but the postoperative phase may be rough."

Then, obviously concerned, he put a fatherly arm around each of us and continued, "Do you kids have any money to pay this hospital bill?" Replying that our hospital insurance would cover most of the bill, we thanked him with all our hearts for his surgery and solicitude. Dr. Potts charged nothing for the surgery. We walked back across the street to the little chapel and prayed our thanks to God, asking for His help and healing touch during the postoperative period.

Dr. Potts' words, "The postoperative period may be rough," were accurate. For two weeks Lynne struggled to remain in the "barely alive" column, sometimes improving, other times deteriorating. Three times she very nearly slipped away. But the third week she slowly improved. We left the hospital with full hearts and a precious daughter in our arms.

Despite my limited salary, we were able immediately to pay the incidental expenses of blood transfusion, traveling, etc., because unexpected money had come to us. During the month just before Lynne's surgery, four letters containing checks arrived in the mail. One came from an elderly lady in Brooklyn, another from the Metropolitan Fellowship of Ministers I had addressed in New York City, a third came from a beloved aunt in Chicago, and a fourth from another friend. On each of the four checks was written exactly the same figure: one hundred dollars. The coincidence seemed more than a coincidence and signaled us that God was at work looking after His children.

My *second year of surgical residency* began in the second death house of my experience. The first had been that anatomy laboratory back in the freshman year of medical college. The department of pathology, the second death house, received the bodies of patients who died in the hospital or who reached the hospital DOA (dead on arrival). The cadaver in the anatomy hall had been dead and embalmed for many weeks before we saw it. In the pathology laboratory, however, the bodies were not yet embalmed and often still warm to the touch. Our scientific instincts, however, soon overcame our emotional reactions and helped us to view an autopsy as a surgical operation after death, undertaken to determine the cause of demise and to help others in the future with the knowledge gained.

Because we physicians and surgeons possess a fierce desire to preserve life, a patient's death is extremely painful to us. It is not enough, however, to accept death; it must be studied and analyzed to provide clues for future cures. At the time of autopsy we inspected, handled, felt, cut, and weighed the various organs. After slides of the tissues were prepared and stained, we spent hours peering at them through the microscope. We carried out the same analysis and study of tissues removed each day in the operating rooms. Through this process we gained a new and deeper understanding of disease and death.

The more I saw and understood death, the more impressed I became with the miracles that Christ did when He raised people from death to life and returned Himself from the dead. My faith increased as I came to understand more fully the power of my Saviour who is stronger than death.

Early in the second year of residency, Pastor Kuhnle requested me to teach a large Sunday school class of young married couples. I pondered the request and prayed. My Sunday mornings would be free the next seven to eight months while I worked on pathology and anesthesia services. Teaching would give me an opportunity to serve my church and would be for me a "spiritual residency." I agreed. I loved that class of bright, alert men and women. Most of the husbands were business or professional men and up to eighty persons would attend on Sunday mornings. Because my schedule was extremely heavy, occasionally I could find no study time until Saturday night. On several such Saturday nights I remained up the entire night to be properly prepared for that tremendous class.

Spurred by the insights we were gaining from the Scriptures, our class became eager to serve. Because one of the couples had a severely retarded child, Larry, we began to search for ways to help such children and their families. Ultimately, an organization, Shepherds, Inc., was formed. God used the prayerful promotion of Shepherds powerfully in the lives of many Americans. This organization now operates a beautiful home and school for retarded children in

Union Grove, Wisconsin, worth three-quarters of a million dollars. Little Larry has become big Larry in the warm, loving environment of the Shepherds home. He and many of his retarded friends, despite their limited mental capacities, were found to have remarkable spiritual potential. Many of them have understood and believed the good news of God's love and Jesus' death for them.

Dr. Kuhnle launched Joan into her "spiritual residency" also. She became superintendent of the Sunday school's junior department which involved considerable organization, program planning, and teacher training. Later he selected her to head up the summer daily vacation Bible school (DVBS). She agreed, with inward reservations about her ability to do the job, for the task of organization was complex. She needn't have worried. Under her direction, more than sixty teachers and helpers brought in, inspired, and instructed four hundred children. In the process many of these young people found spiritual life.

Lynne continued to improve and grow while her big sister Wendy kept us constantly entertained. Wendy was blond and pert, full of life. One day, during a bout of intestinal flu, she inquired, "Am I going to heaven today, Mommy?"

"Of course not, honey," Joan responded, "Why do you ask?"

"Well, Mommy," Wendy replied, "you said I have 'die-arrhea.' "

An unexpected visitor arrived literally out of the blue. The Rev. C. Victor Barnard and his pilot-preacher companion came by private plane to present the need for a Christian doctor in East Pakistan. Rev. Barnard, an Australian, had given a stirring address at our church several months earlier so we recognized him immediately. He reviewed for us his survey trip to East Pakistan sixteen months earlier on behalf of the Association of Baptists for World Evangelism (ABWE). Having served there with another mission for years prior to his ABWE connection, he knew the country exceedingly well. Following the survey, ABWE decided officially to open up mission work in East Pakistan and within a few weeks Rev. Barnard planned to set sail for that land of rice and raindrops. He hoped that if we shared his view of medical missions and applied to serve in East Pakistan, the ABWE board might favor such an application.

Mr. Barnard's view of medical missions, however, clashed hopelessly with mine. He pictured a doctor moving about from village to village with a black bag in hand, treating minor illnesses as best he could. I visualized a small but capable hospital as the essential beginning. I felt we needed a team of doctors and nurses and other workers to provide excellent medical-surgical care worthy to represent the Lord Jesus Christ, and in that environment of love and concern, daily share His good news with others. As we discussed medical missions, I found that Mr. Barnard's views were fixed and nothing I presented changed them. As much as I appreciated this fine dedicated man of God, I was sure East Pakistan was no longer an option because I could not accomplish God's revealed plan for me within that framework.

Anesthesia service followed pathology. Finding anesthesia intriguing and recognizing its importance to my future program, I devoted myself to learning all I could in the three-month period. We learned many techniques of relieving pain and putting operative patients to sleep, or paralyzing the area of incision.

As surgical residents we worked terribly hard during our residency. We always had after-hours duty at least every other night and every other weekend. To supplement the Olsen income I sometimes worked at an emergency hospital throughout the night for sixty dollars. But this meant four days and three nights straight on duty. That fourth night home was only a greeting, supper together, a few minutes of conversation, and collapse into bed.

I felt somewhat prepared for my next service, neurosurgery, by my experience as a neurosurgical intern in Brooklyn. I had to learn much more, however, and learn it quickly, for my responsibility was great. Sometimes we received patients at the emergency hospital and shipped them to our own services at the main county hospital for surgery.

One night, with several sirens screaming simultaneously, the police brought three patients to the emergency hospital. The first patient, a woman, arrived too late — dead from bullet wounds. The second patient, her paramour, I found in shock from bullet wounds causing internal bleeding. The third patient, husband to the dead woman, had shot them both, placed the revolver to his own temple, and pulled the trigger. I concentrated my immediate attention on the second patient. After bailing him out of shock, I shipped him by ambulance to his private surgeon at another hospital. The husband, with gray-white flecks of brain oozing out of a neat round bullet hole in the left temple, still lived. After emergency treatment I sent him by ambulance to my own neurosurgical service at the county hospital. Several hours later, after the X rays were taken, I operated on him to remove the bullet, shattered chips of bone, and the damaged segment of brain.

During the days that followed, I found the patient had completely changed his personality when he tried to blow his brains out. Previously a sensitive person, after the injury he felt no anxiety or remorse about the murder of his wife and attempted murder of her friend. I discussed God's truth with him on various occasions, but he never seemed to feel any sense of sin or need of spiritual help.

Also, during that second year of surgical residency, I worked on the ear, nose, and throat service, which I tolerated, and the thoracic (chest) surgery service, which I loved. On the plastic surgery service I learned many valuable techniques including skin grafting, repair of cleft lips, cleft palates, and meticulous stitching techniques. On the children's surgery service I cared for numerous burned children who required very careful care and frequent skin grafting. The onset of infection frequently complicated the long, tedious process: sometimes the infants and children died from the infection and other complications. These were the cases I had worried about when I admitted them to the emergency hospital the previous year. *There must be some better way,* I thought.

To find the better way to treat children with burns, I ransacked the surgical literature for some technique which would speed up the treatment process and decrease the mortality figures. In a key research article I found the technique for which I had been searching. From that day forward, whenever possible, I did not wait for the burned, dying tissue to undergo the three- to four-week process of crusting and separating itself from the underlying living tissue. As soon as the patient recovered from shock and his condition stabilized, I took the child to the operating room and cut away the dead and dying tissue with an electrical knife called a dermatome. Within two or three days the area would be ready for skin grafting. We saved weeks of time and thousands of dollars by this aggressive procedure. Infection and complications decreased, and all of my small friends survived.

As we studied, considered, and prayed over our file of many mission boards, one finally stood out above all the rest, the Association of Baptists for World Evangelism. The leaders were fine spiritual men. Dr. Harold Commons, president of ABWE, a man of warmth, wit, and perception, qualified as a missionary statesman. ABWE successfully followed the wise indigenous principle of missions which brooks no interference in the affairs of Christian foreign nationals once they and their churches are firmly established.

The various facets of the ABWE financial policy impressed us. We had decided early that we wished to affiliate with a mission that did not have money in the bank to send out a new appointee immediately. Rather, we would have to travel about the churches in deputation, presenting our program, and praying that God would stimulate the churches to undertake the necessary support. In this way we would learn how to trust our heavenly Father more fully and would become acquainted with dozens of churches and hundreds or thousands of individuals. These churches and individuals would likewise know us personally, understand our work, and would pray earnestly for us and our activities. Such prayer support would be priceless. ABWE followed this system of support.

We also appreciated ABWE's substantial doctrinal statement which ensured that the mission's members share the same views on doctrine, thus preventing useless squabbles overseas over doctrinal differences.

We greatly appreciated the ABWE attitude toward missionary children. We did not agree with the principle of some missions that children at age six must be sent back to America or off to some distant school. ABWE stated that family problems and children's education problems of missionaries were very personal. The mission would not interfere, but would do everything in its power to help each family find the very best arrangement for their own children's education.

We tentatively approached ABWE about the possibility of service. Our discussion quickly disposed of East Pakistan. We explained that we were not interested and the mission representative stated that, despite Rev. Barnard's hopes, ABWE had no plan to send a doctor to East Pakistan. In fact, the mission had no program for a new medical mission in any unreached area. Yet God had given us two certain provisos about the kind of pioneer place where we should work. ABWE planned for its next doctor to go to the Philippine Islands to an excellent existing medical work, but one which did not match the provisos God had given us. We were confused.

My *third year of surgical residency* began with Joan threatening to miscarry with our third child. Nothing seemed simple or easy or straightforward those days. Back on the general surgery service, I continued to improve and mature as a surgeon. While the chief resident concentrated on the biggest and most complex cases, I concentrated on cases which were major but less intricate: gall bladder operations, gunshot wounds, excision of tumors, et cetera.

One day I admitted a young husband and father named Joe. Even as he began to relate his symptoms, I sensed a deep fear and dark foreboding within Joe. I soon understood why. From his medical history I suspected a tumor in his lung, and I could feel a tumor mass in his left lower abdomen. I mentally connected these findings with the black mole which another surgeon had removed previously. Positive that he was dying with black melanoma cancer, I ordered the necessary tests and X rays to prove that grim diagnosis. I felt constrained to understand his spiritual diagnosis, also, for his life could not last longer than a few months.

In response to my questions, Joe, laughing tightly, said, "Oh, Doc, you don't have to worry about me. I've gone to church for years and, as far as Christ is concerned, I have always believed that he died to be the Saviour of the world." Although I tried, I could not seem to get across the absolute necessity for each of us to recognize his own sin and to decide personally to believe and receive Christ as his own Saviour.

I saw Joe the next day, Sunday morning, in the hospital chapel. As I came from my ward a little late and sat down in the back pew, I could see Joe, clothed in hospital nightclothes and bathrobe, sitting down in front. At the close of the service, Joe — ordinarily a shy, quiet person — stood, saw me in the back, and impulsively shouted out, "Doc! Doc, I've got it!" While the other worshipers looked about in surprise, I headed toward the front to meet Joe halfway down the center aisle.

"You've got what, Joe?" I asked.

"Doc, I've got it," Joe repeated. "After you left yesterday, Doc, I kept thinking about what you told me. Suddenly, I understood that it really wasn't enough to believe in my head that Christ died for the sins of the world. I thought about my own sins. Then I understood that Jesus died for those sins of mine. It was great! So I prayed to God — I asked Him to forgive my sins — I asked Christ to come into my life to be my Saviour. Then I could feel everything was all right. Whatever happens to me, my future is OK. Doc, I've got it!"

Ten months after the courageous Barnard family reached East Pakistan to work with the Rev. Paul Millers planting the ABWE mission in Chittagong District, tragedy struck! Lovely fourteen-year-old Winnifred Mary Barnard died from a small bowel obstruction because her father could find no surgeon to operate. Six months earlier she had undergone an emergency appendectomy in a hospital near her boarding school in South India; the appendicitis and surgery had caused adhesions which, six months later, suddenly obstructed her intestinal tract. After Mary's burial in the Chittagong cemetery, Rev. Barnard wrote to us a deeply moving letter con-

Winnifred Mary Barnard

taining an arresting passage:

> Just last week our precious child, Winnifred Mary, went home to be
> with the Lord. Although we rejoice in the blessed hope, which is
> far better, precious memories crowd in upon us forcing the tears
> from our eyes. But we have no complaint to make, for He doeth
> all things well. . . . The fact came home to me so strongly when in
> desperation I raced around Chittagong seeking a surgeon or medical
> man to relieve her terrible suffering; and in this city of 300,000 I
> could find no one to help, not a surgeon who could operate. You can
> travel the coastline from Akyab in Burma to Dacca in the heart of
> East Pakistan and along this line of over 400 miles there is not one
> skillful surgeon . . . Though our hearts are crushed and bruised, we
> have no complaint to make, for He doeth all things well and our
> prayer is that her passing may be as a corn of wheat falling into the
> ground that it might die and bring forth much fruit.

A few weeks later the ABWE board, shattered by the death of
Mary Barnard and shocked by the lack of medical facilities her death
revealed, acted unanimously to authorize an ABWE medical mission
in East Pakistan. The news soon reached us, but we did not feel this
could be God's place for us. Victor Barnard's letter contained another paragraph which revealed that he still believed in only a very
limited type of medical missions, and our divine guidance was otherwise. Without a suitable hospital, anesthesia, instruments, etc., I could
not have saved Mary Barnard. Besides, we had developed a keen
interest in Nepal and Bhutan. Perhaps through a medical program
we could open up Bhutan, a country closed to Christian missions.

During my third year program, a new chief of surgery, Dr. Edwin
Ellison, was installed. He was brilliant, driving, hardworking, and a
capable teacher and administrator. He traced his surgical lineage
back to the founder of American surgery, Dr. Halsted himself; he
counted himself fifth in succession in the Halsted line of surgeons. He
expected to reorganize the training of surgeons in Milwaukee. A
friendship, based upon mutual respect, developed between us.

During this period, Joan passed through another long, complex,
delicate pregnancy. She spent most of her time in bed for five
months. Frequently she threatened to go into labor and lose the
baby. The infant's tendency to kick like Earthquake McGoon
played its part in the tendency toward premature labor.

Joan, after a difficult day, knowing that the next week might be
worse, joked, "I hope this is not a preview of coming contractions."
During all this time, she kept her mind off her troubles by studying
the Scofield Bible Correspondence Course. With remarkable speed

she traveled through various stages of the complicated Bible study and theology course. She devoted herself wholeheartedly to that study, knowing it was her great opportunity to become proficient in the sacred Word. The weeks and months passed and she finally completed the course; her certificate was dated three days before the birth of Mark Viggo Olsen. We were delighted to have a wonderful, strong, healthy son and thanked God for him.

It was winter, the perfect time to be in charge of the orthopedic surgery service. Falls and automobile accidents on icy streets kept the bones breaking and our service busy. During that period I set fractures and applied casts, rigged up traction systems, operated on broken bones, and nailed or pinned many of these fractures. One month two of my interns were women who felt we should improve the esthetics of our casting. As a result, many "tough guys" whose bones had been broken in barroom brawls went home that month with casts colored baby blue or delicate pink.

Broken hips were common among the aged. One day an elderly woman with just this problem came to us from another of the county institutions. She spoke an eastern European language but not a word of English. I examined her with care and placed her on the operating room schedule for the following morning. Because nailing the hip would allow her to get out of bed soon, surgery gave her the best chance for survival. Within an hour her relatives arrived to ask about the treatment. When I explained that I intended to operate the following morning, they said, "But doctor, she's 108 years old!" Excusing myself, I went to examine the patient again. My findings and conclusions were the same, and the family agreed to the proposed surgery.

Promptly at 8:00 A.M., after the anesthesia had been given, I made the incision over her hip. Operating quickly, I drove the stainless steel nail into place and finding the check X ray satisfactory, closed the incision. She sailed through the surgery beautifully; on the fifth postoperative day we celebrated her one hundred and ninth birthday. A study of the surgical literature revealed no other patient who had undergone such a major operation at that advanced age.

I moved from orthopedic surgery to gynecological surgery (surgery of the female reproductive organs). Through abdominal incisions we removed various cysts, tumors, and cancer-stricken wombs. When babies could not be delivered normally, we removed them abdominally using a valuable operation called the Cesarean section. Some diseases or abnormalities are better operated on from below by the vaginal route. Every vaginal operation I carried out helped prepare me for the very difficult fistula cases I would see in the years ahead.

Despite our attraction toward the ABWE mission, we had turned away from this board. Probably they had no connections in Nepal and Bhutan, and we could see no possibility of a sound medical mission in East Pakistan. We attended as observers the conference of another mission agency which greatly needed doctors on several fields. A few days later, at a church convention, we met, providentially, Dr. Harold Commons, president of ABWE. We learned two helpful facts from him. First, the mission did not necessarily agree with the "black bag" system of medical missions. They operated an effective small hospital in the Philippines. Second, Paul Miller, ABWE missionary in East Pakistan, had worked several years on the Bhutan, Nepal, and Tibet borders, had translated Mark's gospel into Bhutanese, and could answer our questions about these countries. Dr. Commons promised to write to Paul Miller on our behalf.

The crowning year of surgical training was that fourth and *last year of residency*. At the Milwaukee County Hospital the senior resident was responsible and more or less on duty twenty-four hours a day for 365 days. I could never be away from the telephone during that year more than thirty or forty minutes at a time. The picnics we tried were more like track events than family gatherings. It was the year for big responsibility and the big cases.

I started as chief resident on the thoracic surgery service. Because I loved chest surgery this pleased me greatly. During that period I operated on fifty heart and lung cases, the most ever done by a resident on that service. God answered my prayers and there were no fatalities among those fifty patients. The operations that went smoothly and easily without complication I scarcely remembered. The difficult or complicated cases, however, remained indelibly inscribed on my mind.

One patient, a child, harbored an illness which no medicine could cure. The offending section of the lung had to be removed. He seemed very small as we placed him upon the operating table and I gave the order, "Put him to sleep." It was a great morning. Everything was going smoothly. I had located the sick lobe of the left lung and removed it without difficulty. I felt happy and carefree as I closed that incision.

"Stop!" the anesthesiologist barked, "We're in trouble. The blood pressure and pulse are gone!" He had spoken the most devastating words a surgeon can hear — words which meant the child's heart had stopped.

As my hand quickly grasped the scalpel, my soul cried out in agony, *Oh God — help!* Within ten seconds I had slashed the chest open again and seized the boy's heart; it lay in my hand, quiet, not beating at all. I began to squeeze and massage the flabby ball of tissue in my hand. I felt no response. Rhythmically, methodically, as I had been trained, I continued the massage. Still no response. The anesthesia machine breathed pure oxygen into his lungs. As I continued the squeezing motion with my right hand, at last I thought I felt a tiny flicker. Then suddenly, I felt a definite flicker of movement in my hand. A few seconds later I felt a sure beat of that heart; and fifteen seconds later, *dup — dup — dup.* To my immense relief the little heart was beating again, normally, rhythmically. *Thank You, Father,* I breathed inwardly.

I spent my last six months as senior resident on a general surgical ward. Some cases were once-in-a-lifetime types. One morning an excited ear, nose, and throat specialist called me to the recovery room to see a child whose tonsils he had just removed. *Color blue, respirations labored and gasping, pulse racing,* I ticked off mentally as I checked the dying child. Stripping off the sheet, I asked myself, *Why is his abdomen so prominent if he had nothing by mouth before surgery?* Before our eyes his abdomen grew larger and his color bluer.

"I've never seen or heard of anything like this before," I said as we snapped an immediate X ray with the portable unit. The dripping film revealed the child's abdomen to be filled with free air. Instantly I plunged a hypodermic needle into the bloated abdomen and heard *ps-s-s-s-s.* As his abdomen deflated noisily like a tire going flat, the boy's breathing and color returned to normal. I took the child back to the operating room, opened his abdomen and sewed up the inch-long rent we found in his stomach. He returned home well a week later.

But what had caused the strange sequence of events? The valve in the boy's throat, which ordinarily remained closed, had opened, and every inspiration sucked air into his stomach until it had burst like an overdistended balloon. I could find only three similar cases in the surgical literature. Because no name had been given the illness, I wrote a scientific article for the *American Journal of Surgery* and named the sickness "The Air Sucker's Gastric Rupture Syndrome." My chief, Dr. Ellison, considered the title rather crude and suggested substituting the more elegant word *aerophagic's* in place of *air sucker's.* He relented, however, when I explained that our title was scientifically more accurate. Aerophagic means air swallowing and, in these cases, the air was actually sucked into the stomach.

During this period the news reached us from Paul Miller and the ABWE president that Bhutan remained a country closed to Christian missions, and that medical missions were already established in Nepal. In Nepal, moreover, the government did not allow full religious freedom. Dr. Commons reiterated that ABWE was not necessarily committed to a "black bag" or small clinic concept of medical missions.

This information cleared our minds to focus in seriously on the land of East Pakistan. Although our call to prepare for service on a foreign field had come five years earlier, the provisos attached to it remained fresh in our minds. *And they matched East Pakistan with precision.* A country having a great medical need? The death of Mary Barnard had revealed an area of remarkable unmet medical need. A land possessing very limited knowledge of the good news of Christ? With one missionary for every three-quarters of a million people, East Pakistan was more neglected by the Christian church than any other open land. No Christians or Christian work graced the extreme southern end of the country. There was a great Christian vacuum between the works of the earliest missionary pioneers, William Carey of India and Adoniram Judson of Burma. Visas were readily available to East Pakistan and religious freedom prevailed. Our eyes, furthermore, had been fixed on this very area of the world, for Bhutan and Nepal are quite near to East Pakistan. And ABWE seemed to be the mission agency to which all our guidance pointed.

However, we still did not know whether the ABWE board believed in the really sound principles of medical missions. We shared with our own pastor, a member of the ABWE board, our deep feeling that certain principles of medical work should be followed.

"Vic," he replied, "I don't believe our ABWE board has ever settled on any particular principles of medical mission work, for our experience has been limited in this area. But I certainly agree with the importance of it."

In March 1959, the unexpected happened, and we were delighted. The president of ABWE wrote requesting me to appear before the board as a consultant to present and discuss principles the board might follow in establishing their proposed medical mission in East Pakistan. If they agreed with the important principles of medical missions, we would be assured of a good head start toward a sound medical work should we elect to serve there. If, however, they rejected the principles, we would know we must look further for another board and field. The April meeting was exciting. I presented, one by one, thirteen basic principles* of medical mission work.

For six long hours the ABWE board studied, considered, and questioned the thirteen basic principles. They asked penetrating and analytical questions. But because the principles were sound, I could respond with a suitable answer to every question. At the end of the long session, the board voted unanimously to go forward in East Pakistan on the basis of the thirteen principles.

*See Appendix B. Basic Principles of Medical Missions.

Within days thereafter, our sense of direction and call to serve with ABWE in the land of East Pakistan was finalized. The decision gave us a deep and satisfying peace of heart.

A few days after finalizing our decision, we received a distressing letter from ABWE headquarters which stated, "We just received news yesterday morning that Rev. Paul Miller (one of our missionaries in East Pakistan) went to be with the Lord last Saturday morning from an attack of polio. . . . This brings to our attention all the more forcibly that we are moving in the right direction in establishing a medical work there in East Pakistan."

On afternoon ward rounds one day, I sensed considerable anxiety in a patient being prepared for surgery the next morning. At 10 P.M. I returned to explain to him that because his cancer of the rectum was serious, his operation would be extensive. I talked to him about God and faith and God's Son who loved him and gave His life for him. Before our interview concluded, he expressed his desire to finalize the great transaction. Praying, he accepted Christ, then fell off to sleep. The operation went well.

On the second postoperative day, on grand rounds, I approached his bed with my entourage of nurses, surgical residents, interns, and senior and junior medical students.

The patient thanked everyone for his care and then spoke up before the assemblage, saying, "Doctor Olsen, are you just a surgeon or are you a surgeon and a minister?"

Hearing my response that I was not a minister, he replied, "Whatever you are, you helped me more than you will ever know by explaining to me the way of eternal life. I feel pain from the operation, but I have a peace of mind and happiness that I never knew before."

Some of my atheist and agnostic friends in the group accompanying me smiled as if to say "Olsen has been at his missionary work again." Later I found an opportunity to explain to them the simple principles which motivate a Christian surgeon.

"First, we do not treat sickness; rather, we care for human beings afflicted with sickness. And second, we must care for the whole man, not just his sick body. Man is body, mind, and spirit. Illness striking any one of the three parts of man almost always upsets one or both of the other segments of his being. The complete physician or surgeon sympathetically and compassionately treats the whole patient — body, mind, and spirit. Our Lord, the great Physician, worked in just this way."

It is difficult to say when a senior resident passes from being a surgical trainee to becoming a surgeon. Perhaps it happened at the time of one of those earlier cases. Perhaps it occurred when I was

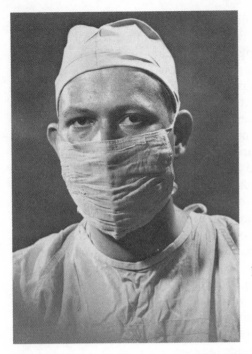

Dr. Olsen, surgeon

Courtesy of the Roob Studio

called upon to operate on a fellow physician's ninety-two-year-old mother. Her bowel was not only obstructed, but also a section of it was black and dead. Because of her great age and precarious condition, I decided against a general anesthetic. After a substantial dose of morphine and injections of anesthetic into the lower abdomen, I removed the black segment of intestine and hooked up the two remaining ends. I feared, because of the limited anesthetic, she might feel some pain which would make her moan and move, upsetting her watching son — to say nothing of her surgeon. Fortunately, she did not quiver throughout the operation and made a speedy and remarkable recovery.

Hattie was another challenging case. Following a nearly fatal massive heart attack, a blood clot developed inside her damaged heart. One night a piece of the clot broke off and lodged in the large artery in her left upper leg. Her mottled blue-white leg would not survive long unless its blood flow could be restored.

Again using local anesthesia, I opened the artery, delicately fished out the clot, and the leg survived. Her sick heart, however, only barely kept her alive.

On Sunday night the ward nurse reached me at the evening church service, "Hattie has developed severe pain in her abdomen, Dr. Olsen, and she looks even worse than usual."

"I'll be there in fourteen minutes," I responded. Before the telephone conversation was completed, I was sure in my own mind that another clot had broken off, despite our medicines, and lodged in a main artery in Hattie's abdomen.

As I flirted with the speed limit, I remembered an article I had read in a prestigious journal two weeks before. The author for the first time had actually removed a clot from that artery deep in the abdomen. When I read the article, I had made a mental note that the principle was sound and the operation feasible. My examination of Hattie convinced me that we should be the second to try this operation despite her precarious condition. If we did nothing, she was doomed.

Under light anesthetic we opened her up, located the blocked artery, and removed the purple, jellylike clot from it. Immediately, the large section of intestine fed by that artery turned from blue to beautiful pink.

As I came to the end of those long, tough four years of surgical residency training, I felt a deep sense of having been helped, guided, and empowered by God through numberless cases and exceedingly difficult problems. Every single time I had picked up the scalpel, I had stopped and silently prayed to God, asking for His help and direction. Every doctor and nurse in those operating rooms had come to know and silently respect that moment, sacred to me, before the keen edge of the scalpel slashed the red spurting line of my incision.

During the last month of training, my chief, Dr. Edwin Ellison, called me into his office. I was not prepared for the offer he made.

"Vic," he said, "I would like you to give up the idea of going to that God-forsaken country on the other side of the world. Just as my old chief, Dr. Zollinger, chose me to be his right-hand man, I would like you to become my associate."

The implication was instantly obvious to me. I would be sixth in the grand lineage of surgeons, extending from Halsted through Ellison, and I would be a professor of surgery at an early age.

"You may have whatever you feel you need for a salary," Dr. Ellison resumed. "Don't answer me now. Go home and discuss it with your wife before you finalize any decision. I am hoping and expecting that you will answer yes to my proposal."

Although my heart said, *no!*, I responded, "I don't know how to thank you sufficiently. It means a great deal to me that you made the offer, and I will discuss it with my wife as you requested."

How will Joan react to this incredible offer? I thought to myself. *She worked so hard those first four years; she's had so much difficulty bearing our children. She's pregnant again now. She's had very little help from me around the house these last four tough years.*

I walked into the house, gave her a big kiss, and dutifully explained the proposal. "What do you think?" I asked guardedly.

She thought for a moment, just long enough to understand the full impact of my announcement, and said softly, "But I thought God called us to be missionaries in East Pakistan."

"That's right, honey," I said, "But do you think this changes any of that?"

"I can't see how it changes it in the slightest," Joan responded.

"Wonderful!" I exulted, "I agree it doesn't change a single thing."

The next morning I faced my chief.

"Thanks again, Dr. Ellison," I said, "I have discussed your fine offer with my wife as you requested, and I am afraid we cannot accept. I respect you greatly, but you see, I have a previous commitment to the great Physician."

A few days later I said my good-byes all around, received a thoughtful gift from my nurses, and walked out of the hospital into a new world and a new life.

*   *   *

Distance in no way lessened the feelings of closeness between the Olsens and Lockerbies. Vic, Joan, and the children were "family," and when some propitious circumstance took us within a few hundred miles of Milwaukee, we just kept going for an impromptu visit. Usually we found Joan alone with the children, and after a joyous reunion, she would regale us with enthusiastic accounts of the cases that came Vic's way.

Fifteen years beyond high school Viggo B. Olsen completed his formal training as a physician and surgeon. His refusal to be less than highly prepared paid off. The chief of the department of chest surgery said: "Dr. Olsen is the finest resident who has ever gone through this department."

The chief of the department of surgery once referred to Vic as "the conscience of the surgical department." He added his commendation as he wished Vic good luck in his overseas service, "We have never had a better surgical resident." No wonder he had selected Dr. Olsen for one of the most prestigious posts offered to any young surgeon in the country that year: the honor of becoming his own associate, including a teaching appointment at the Marquette University medical school.

A few years earlier, both Vic and Joan would have been overjoyed. This was the vision Vic had shared with Joan along the banks of the Maumee River the night he asked her to be his wife: a lucrative practice and the challenge of teaching in medical school.

"We'll have lots of money and I'll build you a dream house," he had told Joan.

Now with this most enticing of all professional plums dangled before him, Vic was not even tempted. Graciously he acknowledged his gratitude.

But East Pakistan was still half a world and many months away. Thousands of miles of the United States and Canada would be traveled before the Olsens and their children would set foot in what is now Bangladesh.

"When I'm in a steaming jungle," the doctor reasoned, "I'll want to know who my colleagues are." To this end — recruiting doctors, nurses, and other missionary personnel, and raising funds to build and operate a hospital — Vic Olsen now started out on the deputation trail. During his crosscountry travels, Dr. Olsen also had opportunities to challenge churches and young people to greater and deeper dedication to the Lord's service.

He also did some key work for Shepherds, Inc., the Sunday school class committee which had established a home and school for retarded children and their families. Traveling to New Jersey for a missionary conference, Dr. Olsen encountered Andrew ("Bud") Wood of Hackensack, a man highly qualified to be executive director of the Shepherd's home and school in Wisconsin. The Woods had every reason to remain in New Jersey. They loved their work, home, and fine church. Loved ones lived nearby. Bud's future looked bright in the local school system. It seemed a big move to put all that behind and strike off for the unknown Milwaukee. Deeply sympathetic with their feelings, Dr. Olsen did his best to bring some perspective to the struggle. The perspective came, and the Woods heard God's call.

Along the way, Vic passed the difficult examinations which made him a diplomate of the American Board of Surgery. His list of professional degrees served a great advantage. East Pakistan was a country where degrees were almost worshiped, so important is a college or university education. Undoubtedly, through the correspondence that flowed between Dr. Olsen and the medical authorities of East Pakistan prior to the arrival of the Olsen family there, a healthy respect was created for the American doctor with all the degrees who proposed to practice medicine and build a hospital in their country. In the ensuing years, as God's plan unfolded, Vic was destined to meet dozens of high officials. Numbered among his friends and acquaintances would be commissioners, secretaries, ministers, governors, ambassadors, a king, the president of Pakistan, and the prime minister of Bangladesh.

9

Cross-Country Doctor

BUT WILL I EVER PERFORM ANOTHER OPERATION? I asked myself in that Bangladesh bedroom. No one could predict whether my shattered elbow would ever move properly again and allow me to wield a life-saving scalpel. *What will I do,* I thought, *if we get out of tonight's mess and my elbow does end up being stiff?* Despite the potential mental anguish of the idea, I found myself surprisingly at ease. Step by step, Joan and I had searched for and found God's personal plan for us. Despite the danger of the night and the uncertainty of the future, I felt I was exactly where I belonged, doing what I should be doing. I would do my best on the human level, pray earnestly, and leave the outcome with the One who loves us. Besides, if my surgical days were over, I could teach or preach or even revert to my original dream — being a specialist in internal medicine. But it would seem mighty strange never to do another operation.

*　　*　　*

I felt momentarily lost after I walked out of Milwaukee County Hospital and away from the four years of unbelievably hard surgical work. But the feeling passed. A few days later, on July 18, 1959, our youngest daughter, Nancy Gay, was born. We were delighted to have her, our only brown-eyed child. For the next two months we enjoyed Nancy and the rest of our brood, and studied Bible and theology in preparation for the mission candidate classes to be held in Philadelphia.

We arrived at the candidate school childless. The mission leaders knew that the heavily scheduled month would leave no time for child care. The first day, each of the twenty candidates shared his or her personal spiritual experience of conversion, consecration, and call to serve. It was a surprisingly emotional experience for all of us.

94

In succeeding days we received courses of instruction on the ABWE principles and practices, financial policy, history of the mission, the indigenous principle of missions, methods of deputation to the churches, how to take good color slides, et cetera. On Sundays we launched out as a team to various churches in the area.

All the candidates shared the household and yard work. All this time the mission officials were quietly and carefully studying each candidate and his or her reaction to the group, the studies, and the assigned tasks.

We spent hours discussing and planning with Donna Ahlgrim, another candidate for East Pakistan. Donna, a friendly, vivacious girl, looked forward to working with women and children overseas. We were also corresponding at this point with Jeannie Lockerbie, R.N., the daughter of Rev. and Mrs. Lockerbie. As a teenager, several years earlier in Brooklyn, Jeannie had told us with stars in her eyes that she would be a nurse.

At candidate school we met visitor Lynn Silvernale, an accomplished nurse with linguistic abilities. Interested in nursing, linguistics, and translation work, she pumped us for information about East Pakistan. All that we could tell this bright, brown-eyed girl seemed to strike responsive chords, and God's direction clearly indicated that land to be Lynn's place of service.

During that month we also met Dr. and Mrs. Ralph Ankenman. Ralph and Lucy were a "paradox"; that is, they were both doctors. Lucy — an amiable, soft-spoken MK (missionary kid) who had grown up in India — had known for years she should serve overseas. Ralph, a well-built, direct-speaking, rugged individualist, had planned on foreign mission service even before meeting Lucy. Lucy's interest in India and Ralph's idea of jungle missions in Africa found a meeting ground in pioneer missions in East Pakistan, a section of old India.

At the end of candidate school came the scary final oral examinations. As we took our seats before the board, Dr. Commons introduced us and said, "You will remember, gentlemen, that Dr. and Mrs. Olsen have had no formal theological training. They have, however, taken correspondence courses, studied extensively to teach their Bible and Sunday school classes, and actively given witness to their faith in Christ. It is our duty to determine whether or not they will need to take a year of formal theological training. So, go to work on them, gentlemen. Let them have it."

The questions came hot and heavy. "Can you give the biblical outline of redemption with scripture references to prove your analysis?"

"What are the five main points of Calvinism?"

"Is it appropriate to pray to the Holy Spirit and why?"

"When is the last time you led a person to faith in the Lord Jesus Christ?"

"Can you outline the sequence of events which will occur in the end times and prove your assertions with appropriate scripture references?"

The years of personal study, teaching, preaching, and correspondence courses paid off. We succeeded, with God's help, in answering the questions satisfactorily, making the additional year of study unnecessary. We received the congratulations of the board and appointment to serve in the land of East Pakistan!

In retrospect, we appreciated the way Dr. Commons "threw us to the pack." He and the board members were warm and considerate, but careful not merely to ease us through because their need for a medical doctor was great. We developed deep appreciation for our board, and that sense of esteem has continued throughout these years.

A few weeks after candidate school, I participated in my first missionary conference two thousand miles from Milwaukee. Our old friend, Pastor Lockerbie, had finished his work in Brooklyn and accepted a call to a church in Seattle, Washington. To save money I traveled the long distance by train. I knew that during that journey I would have to prepare a message that would somehow deeply move and challenge the listeners, for God would have to start recruiting a staff of twenty and tens of thousands of dollars for the proposed hospital.

For my personal devotions I opened the Bible to Matthew's gospel and read words which seemed strange to me. Jesus said: "But when you fast, perfume your head and wash your face so that your fasting may not be noticed by men but by your Father who sees in secret. And your Father who sees in secret will reward you openly."

In this modern day and age, no one fasts, I thought to myself. *I have neither known a Christian who fasts nor heard any Christian speak or teach about fasting.* Suddenly, however, in my moment of great need, my Lord's Word had told me to fast, quietly and secretly, and He would help me and reward me openly. *What difference does it make,* I asked myself, *that my friends and acquaintances do not observe this teaching?* The passage did not say, *"if* you fast" — it stated, *"when* you fast." *I'll do it,* I decided.

Throughout the day, I fasted, prayed, and searched the Scriptures for a suitable passage upon which to build my main deputation message. When I reached the great Palm Sunday narrative in the gospel of John, chapter 12, I leafed quickly past it. There would be nothing about Christ's triumphal entry into Jerusalem relative to missions, our conversion, or call to serve in East Pakistan. I paused, then turned back to the seemingly unlikely John 12.

There, spread on the page before me, I saw the perfect vehicle for my message. Each of the five groups of people mentioned in the narrative portrayed Joan and me at five different stages of our spiritual development. One of the groups had literally seen the great Physician's healing miracle of raising Lazarus from the dead. John 12 recorded the fulfillment of the fantastic prophecy in Daniel 9, studied so carefully by Sir Robert Anderson. This prophecy could introduce the subject of Christian evidences which played such an important part in our conversion. And Rev. Barnard had quoted from this very chapter when he wrote us about his daughter's death and prayed that her passing might be like a grain of wheat falling into the ground to die and bring forth much fruit. This passage portrayed Christ as King of kings and ended with the powerful twenty-sixth verse: "If any man serve me, let him follow me; and where I am, there shall also my servant be. If any man serve me, him will my Father honor." The whole passage was perfectly relevant to the story and teaching I wished to present.

Thank you, Father, I prayed, and the next morning resumed eating — with relish!

For the next eighteen months I traveled the length and the breadth of the land and crossed over into Canada. I drove and flew tens of thousands of miles to meet thousands of people, present hundreds of messages, and participate in dozens of conferences like the one in Seattle. When my automobile gasped its last, three fine businessmen from our Milwaukee church provided another one.

In Grand Rapids, Michigan, I met Dr. and Mrs. Donn Ketcham. Donn, in surgical residency training, was not only a budding surgeon, but also an ordained minister. His father, also a minister, was the well-known and beloved leader of the General Association of Regular Baptist Churches (GARBC). Kitty — attractive, artistic, creative — mothered three children (ultimately four) and "wived" a very busy, dynamic *kajer lok* (man of action). Donn, in his characteristic outgoing, freewheeling fashion, later told me what transpired behind the scenes during our days of meeting in Grand Rapids.

"From the age of four," he explained, "I knew I was going to be a missionary. At age twelve I knew I would be a missionary doctor. I fully expected to do pioneer mission work in Africa under Baptist Mid-Missions; my dad was a founder of that agency and still sits on the board. Kitty, however, had a mental image of loving and helping the sari-clad women of India. As my surgical training neared completion, I met with the Mid-Missions director only to find out that the mission felt uneasy about sending a new doctor to any of their African fields because of current political unrest, stringent government requirements, and other problems.

"Returning home," Donn related, "I felt let down that the African fields seemed closed, and Kitty felt let down because I hadn't the slightest interest in going to India. After hours of fruitless discussion, we declared a two-week moratorium on talking it over any further. For fourteen days we would do our own private thinking and praying. During that period, my thinking cleared up considerably. It was not Africa to which I was called, but a particular type of work commonly carried out in Africa. That work had to meet three criteria: (1) it had to be a pioneer work; (2) it had to be a place where I could teach and share my faith openly; (3) it had to be an area where loving men through medical care would open minds and hearts to spiritual truth when other methods might fail to do so. I told God I could go to any place fulfilling these three criteria, Africa or not. At the same time Kitty came to the place where she could pray, 'All right, Lord. If You want me to go someplace besides India, that's fine. But You will have to give me as deep a love for the people to whom You send me, as for the Indian women.' The moratorium over, we shared our ideas.

"Two weeks later, Vic, you spoke at a men's banquet that I attended. You spoke as though you had an inside track on my three criteria. First, you explained that a pioneer work would soon be started in East Pakistan. In your message, you mentioned second that religious freedom prevailed in East Pakistan; and, finally, that compassionate care of East Pakistanis would naturally make them desire to know more about Jesus Christ. And East Pakistan, part of old India, was filled with sari-clad women like the ones in Kitty's dreams. Fantastically, the whole thing fell into place. I went home so excited I was incoherent and babbled for an hour or so. Finally Kitty said, 'Will you please be quiet and go to sleep? You don't even make sense.' So I lay bug-eyed all night. The next morning I made more sense to Kitty, and within a few days it became crystal clear that East Pakistan would be our target."

Later, speaking in a small Indiana town, I met Harry and Nancy Goehring. Nancy, a sweet and capable homemaker, was devoted to her family. Harry, in the final stages of seminary training, made excellent marks in theology and the biblical languages Greek and Hebrew. Harry was athletically built, good-natured, and slated to become a professor. But the divine slate listed an entirely different program. Harry and Nancy sensed the call to tribal and translation work in East Pakistan. An unexpected secret in God's personal plan for Harry would one day be revealed on the other side of the world.

In another town, before a missions conference, the participants enjoyed a social afternoon in a church member's home. The host took us to his basement recreation room for a game of pool. My skills at the game, developed by years of experience in smoke-filled pool halls during high school days, returned quickly. I lined up a shot and hit it better than I had expected. As the pastor of the church walked down the basement stairs, he saw and heard *plop-plop-plop;* three balls dropped neatly into separate pockets. He looked at me oddly as though to say, "Where did a missionary appointee learn how to do that?"

In New Haven, Indiana, I met Rev. and Mrs. Jesse Eaton. Joyce Eaton, a tall, talented, proficient nurse, was doing more mothering than nursing at that time. Jesse was a tall, big, athletic fellow with a rich baritone voice. Deeply interested in communications and visual aids, his orderly mind focused intently on the charts and maps Joan had prepared for me on white windowshades; made to fit a school-type map rack, they could be pulled down, one by one, at the appropriate points in an address. The Eatons, then in a pastorate, were studying mission boards and fields, and East Pakistan turned out to be the place for them. Jesse would one day deploy his excellent organizational ability as the hospital administrator and business agent.

Like a bolt out of the blue, as I sped along a highway one day, the thought struck me: *If I have to supervise the contracting and construction of the hospital we hope to build, the result will be poor. Not only will the construction be second-rate, but also I will have but a scanty knowledge of the Bengali language the day the hospital opens.* The solution to this problem was instantly obvious: we needed a competent, trustworthy contractor or builder to supervise construction of the East Pakistan hospital! This would ensure properly constructed buildings and provide me and my colleagues protected language study. We could conclude our two years of Bengali language study while the buildings were under construction.

A few days later, I drove nearly a thousand miles to ABWE headquarters in Philadelphia to discuss at length this obvious need. We reached agreement quickly, but the mission had no such contractor available. We made a pact to ask God earnestly and often to provide such a man to build the East Pakistan hospital.

About ten days later, Mr. Paul Goodman, a man well named and a contractor by trade, traveled three thousand miles from his home in California to Philadelphia on business. His business completed, he looked up an acquaintance at ABWE headquarters. After being introduced to the staff and following the greetings and small talk, a staff member said to Paul Goodman, "Mr. Goodman, you're a Christian and a contractor. What would you think of doing some building for God in a little country on the other side of the world?"

Paul smilingly responded, "I don't think that would be a job for me. What country do you have in mind?" The response "East Pakistan" wiped the smile off his face. Something about those two words, like a laser beam penetrating a human brain, slammed into Paul's mind bringing him to instant alertness.

"Gentlemen," said Paul quietly, "don't rush me, but tell me everything you know about this job. You see, I have lived two years of my life in a little country on the other side of the world called East Pakistan. I was a pilot there during World War II. I know a little something about construction there and a few words of the language. I'll have to go home and start praying about this proposition."

Paul Goodman had two months to pray before we could travel to California and meet with him. He did not pray alone. Also, Joan and I prayed daily, intensely. We drove to Los Angeles. With a sense of barely suppressed excitement, we walked into the palatial Goodman home in nearby La Habra, California. Paul and Allene made us feel like part of the family immediately and asked their final questions regarding the hospital proposal. Later, after all questions had ceased, I popped the question. As we stood face to face in the elegant living room of that lovely home, I asked, "Well, Paul, what is your decision about coming to build the East Pakistan hospital?"

Looking almost straight across at me with steel blue eyes, Paul responded earnestly, "Vic, I can see that this project has my name written all over it. What kind of a Christian would I be to say no?" And that was it — that was Paul Goodman's way of saying yes. God had done it again! He had located for us another absolutely open, dedicated man willing to go to the ends of the earth for Him.

A trip to Seattle brought us in contact with another great nurse, Becky Davey. Becky — attractive, alert, and knowledgeable — hovered at just barely five feet tall. She hoped to use her excellent training (M.S. in nursing administration) on some foreign field. Ultimately God's Spirit said to her, "This is it."

While in Omaha, I returned to my alma mater, the University of Nebraska College of Medicine. In the old anatomy lecture hall, where I had listened to so many lectures as a civilized pagan, I stood as a Christian to tell the good news of Christ to fifty medical students.

God did His part, and at least one of those young men came to clear-cut faith in God's Son.

By the winter of 1960 Paul Goodman had taken my rough sketches and produced architect's drawings and blueprints of our proposed hospital. In December the ABWE board met in session in Philadelphia. Outside, snow blanketed the city. Inside, however, as we reviewed the East Pakistan hospital blueprints, we felt a warm glow of elation over all that God had accomplished so quickly. The plans were approved unanimously.

In a Minnesota college a tall, pretty, red-headed girl named Jean Weld was ready for my coming and filled with questions. She had learned of our medical mission to East Pakistan from her mother, who had heard me speak in their church. With her questions answered, a sense of direction to serve in East Pakistan came strong and clear.

"I solemnly swear that the statements made —" In March, 1961, as we stood with right hands raised, our words echoed in the passport office of Milwaukee's Federal Building. Although the necessary pictures, in usual passport photo style, were not exactly brilliant, the occasion lacked no luster, for receiving our passports marked another tangible step toward departure.

Larry Golin, a theology student in Philadelphia, listened with more than passing interest to our presentation on East Pakistan. Conversion to Christ had shifted Larry's gears from forestry to theology and biblical languages. He became especially proficient in Hebrew, perhaps because one of his parents was Jewish. Later, Larry met a sweet, intelligent nurse named Jane who shared his interest in the land of East Pakistan. Larry would later learn physiotherapy and practice that skill there.

I traveled south to speak in churches and visit Rev. and Mrs. W. Eugene Gurganus. Gene and Beth, members of ABWE, had reached Chittagong, East Pakistan, while I was a third-year surgical resident, and had returned temporarily to America. Gene is a big-boned, big-hearted, hardworking preacher and teacher who loves the Bengali people. Beth, a Southern belle and accomplished hostess and homemaker, is a wonderful helpmate to Gene, his righthand woman. The Gurganuses made me feel at home immediately, and from them I learned new details about East Pakistan.

The highway from North Carolina back to Milwaukee wound tortuously, but beautifully, through the hills of Virginia. Weary and ready to eat, I stopped and entered a small restaurant. *Service should be good,* I thought. *There's only one other fellow here.*

I slid onto the counter stool, placed my order, and said, "Hi, how are you this evening?" to the man seated on the next stool.

His "fine" lacked conviction, and I thought I sensed some anxiety or depression in him. Our conversation soon uncovered the fact that he, too, was a medical doctor — not an ordinary doctor, but a specialist in obstetrics-gynecology who had received some of his training in famed Oxford University. He needed someone to talk to. He poured out his dissatisfaction with his successful practice and confessed that the evils of his life, especially his sins of earlier days, now plagued him; he obviously was filled with guilt and remorse.

Praying inwardly, I shared my own faith with him and explained what Jesus had done about his sin and guilt on the cross. Because he had never heard it before, my explanation about God, man, sin, and the cross did not sink in immediately. In an effort to illustrate, I picked up the ketchup bottle to represent God, the steak sauce bottle to represent this man, and placed a salt shaker between them to stand for sin that separates man from God.

Eyes moist with emotion, he brushed aside the salt shaker, took the two bottles from the table, and desperately clinked them together, crying, "If this could happen to me, I'd be the happiest man in the world!"

"Come with me outside to the car," I said. He gulped down the last of his beer, we paid our bills and went to my car where he bowed his head, asked God to forgive his sin, and invited Christ into his life to be his Saviour. In the hush of that sacred moment, I explained to this specialist in the field of the first birth that he had just been "born again."

He was mystified until I opened a New Testament and we read together chapter 1 in the gospel of John. I explained, "Those who receive Christ are given the right to become the children of God. All who believe on His name are born of God." As the significance of the spiritual rebirth which had just happened inside him struck home, the tears came again, and he exclaimed, "Oh, thank you, sir, thank you!"

Later, Joan and I traveled to a mecca of Christendom, Wheaton, Illinois, the home of renowned Wheaton College. We visited, briefly, Dr. Paul Adolph, the missionary physician-surgeon whose writings on the principles of medical missions had influenced me considerably. Because of unexpected car troubles in Wheaton, Joan and I remained overnight with the Adolphs.

Also visiting that night were Bob, the younger Adolph son, and Barbara, his wife. Bob, who specialized in laboratory technology, was a quiet, capable, hard-working young man. Barb, a red-headed

Georgia peach, loved children and was trained as a schoolteacher. They were both deeply committed to foreign mission service, but hadn't the vaguest notion where God desired them to serve.

Dr. Adolph, with a twinkle in his eye, suggested, "Perhaps, Vic and Joan, as long as you are stuck here tonight, you would like to share with Bob and Barb your plans for the medical program in East Pakistan. They can at least know we both heartily approve of the principles ABWE has determined to follow."

We talked together on into the early morning hours, answering questions and telling all we knew about East Pakistan and our plans for a medical-surgical mission to that distant land. Color slides portrayed what our words could not adequately explain. Later we learned that Bob and Barb had decided their target would be East Pakistan. Bob eventually organized and operated the clinical laboratory of the hospital, and Barb participated in teaching missionary kids at the MK school we finally established in the area. (ABWE had readily agreed to my request to establish an MK school to insure proper elementary school education for our children near the hospital so that they could live at home with their families.)

It struck me one day that I should make preliminary contact with the powers that be in East Pakistan. *Perhaps,* I thought, *if I write to the authorities, they might commit themselves in advance to the idea of a hospital in East Pakistan.* I addressed my letter to the surgeon general (later called the director of health services). In the letter I identified myself, explained how I had developed an affection for East Pakistan, and presented my dream of a hospital in Chittagong District to help East Pakistanis. In three weeks I received, on very official-looking stationery, the surgeon general's cordial reply. He stated there was need for a hospital in the region mentioned, and requested that we come to East Pakistan, survey the area, and consult with his office to finalize the site — *precisely the plan we had in mind!* This official letter of the surgeon general would help us greatly in the months ahead.

As the time of deputation ran down, we gratefully took stock of the developments:

1. Tens of thousands had been informed of the projected medical-surgical mission to East Pakistan.
2. Literally thousands, who had come to know us and our plans, were praying down God's blessing and guidance upon us.
3. Hundreds of men, women, and young people had made overt decisions to accept Christ, dedicate their lives to Him and His future direction, or to enter into full-time Christian service at home or abroad.

4. Dozens of churches and individuals had undertaken a portion of our support.
5. Half the necessary funds for the hospital already had been given or pledged.
6. The great Director had tapped at least twenty of us to serve in East Pakistan (in the group were six nurses, four doctors, three missionary homemakers, two ministers, one contractor, one contractor's helper, one laboratory technologist, one physiotherapy technician, and one elementary school teacher.)

God had done a great piece of work for us and for the people of East Pakistan.

The last six weeks before departure were a blur. Every three or four days, immunizations punctuated our schedule — and punctured us. Smallpox, typhoid-paratyphoid, diphtheria, tetanus, and yellow fever injections traumatized our small children. It seemed impossible to finalize the massive job of packing the fifty-five-gallon steel drums with a four-year supply of clothing, shoes, household items, and foodstuffs. In a lovely commissioning service, the pastor and deacons of Milwaukee's Garfield Avenue Baptist Church laid their hands upon us as we knelt before the congregation. With this age-old ritual, initiated by the New Testament church, they sent us off to be missionaries of the cross representing them in a land of the Muslim crescent.

After a few tender days with our loved ones came the inevitable, bitter-sweet good-byes. We traveled by car to Montreal, Canada, to board our ship. There to see us off were Joan's family and ABWE president, Dr. Commons, with Mrs. Commons. On August 17, 1961, standing on the deck of the *Empress of Canada,* Dr. Commons lifted his voice to God, commending us to His everlasting love and care. After the last amen came the last good-byes, and our ship throbbed out into the open water. As those we loved became distant specks, we turned to face the bow and our destination — Liverpool, England.

On my thirty-fifth birthday, August 24, 1961, we arrived in Liverpool for a four-month crash course in tropical medicine. Along with superb training in tropical medicine, we learned much about British life and those who lived it. We located and attended a church which admirably met our needs for worship and fellowship.

No one met our ship, because we had no friends or acquaintances in England. In the customs shed Nancy cried, the older three ran here and there, adding to the general confusion, and Joan sagged, weak from thirty-six hours of flu. The porter in the shed was very helpful and very solicitous — after I accidentally tipped him two or three times too much (I hadn't the foggiest notion about the value of the strange coins in my hand). In an ancient hack (taxi), we

Nancy, Wendy, Lynne, and Mark — England bound

The house on Saltburn Road

bounced and rattled to the office of our estate agent (real estate salesman). He broke the news gently — our house was not ready! The situation was hilariously impossible.

Ready or not, we moved into the "dream house" located across the Mersey River from Liverpool in a section called Wallasey, the "bedroom of Liverpool." The house, situated on Saltburn Road, had deteriorated during occupancy by a number of transient families. The two weeks we had allotted for sightseeing were consumed preparing the house for family living. We cut the high grass, discarded tenement-style pieces of furniture, and arranged for suitable beds and a small refrigerator. We scrubbed every black floorboard in the house twice with boiling water and cleanser in preparation for two coats of paste wax. With the cleanup, waxing, varnishing, and painting finished, we had a pleasant home in an attractive neighborhood.

Before tropical medicine school started, I traveled one hundred miles to the British Land Rover factory in Birmingham, England. A British version of the jeep, the Land Rover outclassed the jeep in several ways. At Birmingham a waiting chauffeur drove me to the factory. The assistant export sales manager gave me a spin around their jungle course which wound through acres of dense timber, over hills, into valleys, down steep embankments, through streams and mud. I was duly impressed with the vehicle, driver, and course. In the executive dining room, I shared my faith with the executives, then brainstormed for two hours with the Land Rover Far Eastern director. I placed my order for a model which would carry passengers, do ambulance duty, be a mobile clinic, provide room for sleeping, and haul supplies and material.

Toxteth Tabernacle in Liverpool became our church home. We loved the church, the people, and their pastor, the Rev. Robert Rowland, a capable Bible expositor with a warm, generous, pastor's heart.

Through our connection with the Toxteth Tabernacle, I met the well-known London preacher, Dr. Martyn Lloyd-Jones, who came as a guest minister to Liverpool. We had much in common because he, too, had been a practicing physician. When he left medicine for the ministry, he was the understudy of the king's physician; if he had remained in medicine, he would quite likely be treating royalty. But God called him to preach, and he did so with consummate skill. Some called him the greatest preacher in Christendom today. As we sat chatting together in front of a crackling fire in the pastor's study, neither Dr. Lloyd-Jones nor I could have guessed that a few months later we would cooperate together, long distance, in vital work for God.

The fiasco of our unprepared house was a harbinger of further trauma to come. Without modern conveniences, Joan's workload was heavy at home. We had no automobile. Through a shipper's error, our winter clothing and other belongings never arrived in Liverpool, and I survived with long woolies under my one summer suit. The house possessed neither storm windows nor central heating. The living room, dining room, and kitchen were heated only by small fireplaces. The front hall and upstairs bedrooms and bathroom had no source of heat until we purchased two electric heaters. That winter of 1961-62 was the most bitter in Liverpool's recorded history; more than once the temperature dropped below freezing in our front hall. The children, accustomed to central heating, were almost continually sick with colds, flu, or other infections. Lynne suffered five attacks of severe bronchitis, and Mark five acute ear infections which resulted in temporary partial deafness. Nancy required plastic surgery with a week of hospitalization when she lacerated her forehead in a fall.

Surprisingly, we also faced a language barrier. We had difficulty at first understanding the Liverpool brand of English, and they had trouble comprehending English served up American style. Joan, on her first shopping trip, asked for butter. The shopkeeper, confused about this strange commodity, asked a clerk if she understood the request. The clerk, too, was stumped. They asked Joan to repeat and she said again, "Butter, butter." By then several other women shoppers crowded around to ask her to repeat it again. "Butter, butter," Joan repeated. The light finally dawned for one woman, who burst out, "Oh, shay mayns booteh — ha, ha, ha!"

The bright spots in all this sickness, freezing cold, hard work, and cultural adjustment were our church, our helpful neighbors, and my school. The famed Liverpool School of Tropical Medicine for decades had trained men from dozens of countries in the field of tropical medicine. The course was well organized, high pressure, and packed to the brim with things I would need to know. After four months of study, followed by oral examinations plus eighteen hours of written examinations, I received a certificate authorizing me to inscribe after my name the letters *D. T. M.* and *H.*, which meant "Diploma, Tropical Medicine and Hygiene."

Many of my fellow students came from African or Asian countries. Two of the students were Bengalis, one from East Pakistan, the other from India's West Bengal District (next door to East Pakistan). This gave me my first opportunity to develop a friendship with an East Pakistani. Not only his religion but also his name was Islam; we discussed his faith, and he listened with deep interest to my explanation about Christ and the way of eternal life through Him.

One cold winter afternoon, a British medical missionary to India invited me for tea. When my bombardment of questions waned, he asked, "How did you decide to go to East Pakistan?"

I told him the whole story, including the crucial part the death of Mary Barnard had played in our call to serve in East Pakistan.

"During her school year in India," I explained, "Mary Barnard had an appendicitis operation which apparently cured her. Later, however, when she returned to East Pakistan during school holidays, her bowel became obstructed by adhesions from the appendicitis, and she died."

The doctor, obviously shaken by my recital, finally spoke. "I was the surgeon," he revealed, "that operated on Mary Barnard in India! I heard that later she died in East Pakistan."

The fact that God had used the death of Mary Barnard to call a surgeon and a medical team to serve in East Pakistan was a great comfort to my new friend, the British surgeon.

Wendy and Lynne found British school different from American school. The quality of education was high and the children far advanced beyond American children of the same age. Within a few weeks Wendy and Lynne adjusted to their new school life; they would return from school in their smart blue school blazers and speak with a rapidly developing British accent. Wendy earned her longed-for allowance by learning British money and the multiplication tables through the 12's. With sixpence a week to squander, she felt like the Chancellor of the Exchequer. About this time, we received word that in Philadelphia the ABWE candidate school was in full swing; fifteen of the twenty candidates were planning to serve in East Pakistan! Another letter notified us that co-workers Donna Ahlgrim and Lynn Silvernale were en route to East Pakistan to arrive shortly before us.

While we were celebrating Guy Fawkes Day (a British holiday featuring fun and fireworks) in England, Jay and Eleanor Walsh, co-workers-to-be, also were celebrating. After a Chittagong doctor's unexpected announcement, they traveled fifteen hundred miles from East Pakistan. There in the city of Lahore, Eleanor gave birth to twin daughters, Sheryl and Shelley. The life of one of the twins would depend upon our timely arrival in Chittagong a few weeks later.

Before Christmas, I spoke at a squash at the manse (party at the parsonage) for sixty to seventy young people. Some of the teenagers came from mission Sunday schools sponsored by Toxteth Tabernacle. One gang, who called themselves the Scalliwags, came from a mission Sunday school located in one of the roughest sections of Liverpool. After the message, three Scalliwags wanted to talk about Jesus. We went to a private room where I told them about God and about Christ who gave His life for us all. With tears those three tough teenagers believed, prayed, and accepted Christ into their lives.

Church friends and Scalliwags at
Liverpool train station

The Land Rover "jungle"
course at Birmingham

Except for sick children and the chillingly cold house, Christmas was a delight. Jean Weld, the red-headed nurse from Minnesota, brought a friend and joined us for Christmas. Jean was studying midwifery in England to prepare for her future service in East Pakistan. We talked for hours, wondering what the future would hold for us all in East Pakistan.

On one of our last nights in England, we had a tea for our kind neighbors who had generously loaned us blankets, sweaters, hot water bottles, etc. We showed them slides of East Pakistan and shared with them our spiritual experience of faith and conversion. Then, the final scramble of house cleaning and packing completed, we were scheduled to depart on an evening flight. Because of bad weather, however, all planes were grounded, so our plans were quickly changed to travel by train to London.

At midafternoon we raced to the Lime Street Station, and to our surprise, a large contingent of our Christian friends awaited us. How so many managed to leave their jobs on a moment's notice at such an awkward time of day, we never knew. Some of my Scalliwag buddies were part of the crowd. Our friends had the compartment completely prepared with magazines, comics, candy, and gifts for the children.

As the train slowly chugged out of the station, we heard the sound of music. There stood our wonderful friends, with their bowler hats off, singing in the middle of Lime Street Station, "Jesus shall reign wheree'er the sun — " As I looked at Joan, I had trouble seeing her tear-marked face through a sudden mist which fogged my own vision.

We were exhausted after the long flight to Calcutta, India, a city less than fifty miles from the East Pakistan border. Our first official act after arrival in tropical Calcutta was to undress and strip off the long woolen underwear. An Indian woman in the ladies' room giggled as she watched Joan peel the woolies off each of the four kids. That afternoon of January 12, 1962, we boarded Indian Airlines Flight #401 and took off on the hour-long flight to Chittagong, East Pakistan.

10

SURVEY AND Shock

PERCHED ON TOP of the Bay of Bengal, East Pakistan on the map looked like a lopsided amoeba with one finger pointing southward into Burma. As our propeller-driven plane throbbed over the East Pakistan countryside, we craned our necks to catch our first glimpse of its checkerboard fields, palm trees, and hundreds of villages made up of thatched-roof houses. After all those years of mind-bending, body-fatiguing preparations, and propelled by the divine bowstring, we were finally arriving on target. How excited we were!

After banking out over the Bay of Bengal, Chittagong — the main seaport and second largest city in the country — appeared in the distance. Following a perfect landing at Chittagong airport, we were welcomed by Jay and Eleanor Walsh (and children), Mary Lou Brownell (a nurse who had arrived nearly four years earlier), and Donna Ahlgrim and Lynn Silvernale (who had arrived in Chittagong twenty days earlier). We were home!

We lived in with the Walsh family the first three weeks. Tranquilized by exhaustion, that first night we slept like zombies. But we goofed! Because we failed to tuck in the mosquito net properly over Nancy's crib, she awakened in the morning with dozens of red, blotchy mosquito bites. The Walshes' Bengali cook, Shuki, positive the house harbored a smallpox victim, threatened to resign. Only after long explanation did he simmer down and continue his duties.

The second night, sleep did not come. Our internal clocks thrown off by rapid air travel over thousands of miles, we lay starry-eyed. A nearby Hindu religious festival fostered our wakefulness. The rhythmic beat of drums and shrill notes from a native flute joined a cadence of spooky voices which chanted the whole night long.

Our next musical surprise appeared the next day. With bugles blasting, drums rolling, and bagpipes skirling, nearly one hundred uniformed men came marching into the Walsh yard; their perfect formations and precision drills were highly professional. The direc-

110

tor of this railway police band, Major Oliver Ormerod, had come to welcome the new doctor's family to Chittagong. We were impressed, and the children were enchanted.

The Walshes, our host and hostess, cared for us warmly and well. Eleanor, capable nurse and mother of six (later seven), somehow managed to keep our two families fed and functioning. Jay Walsh, a gifted young man with an engaging personality, was chairman of the tiny field council. Because of his leadership ability, he was frequently reelected to that responsible post in ensuing years when the field council became a sizable body. As Jay showed me around Chittagong, I could see that his natural warmth and friendliness had won him many close Bengali friends.

Chittagong seemed like a scene straight out of *Tales of the Arabian Nights*. A sprawling seaport city of nearly half a million people, Chittagong was the gateway to East Pakistan. The downtown streets were endlessly crisscrossed with jeeps, bicycles, rickshas, trucks, three-wheeled motor scooters, bullock carts, brown feet, cattle, dogs, goats, and ancient carriages drawn by tiny horses. Men — men — men were visible everywhere. Women, however, were few and far between and usually covered from head to foot with the *burqa,* a black sacklike garment with peepholes. Most of the people were small, slim, brown-skinned folk. Black-bearded Muslims wearing white prayer caps mingled with Hindus, yellow-robed Buddhist priests, Englishmen, American and Dutch businessmen. The bazaars reeked with local color — and dried fish! White-sailed boats and graceful palms gave the city an exotic, colorful atmosphere. But the attractive elements were countered by open drains, garbage heaps, squawking crows and hawks, sick people, and beggars with outstretched hands crying, *"baksheesh* [alms]!"

Within a week Gene and Beth Gurganus, whom I had visited in North Carolina, arrived, and together we settled into a large, pleasant duplex-type house — Gurganuses downstairs, Olsens upstairs. Clearing customs came next. The Chittagong customs official, who obviously wanted to keep my duty at the absolute minimum, asked me to sign a statement that all our belongings had been in use more than a year. Because many items were new, I could not conscientiously do so. Three times he urged me to sign the false declaration so that he could easily pass my goods with minimal customs charges. Heeding the voice of conscience, I politely refused.

The perplexed official exclaimed to another officer, "I don't understand this man! He will not fix his declaration even though it would save him thousands of rupees!"

I heard myself say, "I believe a man's honor and integrity are worth millions of rupees. We're going to build a hospital. Maybe one day sickness will strike you and you will wonder whether or not you can trust me — now you know."

"Yes, now I know," the officer replied thoughtfully. After a whispered consultation, the two customs officials superficially examined three drums and found some loophole to charge us the absolute minimum — 270 rupees ($60) duty on the foodstuffs.

At home, when I told my adventure to Joan, she dug out a portion of Psalm 15 which said, "He that swears to his own hurt, and changes not . . . shall never be moved." The incident illustrated a principle which seemed important to us: if we expect God to guide us into special paths of usefulness and answer our prayers remarkably, we must follow His teachings on ethics and integrity.

We attended our first ABWE field council meeting eight days after arrival. It marked the end of one era and the beginning of a second era. Era 1, the period of East Pakistan survey and beginning ministry, had extended from 1955 to 1961. This era began with the original survey of the field, the buildup of a sizable staff, and the beginning of the mission's work in the city of Chittagong and a jungle station called Hebron. Era 1 ended with a loss of many valuable workers due to death, sickness, and resignations. The ABWE work in Hebron and Chittagong were temporarily at a standstill. In the transition period between eras 1 and 2, a skeleton crew — Jay and Eleanor Walsh, Mary Lou Brownell, and a linguist named Joyce Ann Wingo — had held things together and "kept the ship afloat." Era 2 would focus on the establishment of our medical mission and the strengthening of the work in Chittagong and Hebron.

Two weeks after our arrival, I faced my first medical emergency — the first patient was Sheryl, one of the Walshes' infant twins, who suffered from an unusual form of dysentery. We awakened one morning to find her cold, ghastly blue-white, in shock. We rushed her by jeep to a local hospital, demanded and got a few surgical instruments. Whether the ancient scalpel was adequately sterilized or not, I could not say, but I took it and quickly made an ankle incision. The tiny, threadlike ankle vein, constricted by shock, would not admit a needle. A second incision in the groin, however, uncovered a vein which did receive the needle — and the life-giving saline solution. Mary Lou Brownell assisted me skillfully and kept the flies shooed away. After a thirty-three-hour vigil at Sheryl's bedside, I knew she would recover and so went home to bed. Mary Lou and Lynn Silvernale alternated the nursing duties.

Before 1947, Chittagong was part of the East Bengal province of India. In 1947 the Muslim majority districts of India were con-

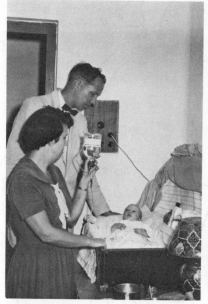

Sheryl Walsh back from the brink (with Mary Lou and Vic)

Muslim muezzin calling the faithful to prayer

stituted as the new nation of Pakistan. Four provinces in the west became West Pakistan. The lone East Bengal province, eleven hundred miles across India, became East Pakistan. Most East Pakistanis were Bengalis, members of one of the largest racial groups of the Indo-Pakistan subcontinent. Casual observation of dozens of mosques and thousands of men wearing prayer caps, calling each other Arabic-sounding names (Ibrahim, Rahman, etc.) made it obvious that the majority of East Pakistan Bengalis were Muslims, believers in Allah and followers of their prophet, Muhammad. Also there were a few thousand Christian Bengalis, considerably more Buddhists, and several million Hindus. The Hindus were of all castes. One group, the Hindu sweepers of Chittagong, were casteless — they were outcasts. Gene Gurganus, who taught and helped these people, took us to two of their squalid villages. The people lived, in their decrepit bamboo houses, very close to mother earth. Under Gene's direction the unkempt children sang and smiled broadly, appreciating his teaching.

In the small, moldering Christian graveyard we viewed with much emotion the graves of Paul Miller and Winnifred Mary Barnard. Joan and I looked at one another and remembered how Mary Barnard's death had moved ABWE to open this field to medical missions; because she died, we were there. A few days later we learned

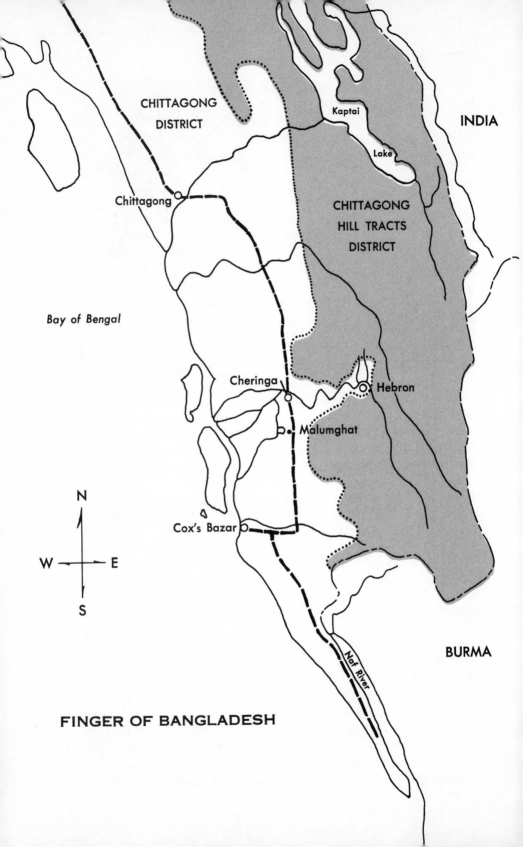

that Mary's parents, Rev. and Mrs. Victor Barnard, had resigned from the mission to go, as independent missionaries, to a needy section of India. These pioneers had left a very precious part of themselves in the Chittagong graveyard.

Within East Pakistan's "finger," two of the country's nineteen districts lay side by side. Chittagong District, the seaward half of the finger, was plains land jampacked with Bengali people, their villages, and their rice fields. The eastern, interior half of the finger, lying adjacent and parallel to Chittagong District, bore the name Chittagong Hill Tracts District. On its jungle-covered low mountains and hills lived non-Bengali tribal peoples, many having Oriental eyes and yellowish-tan complexions. More than a dozen different tribes inhabited the Chittagong Hill Tracts.

In mid-February contractor Paul Goodman and ABWE treasurer, Rev. Edward Bomm, arrived to participate in surveying for hospital location. The survey team visited both districts in the finger. We started with aerial reconnaissance on the Pakistan International Airlines (PIA) flight from Chittagong south to Cox's Bazar. Because Cox's Bazar was situated less than one hundred miles from Chittagong, the plane never flew higher than fifteen hundred feet altitude. The orderly countryside looked like a giant chessboard. Each rice paddy was surrounded by a six-inch earthen wall clearly visible from the air. Every clump of trees signified a village, and in the village bamboo homes lived some of the millions of East Pakistan. Great serpentine rivers writhed sinuously inland from the coast. Around the offshore islands, the tiny white sails of the fishing fleet dotted the glittering sea.

At Cox's Bazar, the surf rolled in upon a broad, white sand beach stretching nearly one hundred miles to the south. Near this subdivisional town of eight thousand, the jungle-clad hills became abrupt cliffs that descended to the beach below. Cox's Bazar would be our base of operations for the next few days. In the blistering hot March days that followed, we traveled many miles by plane, by foot, by jeep, by Land Rover, and by boat. One rugged trip took a portion of the team up the Matamuhari River, beyond our jungle station (Hebron), deep into the Hill Tracts jungle where monkeys raced along treetop trails and elephants hustled giant teak logs to the riverbank. During the survey Paul Goodman shot four thousand feet of color film to produce a moving picture on East Pakistan.

After our survey, we determined not to build the hospital at Hebron; it was too far off the beaten track. We decided against the city of Chittagong because the government had begun building a medical college there, which would ensure that medical care in the city would steadily improve. We had no desire to compete with government doctors and hospitals; rather, we wanted to locate in some area where the Ministry of Health could not yet provide suitable medical services. The survey directed our sights to the area between Cox's Bazar and Cheringa, a town thirty miles to the north. We were disappointed to learn that several tracts of beautiful, wooded, "unfloodable," high plateau land in the area were classified government "reserve forest," a special, sacrosanct type of land unavailable to private organizations.

Back in Chittagong, Joan had dreamed up a title for Paul Goodman's film. The title "Such As I Have" was taken from the words of Peter who said to a lame beggar, "Silver and gold have I none, but *such as I have* I give to you." Each member of the team was giving such as he had (medical skills, linguistic ability, teaching talents, etc.) to God's work in East Pakistan. The film opened with a beggar approaching Joan and Wendy seated in a cycle ricksha. On location, we lined up a beggar who limped up to the ricksha whining, "*baksheesh! baksheesh!*" Within moments a huge crowd gathered to watch the filming. Feeling that beggars were not the best public relations subjects for their country, some became disturbed, and the throng turned noisy and unruly. Before the crowd exploded, we grabbed our props and people and raced for home in another section of the city.

Paul Goodman filming *Such As I Have*

"Baksheesh!"

On a blazing hot day, late in March, the Olsens and Gurganuses drove by Land Rover to Cox's Bazar to begin phase two of the hospital land survey. Where in the thirty-mile radius area should we construct the hospital? That question we hoped to answer by examining the countryside, brainstorming with government officials, analyzing government documents, etc. The next morning, as we consulted in a government office, a breathless Beth Gurganus burst in to say that Joan, at the motel, had been stricken with excruciating abdominal pain. Racing back to our room, I found her in agony. Finally, in a local dispensary I located some pain-killing Demerol (they called it Pethidine) and someone said, "The airplane has landed at our Cox's Bazar airport." Knowing the plane came only twice a week, I sped to the airport and drove the jeep in front of the roaring plane so it could not possibly take off without us.

We brought Joan by Land Rover, placed her stretcher on the plane, and flew to Chittagong, only to learn there was no connecting flight to Dacca, one hundred seventy-five miles to the north. Placing Joan's stretcher on the floor in a quiet corner of the airport, I prayed, "Father, I need You to do something special; Joan can't lie here hour after hour till this evening's flight. Please help us."

I couldn't imagine how God would solve this problem — but I did not wonder long. A PIA official, wearing a puzzled expression on his face, came to report, "Dr. Olsen, something unexpected has happened. Flight control, Dacca, is sending us a plane immediately in exchange for the aircraft we have here in Chittagong. I do not understand why they want this plane so badly, but we are sending it in a few moments; you and Mrs. Olsen will be the only passengers!"

"Thank You, Father," I breathed and asked the officer if he would try to contact, by phone, the Holy Family Hospital in Dacca concerning our arrival. He said he would try, but we both knew it sometimes took a day or two to reach anyone in Dacca by phone.

After another injection for pain and a smooth forty-five minute trip on our "private" passenger aircraft, we circled over Dacca airport. As we breezed in for the landing, I saw the Holy Family Hospital ambulance drive off the main road into the airport! Tests at the hospital confirmed the diagnosis: kidney stone. The final outcome was an "outpassing" of the stone. My cable, garbled in transmission, as usual, did not greatly enlighten my colleagues in Chittagong. The cable read: KINNEY STORE PASSED SPONTANEOUSLY STOP SURVERY NOT NECESSARY STOP DOXOLOGY OLSEN. (When I wrote the cable, it had said: KIDNEY STONE PASSED SPONTANEOUSLY STOP SURGERY NOT

NECESSARY STOP DOXOLOGY OLSEN.) A few days later we returned to Chittagong.

Mary Lou Brownell and Joyce Ann Wingo, after traumatic but productive first terms of service, returned to America on furlough. Joyce Ann had trekked jungle trails and lived in tribal villages deep in the Chittagong Hill Tracts, a remarkable feat for a girl alone. She learned the Tippera language, translated a portion of the Scriptures into it, and helped Tipperas find Christ and release from their life-shattering fear of evil spirits.

Mary Lou, with Juanita Canfield, another nurse then studying midwifery in a West Pakistan hospital, had operated a dispensary in Chittagong. They also conducted occasional clinics in villages near Chittagong. Mary Lou, a competent nurse with snapping brown eyes, later operated the first dispensary at the jungle outpost, Hebron. She planned to take a course in missionary dentistry and return within a year and a half to work in the hospital when it opened.

Fortunately, a good architect with hospital design experience was available in Chittagong. An aggressive, competent Englishman, he directed a company known as ABC (Associated British Consultants). We began working with him on refining our hospital design.

In May our family located for two weeks in Cox's Bazar to continue the interrupted phase two of the hospital land survey. Jay Walsh joined us for part of that time. We met the SDO (subdivisional officer) in charge of Cox's Bazar Subdivision, one of the three subdivisions of long, narrow Chittagong District. We brainstormed with him for hours, talked to many citizens, explored the whole thirty-mile radius area, etc. We made copious notes and discussed all the factors for hours. The SDO's wife, a pretty German girl, often brought her sister and children to spend time with Joan.

Because of the proximity of this subdivision to Burma, we found that the Muslim and Hindu communities were diluted by numerous Buddhists. Their temples were intriguing, and we found that one Buddhist temple contained a massive and exquisite brass Buddha. We encountered difficulty photographing one of the yellow-robed priests; every time the lens pointed his way, he fell into a trance.

Unexpectedly, I met in Cox's Bazar the Chittagong Divisional Commissioner, the prestigious chief officer over five of East Pakistan's nineteen districts, including Chittagong and Chittagong Hill Tracts Districts. In front of twenty other government officers, he asked, "What brings you, doctor, to Cox's Bazar?" I told him my story of conversion to Christ, Mary Barnard's death, and my sense of call to serve in East Pakistan.

"Extraordinary!" he exclaimed, "I've never heard anything like it. We're glad you have come. I will help you any way I can."

In that meeting, my first encounter with a really senior government official, I began to realize that relatively few men in East Pakistan had the power to help us accomplish our objectives. We would have to pray that God would give us favor in their sight.

Back in Chittagong, we analyzed, sifted, and refined the mass of information we had obtained. Although many factors favored the Cox's Bazar area, careful analysis revealed that most of them were physical, convenience, or comfort factors. We had come to care for the sick, share our faith with interested people, help Christians to organize their churches and train their leadership. Because each of these aims could be more effectively realized if we were located in the Cheringa region, that area became our choice. That location would place us in the area of greatest medical need and keep us out of competition with government medicine. The Cheringa location, furthermore, would tie us into our existing stations, keep us from overextending ourselves, and relate us to the fruitful tribal work. After the unanimous field council decision, we were ready to approach the people of Cheringa and medical authorities in Dacca.

Then the rains came! In mid-June, the southwest monsoon winds began to dump tons of rain water on East Pakistan, thirteen inches the first day. The rain continued fiercely every day for five days until the city looked like a lake.

In late June, Jay Walsh and I, according to the original plan, traveled to Dacca to meet with the director of health services. We hoped to obtain his approval for our proposed hospital in the Cheringa area. He listened with interest and appreciation — and punted. He sent our petition up the ladder and stated the decision would be communicated to us "in due course."

In July, Jay and I traveled to the Cheringa area to talk with local leaders at the grass roots level and select possible land for the hospital buildings. Our friend, the SDO from Cox's Bazar, had rounded up the four key union council chairmen representing some fifty thousand people. They were more than happy to have the hospital located in their area. We brainstormed with these men and looked around for the most suitable land. After reconfirming the unavailability of the prime reserve forest land, we tentatively selected a fifty-acre plot of farmland one mile north of Cheringa town. We chose the highest, most flood-proof farmland in the area. Then we met to begin the preliminary bargaining over land price.

Hearing of heavy flooding in the Cheringa area, we recognized we had been given a golden opportunity to see if our potential hospital land was flood-safe. Arriving there we found the land inundated

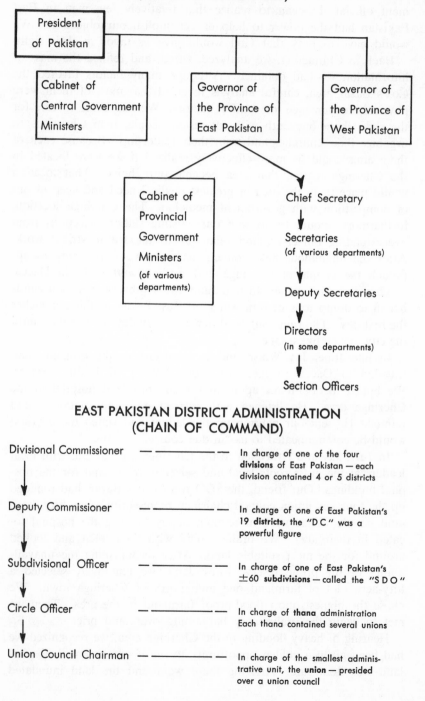

PAKISTAN HIGH LEVEL ADMINISTRATION
(CHAIN OF COMMAND)

President of Pakistan

Cabinet of Central Government Ministers

Governor of the Province of East Pakistan

Governor of the Province of West Pakistan

Cabinet of Provincial Government Ministers (of various departments)

Chief Secretary
↓
Secretaries (of various departments)
↓
Deputy Secretaries
↓
Directors (in some departments)
↓
Section Officers

EAST PAKISTAN DISTRICT ADMINISTRATION
(CHAIN OF COMMAND)

Divisional Commissioner — In charge of one of the four **divisions** of East Pakistan — each division contained 4 or 5 districts
↓
Deputy Commissioner — In charge of one of East Pakistan's 19 **districts**, the "D C" was a powerful figure
↓
Subdivisional Officer — In charge of one of East Pakistan's ±60 **subdivisions** — called the "S D O"
↓
Circle Officer — In charge of **thana** administration Each thana contained several unions
↓
Union Council Chairman — In charge of the smallest administrative unit, the **union** — presided over a union council

with two to three feet of brown, swirling river water. Dismayed at first, we later relaxed and rejoiced that we had learned in time our proposed site was unsatisfactory. Then, fortified with proof that no farmland in the region would serve our purpose, we gained courage to try for the impossible.

We headed back to the tracts of reserve forest land below Cheringa. Three miles to the south, we located a beautiful sixty-acre plot of high plateau land. Because the valuable, tall, stately trees had been cut from the land, we hoped the government might be more willing to part with this plot. But the divisional forest officer said no. His superior, the conservator of forests, said no. The Dacca-based chief conservator, in charge of all East Pakistan forest land, also said no.

Our last court of appeal was the governor, the head of the total East Pakistan government. When we were thoroughly "prayed up" and when the time was right, I took our architect and entered the "lion's den," the office of the governor of East Pakistan. I made two requests: first, that our hospital project be speedily approved and, second, that we be granted the special reserve forest land needed for our project. Governor Faruque, a stout man with a bristling gray mustache, listened impatiently to my defense of these two propositions.

When he had heard enough, he barked. "This is not my business! The secretary of health must deal with your hospital proposal and the secretary of agriculture, who is responsible for the Forest Department, must deal with your request for reserve forest land. Doctor, present your petition to the secretary of health."

"It has been on his desk for weeks," I countered.

The governor roared, "I can't help that; my man will arrange the appointment for you!" and dismissed us.

Outside, the architect, feeling the meeting had been a flop, shook his head. I had a hunch, however, that Governor Faruque would stir up some action in the secretariat. I had studied and learned all I could about him; he was noted for getting things done.

Governor Faruque did not disappoint me! The next day, the secretary of health handled our request with alacrity and courtesy. On the spot, he provided *a formal, official, written approval of our total hospital plan and location.* He then arranged my appointment with the chief conservator of forests who listened with a new degree of openness. Either God or the governor had softened him up. His previous no turned into a written, official yes. He sent me to his superior, the secretary of agriculture, who quickly ratified the approval, agreeing to release the reserve forest land to us. *For the first time in the history of the nation, this special sacrosanct type of land was granted to a private organization — and we were a Christian mission in this Muslim land!* "Thank You, Father!"

In three days our whole plan had fallen neatly, beautifully into place! And the key to success was the visit to the governor. As Solomon put it, "Where the word of the king is, there is power" — and Solomon ought to know, for he was one. I was beginning to get the feel of how this government and country operated.

With the written approval in hand, I could now take the first step toward registering the hospital as a nonprofit charitable institution, which would open the door to duty-free import of cement, reinforcing bars, fixtures, medical equipment, medicines, et cetera. To obtain duty-free status would save us tens of thousands of dollars. I met with the chief income tax officer in Dacca who explained that approval as a charitable institution actually must be given from his headquarters in West Pakistan. This department did not belong to the East Pakistan provincial government; rather, it was a branch of the central (federal) government with headquarters in West Pakistan.

Then the officer smiled and said, "I have just been promoted to the position of officer in charge of headquarters, so I will very soon be moving to. West Pakistan to take up my post! Just forward the written request for registration of your hospital as a nonprofit, charitable institution directly to me, and I will do the needful!"

That third week in August was one of those rare weeks when everything went right. Such weeks were hard to come by in East Pakistan. The Peace Corps found it so difficult to accomplish anything there, it finally withdrew its workers and quit.

Back in America, contractor Paul Goodman also hit a gusher. Paul, speaking to an adult Sunday school class, explained his sense of call to manage the construction of the East Pakistan hospital. In characteristically honest fashion, he confessed his own lack of expertise in matters electrical.

"What we need now," he said, "is a man who can install generators and wiring. Ideally, he should also know general contracting. If he knew a little something about medicine and treatment, that would be the frosting on the cake, because the mission doctors will be studying language in the city and sick workmen are bound to come to us for help."

As Paul spoke, Tom and Olline McDonald hung on every word. As he ticked off the one-two-three requirements, Tom McDonald was saying to himself, "I could do that — I could do that — I could do that." Tom held an electrical contracting license and owned his own business; he was also an experienced builder holding a general contracting license; and Tom had been a medic in the US Navy. Seated beside her husband, Olline was saying to herself, "My Tom can do that — my Tom can do that — my Tom can do that." When they shared their feelings on the way home from church, they suspected the great Architect was drawing them into a new blueprint. To obviate being swayed by emotionalism, however, they kept the matter even from their family, prayed, and discussed the proposition for over three months. Then that wonderful couple, Tom and Olline, sold their home, their car, and their business to build for God and the people of East Pakistan.

On September 1 the forest department provided two survey teams to survey and demarcate our sixty acres of land. Life was sweet! Although my time was consumed with government contacts, gaining approvals, and finalizing the land purchase, I saw occasional patients. From the Chittagong Hill Tracts town of Bandarban, one day came the prince of the Moghs (rhymes with logs). His elder brother was the raja (king) over all the tribal people in the southern half of the Chittagong Hill Tracts. The Moghs look like Burmese, are related to the Burmese, and speak a language similar to Burmese. In addition to the Hill Tract Moghs, plains Moghs live in villages in the Cheringa/Cox's Bazar area. The Mogh prince came as a patient, responded to treatment, and became a friend of the family. Because of his love for Mark, on every visit he would bring him from the jungle a tribal musical instrument, candy, or some other fascinating memento. He listened with sincere interest as we shared our faith with him.

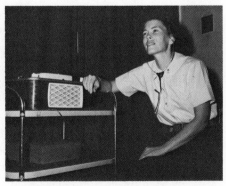

New student — new sounds

Mogh prince with a gift for Mark

In September I finally was able to begin Bengali language study. An educated Pakistani lady taught Wendy and Lynne their Calvert course, freeing Joan, also, for her study of Bengali. By this time we were becoming euphoric over our new life in East Pakistan. Our study of the beautiful Bengali language was under way, a second contractor had volunteered, patients had been cured, our trip to the governor had been successful, the hospital project was officially approved, and the government had granted us the impossible-to-get land. And official registration as a nonprofit, charitable institution, was just around the corner. Life was great!

The shock wave struck on October 1 in the form of a letter from the government. The communication detailed the large amount of money we should pay for the land and concluded with a shocking sentence: "An undertaking may also be taken in writing from the Association that the proposed hospital is a purely humanitarian institution and not an instrument of conversion of people from one religion to another." This demand went completely contrary to the constitution of Pakistan which stated: "No law should prevent the members of a religious community or denomination from professing, practising, or propagating, or from providing instruction in their religion, or from conducting institutions for the purposes of or in connection with their religion."

The demand seemed not only unconstitutional, but also would nullify the mandate given us by our Master who said, "You shall be my witnesses . . . to the uttermost part of the earth," and again, "Go you into all the world and preach the good news." We knew from our own life experience that this news was so good that if we shared or presented it, some would undoubtedly believe and become followers of Christ. And if we lived the Christlike life of loving and helping others, this, too, would inevitably draw people to Him. We could not go forward with our plans to construct the hospital if religious freedom were to be denied us.

On the same day our team gathered together for a special field council session. We decided to lie low for a while, and notify our home board and constituency in an effort to generate massive prayer backing before we made our move. We would also discuss the problem with our legal adviser. When the time was ripe, we would make a careful, discreet approach to the government and request that the demand be dropped.

Three weeks later Gene Gurganus and I flew to Dacca to meet with the secretary of health, the man who ordered that we sign the "nonreligious-instrument" undertaking. We were delighted to find out that a few days earlier a new officer had taken over as the secretary of health. He was a friendly, congenial, intelligent man. We approached him first about reducing the price of the land (the government had asked $23,000 for the sixty-one acres of land). Then we gingerly raised the question of the clause which would affect our religious freedom. Although sympathetic with our dilemma, he said the matter would have to be settled at a higher level — this meant the chief secretary or governor. I had learned by then that the courts could not help us because in Pakistan, at that time, decisions about basic freedoms were made by the government and were not justiciable by the courts.

Our plans to meet the chief secretary were quickly frustrated by a startling development in international politics. Communist China launched a sudden military attack against India in an area northeast of East Pakistan. The United States government, to withstand communist aggression and expansion, began airlifting huge quantities of military hardware to India. Pakistan, an old friend of America, deeply resented America's arming its ancient enemy India. Pakistanis felt sure that Indians would one day attack them with the American weapons which were pouring into India. Because of the violent anti-American reaction, we felt it prudent to delay our approach to the chief secretary regarding our American-sponsored hospital.

As our first East Pakistan Christmas approached, my workload skyrocketed. Gene Gurganus and Jay Walsh, the other two ABWE men in Chittagong, departed for a pre-Christmas trek into the Hill Tracts to visit our Tippera tribal Christian brothers and sisters.

As he departed, Jay said to me, "Vic, look after my family, will you, while I'm gone?"

"Sure, Jay," I responded. As I raced around trying to do the essential parts of three men's work, it struck me that I should arrange for Christmas trees. I sent a trusted Pakistani friend to arrange two trees (the Gurganuses had an artificial one). I was naïvely unaware that pine trees did not exist in East Pakistan. There were, in Chittagong, a handful of tamaracks, distant relatives of the pine; I later learned the only large groves of tamarack were located near Cox's Bazar. By a herculean effort my friend obtained some branches of a Chittagong tamarack. Remembering my buddy's request ("Vic, look after my family, will you?") and my response ("Sure, Jay") and recalling also that the Christmas program would be at the Walsh home, I took the branches there. Eleanor Walsh and I stuck them in a bucket of sand, decorated the makeshift tree with their trimmings, and were pleased with the final creation. Certain that my friend would produce some branches for the Olsen house, I carried on with

SDO of Cox's Bazar

The special Christmas tree

my busy schedule. Suddenly, it was 6:00 P.M. Christmas Eve —
and I had no Christmas tree for my children on our very first
Christmas in East Pakistan. I was crushed. Why it affected me so
deeply I'm not quite sure; I suppose no father feels happy failing
his children. With an aching heart, I took out the Christmas decor-
ations, untangled a string of lights, and plugged them in. As I expected, they didn't work.

After some bulb replacements, I took the lighted string in hand
and wondered what in the world to do with it. *Maybe I could use
tape or drive three nails in the wall and install the lights in the form
of a triangle, or something,* I thought. Feeling poignantly helpless
to provide for my family, I held the lighted string of lights against
the wall. At that exact moment I heard a knock at the door. Putting down the lights, I opened the door to see a tall Bengali man
with a huge tamarack Christmas tree over his shoulder.

"Salam alekum," he said, grinning broadly. It was the Muslim
greeting, "Peace be upon you."

He continued, *"Ami ke apni janen?* [Do you know who I am?]"

I recognized him instantly as the jeep driver for the subdivisional
officer of Cox's Bazar. That morning, he explained, the memsahib,
the German wife of the SDO, had ordered the driver to drive six

miles down the beach to the tamarack grove to cut down two trees — one for her and the other for "that American doctor in Chittagong." After delivering the memsahib's tree, he had lashed our tree to the roof of his jeep, driven the one hundred miles to Chittagong, and searched for an hour and a half to find our house. The kids squealed with joy when they saw the tree. We thanked the driver, we thanked God, and we erected and trimmed the tree with indescribable joy. Planted in a bucket of sand, the top of the tree reached to one-half inch below our ten-foot ceiling — a perfect fit!

On the world's first Christmas, God reached down out of heaven and revealed Himself to the human race through the gift of His Son. On our first Christmas in East Pakistan, God reached down out of heaven, through quite a different kind of gift, and revealed Himself anew to us. God did not meet me in the *hour* of my need — He met me in the exact *second* of that need! Despite the cloud of the nonreligious-instrument clause, difficulties in Bengali language study, and the menace of a nearby war between the world's two largest nations, we were content. We knew God was real and that He had not forgotten us. *Salam alekum* was true for us — His peace was upon us.

11

Clause and Colleagues

SITTING in a Bengali-made rocking chair in our Bangladesh bedroom, I found that I could relieve partially the steady pain in my elbow by resting the plastered limb on the arm of the chair. Sitting there, my thoughts turn to a colleague: *I wonder how Reid is getting along in Chittagong?* As Donn Ketcham and I had elected, at the time our families evacuated, to remain at the hospital, so Reid Minich had decided to remain in Chittagong to help our Bengali brothers and sisters and protect mission property there. We had no way to know how much danger he was facing.

Reid had come first in 1963, the year we suffered seemingly endless frustration over "the clause." In 1963, a big year for newcomers, we had received with joy and open arms thirteen new, first-term colleagues.

* * *

Our old friends, nurses Becky Davey and Jeannie Lockerbie, arrived in January. Jeannie and Becky were to live with Juanita Canfield who also arrived in January. "Nita," a jolly, experienced nurse, had worked in the early days with Mary Lou Brownell in Chittagong. More recently, she had lived in West Pakistan where she tackled the Urdu language, studied Islamics at Lahore's Punjab University, and learned midwifery at the huge government hospital in Multan.

When the Chinese army retreated back behind the bamboo curtain, the cessation of the Sino-Indian war somewhat cooled down anti-Americanism in East Pakistan. So I flew to Dacca for the fateful meeting with the chief secretary regarding the nonreligious-instrument clause and some concession in the price of the land. We had prayed for two months about this crucial meeting. In Chittagong our mission team kept a two- to three-hour prayer vigil going at the time of my Dacca meeting with the chief secretary. He received me graciously, heard my story, accepted the written petition, and said,

"I'm leaving the country tomorrow for several days of work in West Pakistan. Contact me in a week."

I returned to my breathlessly expectant family and colleagues to report again, "Nothing definite." Ten weeks earlier I had returned from my meeting with the secretary of health to report the same indecisive response. For weeks to come, my negotiations would have the same mushy, unsatisfying, patience-devouring result. Three more times in the first quarter of 1963, I flew to Dacca, met the chief secretary, and returned to Chittagong with the report: "Nothing definite." I thought drearily I might someday qualify as the "hero" in the Rudyard Kipling poem which reads:

> And the end of the fight is a tombstone white
> with the name of the late deceased,
> And the epitaph drear: "A fool lies here
> who tried to hustle the East."

Akotoshee and Lynne

Akotoshee, the gardener's daughter, ten years old like Wendy, played daily with Lynne and Wendy. When Joan groomed our girls' very blonde hair, she also combed and brushed Akotoshee's glistening jet black hair. She called Joan "Mommy," for her own mother was dead. When Wendy told Akotoshee about God's love and about Jesus dying on the cross for her, Akotoshee wept; she was learning more about love than she had ever known.

On a bright February morning I drove my Land Rover into the motor workshop of Steel Brothers, Ltd., the Land Rover agency in Chittagong. I was delighted to see Percy Bamber, workshop superintendent, who had been away for three months in England on home leave. I had never yet found a suitable opportunity to discuss spiritual matters with him.

"How are you, Percy?" I asked.

"Fine, Doc," he replied. "Would you care to have a cup of tea with me?"

Over tea, Percy immediately took the initiative and began to discuss spiritual truth. I had never heard him talk like that before.

"Percy," I asked, "where did you learn all this?"

"While I was in England, Doc," he responded, "my cousin took me to a fine church with a wonderful minister, and I liked what he preached so much that I kept returning to hear more."

"What's the name of this church and who is the minister?" I asked. When Percy replied, "Dr. Martyn Lloyd-Jones of Westminster Chapel," I understood how he had learned so much and why he had gained such an interest in spiritual things.

"Percy," I asked, "what else did you learn from Dr. Lloyd-Jones?"

"Well, Doc, I learned that you've got to be born again." When I asked Percy how a person is "born again," I found we had reached the limit of his new knowledge. He wasn't quite sure but feared it would be a difficult procedure. I invited him for dinner on Friday night.

At dinner, Percy was eager to discuss the Bible and its teachings. Joan and I explained to him the good news of Christ and how, through sincere faith and acceptance of the Saviour, a person is "born again."

"Explain it again," Percy requested. "I want to understand it perfectly." I did explain it again, and Joan gave Percy a booklet from our files for his further study. At the end of the evening he seemed moved when we prayed with him before his departure. Ten days later we met again.

"Did you ever read that book, Percy?" I asked.

"Oh, yes, Doc, I've read it five times."

"Well, Percy, when are you going to get born again?"

"Oh, that's already happened," Percy chuckled. "Over in my digs the other day after I read your book the fifth time, I put everything aside, prayed to God, and accepted Christ into my life. It's wonderful to have it settled."

In March, when the ABWE executive committee met in Philadelphia, they found little to encourage them regarding the medical-surgical mission to East Pakistan. The nonreligious-instrument clause still hung over our heads, our negotiations had produced "nothing definite" results, and anti-American sentiment flared up again in Pakistan. In the meeting a board member quoted Dr. Donn Ketcham. Donn, nearing the end of his deputation, had been doing some rethinking; naturally enough, he wondered whether or not we should start small and not put all of our eggs in one basket.

"Perhaps we should hold up our plans until Dr. Donn Ketcham arrives on the field for further discussion," suggested one board member.

Another proposed, "It might be wise for Dr. Olsen to fly to the Philippines and study the ABWE nine-bed hospital-clinic setup there." The ABWE president wrote quoting the minutes of the meeting and added, "No action was taken, but this minute is designed to reopen the whole matter for review and fresh evaluation." To receive this new directive, after fourteen months in the country, during the blazing hot season when we were physically and mentally exhausted, with negotiations stalled and our whole dream teetering on the knife edge of Muslim sufferance, seemed almost too much.

In April we met three times with the new governor of East Pakistan. Governor Abdul Monem Khan, sworn in five months earlier, knew something about medical matters. He had been previously minister of health for the central government of Pakistan. At the first introductory meeting, Juanita Canfield, Gene Gurganus, Jay Walsh, and I spent twenty minutes conversing with the governor. Although the file had been with him for many days, he knew nothing of the case. While he chewed betel nut and listened attentively, we outlined the background of our project and problem. He did not seem to be sure what the constitution declared about religion. Apparently he had not faced a problem like this before. Assuring us he would study the case with care, he asked us to return in a few days.

At the second meeting Gene Gurganus and I spent an hour with this Muslim governor of a Muslim land. He was cordial and hospitable, serving us tea in his chambers. In a talkative mood, he spoke of his hopes for East Pakistan and the problems he faced in bringing those hopes to fruition. He spoke also of spiritual things, relating an incident in the life of Muhammad which emphasized the value of service to mankind and the doing of good works. He made us feel very much at home and we appreciated his cordiality. After expressing our admiration for the constitution and its guarantees of religious freedom, we raised the question of the clause. Governor Monem Khan, who had evidently done his homework on the constitution, affirmed that Islam as a religion and Pakistan as a country were committed to the principle of freedom of religion. Those words were music to our ears!

The governor then asked us to redesign our proposal to request a smaller amount of land. He explained that due to the terrific population pressure, his superior, the president over all of Pakistan, recently had ordered him to hold land grants to the minimum. He asked us, further, to have one final consultation with the minister of finance regarding the concession we had requested on the price of the land. We thanked the governor for his time and kindness to us. He seemed touched and grateful when we explained that it was our habit to pray for him.

After slashing our land request to twenty-five acres and enjoying a profitable meeting with the minister of finance, Jay Walsh and I held the final forty-minute interview with Governor Monem Khan. During our discussion, he strongly reiterated his stand that Islam teaches and promotes freedom of religion, adding that he also believed in religious freedom. He said he fully expected that some East Pakistanis would become Christians as a result of our influence and kindness to them; he seemed quite unconcerned about the prospect. He closed the interview, indicating he had decided in our favor!

When we picked up the written order, we knew that God had answered our prayers. We were allowed twenty-five acres of reserve forest land on a perpetually renewable lease at the concessional rate of one thousand rupees per acre. (This meant the total cost of the land would be five thousand dollars, the exact amount originally designated for purchase of property!) The nonreligious-instrument clause was thrown out. The highest level of government had upheld the Pakistan constitution. The document given us further stated that if the government ever reclaimed the property, it would be legally bound to pay compensation to us according to the stated rules of compensation. April was a great month! "Thank You, Father!"

According to the home board's instruction to reevaluate the total program, the field council members met together to analyze and brainstorm. It seemed to us the light was very green. Not only had the special land been granted us for the first time in the history of the country, but also it was being given us at a concessional rate. Through traumatic experience we had learned that the government held a high view of the religious freedom guaranteed by its constitution.

We found Solomon's words again applicable to our situation: "He that observes the wind shall not sow; and he that regards the clouds shall not reap." The entire team was in unanimous agreement that the program should be carried on as originally planned. We fired off our analysis to the home board in Philadelphia.

In May, as we waited for home board response, Jeannie, Becky, and Donna started a great program. Recognizing that all kids, junior age and up, need supervised group activity, they started the Torchbearer's Club. The Torchbearers had uniforms and earned badges for health, safety, Bible, patriotism, art, crafts, etc. Because American children who live most of their years overseas often have little positive feeling of identification with America, the nurses emphasized the national anthem and American sports and games. Whenever these nurses saw a need or sensed a problem, they pitched in and helped; they put the spirit of teamwork into action. Teamwork was a big thing with us.

On May 20 we visited the rural home of Mr. Mitro, my Hindu language teacher, in a village area several hours from Chittagong. It was the fifteenth day following the death of Mr. Mitro's grandmother, and Hindu social law dictated that he and his father must give a banquet for over twelve hundred people from neighboring Hindu villages.

"Where will they get the plates?" we wondered. No problem — banana leaves served as plates for the rice and curry dished up out of huge tubs. Because this Eastern food was eaten with fingers, silverware also posed no problem. The occasion was a festive and carefree one. But ten days later scores of those same people were dead! On May 30, the 1963 cyclone and tidal wave struck with terrible fury.

Torchbearers pledging allegiance to the flag

Festive crowd — scores dead ten days later

East Pakistan is cyclone prone. Two cyclonic storms hit in October, 1960, and two more followed in May, 1961, prior to our arrival in the country. Because we seldom had time for radio listening, we had no warning at all before our first cyclone. We awakened at midnight to the unearthly scream of one-hundred-mile-an-hour winds and banging of windows. Stepping out of bed onto the unexpectedly wet floor, my foot slipped. In the living room, glass shattered as the wind velocity picked up. I tucked Joan and the children into the one dry room with unbroken windows, then went from room to room trying to close other windows. Several windows, with nonfunctioning handles, could not be secured. Back in my bedroom, straining and tugging at a window, I learned that the strength of the wind had become greater than my strength; that window, seized by raging blasts of wind, began to pull me outward. Abandoning the window and the room to the storm, I retreated to the safe room.

In awe, we wondered what people in bamboo houses could possibly do against the fury of the wind and the wall of water that such a massive storm usually vacuums up from the Bay of Bengal to hurl at the unprotected coastline. Hour after relentless hour, the gale attacked the defenseless people and property in Chittagong District. And, hour after hour, more hundreds and thousands succumbed to the fury of the wind and water. The low pressure in the center of that storm popped our ears as though we were climbing fast in a jet plane. As we felt and heard the power of the elements, I suddenly gained a new comprehension of what was involved when Jesus stilled the storm — how mighty was His power! We comforted the children throughout the night.

On the other side of town, Percy Bamber, lying in bed when the cyclone reached its peak, heard a strange noise in the bathroom. He leaped from bed to investigate but found nothing in the bathroom. At that precise moment a huge chunk of his brick wall and ceiling, torn loose by the furious wind, crashed down on the pillow where his head had been seconds before. It was his turn to say, "Thank You, Father."

As a new day came to life, the seven-hour storm died. A pallid sun rose to view the horror: tens of thousands of animal corpses, twenty-five thousand dead men, women, and children, and hundreds of thousands rendered homeless. The daily *Unity* reported the effects of the storm on Chittagong city:

> One more great calamity has overwhelmed our city and suburbs. A "horde of mad elephants" ran amuck and tore our delicate "queen city of the east" to tatters, and ripped her open. Even angels must have shuddered to see that ghastly sight.

We went to work to help the stricken people with food and clothing. That, too, became a nightmare, for as people poured in through doors and windows of the relief center, rioting and fighting broke out. Mothers and babies were squashed as they tried to get a handful of rice. We organized our team to help the government give immunizations, but no vaccine was available. So typhoid and cholera claimed the lives of hundreds more. We could never be quite the same again.

In early June we received by cable good news from Philadelphia. The home board had accepted our evaluation of the hospital project and agreed that all systems were go. That grand group of men then went all out for the project! Despite the great strain it would place on ABWE resources, the board guaranteed the contractors would have in hand to work with, the full amount of money for hospital and housing construction. Contractors Goodman and McDonald previously had been released by the board from their commitment, but, wonderfully, their schedules allowed them to step back into the project. They were urgently requesting hospital plans. We worked day and night to finalize the floor plan and fire it off to them.

Before mid-June the monsoon rains appeared to begin their annual window-washing work. Where our window panes were missing, the rain came right in. We found Mark, Nancy, and Lynne, one day, playing in puddles in the hall and bedroom. Mark was down on his tummy, clothes and all, pretending to swim in a big one in the hall. It took ages for the overworked glass *mistris* (workmen) to come and replace the broken window panes. At last, on a wet June nineteenth they arrived to delight us with the best possible gift, window glass — on our *crystal* wedding anniversary.

With the hospital project approved, we could now apply to the income tax department of the central government for registration as a bona fide, nonprofit, charitable institution. We cranked out the required constitution for the hospital, filled out the necessary forms, prepared a cover letter, and sent the package to the friendly officer who had become the "in-charge" of the headquarters office in West Pakistan. Almost by return mail, the letter of approval came — it was dated the fourth of July. With this letter and other documents in hand, I approached the Chittagong customs authorities. Within days I received from them the official letter stating that all goods, materials, and supplies for the hospital would be admitted free of duty or sales tax! That would save us tens of thousands of dollars. "Thank You, Father!"

We enjoyed a brief vacation at Kaptai, an hour and a half due east from Chittagong in the Hill Tracts. An American company had constructed a huge dam on the Karnaphuli River at that point producing, behind the dam, the largest man-made lake in Asia.

Shortly after our return to Chittagong, I tackled my first major surgical operation in East Pakistan. A patient named Kahloo (Bengali for "blackie") sustained a badly broken lower jaw. The usual treatment in Chittagong for such a case was to shoot the patient; Kahloo was a young cocker spaniel, Wendy's beloved pet. One look at her tear-stained face convinced me that the usual treatment would not suffice. At a bamboo hardware store in the bazaar, I purchased some baling wire and an imported carpenter's hand drill.

Our team went into action on the nurses' back veranda. Anesthetist Canfield put the patient to sleep with intravenous Pentathol. Circulating nurse Lockerbie kept the sterile instruments coming to the table. Assistant surgeon Davey rendered invaluable assistance to surgeon Olsen who made the necessary incision, drilled the broken bones, and wired them together with the bazaar wire. To be doubly sure the broken fragments would remain in proper position, I designed a circular cast for Kahloo's nose — but that was my big mistake! I left Kahloo with Joan and Wendy and went out.

Awakening from the anesthesia, Kahloo had a prolonged excitement phase. Plunging out of Wendy's arms, he staggered about until captured by Joan. Lunging, he escaped again to run smack into the wall. Joan grabbed him again and noticed, to her dismay, that the dog had forced his tongue out between tightly clamped teeth, obstructing its circulation. The end of Kahloo's tongue began to blow up like a balloon. I returned just in time to remove the cast, free

First surgical patient, Kahloo (with Wendy)

Sinking first tube well at Malumghat

Kahloo's tongue, and quiet the jangled nerves of the Olsen girls. Within a month Kahloo could chew anything.

Late in July the time was right to resurvey our forest land to fit the twenty-five acres allotted us. Without the survey and demarcation of the land, we would be unable to sign the necessary lease. The rain would be a problem, for it had rained heavily for days. Somehow, however, the feeling came to me strongly that our efforts would succeed. Our first stop would be the surveyor's office, Cox's Bazar. Jay Walsh and I took the hour-long trip to Chittagong airport only to find that the Cox's Bazar flight was booked solid. Because a section of the road had washed out, air travel was the only way to Cox's Bazar. But two of the forty-four passengers failed to show up by boarding time, so we got the seats. Despite the rain, the flight was not canceled, and we flew the cloudy skies to Cox's Bazar.

We presented our papers in the surveyor's office and, as the rain beat a tattoo on the roof, the surveyors laughed at us.

"It will be impossible for us to survey tomorrow because of the rain," the chief surveyor informed us.

"But we *must* survey tomorrow," we responded. "Our whole hospital work depends upon getting this survey done immediately."

"But it is impossible to survey in such rain," the surveyor countered. "It has been raining like this for days, and it will probably rain for days to come."

I could hardly believe the next words I heard myself say: "Don't worry about the rain, gentlemen; we are God's men doing God's work, and He will take care of the rain. We will be back at 8:30 in the morning for the survey."

Great Scott! What had I said? I had spoken as though possessed — I hoped I had been possessed by God's Spirit and not some other spirit. I had opened the door either to one of life's greatest experiences or one of life's biggest fiascos. My buddy Jay, that great guy, was game. Our friend, the SDO, gave us rooms in the VIP circuit house for senior officials. As the rain beat down on the circuit house roof, Jay and I prayed urgently that God would stop the rain.

We awoke in the morning to the sound of rain. We prayed again, as though our lives depended on it, ate a little breakfast, donned our raincoats, put up our umbrellas, and proceeded to the surveyor's office. As we entered, they smiled as if to say, "We told you so."

We said, "Gentlemen, get your chains and other tools. It's time to get started." Convinced that we were surely mad, they remonstrated with us. Because we were adamant, they finally gathered their umbrellas and tools, and we piled into the jeep.

As we drove along to our destination, thirty-two miles to the north, the monsoon rains increased in intensity. From the slate gray sky, rain poured down in such blinding sheets that the driver was forced to slow down to a crawl. The surveyors smirked overtly to each other. Ten miles, fifteen miles, twenty miles — the heavy rain continued. My lips were dry and my heart beating a little faster than usual. I wondered what was going on in Jay's mind. Twenty-six miles — twenty-seven miles — twenty-eight miles — the rain kept slashing down. The surveyors smiled.

In the depths of my soul I cried out silently, *Oh, Father, will You help us now? Will You uphold Your own name and do something to help us for Your project's sake and for Jesus' sake? Amen.* But the rain kept pouring from that inscrutable sky. Seconds ticked by. Then, suddenly, as though a giant hand had sealed the heavens, the rain abruptly stopped! The smiles vanished from the surveyors' faces. I looked up to see a tiny patch of blue in the gray sky, which seemed to me a symbol of the goodness and love of God. A half hour after our arrival, the high, firm, gently sloping land was sufficiently drained for us to survey, demarcate the twenty-five acres, and install concrete corner posts.

James, Jesus' brother, knew what he was saying when he wrote that earnest prayer can accomplish much. In this regard, James mentioned Elijah. We certainly had a new fellow feeling for that old prophet who was a man subject to the same feelings we have, "and he prayed earnestly that it might not rain: and it rained not." The fiasco was averted and it was one of life's great experiences. "Thank You, Father!"

Back in Chittagong, we continued to work more hours with architect Tony Adams on hospital plans. I first met Tony and his wife, Myra, in Dacca shortly after their arrival some months earlier. In that very first meeting, he listened with exceptional interest to my experience of conversion from agnosticism to Christianity. But I did not learn until much later that Tony had arrived in East Pakistan an atheist. We loved Tony and Myra, and grew very close to them as we worked countless hours together on the hospital plans.

Over the months, different members of the team shared their faith with Tony and Myra. Tony, convinced by all that he had heard, chucked his atheism in exchange for faith in Christ. When Myra wanted to learn more about the Bible, Becky Davey helped her get started on a correspondence course. One day, in her bedroom, while studying John's gospel, Myra awoke to the fact that her

Christianity was very nominal. The Father's Word and His Spirit had done their perfect work. In her bedroom Myra made the great decision and accepted Christ as her Saviour.

Myra had been one of the first students in the Chittagong branch of the East Pakistan Correspondence School. Gene Gurganus had seen the need to bring the correspondence school approach to our end of the country and had beautifully organized the program. Within weeks, hundreds of students from Chittagong District and the Hill Tracts were not just reading, but actually studying, God's Word. Joan did the art work for the correspondence school's promotional literature and lesson sheets.

On August 7 the Ketchams and Goehrings arrived at Chittagong's outer anchorage aboard the S.S. *Hellenic Spirit*. The outer anchorage was dotted with many ships carrying relief supplies for cyclone-stricken Chittagong. To expedite customs clearance, they remained on board until their ship could, in turn, dock at Chittagong port. A friend in the Port Trust Authority arranged for Jay, Gene, and me to take the pilot launch out to the *Hellenic Spirit*. As we approached across the choppy bay, two white spots at the rail became Dr. Donn Ketcham and Rev. Harry Goehring. (As we climbed the small swaying ladder up the steel hulk of the ship, I remembered my teenage escapade, climbing to the top of the grain elevator.) What a wonderful reunion we had! We spent four grand hours together before the pilot launch returned for us. Their ship rocked at outer anchorage for eleven days before entering the port.

On August 13 Paul Goodman and family arrived for six days of brainstorming and planning. We were thrilled to see them again. During the Goodmans' brief visit, we had nine meetings together involving, at one time or another, the medical team, architect, tube well contractor, plumbing contractor, and electrical contractor. Paul, delighted with the high and dry new site, put his builder's stamp of approval on it.

We showed Paul our hospital plans, explaining that our calculations showed that these plans put us twenty thousand dollars over our budget. Paul opened the ninth meeting with a startling offer.

"Since you told me you were twenty thousand dollars over on your plans," Paul said, "I have been doing some soul-searching. If Drs. Olsen and Ketcham could supervise hospital construction, it would save you ten thousand dollars in contractors' expenses and I could then afford to donate ten thousand dollars which would add up to the needed twenty thousand dollars." How like Paul to make a thoughtful sacrificial offer! He made it clear that he wasn't trying to duck out on the job, but felt that he should raise the point.

We thanked him with all our hearts for his generous offer, then explained that we wanted him and Tom McDonald more than his money. We felt Goodman-McDonald could build a better hospital than Olsen-Ketcham. Besides, Olsen and Ketcham had to complete their language study before the hospital doors opened, or they would never have a really good, fluent use of the Bengali language. Without a knowledge of Bengali, we could neither properly diagnose our patients' problems, nor could we share with others our knowledge of Christ and the great joy to be found in following Him.

In mid-September a ship arrived bearing "gifts." Down the gangplank walked Jean Weld, the red-headed Minnesota nurse who had shared Christmas with us in Liverpool, England. Following Jean came Mel and Marj Beals, a handsome young couple from California with two small daughters (later three). Marj had dark hair and dark eyes, possessed artistic ability, and became a fine language student. Mel, a tall sandy-haired minister, would work closely with the church and one day study missionary dentistry. Our team, a group of people who would experience many things together, was growing.

Later in September the great day arrived! At our hospital site, I met with the divisional forest officer (DFO) for him officially to hand over the land to us. The ceremony was postponed for a day because the tube well contractor suggested two small changes in the boundary in order to help him strike good water. The following morning I met again with the DFO for the ceremony.

Then came the bombshell!

"I'm sorry, Dr. Olsen," the DFO intoned gravely, "but I cannot hand this land over to you!" He finally explained that a special messenger had driven from Chittagong the previous evening to deliver to him the order from Dacca that *this site would not now be given us* and that we must look for another site.

Crestfallen, I knew the order must have come from the governor, for he had granted us the land in the first place, and only he could take it away. Would our dream be thwarted after all? No reason was given for this action.

Returning to Chittagong, I immediately contacted my friend, the commissioner of Chittagong Division. He said, "Land matters are cared for by the deputy commissioner (DC) of Chittagong District. I will give you an introduction to him and ask him to deal with your case immediately. Don't worry — everything will work out all right." I silently thanked God for the day I had accidentally met this man in the little town of Cox's Bazar.

The DC, Mr. Ahmed, was a crackerjack. Nearly every finger

sported a glittering ring, but more brilliant than the rings was the keen mind of this ebullient Bengali. Although a young officer for such a responsible post, he managed his duties skillfully, imaginatively, and boldly. Donn Ketcham and I presented our problem to him. Sensing our anxiety over the unexpected development, he said, "Why don't you two gentlemen bring your wives for tea tomorrow afternoon?"

At tea, we found Mrs. Ahmed to be a warm and hospitable homemaker who knew everything worth knowing about Bengali cookery. The DC listened to our hopes and dreams and then shared his own plans and programs for helping the people of Chittagong District. We hit it off together, and the Ahmeds became not only our patients but also our friends. He set a date for us to view other property in the Cheringa area.

On a blistering hot September day, the DC's subordinates showed us four miserable properties, not one of them government reserve forest land. Meanwhile, the DC sat in the Cox's Bazar circuit house, wearing a silk bathrobe under a cooling fan and sipped a cold drink, knowing all the time that he would show us a fifth property. He sent us on the wild goose chase partly for fun, for he was a fun-loving man, and partly to prepare us to really appreciate the site he would finally recommend to us. Bedraggled, hot, dripping with sweat, we returned to him and reported that none of the four sites would do. With an enigmatic twinkle in his eye, he advised us to shower, enjoy dinner with him, and get a good night's sleep, for "Tomorrow morning we will see another site."

Malumghat was simply beautiful! We had discovered it months earlier in our very first survey of the area. Because it was the absolutely choicest reserve forest land in the area, we hardly thought twice about the possibility of obtaining it. The denuded reserve forest land closer to Cheringa seemed the best bet. Now our new friend, the DC, was offering us this prime land on a silver platter. Until this point we had darkly wondered whether or not the government decision to snatch our land away from us at the last minute was a satanically inspired move to thwart us on the threshold of victory. Now it was clear that such was not the case. Rather, we were seeing the hand of God moving and influencing the rulers of a nation to grant us a site wonderful beyond our wildest dreams. The words of Scripture, "O you of little faith!" leaped into my mind and, "He is able to do exceedingly abundantly above all that you ask or think."

The advantages of Malumghat were many. During World War II, this location on a navigable river, Ringbhong Khal, made it a valuable site for the Allied military forces. The river would be a high-

With DC and Mrs. Ahmed

way for those living on the offshore islands and at the seaside to bring their sick to our hospital. Where the boundary of the Chittagong Hill Tracts swooped down very close to Malumghat, three of the tribal people's foot trails exited near the site. And the property fronted on the main north-south concrete highway. Scattered over the land were lovely, tall, straight gurjun trees which provided beauty and shade. There was direct river communication all the way from Malumghat to our jungle station, Hebron.

When the DC offered us Malumghat, I wanted to jump up in the air, click my heels three times, pound him on the back, and shout, "Hallelujah, we'll take it!" Instead, I told him in a reasonably controlled voice that we liked it and would discuss the matter with our mission. Of course, the mission team approved of Malumghat.

The first week in October, despite many obstacles and problems, I supervised the survey and demarcation of our Malumghat site. In the densest parts of the Malumghat forest, I walked the survey line with a gun over my shoulder. The Malumghat leopard had lived in the area for many years. Having never met a leopard before, I was not sure he wouldn't resent our intrusion. When the survey was completed, the Malumghat site was officially, in writing, handed over to us.

During the second week of October, Donn Ketcham, along with the tube well contractor, started the sinking of the first tube well. I organized the clearing of the underbrush off the land. Because I could not be present throughout the clearing operation, I needed some scheme to keep the work moving. A plan came to me based on the good old American competitive system. I hired two contractors, one to lead a team of local Bengalis and the second to direct the efforts of a team of Tippera tribal people from the jungle. Whichever team cut the most underbrush would receive an attractive bonus. They cleared the site in record time — the Tipperas won.

In the fertile brains of Goodman and McDonald, several new ideas about construction were percolating. Until the ideas were finalized, we could not order from abroad essential materials like cement, steel reinforcing bars, etc. Yet we had to get some of these items on hand to be prepared for their arrival. The obvious solution was to borrow the materials and repay later. But the obvious was difficult to accomplish. We looked for cement all over Chittagong, even visiting two or three government agencies in Dacca, but we failed miserably. East Pakistan was facing a severe cement shortage.

On a Saturday morning Donn Ketcham and I jumped into the Land Rover to tackle some other work. Deciding we'd need all the help we could get that day, we took off our hats, bowed our heads, and prayed: "Father, there are so many problems and difficulties to overcome. Help us with our work today. Give us some new idea about getting cement."

Later, as we drove along, Donn said, "Vic, that new American in town is here to help the government build a sewer system for Chittagong. Do you suppose he's got any cement? You know — his name is Chuck Kline."

The very instant Donn said the word *Kline,* a car horn blasted behind me, and I looked in the rear view mirror to see the face of Chuck Kline who was driving the truck just behind us. A thrill of excitement stabbed me; I *knew* God had moved into action! Waving to Chuck to pull up, I stopped smack in the middle of the overpass bridge. As the traffic piled up behind us and horns honked, we leaped out of the Land Rover and talked with Chuck about cement.

"Well, fellows," Chuck said, "I'm sorry I don't have any cement. But, listen — I know someone who may. Go see the public health engineering department."

"Thanks a zillion, Chuck," we shouted. "You're the answer to a maiden's prayer — and ours, too!"

Chittagong's public health engineering department, according to the chief engineer, had a problem. They were far behind schedule on a big project, but they kept receiving the shipments of cement right on schedule. The engineer feared their cement would spoil in the next rainy season before they could use it. So he was delighted to give us a loan and, as rarely happens, we made phone contact with his superior in Dacca within ten minutes and received the final approval on the spot. "Thank You, Father!"

In the days that followed, we miraculously obtained similar loans of steel reinforcing rods, corrugated iron sheets, steel pipe for plumbing, and even bricks.

At the end of October our mission ranks were increased by one. Bachelor Reid Minich, an old friend of Jay and Eleanor Walsh, arrived to begin his first term of service in Chittagong town. Reid, a capable man with leadership ability, developed a particular desire to help teenage Bengali boys and later organized for them a boys' club. He would one day serve for a time as field council chairman.

The Goehring family moved to Hebron in time for our first Tippera short-term Bible school in early December. Simultaneously, Drs. Ralph and Lucy Ankenman and family arrived in Chittagong; what a delight to see them! Jay and El and family, after four years of devoted and productive work, departed for their first one-year furlough in America.

Joan greatly enjoyed her English-speaking Sunday school class of older girls. December was a climax month for that group, for three of the American girls, deeply moved by truths from God's Word, made the great faith decision, each one accepting Christ as her Saviour. Their eyes, and their lives, shone for Jesus. One reported awaking in the middle of the night at the sound of a knock on her door. Sitting up in bed, she thought she heard it again. Then she knew no person had knocked. "Jesus was knocking at my heart's door," she said, "and I was ready to let Him in."

Before Christmas the contractors' team arrived! Paul Goodman brought his teenage son, Bobby, along with Bob's buddy, Dave Gault. We were delighted to meet Tom and Olline McDonald, for we had heard so much about them. We could not find words adequately to express our appreciation to these dedicated people, willing to make great financial sacrifices and to give themselves to God's work in East Pakistan. The McDonalds had sold their car, their home, and their business, to come! Christmas was a joy, and 1963 ended on a triumphant note.

12

Building and Bengali

WHEN THE ATTACK COMES, I thought looking at the bedroom walls around me, *these brick walls will be my fortress or my tomb!* The walls had been erected in 1964, the year that hospital construction had begun and boomed under the aggressive direction of contractors Goodman and McDonald. The rest of us remained in Chittagong or Hebron tediously gutting away at Bengali language study, the nemesis of all first-term workers. We had to let the Bengali language and thought patterns permeate our minds like the pungent Bengali spices penetrate every fiber of their curried fish or meat. If we failed to do so, we would never amount to much in East Pakistan.

*   *   *

After three weeks of investigation and cost analysis, the contractors called for an evening meeting where we, the medical team, would have to face the music.

Paul and Tom reported, "Our calculations tell us that we cannot build all you have envisioned with the budget allowed us. You must cut the hospital from thirty-two thousand square feet to twenty thousand square feet. You also must redesign the nurses/teachers' residence and the family houses a bit smaller, and forget about one of them entirely."

Recovering from our shock, we were thankful for these men, God's gift to medical people ignorant of the building trade. Immediately,

What to cut? What to keep?

the medical team huddled at the Olsen house to start the slashing operation. We found it distressing to cut away various attractive refinements and carefully designed rooms, but kept on until 1:30 in the morning. It took more meetings over several days to complete the painful amputation of the excess square feet — without anesthesia.

The drama of obtaining the Malumghat land was not quite complete. Although the land had been handed over to us, and the order passed regarding the price, one last act remained — signing the lease. I had worked for days on this project. With legal counsel, we thoroughly analyzed the proposed lease agreement. Wanting some changes in several provisions, I flew to Dacca to negotiate these lease provisions with the Board of Revenue; Paul Goodman traveled with me. Our negotiations were fruitful.

By then the government had discovered there was no legal provision to lease out the reserve forest land directly to us. This meant that, somehow, our land had to be removed from that special classification and declared ordinary land. It required an act of the Provincial Assembly (Senate) of East Pakistan to accomplish this change.

At this point the next problem raised its ugly crosscut saw. The forest department decided to cut down our twenty-five acres of exquisite Malumghat trees for their own gain, before the lease was signed! Officers from that department came, marked each tree, and calculated the cubic footage of timber they would realize. (What nerve!) Neither the local official nor the Chittagong-based conservator of forests paid any attention to our protests. Our written orders from the government granting us the land were slightly ambiguous in regard to the trees, but the intent of the documents seemed clear: that we receive the land — plus trees — at the concessional rate. We had to make some speedy moves to block the tree cutting and obtain an immediate settlement of the problem in our favor.

At first we were not sure how to move (it never seemed easy to decide which level of the East Pakistan government to tackle about each new problem). I feared that any high-level approach in Dacca might bog us down in endless negotiations and delays which we could ill afford. As we prayed, the guidance factor began to operate and pointed us to the Chittagong DC. We knew he had no jurisdiction over the forest department, but hoped he could at least give us some good advice.

"Here are the documents," I said, placing the papers before him, "I feel the intent is clear that the trees are ours."

Rereading the official words, the DC responded, "Yes, I agree. Besides, a hospital should be built in a beautiful setting with trees and flowers; that is part of the cure." Pondering how to solve this problem involving another department, yet protect his own skin and avoid endless delays, he looked off into space — thinking. I, too, looked off into space — praying.

A look of "Aha, that's what I'll do" lighting his face, he picked up the telephone. The rings on his fingers flashed as he dialed Dacca; remarkably, he contacted his party almost immediately.

"Peace be upon you, brother," he greeted his friend, the secretary of agriculture, head over all forest department officials.

After a personal chat about family members and mutual friends, he continued, nonchalantly, "You remember the case of the Association of Baptists' hospital land at Malumghat? Of course you have in mind including the trees which are so necessary around a hospital."

The gleam of triumph in the DC's eyes told me the answer had been yes or a reasonable facsimile thereof. Without a word to me, he wrote in the file that at 3:15 P.M. on that day the secretary of agriculture had "decreed" that the trees be granted us!

Then, glowing, he announced, "The trees are yours. Allah has been good to you. I will notify the conservator of forests to stop troubling you." I thanked the DC — and the "Allah" who had been good to us.

When the East Pakistan "senate" acted to declare our twenty-five Malumghat acres "ordinary" land, the notice of the act duly appeared in the official *East Pakistan Gazette.* After many more hours of work finalizing the wording of the lease and getting sufficient copies typed on special government-stamped paper, we were within striking distance of getting the lease signed. On January 15 we gathered for the signing ceremony in the office of the deputy commissioner, Chittagong. Delighted with the occasion, the DC signed dramatically on behalf of the government of East Pakistan. With a flourish, I, too, signed each copy on behalf of ABWE. Paul and Tom donned Pakistani caps and presented the DC with an American cowboy hat. Smiling broadly, he placed it on his head at a rakish angle.

When I put into my briefcase the doubly signed copy of the long-term, perpetually renewable lease for twenty-five acres of choice Malumghat land (including trees), the words from Psalm 44, given us long before, were at last fulfilled: "For not by their own sword did they possess the land, neither did their own arm gain deliverance for them; but Your right hand, and Your arm, and the light of Your face; because You did favor them."

Five days later we finalized the name of the hospital to be constructed at Malumghat: *Memorial Christian Hospital.* Several years earlier Winnifred Mary Barnard lost her life because in Chittagong there was no surgeon to operate. Then Rev. Paul Miller gave his life in his Master's service. This hospital was to be a *memorial* to them, but most particularly, it was being built in memory of our Lord Jesus Christ who died some nineteen hundred years earlier for our sins and the sins of our Bengali and tribal neighbors.

After Sunday school one Sunday morning, another of Joan's girls came at the end of class period to say, "I want to be sure I belong to God — will you help me, Mrs. Olsen?"

"Do you really know and believe that the Bible is God's Word?" Joan began.

The teenager replied, "Yes, it's like you said about the sheep knowing the shepherd's voice — I can hear God's voice in the Bible." Accepting Christ into her life, she was sure that she belonged to God.

January was a big month at our Hebron jungle station which hosted our first Tippera short-term Bible school. Not only do the Tipperas' oriental appearance and scanty dress set them apart from the Bengalis, but also they speak their own tribal language. Of the forty thousand Tipperas (also called Tripuras) who inhabit the Chittagong Hill Tracts, about four thousand profess the Christian faith and worship in bamboo "Jesus houses." Ancharai Tippera, spiritual leader of his people, is a grand, warm-hearted Christian brother.

By February a huge *basha* (bamboo-thatch house) was ready for occupancy at Malumghat. So Paul and the two teenage boys, Bob and Dave, moved to the site. Kitty Ketcham designed an attractive letterhead for the project, and Donna Ahlgrim left Hebron station to do the contractors' secretarial work in Chittagong. In February Joan, Juanita Canfield, and I took a quick trip to the hospital site. After viewing the progress we traveled by sampan up the Matamuhari River to the Hebron station.

Lynn Silvernale, hardly able to believe her eyes, exulted, "Am I glad to see you! I have a patient who badly needs a doctor." I could see it was my turn to be an "answer to a maiden's prayer."

The patient, a fourteen-year-old Mogh tribal girl, had an extensive, infected, third-degree burn of her right thigh and knee. A cooking fire had ignited her skirt. It took me an hour to remove all the crusted scab and debris, exposing a large expanse of raw, infected flesh.

If only our hospital were ready! I thought, *I could admit this girl, give her antibiotics, apply hot soaks to the wound for a week, and, using our dermatome, skin graft the wound.* But I had no hospital, dermatome, or anesthesia machine. I made up my mind quickly. I must somehow *try* to graft the wound; perhaps I could cut small pieces of skin freehand with a disposable razor blade. It all had to be accomplished in twenty hours. I ordered additional

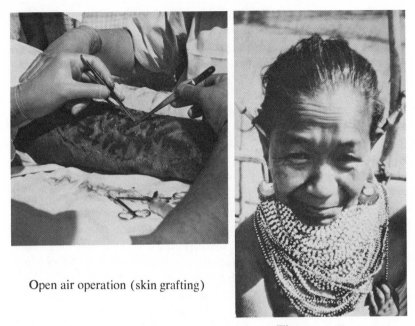

Open air operation (skin grafting)

Tippera granny

antibiotics and hot soaks to be applied nonstop, hour after hour, throughout the day and night.

Early the following morning, as the mists came swirling off the Matamuhari River, I awakened, sat on the side of my bed, and asked God a question: "Heavenly Father, how can I possibly cut enough skin with this disposable razor blade to actually cover that wound? You know that's a Mickey Mouse surgical instrument. Besides, I haven't a suitable clamp to hold it — and I haven't been in an operating room for a long, long time. Father, I've got to have a better instrument for this operation."

Heavily, I walked to the bathroom. While brushing my teeth, my eyes fixed on a small black case. I stopped brushing, opened the case, and withdrew from it a beautiful, hollow-ground, straightedge razor — with a handle! Perfect! Even though I had been out of the operating room three years, I was sure that I could cut skin grafts with that neat instrument. "Thank You, Father!"

We placed the girl on a wooden table under the open sky, our only light. Using Lynn's last injection of pain-killer and last bottle of local anesthetic, I numbed the skin of her good thigh. The straightedge razor worked like a charm! With it I successfully cut long, satisfactory skin grafts about 11/1,000ths of an inch thick and applied them to the raw wound. After bandaging the legs and eating a bit of early lunch, we left Hebron — and we left the little patient in the hands of Lynn and the great Physician. Ten days later came the unveiling. Lynn removed the dressings to find a ninety-nine percent take! Then it was her turn to say, "Thank You, Father!"

We returned to Chittagong to learn that Peter and Nina Rowley had come to Christ. Peter, a tall British latex technologist, came to Chittagong as a consultant for a new industry utilizing latex. Nina, Peter's attractive wife, had plans to present him with their first son. Under Dr. Ketcham's care, she listened enraptured at each visit to his explanations of how her unborn child was developing.

One day she decided, "If something that complicated and wonderful is going on inside of me, there *must* be a God and He *must* love us." Within days she made her decision for Christ. Peter, a more skeptical person, listened intently to all I could tell him about Christian evidences; he read with deep interest the book I gave him on the subject. Finally convinced about God, Christ, and Christianity, he made the great faith decision.

During hospital construction, huge amounts of material had to be shipped from Chittagong and other towns to Malumghat. We calculated the total tolls on the two intervening bridges might approach four thousand dollars. In an effort to save that money for actual construction purposes, we applied to the government for exemption of bridge toll payments on the grounds that we were constructing a hospital for the people, not for our personal gain. After several visits to Chittagong offices, I learned that a high-level decision would be required. At Dacca I found that the finance ministry had to decide the matter. After hearing my story, the finance secretary responded brusquely, "I don't think there's much chance of getting your request approved, Dr. Olsen. Such exemption has never been given before, and to give it to you would start a dangerous precedent. Why, some of our own government departments have requested this type of exemption and we have denied them. If we grant your request, these departments will complain; also, we will be forced to grant such exemptions to all the other private organizations." Reluctantly, he agreed to give it more thought and talk with me again the following morning.

Back in the quiet of my hotel room, feeling defeated, I knelt down, placed folded hands upon the bed, and prayed. "Gracious Father, I am really stumped on this one. To get the approval would help Your work. Give me some idea, some new plan of how to approach this officer." Within thirty seconds the idea came!

The following morning I found the finance secretary in a big hurry. He was preparing to ride by limousine to the airport to receive Chou En Lai from China. As he hastily donned white gloves, he stated with finality, "I have given your problem more thought, but I see no way to approve your request. The answer is no."

"I know you are concerned about opening the door to a flood of other organizations," I responded, unleashing my new idea, "but that will not be a problem. We have three things that no other organization in the country possesses. These three items put us in a class by ourselves: written government approval of our total project, registration as a bonafide nonprofit charitable institution under Section 15D of the Income Tax Act, and duty-free status. Because of these three points you can rightfully grant us our exemption, yet not be forced to approve all other applications."

Impatiently he said, "All right, write that on your application and I'll forward it on to the finance minister. Let him decide. Excuse me, I must go now."

Neither his words nor his manner were even slightly encouraging, but I appended in handwriting the additional, God-given idea and returned to Chittagong.

We gathered together for the weekly prayer meeting, gave some attention to the Scriptures, and prayed together about many things, including the finance minister's decision and our upcoming annual field council meeting. As the prayer meeting came to a close, the whole room began to dance and shake, and suddenly we were plunged into darkness. The earthquake tremor ceased as suddenly as it began — and *terra* was *firma* once again. After a moment of startled silence, some wag quoted from the book of Acts, "And when they had prayed, the place was shaken where they were assembled together."

In the field council meetings which followed, it was decided that I should travel to West Pakistan, see the top man in the import-export department, and attempt to gain some special concessions from him. Our contractors were having great difficulty obtaining import permits.

On our way to West Pakistan, Joan and I stopped off for a day in Dacca. From the finance minister's office we picked up our letter of authorization exempting us from payment of the bridge tolls! Because our Father stepped in, the seemingly impossible had happened. Never before in the history of the country had such an exemption been given — and now it was granted to us, a Christian mission in the world's largest Muslim nation. "Thank You, Father!"

We flew next to Rawalpindi, Pakistan's "Washington, D.C." Here, I would tackle the main assignment: obtaining from the department of imports and exports a blanket prior permit for all our building and medical materials and equipment. We hoped, in addition, to gain approval to import banned items such as steel reinforcing bars, a motorboat, etc. If we could obtain the blanket permit and approval to import banned items, we would save thousands of dollars, miles of red tape, and hundreds of hours of precious time in government offices. Because such approvals were not known to be granted by the Pakistan government, we prayed urgently before the first appointment. The tough but fair-minded officer interrogated me, demanding documentary evidence for all my assertions. Because over the months we had worked carefully and methodically, and because God had helped us, I had documents galore to prove everything. Three days later, with negotiations completed, the double approval was granted us! Thrilling! "Oh, thank You, Father!"

Late in March, an American missionary in Dacca, the Roman Catholic Archbishop Grainer, preached and published his famous Easter message. His message, critical of the government of Pakistan, would have profound repercussions on our lives. A long series of events had preceded his declaration. For centuries Muslim-Hindu reciprocal animosity had smoldered, periodically breaking out into open flame. Some weeks earlier, in the disputed state of Kashmir, a sacred relic of the Muslims, a hair of the prophet Muhammad, was stolen. Enraged Muslims blamed their ancient enemies, the Hindus.

In the riots which followed, some were killed. Then, like jumping wildfire, riots exploded across India and Pakistan. In India, Hindus killed Muslims. In Pakistan, Muslims killed Hindus.

Then India disowned many Muslims, sending them across the northern border into East Pakistan. Many Christians, non-Bengali members of the Garo tribe, lived in this hilly border area. Following altercations between Muslims and Garos, thousands of Garos in a mass exodus crossed the border into India. In his Easter message the Dacca archbishop criticized the East Pakistan government for failing to protect the Garos and prevent their exodus. The government, enraged, printed a rebuttal in the newspapers saying that President Ayub Khan himself sent the governor to the Garo area to bring the situation under control.

Joan and I were invited to a reception and dinner party for a favorite personality, Pakistan's ambassador to Italy and widow of the first prime minister of Pakistan. We enjoyed meeting this famed elder stateswoman and appreciated, too, the opportunity to meet and make new friends among the attending guests who were the elite of Chittagong Bengali society. Some of them we already knew as friends or patients, and others among the guests became new friends and patients.

The building operation progressed steadily at Malumghat. But the local populace seemed strangely restless and unsettled about the hospital. Only years later did I learn about a fantastic drama then going on behind the scenes. It all started at Dacca University. Twelve upper-class Muslim boys, very active in student politics, had demonstrated passionately against the government. As a penalty for their antigovernment activities, they were expelled from the university and denied their degrees. Angry and rebellious, they lashed out at whatever target they could find. One, named Akand, a violently anti-Christian fellow, heard about two Christian hospitals then in the offing.

Through his close friendship with the governor's son, Akand arranged an appointment with the governor of East Pakistan, the official who had granted us the reserve forest land. Akand bitterly criticized our hospital. He also attacked another mission organization which hoped to build a hospital in another area where medical care was desperately needed.

The governor defended our hospital to the vitriolic, anti-Christian young Muslim.

"I do not see anything wrong with allowing this hospital to be built," he said. "The project has already been approved and they are building it now."

Then (shades of Pontius Pilate) he continued, "There's nothing I can do to stop it anyway. Only if the local people protest could any such action be taken." Behind Akand's intense black eyes his brilliant mind instantly concocted the next move.

Traveling to Chittagong, Akand gained the support of a prominent intellectual, author of many books and translator of the Muslim's Arabic *Koran* into the Bengali language. Through another pal, Akand made contact with my friend, the powerful commissioner of Chittagong Division and lived in his home for a few days. He tried to poison the commissioner against us — unsuccessfully.

"Why stop them?" the commissioner countered. "These Americans bring in valuable dollars from the outside. And Dr. Olsen, that tall guy, is a good man who wants to help our people. So what's the harm? Even if he talks to people about God, so what? His God is not as efficient as my clerk; He knows nothing about how to distribute wealth equally to people. Would you like to meet the tall guy? He's sitting next door in my office right now."

So we met. I knew nothing of Akand or his intentions; he knew plenty about me. Belligerently he quizzed me about our hospital and "activities." Question by question, I answered him.

Sharply he asked, "Do you make Christians out of Muslims?"

"No," I responded, "only God can make a person truly Christian, but if anyone wants to learn about Christ, I am happy to tell him what I know, and —."

Akand jumped to his feet. "That's enough," he stormed, "I got what I wanted. You *do* make Christians out of Muslims." Puzzled by the confrontation, I watched him stalk angrily out of the room.

Akand established an anti-Christian center in a rented house in Chittagong, then began his agitation in the hospital area. He harangued people and priests alike to convince them that Islam would be endangered by our hospital. Cleverly, he told the local village medical practitioners that we would put them out of business. A certain restlessness gripped the countryside. Wild rumors circulated:

"If you go to that hospital, the Christian doctors will put rupees in your hand and stamp the mark of the pig on you, forcing you to be a Christian."

"In the daytime those Christians at the hospital site unload cement and bricks from the trucks and country boats. At night they unload guns and bullets and hide them under the hospital. Some day they will rise up and conquer the whole district."

Our friends in the Malumghat area, however, worked on our behalf to counter the propaganda efforts of Akand and his recruits. One of my patients, Fazlul Karim Choudhury, respected head of the leading Muslim family of the locality, spoke eloquently to many in favor of the hospital. His son Shahabuddin, nephew Rafique, and grand-nephew Momin, men whom I had met on my first visits to the area, spread the same message to their many contacts. The simmering agitation never exploded. Akand retreated to Chittagong to hatch new plots against the infidels.

As field council chairman, I also devoted myself to administrative duties and found ways to improve our administration and team efficiency: instituted an executive committee, initiated mid- and long-range planning, established a system of appointing members to the committees where they function best, et cetera.

The demands of those early days prevented us from enjoying the privilege of "protected" language study. Despite our late start and impossible schedule, however, we completed Bengali I in May with good marks. Overjoyed, we eagerly moved on into Bengali II.

In early June, Paul Goodman, Bob Goodman, and Dave Gault returned to the United States. While East Pakistan monsoon rains slowed hospital building, Paul planned to care for business matters

Tom McDonald on the job

and return when the monsoon ceased. Tom McDonald, meanwhile, was to build as much as the rains would allow.

On the last day of June, Joan and I visisted the McDonalds on site and found the monsoon hampering Tom surprisingly little. Although in Chittagong it usually rained during working hours, at Malumghat the rain poured at night and during the midday rest period. Little rain fell during working hours. Tom had lost only three half days of work during the first three weeks of strong monsoon rains.

A local Muslim gentleman marveled to Tom, "Your God is good to you. He is giving you building weather even during the rainy season."

On the fourth of July a "Bomm" dropped on Chittagong. ABWE treasurer Edward Bomm arrived for another brief visit to consult with the mission team and see the progress of hospital construction. With him was Fenton McDonald, the teenage son of Tom and Olline.

After Mr. Bomm's departure, Fenton McDonald settled in at the construction site with his parents. A handsome, talented young fellow, Fenton was passing through a listless, drifting period in his life. For that reason Paul Goodman had sent him from California to be with his folks in East Pakistan. When a period of sleeping long hours and loafing around soon passed, Fenton became aware of his dad's busy schedule. Then plunging into the work, he did a man-sized job. Working among them, he came to love the Bengali people, who responded warmly to his bright smile and friendly manner. Through long talks and sharing with his parents and various members of the mission team, something of their love and devotion to Christ reached into his heart. By the time he left East Pakistan, Fenton had determined to serve God.

Several hospital workmen, preparing to go to bed one night, heard outside their bamboo basha the sound of a heavy animal moving about.

"Where did that cow come from?" one of them groused.

Grabbing a flashlight, he pointed it out the window to locate an unexpected target. One look down that shaft of white light so upset a teenager standing on a bed that he fell panicstricken to the floor. The handful of men gaped at a beautiful, monstrous royal Bengal tiger! The next day, a government official who also had seen the tiger described him as a beautiful adult male. His pugmarks (footprints) measured nineteen inches in circumference. Was he just passing that way on a trip from the Hill Tracts? Had he come to take over the territory of the Malumghat leopard? If he had come to observe the progress of hospital construction, he returned to the jungle a happy beast, for the foundations of the family houses and school were completed, and the walls of the nurses/teachers' residence were rising rapidly.

On July 26, our Wheaton friends, laboratory technologist Bob Adolph and "Georgia peach" Barbara Adolph sailed into Chittagong. With them was Lois Cooper, a nurse from Michigan. They received the useful welcome packets produced by Joan's orientation committee. By that time we had become the largest of ABWE's field councils scattered throughout the world.

My birthday in August was marred by the news I sent to the home board in a cable which read: AMBACHER VISA DEFINITELY REJECTED STOP NOW APPROACHING HIGH OFFICIALS OLSEN. Until that point, visas had been automatic for our people — excellent four-year multiple-entry visas. Now, for the first time, one of our appointees had been rejected. Then we learned of others, from other mission groups, receiving rejection notices. I called for a special field council meeting to pray and plan out our strategy.

In Dacca Gene Gurganus and I visited my old friend, previously the commissioner of Chittagong division, now secretary of the East Pakistan Home Ministry. After our discussion of old times concluded, we learned several things from him regarding the visa problem. With emotion, he explained how India had used the migration of Garo Christians to inflame Christian countries against Pakistan for "persecuting" Christians. Angrily, he blamed the Easter message of the Dacca archbishop for causing the trouble. He said that the pope, after receiving a written copy of that Easter message, wrote a letter to Pakistan officially indicating his displeasure; the Pakistan foreign minister had to travel to the Vatican for a talk with the pope. Pakistan had to make further explanations in the United Nations.

"At that time," the home secretary continued, "I traveled to India for official meetings with my counterpart, the Indian home secretary, about various border problems. As I walked into the conference room, the Indian home secretary placed on the table before me pictures of Garo Christians who had fled East Pakistan for India and the text of the archbishop's Easter message. My negotiations were ruined!"

Further investigation revealed that nothing further could be done about reversing the Ambacher visa decision without a trip to West Pakistan. In another special field council meeting the group decided that I should proceed to Karachi, West Pakistan, to contact the director of immigration and any other pertinent officials. The West Pakistan trip consumed six weeks of precious language study time. In Karachi, after two interviews with the director of immigration and one with his deputy director, I learned more of their resentment about the Garo migration and the Easter message which had embarrassed them around the world. However, the director finally appended a handwritten note to the file, reopening the case. The rejection could be reversed, he said, only at the Central Home Secretariat level in the capital city of Rawalpindi. So I flew on to 'Pindi.

Despite superficially congenial meetings with officers in the Central Home Department, our appeal for the Ambachers was denied. Written encouragement was given us, however, regarding visas for our medical workers. Then the American embassy stepped in, at my request, to help find out the actual details of the new policy. I enjoyed a cordial meeting with the American ambassador to Pakistan who became vitally interested in the problem. He determined to take up the matter personally, even with the president of Pakistan if necessary.

Looking at it from a doctor's point of view, it seemed important to make the diagnosis of where the holdup originated. If the order came from the president or cabinet, probably little could be done to change the situation. If, on the other hand, the visa problem had originated from a lower level of government, there might be a chance to influence the situation for good. I hoped that the American ambassador would be able to make this diagnosis.

In 'Pindi I stayed with friends at Gordon College. During the days of waiting for government decisions, we stumbled on a system of spiritually helping college students. Our hosts held a tea party for a group of students previously known to them. During the party we discussed Bible teachings, for Gordon College is a Christian institution with many Christian students. Soon Urdu and English Bibles were on the table for use in the lively discussion. It became quickly evident which were spiritually reborn students and which ones had not yet reached that point. I arranged private appointments with those students who desired help. Repeating this tea party evangelism twice more, six or eight young men found the Saviour through warm experiences of faith.

Building at Malumghat was costing more than the estimated four dollars per square foot. So, we slashed another two thousand square feet from the hospital and decided to build wards and the outpatient department "semipukka" style (concrete floor, three-foot brick walls, timber and bamboo upper walls, corrugated aluminum roof). The rest of the hospital would still be pukka (first class brick and concrete).

Word then came from Paul Goodman that he was facing unexpected business problems. Assured that Tom McDonald had the construction work well in hand, the board released Paul who continued to help the project greatly on the home front. Paul reported that the film *Such As I Have* was receiving a good reception throughout America.

The Hebron station received a notable Christmas present to help them travel the shallow, dry-season waters of the Matamuhari River to and from civilization. The Aircat was a flat-bottomed boat pow-

Mru dancer

Mru musician

ered by a Lycoming aircraft engine and propeller; the shallower the water, the faster it skimmed, unhindered even by sandbars. Ralph Ankenman expressed it perfectly, "The Matamuhari River was just made for this boat!"

At Hebron, fourteen students graduated from the Tippera short-term Bible school having learned much about reading, writing, and God's Word. The spiritual growth in Ancharai was phenomenal. Several animistic tribesmen found Christ as they stopped to visit and heard Ancharai preaching and teaching. Five of them were Mrus (or Murungs),[1] the most primitive of the hillmen. Athletically built, Murung men wear scanty clothing. Their hair, grown to waist length, is twirled into a bun and skewered by a huge comb. Sometimes, wearing flowers in their ears, they smear their faces and chests with red paint.

The Chittagong DC played a big part in our family's Christmas. He had a beautiful tamarack Christmas tree brought to us from Cox's Bazar; then his two children came to decorate the tree with Wendy, Lynne, Mark, and Nancy. Decorating the tree was the first experience these Pakistani children had with Christmas in a Christian home. On Christmas night, the DC's family members, bringing a huge roasted goose, joined us for the evening meal. They were delighted with a Christmas carol serenade by our talented nursing staff.

We visited Bandarban in the Hill Tracts at Christmas and saw my patient, the Mogh prince. This Buddhist prince praised the Christian tribal people. He explained that when tribal men became Christians, their behavior improved remarkably, making it easy for him and his brother the raja (king) to manage the administration of their area.

Turning to me, he said, "Doctor, you should come with me to the animistic and Buddhist villages along the Sangu River and preach

Mogh raja

your good news of Jesus to my people. They need your words —
and I will be your interpreter!" Sadly, an unexpected development several months later frustrated my follow-up of this tempting
invitation.

Our friends the Lockerbies arrived in December to visit their Jeannie and the rest of us. We remembered together our life-changing
decision and "spiritual internship" in Brooklyn, also that very first
missions conference in Seattle. How delighted we were to see them,
chew over old times together, and show them "our land."

*   *   *

*The PIA prop plane circled low over the lush green, pond-
spangled countryside that is East Pakistan, to land in Chittagong's
airport. Expedited through customs by the able team of Doctors
Ketcham and Olsen, to whom untangling red tape had become a
way of life, my husband and I were soon on our way to a welcome
party which was Pakistani all the way.*

*Struggling into six yards of beautiful sari loaned to me for the
occasion, I was conscious that my ears were playing tricks on me.
I actually thought I was hearing the music of my native land:
bagpipes!* Too much airplane, *I told myself. But — no! A knock
on the door, and a bevy of giggling missionary kids urged,* "Hurry
downstairs!" *And there, to my wonder, was a real live pipe band,
lined up in precision array, especially to serenade the visitors from
the US.*

*Christmas preparations were in full swing when we arrived. A
Christmas play was written for the poetic and drama-loving Bengalis, who eagerly rehearsed it. A hall was rented, scrubbed, and
decorated; and four hundred men and three women (in addition to
missionary families) jammed the place. The men ingeniously rigged
up a star that really did travel, at least from the balcony "to where
the young child lay" on the stage. And since the original Herod
himself, there has never been a more impressive King Herod; his
throne was a folding garden chair draped with a purple satin robe.*

*At prayer meeting the following week, I noticed Dr. Olsen and
"King Herod" sitting together engrossed in conversation. Before long
they bowed their heads. Moments later the Bengali youth, short of
stature as are his people, stood up with a broad smile on his face.
Dr. Olsen put his arm around the young man's shoulders and said,
"The Bible says that all who have received Christ are brothers in
Him. That means that now you and I are brothers." The boy's
eyes widened as he said in an awed voice, "I have little brothers —"
He looked up at the tall doctor and exclaimed, "but I've never had a
big brother!"*

With the slow smile that lights up his face, Dr. Olsen took the boy's hand, shook it, and said, "Now you have lots of big brothers."

Our missionary daughter Jeannie had saved her vacation that year so that we could see East Pakistan together. We fought our way in her Taunus through the maze of oxcarts, goats, baby taxis, sacred cows, army vehicles, and buses that, as Jeannie says, "dare anything to hit them." Sixty-five miles of such driving took us to Malumghat, the site of Memorial Christian Hospital.

The early morning scene at the hospital site opened with the workmen converging on the grounds, each wearing what his culture decreed: some in lungis, *some in* punjabi *attire, and some in a G-string, hair adorned with exotic flowers. At dusk they lined up to collect their rupees for the day's labor.*

The hospital itself was a network of scaffolding at that time. Men, like ants, ran up and down bearing loads of building materials. In this country everything is done the hard way; there is almost no mechanized equipment. Supervised by contractor Tom McDonald, the staff homes and the nurses/teachers' residence were built.

As the hospital was under construction, the medical team busily studied the difficult Bengali language. Meanwhile they operated a first-class clinic, serving the missionary families, other foreigners in diplomatic and professional service, and the people of Chittagong. Many of Dr. Olsen's strategic contacts with the leading men in East Pakistan were made as they came to the clinic in Chittagong for medical help.

The medical team practiced their convictions about treating the whole person. They did not hesitate to share their faith with those having a spiritual need. A young couple from Britain admitted, "We had to come all the way around the world to meet God."

From the hospital site our itinerary next took us to the jungle station Hebron. We skimmed the Matamuhari River in an Aircat, a fifty-minute jaunt that takes eight hours by the hand-poled country boats. At our approach everything near the river banks — cows, chickens, women washing their clothes, children frolicking — skittered off in fright. At Hebron we slept in a bamboo house. Looking out the bedroom window, we could see a bullock treading corn.

New Year's Eve at Hebron consisted of a lantern-lit watchnight service in the living room of our hosts, Harry and Nancy Goehring. We sang all the verses of "Unto the Hills Around Do I Lift up My Longing Eyes."

We said goodbye to our daughter and our friends in the chill of a January morning in Chittagong. It would be more than two years before we would see Jeannie and the Olsens again.

13

President and Pressures

What a year 1965 was! I mused in my Bangladesh bedroom. Then, also, war had come our way; India was on the offensive against East Pakistan. In 1971, however, West Pakistan was the attacker furiously smashing East Pakistan, with India on the sidelines. India, this time acting quite friendly to East Pakistan, was helping the millions of East Pakistani refugees pouring across her borders.

In early 1965 Pakistan President Mohammad Ayub Khan had appeared on our horizon in a new way. Then, throughout the year, crisis after crisis pressed in upon us as never before. We were hit from all sides by continuing visa obstructions, crippling of our tribal work, employee problems, storms of wind, storms of war, bombing, illness, and death! In 1965 I had to call twenty-five special field council sessions to deal with the recurring problems and crises. But, in this Bangladesh war of 1971, field council meetings were a thing of the past — humanly speaking, there remained only my buddy Donn, my Bengali guards, and my clock ticking inexorably toward 10 P.M.

*   *   *

President Ayub Khan had been at the helm of Pakistan for six years. To direct the affairs of his turbulent developing nation required the patience of Job (the name *Ayub* actually is the Muslim word for Job). As the army commander-in-chief, he took the reins of government from the hands of inept politicians who had failed to lead the country forward. On the world scene he became one of Asia's greatest statesmen. No other foreign dignitary addressing the United States Congress on such an unpopular subject (foreign aid) ever received a standing ovation as did Ayub.

On the second day of the year 1965 he faced the elections he had called. While many applauded President Ayub's call for elections, others complained that the presidential election was only a vote for electoral college members who would really elect the president. Those who complained demanded full adult franchise with the voters casting their votes directly for the presidential candidate of their choice. Throughout election day I listened in snatches to Radio Pakistan election returns. By evening it was clear that Ayub Khan would win. The final tally showed 63 percent of the votes for Ayub and 36 percent for Miss Jinnah — a conclusive majority! Next would come elections of the national and provincial "senators."

Aircat adventure
(Vic and DC)

We learned that President Ayub would come in January, on behalf of his party, to our area to hunt for votes — and jungle chickens. Ayub Khan was known to be an excellent marksman. When the Chittagong DC contacted me for assistance in locating a suitable hunting site for President Ayub, I agreed to help. He wished to visit a place called Alikadam, deep in the Chittagong Hill Tracts, miles beyond our Hebron station on the Matamuhari River. The trip during the dry season ordinarily required four days' travel by car and riverboat, but our Aircat could drastically slice that timetable.

In January we traveled by government car to Cheringa (with a stop to shoot a few jungle chickens ourselves). Meeting us at the bridge with the Aircat, Harry Goehring zipped us up to Hebron station in an hour. After a tasty curry we headed upstream again, reaching Alikadam in another hour. Our investigation soon revealed the place to be unsuitable for the president's hunting trip. The terrain was too rugged, and two rogue (dangerously insane) elephants were troubling the area and could endanger presidential safety. I suggested an alternative hunting site: the Dulahazara jungle near Malumghat.

Returning, we reached Cheringa before sundown and Chittagong before bedtime. That was the first time anyone had ever traveled by surface in the dry season from Chittagong to Alikadam and back in the same day!

Several days later I contacted the DC about a new idea: meeting with President Ayub and inviting him to visit the hospital site as a preliminary to his inaugurating the hospital on opening date. He agreed to try to help by applying, on our behalf, to the president's

military secretary. The next day, unable to contact the DC in Cox's
Bazar by phone, Joan and I felt we should drive there to talk with
him directly. In Cox's Bazar he broke the news to us that the president's military secretary had denied our request for an appointment
with President Ayub and stated it would be impossible for him to
visit the hospital site. Disappointing! Later Joan and I returned to
our room and prayed a very contrite prayer: "Gracious Father, we
have come all this way for nothing and apparently have missed Your
guidance. Please forgive us for being presumptuous."

The following morning, waiting at the airport to watch the presidential plane arrive, we met some of our friends from the Malumghat
area: Fazlul Karim Choudhury, elderly Muslim patriarch of the hospital locality, his nephew Rafique, younger son Shahabuddin, and elder
son Giasuddin. All of these men, or their family members, were my
patients. Giasuddin, a prominent Chittagong businessman and president of the Chittagong Chamber of Commerce, would be elected to
represent our area in the National Assembly (Senate) of Pakistan
when it met in 'Pindi. The old gentleman, Fazlul Karim, greeted us,
"Salam Alekum!" He then asked if we would "honor him" by join-
ing a breakfast party at his home the following morning. Thanking
the old gentleman, we agreed to the breakfast date.

Then, with a twinkle in his eye, he added, "Oh yes, by the way, I
think my president will be there." Joan and I exchanged glances —
maybe we hadn't missed that guidance factor after all!

The presidential Viscount appeared, landed, and the president dis-
embarked amid earsplitting cheers and throwing of flowers. Leis of
flowers were placed around his neck as he gaily proceeded down the
reception line. Presented to the surging crowd by the DC, he made a
speech in Urdu, then retired to the circuit house on the hill.

Later, back in our motel, the DC arrived to say dejectedly, "I
went to tell the president the afternoon schedule, but couldn't even
see him. He was reading a book on the verandah and had ordered
that no one — absolutely no one — could disturb him. I have never
seen him act like that before." (I chuckled years later when I read
Ayub's autobiography, *Friends Not Masters*,[1] in which he mentioned
on page 1 that very moment in Cox's Bazar as one of the few occasions he had ever as president taken time simply to sit peacefully
and reflect.)

That night I met the president's military secretary who confirmed
that it would be impossible for me to meet with the president on this
trip. The DC reported to me, however, that President Ayub had
decided to accept Fazlul Karim's breakfast invitation before hunting
in the Dulahazara jungle near Malumghat! Leaving Cox's Bazar in

our Land Rover, Joan and I reached the hospital site before midnight.

Up at 6:30 A.M., accompanied by Fenton McDonald, we arrived in good time for the breakfast party. Behind the gaily decorated guesthouse, located a mile from the hospital site we saw a huge red-and-white-striped *shamiana* (decorative canvas canopy for shade). Under the *shamiana* the heavily laden breakfast table awaited its hour of glory. Promptly at 8:00 A.M. the imposing retinue of cars arrived; the president stepped out to be greeted warmly and be embraced by members of the Choudhury family.

Joan and I took our places on the far left sidelines of the gathering. President Ayub, with military bearing, looked tall, strong, handsome. The greetings finished, this leader of the world's fifth most populous nation walked towards the breakfast area. The air was tense with excitement. We were the only foreigners there. Coming abreast of our location and catching sight of us out of the corner of his eye, President Ayub stopped, then turned ninety degrees to look me straight in the eye.

He walked the fifteen steps to where we were standing, put out his hand to me, and said in impeccable British English, "Hello, there! What are you folks doing here? Are you just passing through this area?"

"No," I replied, "we thought we'd stay awhile — we're building a hospital a mile up the road."

"Oh," he said, "that's something new. I'm happy to hear about it. Now you'll have to excuse me; they want me for breakfast." Joan and I looked at each other. I could feel in my bones that God was doing something — I wasn't quite sure what. The president had noticed us even though we had followed the precept of old King Solomon who advised, twenty-nine hundred years before:

> Do not put yourself forward in the presence of the king, and stand not in the place of great men, for it is better it should be said to you come up hither, than that you should be put lower in the presence of the prince whom your eyes have seen.

Two minutes later a Bengali man rushed breathlessly up to us with the words, "Come quickly! The president is calling for Dr. and Mrs. Olsen!"

As we approached and stepped under the *shamiana,* President Ayub stood to his feet. Like the perfect gentleman he is, he walked over, picked up a chair, and seated Joan beside him. Another chair appeared for me and we proceeded to enjoy breakfast with the president of Pakistan! Protocol had planned for him to eat alone, but even protocol is subservient to the ruler of a nation — and he

Breakfast   with   Pakistan   President Ayub Khan

wanted company for breakfast. Bypassing generals, civil officials, his private physician, and even old friends, for some reason he selected Joan and me to be his breakfast partners.

We ate eggs, fruit, and even a piece of "Welcome President Ayub" cake. He was a warm and charming breakfast companion. We talked of many things during that hour. We answered his questions about the hospital; he approved heartily all we explained to him. He willingly agreed that if we could time the opening of the hospital with one of his periodic visits to East Pakistan, he would be happy to inaugurate the hospital. We discussed his plans for Pakistan and learned more of each other's families and backgrounds. President Ayub explained that the old gentleman, our host, had been his friend for years. During World War II, President Ayub had been a military officer in the area and their close friendship dated back to that time.

When various leaders began coming to the breakfast table with petitions, Ayub received them graciously and listened to their requests. Some he approved, others he denied. Fazlul Karim presented a petition from one of his old Muslim cronies who for many years had wanted to make the pilgrimage to Mecca, but never succeeded in getting a seat on the special Hajj ship. He wanted special presidential approval for a seat on the next ship. President Ayub, feeling the matter was quite out of his purview, steadfastly refused to approve the petition.

A moment later, a village school principal came with a petition in his trembling hands. When Ayub learned that a number of local children were unable to attend school because they lacked the few rupees necessary to purchase textbooks, he called immediately for one of his secretaries who, at the president's direction, peeled off six 100-rupee notes for school books. Education, medical care, public works, and the advance of his people and nation seemed close to Ayub's heart. By the time breakfast was finished, a friendship had developed between us.

Then came the hunt! We watched the president and his party head out for the hunting site. Moments later an officer said to me, "We must take more firearms to the jungle. Please drive us there in your Land Rover and join us at the hunt." Calling for Fenton, we jumped into the Land Rover and shared in the president's hunt. To everyone's great delight a number of jungle chickens and a rare jungle pheasant were bagged.

Later, back at the rest house, a huge crowd of countryside people gathered to see and cheer their leader. With great swelling cheers they shouted, *"Ayub Khan Zindabad! Pakistan Zindabad! Ayub Khan Zindabad!* [Long live Ayub Khan! Long live Pakistan!]" I met and talked with the president's personal physician; he, too, showed great enthusiasm for our hospital project. After photographs and a few last words together, we thanked our host and President Ayub for their kindness to us and departed.

We learned later that after our departure the president spoke earnestly to the local leaders, saying, "Dr. Olsen and his colleagues are doing a wonderful thing for you people of this area. Just think! They have left their friends and loved ones and their beautiful country with all its luxuries to help you people who never have received proper medical care. You must give them all possible help and assistance."

As we drove away from the scene of the day's astounding events, I mused to Joan, "I wonder why God arranged that? Just so the president would inaugurate the hospital?"

"I don't know," Joan replied, "but the day will come when we will know for certain." She spoke prophetically — that day did come!

Meeting in January the American consul general to East Pakistan, I learned that the American ambassador had not yet made a high level approach regarding our visa problems, nor had he diagnosed the level from which the problems emanated. In February I flew again to Dacca, at the consul general's request, for an updating session. From him I learned that the American ambassador still had not acted. Most mission personnel requesting visas, however, continued to receive rejections or experience interminable delays. The consul general advised withholding further visa applications until after the upcoming elections when the excitement of political campaigning would die down. How to manage future visa applications was an urgent concern — one-half of those attending the recent ABWE candidate classes were candidates for East Pakistan!

Meanwhile language study consumed the gang in Chittagong, and at Malumghat hospital construction proceeded steadily. The McDonalds moved from their bamboo *basha* into the attractive nurses/teachers' residence.

Two miles from the hospital site, on a hot March day, five Bengali men and a boy stood beside a jungle road waiting for a timber truck to pick them up. Suddenly, from the thicket, a great royal Bengal tiger appeared. With a spine-chilling snarl he leaped, nailing one victim. While four men scrambled for trees, the horrified twelve-year-old boy screamed as he watched the tiger drag his father away — the man's head in the tiger's mouth! Unnerved by the boy's piercing shriek, the tiger unexpectedly released his prey and bounded off into the jungle.

Moments later at the hospital site, Tom and Olline McDonald were not alarmed to see a group of men bringing a patient, a common enough sight. But the injury was not so common. Tom found a hole completely through one cheek where a great fang had impaled it, also another tooth perforation, and cuts on the back of his neck. Blood trickled from other lacerations dealt by lashing tiger claws on the unfortunate victim's back, neck, and leg. Tom, with his limited background as a Navy medic, knew he would have to be the surgeon.

Later he told me his feelings: "When I saw the seriousness of the injury, I must admit I felt pretty helpless. I called on God for strength and had everyone bow while we prayed for the man. I gave him sedation for the shock and pain. Fenton, Olline, and I went to work cleaning off the dirt and blood and cutting away his clothing. I gave local anesthesia to the deep cuts and began to sew. It was 9:00 A.M. when we started, and at 1:00 P.M. we put in the last stitch and bandage." The patient recovered.

All of us who were well into Bengali II study, or beyond, were actively involved in teaching and sharing our faith in the Bengali language. Joan and I were requested by our old barber, Anungo, to hold meetings in his Hindu village. Using Anungo's home, we showed filmstrips and taught great truths of God to the simple village people. I treated the old barber, too, when recurrent bronchitis and pneumonia struck his weak lungs. During one illness, while I attended him in his bamboo house, by the light of a kerosene lamp he told me of his great desire for eternal life. Explaining that his Hindu faith did not provide any such wonderful thing, he said he was ready to accept Christ.

So he bowed his aged head and prayed, *"Hay, probhu Jishu, ekhuni amar antare ashun!* [Oh, Lord Jesus, right now come, enter into my heart and soul!]" And the great miracle happened in the life of the old Hindu barber, the first person I ever helped to find everlasting life using the Bengali language.

Handing me his Hindu scriptures and pictures of a god and goddess from his wall, he said gravely, "Please take these; I won't need them any more." Later, in our home, Joan and I counseled with another from that village and she, too, became "accepted in the Beloved One."

Wendy and Lynne went downcountry to visit our other stations before school began again. Lynne watched "Uncle Tom" build the hospital and helped her "Aunt Olline" care for sick people. Olline had found her slot! Before coming to East Pakistan she thought there would be little or nothing for her to do except keep house for Tom. Then the sick people began to come: workmen who dropped bricks on their fingers, children with burns, and scabby babies. Guided well by her motherly instincts, she spent hours each day lovingly caring for those who came.

Wendy, at Hebron, helped Jean Weld in the dispensary — running errands, filing cards, etc. A born animal lover, Wendy was delighted with a tiny monkey brought in by a Mru tribesman. We smiled at the letter describing her new friend: "The baby monkey is so little that you can hold him in one hand and still you can see lots of hand left over." She wrote about patients, too: "A lady came and said a bug went in her ear and sixteen came out her nose."

I enjoyed reading Harry Goehring's May Hebron station report. He wrote that Shudhir, who a year or two before had determined to follow Christ, had now gained courage to be baptized. Progress continued with Tipperas and Mrus. Recently, a member of the third big tribe in our area, the Mogh tribe, had decided to follow Christ. Excited and enthusiastic about the future, talented Harry Goehring looked forward to completing his Bengali language study in record time, then launching into Tippera and his life's work among the tribes of the Chittagong Hill Tracts.

Then on a cloudy day in June, Harry went to bed with fever. When word of Harry's illness reached Chittagong the following evening, Donn Ketcham drove immediately downcountry to Malumghat. Early the following morning Donn and Ralph Ankenman traveled upriver by outboard motorboat. They treated Harry throughout that day and night then evacuated him by Aircat and Land Rover to Chittagong where we settled him in our medical room.

Harry was gravely ill. After examining him I added up the findings to indicate that Harry's kidneys were so terribly damaged (presumably by infection), that they had shut down completely, producing no urine at all. Overnight, in response to treatment, Harry's temperature dropped dramatically from 104 to 100 and he felt somewhat better. His kidneys, however, remained steadfastly shut down throughout the day. During the night, however, small quantities of urine began to flow and tenderness over the kidneys was decreased. I was delighted!

Early the following morning, Dr. Ralph Ankenman flew to Dacca to obtain chemical tests on Harry's blood and bring back materials for a treatment called peritoneal dialysis, which we would use, if necessary, to help remove waste products from Harry's blood until his kidneys could do the job again. At midmorning, Harry took a turn for the worse. Over several hours his condition continued to deteriorate. His strong heart was failing. We applied every conceivable treatment to his dying heart, but finally Harry gasped, "Let me go!" — and he was gone! Crushed, I remembered that through my presentation of the needs of this land, back in Indiana, Harry had sensed God's call to serve in East Pakistan; now, under my hand, he had died in East Pakistan! His death was to us a harsh, painful, agonizing blow.

Loss of a brother beloved
(Vic and Donn beside
Harry's casket)

Telling Nancy that Harry was gone tore my heart out. But she was superb. That night, devastated and benumbed, Donn, Ralph, and I autopsied our brother. Like unwilling robots, we carried out our painful task, mechanically making our notes, taking the specimens and cultures.

Several days later the microscope slides confirmed that Harry's kidneys had been shattered, not by infection, but by some toxic substance. But where had it come from? A minute, careful, extensive, prolonged investigation of every factor surrounding his illness and death failed to answer that mysterious question.

At Nancy's request, Harry was buried at the hospital site near the foot of two tall, stately gurjun trees. Many came from the Hebron area — Christian, Hindu, Buddhist alike — to pay their respects at the burial of their dear friend. The service was simple and beautiful.

We proceeded to the graveside. There, under a tarpaulin in the driving monsoon rain, first in English and then in Bengali, I committed my brother-patient-friend to the cold, wet earth. I have missed him deeply ever since and await expectantly my next meeting with Harry in God's great beyond.

Divine grace glowed forth in Nancy's life. What a stalwart she was! She wept and smiled, worked and prayed, reminisced and remembered, and many times gave witness to her faith to those who had known Harry. After her return to the USA a few days later, her messages in American churches touched the hearts and lives of many. Through Harry's death some were challenged to serve God in foreign lands — including East Pakistan.

US-Pakistan relations continued to deteriorate. President Ayub Khan, conscious that his nation was surrounded by India, Russia, and China, decided it was time to establish more friendly relations with the two massive Communist nations. (There was no hope for early rapprochement with India.) America reacted strongly to the friendship developing between Pakistan and its neighbors. These tensions played their part in our visa crisis. In May, when the American ambassador visited Chittagong, he called for me. During our meeting he had nothing encouraging to report regarding our visas. He had not felt it feasible to go to the top, nor had he been able to diagnose where in the Pakistan government structure the visa problem originated.

In July came the devastating blow to our plans to help and teach the tribal people — the Chittagong Hill Tracts were closed to travel by foreigners! As long as that ban continued, our Hebron team would be unable to trek to the Christian villages, and I could not follow through on the invitation of the Mogh prince to visit his villages and teach his people.

At Malumghat, the explosion of Tom McDonald's twelve-gauge shotgun fired inside his living room was deafening! As the concussion snuffed out the kerosene lamp, some of the slugs tore furrows in the concrete floor while others found their mark in the sinuous, brilliantly black- and yellow-banded krait, one of Indo-Pakistan's most deadly poisonous snakes. A moment earlier, as Tom had walked past a chair, he saw a faint movement in the shadows. He stopped — just in time — for the krait was poised, ready to strike. Olline, deathly afraid of snakes, was thoroughly traumatized. A few days in Chittagong, however, eased off the strain.

While working on visa renewals for two of our members one day, I encountered a rather cool attitude at the Chittagong DSB office. That was bad news. Because the DSB (police intelligence branch) is responsible for registering and keeping tabs on all foreigners, they have considerable control over us, our visas, and our future. So the brusqueness of the officer-in-charge concerned me. On the following morning I awakened with the overpowering impression that I should go that day to talk with the officer in an effort to improve relations with him. As he and I arrived at his headquarters simultaneously that morning, I was able to enter directly into his inner office without being stopped by a junior officer. Because I had no business to transact we simply talked. For nearly two hours we discussed the Bengali language, our families, the problems and progress of East Pakistan, the work of our mission, and Memorial Christian Hospital. I tried subtly to correct some of his rigid, stilted notions about missionaries. When I offered our help should sickness strike his family, he immediately spoke of his thirteen-year-old daughter who was quite deaf. He reported that a specialist had described her hearing as permanently damaged and had offered no treatment; I feared there was no hope for the girl.

"Would you examine my daughter?" the official asked.

"Of course, " I agreed.

Upon examination I found to my great delight that the hearing damage was not permanent. I arranged a treatment which markedly improved the attractive child's hearing. In the process, as the officer gained new appreciation for Christian love and concern, his brusqueness changed to cordiality. From that time forward, not only was his door always open to us, but he continually extended himself to help us to the limit allowed by his rules and regulations.

Then came that morning in early September. At the crack of dawn, four unannounced, unexpected aircraft appeared over Chittagong airport. One detached itself from the pack, fell into a screaming dive toward the main runway, releasing four black whistling objects. Two of the bombs were duds. The other two bombs dropped by the Indian Air Force fighter bomber exploded, gouging out house-size holes in the turf beside the cement strip. Several in our group, although they lived twelve miles from the airport, were awakened by the explosions and rattling windows. The day before, we had heard rumors of possible warfare on the West Pakistan-India border. For weeks, border incidents and a vitriolic war of words had kept Indo-Pakistan feelings high. Now there was no doubt; India was at war with West Pakistan — and East Pakistan.

I called our group together to analyze the situation and make our plans. Because September, the "month of rot," was a good month to be elsewhere, some of the team were out of the country on vacations. Mary Lou and Becky were en route to south India. Jean Weld, Jeannie Lockerbie, and the McDonald family were on the high seas between Chittagong and Ceylon. The Walshes were at the hospital site where Jay was filling in for Tom McDonald. In Chittagong the rest of us gathered to decide what to do next. We all felt quite green and inexperienced at dealing with wars!

"Careful there!" (Mark and Anungo)

To help solve the communications problem I declared our house the nerve center. Anyone receiving significant information would come, record it in the book, and learn whatever news others had picked up. We made assignments to monitor various shortwave radio broadcasts. Then, on the grounds that our brick homes were strong enough to tolerate anything but a direct bomb hit and were located some distance from what we considered military targets, we decided to sit tight. Each family was to gather together six drums of foodstuffs and other important items for immediate shipment to the hospital, to be ready in case circumstances forced us to evacuate there. Attempts to phone the US consulate in Dacca failed.

The next day no hard information reached us, but on the following day our American friend Chuck Kline arrived from Dacca. He reported that some in Dacca feared the hostilities might become a holy war. The American consul general had called for the evacuation of all dependents and nonessential Americans. Chuck considered the directive to get out a strong order. When we actually read the directive, however, it did not seem quite that potent. In it the consul general reported that American government dependents and nonessential personnel were being evacuated, and advised that other nonessential Americans evacuate on the same planes; but he did not say, "You must go."

Again I called our team together. To evacuate or not to evacuate, that was the question. None of us wanted to see our wives and children killed. The morning's Voice of America broadcast reported that the Pakistan government desired all foreigners to leave Pakistan immediately. Rumors had it that an Italian ship at Chittagong's outer anchorage would accept all who desired to evacuate immediately — and that it would be the last ship out of Chittagong!

At the beginning of our meeting a wide range of opinions were expressed. We decided quickly that each family or individual could evacuate or stay put, as he decided; all did not necessarily have to make the same decision. Certain obvious factors supported evacuation: active warfare had begun and Chittagong had been bombed. The American consul general had called for evacuation. Civil strife might develop and make later evacuation difficult or impossible. The last ship would soon leave Chittagong port. If the Chittagong or Dacca airfields were successfully bombed, later evacuation would be impossible. Because America had cut off military aid to Pakistan (and India), anti-American feeling was running high. China might become involved in the war.

Despite all these factors, in the end the gang had no peace of mind about evacuating. After all, our work was very essential. We wondered how the American officials would react if we were to refuse evacuation. To determine the answer to that question and find out how strong his directive really was, we decided I should travel overnight by train to Dacca to meet with the consul general. Despite the potential risk of military action at a touchy point where the train passed very close to the Indian border, my trip was uneventful; I arrived refreshed in Dacca after a good night's sleep.

The consul general's office was a beehive of activity and jangling telephones. Squeezed by pressures on every side, he seemed a bit distraught.

"How strong is this directive you have given us?" I asked Mr. Bowling. He responded that a stronger statement could have been made; this one was medium intensity.

"In that case," I asked with a smile, "you wouldn't really be too upset if we decided to remain, would you?"

His face lit up momentarily with a quirky little smile as he remarked, "No, I wouldn't be too upset. As a matter of fact, I thought you people might just decide something like that."

The tension was broken — his response seemed to confirm our tentative decision to sit tight. I managed to relay the information by telephone to Chittagong. In the meeting there, each person registered his decision to reject evacuation and remain at his post. Happily I cabled the home board: ABWE STAFF COOL CALM COLLECTED STOP REMAINING TO SERVE STOP ALL WELL HERE STOP REJOICING IN PRIVILEGE OF SERVING CHRIST AND PAKISTANI BRETHREN STOP OLSEN

The die was cast!

Upon return to Chittagong I found the local population carrying on full-scale preparation for a long war. Laborers were digging V-shaped trenches by every roadside. All automobile headlights were painted black except for a narrow slit. Blackout was imposed upon the city from dusk to daylight. Whenever light showed in house or vehicle, vigilant young neighborhood wardens blew whistles or threw stones at the offender. Knots of people gathered around every short-wave radio, but listening to Indian propaganda over India Radio was strictly forbidden.

A missionary husband and wife, members of another mission, were picked up by a civilian as suspicious-looking foreigners and grilled for nearly two hours by the police. We were ordered to remain within the municipal limits of Chittagong. On several nights a siren signaled air raid, but no planes appeared. Despite the tension, our folks quietly went about their business — studying language, teaching God's truths, and helping anxious, distraught people.

At the call of the consul general, Americans from every corner of East Pakistan had converged on Dacca. There six hundred of them were stacked on each other awaiting the evacuation planes. Day after day, the planes were either delayed, or landing rights were denied them by the Pakistan government. Finally the great planes came one by one, to land, devour a large group of harried Americans, then carry them off to be disgorged in Bangkok or Manila.

When an RAF plane flew into Chittagong for the compulsory evacuation of all British dependents, we felt it was time to reevaluate our decision. Here was another possible chance to evacuate. Besides, the British are quite cool and experienced, we reasoned; if they are forcing their people out, maybe it's foolish to stay! In the meeting, as we reprayed, rediscussed, and reanalyzed, we redecided that our guidance factor was solid that we should remain at our posts.

We appreciated a timely cable from our home board referring to Psalm 46:1: "God is our refuge and strength, a very present help in trouble." I cabled back a response to them from the same psalm, verses 9, 10, and 11:

> Who makes wars to cease to the ends of the earth; He breaks the bow into pieces and snaps the spear in two. He burns the chariots in the fire. Be still and know that I am God; I will be exalted among the nations; I will be exalted on the earth. The Lord of hosts is with us; the God of Jacob is our fortress.

After seventeen days, the war ground to a sudden, uneasy halt. We gathered to thank God for His protection and guidance which had kept us at our stations. Our work had progressed well in the interim. Government officials and Bengali friends were warmer than ever, grateful that we had remained to catch the bombs with them. Though most of those who evacuated did not return for months, our people who had been caught outside the country soon returned to us, making our mission family once again complete.

The war had given our Bengali friends a new sense of national unity which, for a while, drew together opposing parties. We saw a new light in the eyes of the common man. Throughout the country requests were made for contributions to the national defense fund. To show our sympathy for the war-stricken nation, we contributed fifteen hundred rupees to the widows and orphans left behind in the wake of the war. The DC was quite moved to receive our money and my accompanying note:

> We are proud of the gallant sons of East Pakistan who have given their all to defend the land they loved and which we, too, love. With the advent of cease-fire we are conscious that there will be many homes to which husbands and fathers will never return. Our hearts go out to the widows and their children who are suffering now, and we recall the words of the Holy Injil: "Pure religion and undefiled before God the Father is this, to visit the fatherless and widows in their affliction." We would like to visit them through the enclosed gift which comes from the members of the Association of Baptists.

By then Joan and I were ready for vacation. The war had interrupted our planned trip to India. Wanting and needing a calm, restful type of vacation, we spent three weeks at Cox's Bazar. We loafed, swam, sunned on the beach, played games with the children, and recouped our inner resources so drained by the events of the year.

One day the SDO loaned us his launch and driver for a day to

Brave fishermen of Sonadia

visit Sonadia, a tiny island offshore from Cox's Bazar. The flat sandy island sported very little foliage but plenty of fishermen. They were brave, devil-may-care, dark-skinned men with flashing white smiles. While talking to a group of them who were fascinated by my four white-headed children, I mentioned the name of Jesus. They expressed interest so I told them more. I explained who He was, His connection with the heavenly Father, His love for them, and His death on the cross for all mankind.

But my words were not getting through to them. Suddenly it came to me that my simple explanation was no doubt the first presentation of Christ's good news message on that island in the history of the world.

After a moment I diagnosed the problem — they hadn't a clue what a cross was! Kneeling, drawing a cross in the sand, I asked, "Don't you really know what this is?" I looked up to see blank faces.

Then one fisherman, brightening, suggested, "It's one of those airplane things that sometimes flies into Cox's Bazar."

"No," I countered, "it's not an airplane."

Finally another man suggested, "I think it's a bird."

"No," I explained, "not a bird, it's a cross — one tree trunk pointing to the sky with another smaller one fixed across it. On such a cross they nailed Jesus, whom your Holy Koran calls Hajrat Isa. He died on that cross, not for His sins, but for your sins and my sins and the sins of all the people of the world. He loves all men, wants to fill our hearts, help us, and take us someday to a wonderful place beyond the sea and the sky." When we said goodbye, it seemed almost as though we left a little of ourselves behind with those strong, courageous men who waved us off.

A month later our fishermen friends were dead! Knowing that cyclones never come in December, many of them were fifty miles out to sea, bobbing on the big waves, hoping for the big catch. Precisely then the unseasonable December cyclone appeared out of the blue to consign them to a liquid mass grave. Those left on Sonadia Island also perished, for deflected by some invisible bar from its northerly course, the madly swirling storm made a right-hand turn and smashed across the lower half of the finger of East Pakistan. A fifteen-foot wall of water swept over Sonadia Island stripping it of life and habitation. As far as we could learn, none of the men and boys we had met on Sonadia survived; but God in His grace had given them one chance to hear the message of eternal life. "What is your life? It is just a vapor that appears for a short time, then vanishes away."

The cyclonic winds hit Memorial Christian Hospital full force, stripping the leaves from the trees and snapping some trees like matchsticks. During the evening before the storm, masons working at the hospital had heard radio warnings of the impending storm but neglected to mention the news to Tom. Therefore, he had not battened down the hatches, so the wind shattered glass in many windows and doors. Some corrugated aluminum sheeting was ripped from roofs of our service buildings, and all of the workmen's bamboo quarters were destroyed. The hospital buildings, on the other hand, stood like Gibraltar before the fearful onslaught. The terrible storm proved the wisdom of our decision and the home board's willingness to build substantial homes and hospital buildings.

Rejuvenated by our vacation, Joan and I slogged through the last lap of Bengali II study. On a monumental day we passed the final Bengali II examination with good marks. Getting that "Bengal tiger" off our backs at last we found an immense relief.

Ending the painful year on a bright note, we made an important, far-reaching decision involving nurse-linguist Lynn Silvernale. Lynn had used her several talents well. She deployed her nursing skills at the Hebron dispensary. She exploited her high language aptitude by learning Bengali quickly, then authoring our mission's study courses in Bengali I, Bengali II, and the Chittagonian dialect. That done she was ready to tackle a tribal tongue, first learning the language, then doing the linguistic analysis, and reducing the language to writing. That was her purpose in coming.

The Bengali Bible, however, begged for attention. We learned soon after arrival in East Pakistan that the Bengali Bible, artistic and beautiful to a college graduate, is of little value to the slightly or moderately literate. Written in a high literary style, it is not well suited to the man on the street. We sensed the need for a common language translation of the Scriptures. It seemed to me, as I analyzed the many activities of our mission, that no other work had a priority quite so high, for Bengali, understood by 125 million people, is one of the world's most widely spoken languages.

Once or twice in the early days I had said to Lynn, "Do you think it could be God's plan for you to use your linguistic skills to produce a truly readable Bengali Bible?"

Lynn would respond, "Well, it's certainly an urgent need."

Later we had learned that a Bengali friend, Mrs. Bashanti Dass, possessed superb skills to share in such a work. But she was scheduled to leave Chittagong to live in another district hundreds of miles away. In preparation for departure, Mrs. Dass resigned her teaching position. But, suddenly, her plans changed, and we learned that she would remain in Chittagong. When Lynn heard the news, she felt, with a sense of urgency, that she *must* do this new translation! When I heard the news, separately, that Mrs. Dass would remain in Chittagong, exactly the same thought struck me deeply. When Joan and I got together with Lynn and compared notes we became excited. The guidance factor seemed very strong. We laid out a tentative program to the executive committee who studied it with care and ultimately agreed. The field council analyzed the program with equal care. Then God's Spirit brought the conviction to us all that this great project *must* be done! But I had no idea then that my own involvement in Bible translation would become so deep.

We had started the agonizing year of 1965 *hearing* the words of President Ayub Khan, the raja of Pakistan. We ended the year with a plan for *giving out* the words of One who is the "Raja of rajas."

14

Opening and Overture

As THE CLOCK edged past the 9:30 mark in my Bangladesh bedroom, I remembered 1966 with a warm glow in my soul. Our medical team, in a mass exodus from Chittagong, moved downcountry to open Memorial Christian Hospital! It was the year we had worked and fought and waited for. Our joy was tinged with anxiety, however, when illness found a target in our flock. And the visa situation deteriorated even further, threatening to capsize us. Then came the day of reckoning — we had no idea whether our daring overture would succeed gloriously or fail dismally. But that risk we had to take!

*   *   *

By February, hospital construction was finally nearing completion. At that point Jay Walsh moved to the hospital site to help in the final stages of building and to receive from Tom McDonald all the tools and equipment in an orderly turnover. And that same month we Olsens had our first teenager. On February 13 Wendy became age thirteen! How she enjoyed her party at the Chinese restaurant!

Then, a few days later, illness struck among us. Quite unexpectedly, one of the wives developed a sudden severe mental-emotional breakdown. She suffered, not a garden-variety nervous upset, but a complete collapse of her normal mental processes with extreme agitation. All contact with reality gone, she could not say whether she was on earth or in heaven.

Giving her sedation for anxiety, I pondered, *What next?* The physician in me said, *Ship the patient immediately to America for sophisticated psychiatric treatment by specialists.* The Christian in me spoke up, saying, *Not so fast — how about giving God a chance to do something?* The Bible student in me said, *If there ever was a time for prayer and fasting, this is it.* The field council chairman in me said, *A member of the team is hurting. We must pray and plan together, for she is our sister.*

I called the field council together to explain the developments. We

180

decided to give God a week to do the miraculous. In the meantime, not knowing His plan, we would in a businesslike way purchase air tickets and make all necessary arrangements for evacuation to America. Gingerly I presented the idea of observing a day of fasting and prayer. Conscious that fasting was not a normal activity in our circles, I wondered what the reaction would be.

Jay Walsh, with tears in his eyes, spoke immediately, "That very thought was going through my mind. I think that's exactly what we should do." The point carried. The patient's husband, a man of great faith, approved heartily.

On the appointed day Jay, at the hospital, led weeping Tipperas in their observance of the special day. Each family of American and Bengali Christians in Chittagong spent the day in their own homes in prayer and fasting. In the afternoon we came together to pray fervently from shattered hearts that God would reach down out of heaven and do the miraculous. The children also met to pray. That venture of faith was an unforgettable experience. Finally, the American and Bengali leaders of the church group went to the patient's bedside to pray as taught by James, the brother of the Lord. Then each one returned home to break his fast with the evening meal and await the outcome.

As I objectively examined the patient the next day I found not a single encouraging sign. She remained agitated, confused, disoriented, disconnected from reality.

Back home at lunch, my children asked, "Is she all well now, Daddy?"

"No, kids," I had to reply, "I don't see any change."

Then, with the wisdom of the ages etched in her voice, Lynne said, "Don't worry; it won't be long now. She'll soon be OK." The faith of the mission children was beautiful to behold.

The next day, the day before the planned evacuation, I was forced to give the same glum report — no change. That evening, before our little going-away party for architect Tony Adams and his wife Myra who were returning to England, I checked my patient again; this time I sensed a slight but definite change for the better. Later I returned from the party to find her definitely "back in the ballpark." Anxiety persisted, but she was in her right mind!

Absolutely thrilled, I called Donn Ketcham to check my findings. Sitting down at the bedside, he talked with the patient, asking pertinent questions. He mentioned our plan to send her to America the following morning.

Sitting bolt upright in bed, she responded petulantly, "Donn Ketcham, God called me to be a missionary when I was eleven years old!

That's what I've come here to be, and I don't want to go to America." We could only say, "Thank You, Father!"

I explained to the patient's husband, whose great faith had been rewarded, that follow-up psychiatric counseling would be necessary to uncover the causes underlying the breakdown and help prevent future problems. I explained that a wise Christian psychiatrist would be the person best qualified to manage the psychotherapy. I answered his questions, explaining that I was not a trained psychiatrist, but admitting that I knew more about the subject than the average doctor. His guidance factor suggested that she should remain in East Pakistan for me to carry out the treatment. With God's explicit help, the counseling progressed successfully and that fine, cooperative patient was rehabilitated to carry on efficiently the work which, as a child, God had called her to do.

Our annual field council meeting came in early March. In my swan song report, I reviewed the work of our mission through eras 1 and 2, pointing out that our meeting marked the end of era 2. Era 3 would begin with the exodus of the medical team from Chittagong to occupy the new quarters at Malumghat and begin our medical-surgical mission at Memorial Christian Hospital.

Late in March came the day of culmination, the day for dedication of Memorial Christian Hospital! We gathered for a semiprivate service in a semipukka ward of the semiready hospital. The service, restricted to friends in the Christian community, allowed us to receive the completed buildings from our contractors and dedicate them to God and His glory. By noon cars from Chittagong and boats from the Hebron area began to arrive. East met West at that dedication service in the women's ward. Visiting American women, some with bouffant hairdos, sat among simple Tippera tribal women, one of whom calmly nursed her baby. Western dresses and suits contrasted gaily with loincloths and *lungis.* Bengali Christians from the city, tribal Christians from the jungle, English, Chinese, Japanese, Americans, and missionaries from other organizations sat on straw mats or the few available chairs. The refreshment tables held Kool-Aid and *labonga purri,* plus brownies and *chanachur.*

Jay Walsh opened the dedication service with bilingual greetings, prayer, and Bible reading. The talented medical group graced the occasion with music.

Tom McDonald spoke recounting God's help to him during the long months of construction. I never forgot his story about the huge gurjun tree which needed to be felled very near our meeting place. As workmen chopped nearly through the tree, oddly it remained perfectly balanced, refusing to fall as planned. Seeing potential danger to his men beside the tree, he sent them off to lunch. If a wind came up from the wrong direction, the massive tree would topple on the hospital buildings. With head bowed, Tom prayed for God to do something. As he opened his eyes, the leaves in the jungle behind him began to stir and rustle; a fresh breeze sprang to life, toppling the great tree in just the right spot!

Khoka Sen spoke on behalf of the national Christians. I gave the dedicatory address first in Bengali, then in English, recalling the decision of King Solomon: "Behold I build a house to the name of the Lord my God, to dedicate it to Him." That desire which had stirred in Solomon's heart lived also in our hearts — to build a house, a place of healing, to the name of the Lord and to dedicate it to Him.

Also I touched on the name *Malumghat* which means literally the port of perception. It was our desire that the Malumghat hospital would be a "port of perception," a place of new understanding.

As the medical staff and our wives knelt, Gene Gurganus led the dedicatory prayer. We dedicated not only the building, but also ourselves to the glory of God and to the service of our fellow man in East Pakistan.

A few days later came the final goodbye party for the McDonald family. Our words of appreciation and our gifts were small recompense for all that fine family had accomplished for the project. We remembered, too, Paul Goodman, his answer to God's call, and the months which he selflessly devoted to God's work in East Pakistan. Two days later the McDonalds were airborne, headed for the USA.

By this time our old friend, the DC, promoted to a high position, had moved to Dacca. Before our move to Malumghat, I received an

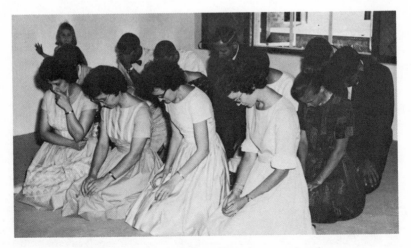

"Not only the buildings but also ourselves"

urgent call from him in Dacca to come to consult on his wife's complicated delivery case. I planned with the Dacca doctor the best method of managing the delivery. Mrs. Ahmed gained strength and confidence as I prayed at her bedside before the delivery. We all rejoiced when a baby daughter was born without complications.

One by one throughout April and May, the nurses and medical families transferred to Malumghat station. Because we all had been a part of the Chittagong work, we left the port city with mingled emotions. Under the leadership of Gene Gurganus, the Bible Information Center had been established near downtown Chittagong. There we preached in English and Bengali church services and the citizens of Chittagong utilized the reading room and lending library. With the exodus of medical workers, just a handful would be left behind to carry on the important work in the great city of Chittagong.

In mid-May the Olsens moved to Malumghat and settled in our new home, house 6. Our homes were located one-half mile off the highway on a lovely nine-acre estate in the forest on the pleasant banks of Ringbhong Khal, a picturesque tidal stream. On the property were six spacious family houses, a large nurses/teachers' residence, and a small primary school building. This was home!

Our sixteen-acre hospital site, beside the main highway, contained the main hospital building, five service buildings, and several bamboo *bashas*. Later, additional structures were added. We designed the housing estate one-half mile from the hospital to keep the children away from the smallpox, cholera, and myriad other diseases. We knew, also, that it would be good for our mental health to be able to go home out of sight of the hospital when the day's work was done.

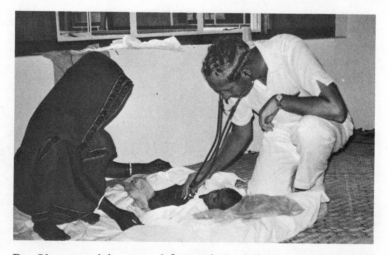

Dr. Olsen examining one of first patients, before the beds arrived

Although our hospital beds had not yet arrived we operated an active outpatient department from the beginning. When a serious case came, we admitted the patient to a floor mat in the ward. My first seriously ill patient suffered from a perforated stomach ulcer with peritonitis. He arrived at the hospital in a bicycle rickshaw, at death's door, with no pulse or blood pressure. Despite our limited facilities, we treated him successfully. Some outpatients, just to get a look at the new hospital, came complaining that their perspiration smelled or that when sleepy they couldn't keep from yawning. Other patients, under cover of darkness, sneaked across the forbidden border from Burma to be treated by the Christian doctors. I was overjoyed to be functioning as a doctor in the hospital at last!

To prevent any of us who were doctors from getting delusions of grandeur and to provide each physician opportunity to utilize his administrative talents, we decided the medical director should be changed annually by rotation. If a doctor disliked administration he could decline the honor, but the position would be offered him when his turn came. This simple administrative device prevented rivalry or position-seeking, and promoted a wonderfully harmonious sense of camaraderie.

Back row, left to right: Mr. Robert Adolph, Dir. of Laboratory; Dr. Ralph Ankenman, Dir. of Anesthesiology; Dr. Viggo Olsen, Med. Dir. of MCH; Dr. Donn Ketcham, Dir. of Surgery; Rev. Jay Walsh, Chapl. and Supt. of Maintenance. *Front row, left to right:* Dr. Lucille Ankenman, Part-time Consultant; Miss Mary Lou Brownell, Dir. of Dentistry; Miss Jean Weld, Dir. of Midwifery; Miss Jeannie Lockerbie, Dir. of Outpatient Dept.; Miss Rebecca Davey, Dir. of Nursing.

Within days after our arrival the Malumghat leopard struck! Less than a mile from our house he sprang from the jungle, caught a village child by the throat, and dragged the lifeless little body into the jungle to feed upon. We were shocked and surprised, for only rarely does a tiger or leopard ever become a man-eater and attack human beings. Sometimes, however, injury, illness, or old age renders the animal incapable of catching its normal prey; then it may begin to attack weak, defenseless human beings who can't run half so speedily as a deer. The Malumghat leopard had become very old with white whiskers and muzzle.

We visited the dead child's family to offer our sympathy. Her father, recreating the attack for us, took us into the jungle to the blood-soaked spot where his daughter had been found. As we looked, two of the Bengalis stiffened, recognizing the sound of the leopard in the thicket. He was watching the whole proceedings! We departed quickly, our guides insisting that Joan, Becky, and Jeannie walk in the middle of the line — instead of the end where women usually walk!

For weeks we restricted our children from entering the forest around us or from walking between our houses at night. But soon all signs of the leopard vanished; thereafter, he was never again seen at Malumghat.

Another leopard, however, did get into the act at our house. The tiny ball of fur brought from the distant Hill Tracts by a Mru tribesman became Wendy's beloved pet. The cub, a rare "clouded leopard," was the closest living relative of the extinct saber-toothed tiger.

Vic with father of slain child, where the body was found

Clyde the clouded leopard and Wendy

Clyde the clouded leopard had large distinct spots and a nature which made him want to climb and live in trees. He revealed this instinct early in life; as I walked past him one day he leaped to claw himself up my leg as though it were a tree trunk. Wendy mothered him, loved him, and fed him with a baby bottle.

At Malumghat I continued to work on a project which had occupied my spare time for two years — a Muslim Bengali-to-English dictionary. Soon after beginning Bengali language study, I became painfully aware that most of my friends were speaking a somewhat different language. As Muslims they spoke Muslim Bengali, not the standard Bengali I was learning. Eight centuries earlier, the Muslims had come to Bengal, learned the Bengali language, and salted it down with many of their own Muslim terms. I felt a compulsion to learn these words, so much a part of the vocabulary and life of my Muslim friends. I was on the verge of completing my collection of nearly five thousand such words. The final step would be to publish them in the form of a pocket dictionary to be sold in bookstores throughout the land. As the first such dictionary to be published in the country, it would have significance to the community of scholars. More practically, I found that when I conversed with or taught Muslim friends in their own Muslim language, it "rang the bell" with them. The dictionary would be a tool for all of us in relating to our Muslim acquaintances.

In June, after many weeks of intense opposition, political activity reached a bloody climax. Early in the year, the Awami League's Sheikh Mujibur Rahman began to blast the existing Pakistan government with withering speeches across East Pakistan. In February he addressed in Lahore, West Pakistan, a convention of all political leaders opposed to the government in power. Convinced that the government (and all preceding Pakistan governments) had neglected the East Wing, treating it as a stepchild, Mujib presented his monumental six points summarizing the changes necessary to redress the legitimate grievances of the Bengalis of East Pakistan.

President Ayub, unhappy about the political attacks, explained he was doing his best to remove disparities between East and West Pakistan. During the next three months Mujib was jailed five times, apparently on the orders of the East Pakistan governor Monem Khan; Sheikh Mujib's Awami League filled the streets with angry Bengalis. The police arrested nearly eight hundred and opened fire on the mobs, killing eleven. Two days later Sheikh Mujib was incarcerated in the Dacca central jail where he remained for the next eighteen months.

For months the visa situation had remained serious. The situation deteriorated further in June when we were notified that our members in East Pakistan would no longer be granted four-year multiple-entry visas, the type of visa which greatly facilitated our life and work. The six-month single-entry visas we were now offered would render a proper furlough impossible and greatly complicate our children's educational program. Then came the even more depressing news that our visa request for a new school teacher appointee, Marilyn Malmstrom, had been denied. The visa situation was now critical! During July we ruminated and made appeals — all to no avail.

One day our old friend and neighbor Mr. Fazlul Karim Choudhury, our host when we enjoyed breakfast with the president, came to talk with me.

"I understand, Dr. Olsen, that you are having difficulties with your visas. Is that so?"

"Yes," I replied.

As I explained the problems we faced, he listened intently. His voice cracking with emotion, he pledged, "I will do anything in my power to help you, Daktar Sahib. If you but say the word, I will travel to West Pakistan and clutch my president by the feet for you."

Fazlul Karim Choudhury

Touched by his love and willingness to help, I momentarily fumbled for words then suggested, "Not now; let us see what happens to our current appeal."

By the first of August our appeal had failed to provide visas. When newspaper headlines reported that President Ayub Khan would spend the second week of August in Dacca, East Pakistan, something clicked! Perhaps the time had come to agree to the old gentleman's offer to help us and go to the top! The words of a respected local leader speaking on our behalf would be even more forceful than our own direct appeal.

In our field council meeting we studied and debated every aspect of the problem. The decision to go to the top is a big decision to make, for failure can produce drastic effects — "The king's wrath is like the roaring of a lion." As we studied and prayed, however, a certain sense of direction and destiny came to us and we decided to go all out.

The old gentleman and I flew to Dacca; we met first with the old DC, Mr. Ahmed, newly appointed to high office in the capital. We put our heads together to think up some last-minute way for Fazlul Karim to make contact with the president.

At last Mr. Ahmed said, "I have it! I will arrange for him a place in tomorrow's presidential reception line at the airport. There he can make the contact and request an appointment." Mr. Ahmed insisted that I stay in his home until my business was finished. Jay Walsh arrived in Dacca the next morning.

As good as his word, Mr. Ahmed arranged the engraved invitation and an automobile to get the old gentleman into the reception line in the nick of time just as the presidential plane came in for a landing. The airport was jampacked with thousands of people. As the plane taxied to its halting place and the door opened to reveal the president of Pakistan, a thunderous ovation rocked the airport. After saluting the crowd, President Ayub walked slowly down the long red carpet greeting each member of the reception line. Finally he reached the old gentleman, Fazlul Karim. His elderly voice barely stretching over the din of the huge crowd, Fazlul Karim greeted President Ayub and asked for an appointment.

"Mr. President," he said, "I have a very important matter to discuss with you and I need a brief appointment." Our whole plan hung in the balance during that critical instant when Pakistan's president framed his response.

Then he answered, "Yes, you may have the appointment. I'll be happy to hear your important matter." Whew!

We arrived for our appointment that evening at the designated time of 6:00 P.M. In President Ayub's office, as soon as he had paid his respects, the old gentleman began to discuss the important matter.

"Mr. President," he said emotionally, "you know that the hospital built by Dr. Olsen and his colleagues is the greatest thing that has ever happened in our area. They are saving the lives of many of my people who used to die. We have a love for these doctors and nurses who have come to help us. Now I have learned from a reliable source that someone in your government is causing Dr. Olsen and his people much inconvenience in obtaining their visas. He cannot even get a visa to take his normal home leave. Mr. President, what fairness — what justice — is there in that?"

The president responded, a bit nonplussed, "I know nothing about this! It does indeed seem strange."

Then Fazlul Karim, with consummate skill, said in his twinkly way, "I have heard that missionaries in West Pakistan are facing no such problems, only those here in East Pakistan. I'm sure you do not love our East Pakistan any less than the West wing."

"Of course not," President Ayub responded indignantly, "I will look into this immediately." Calling for his righthand man, the

principal secretary, he ordered him to sit with me immediately to
learn all the particulars of our problem.

I talked for nearly an hour with the immensely powerful principal
secretary, an intelligent and thoughtful man. He heard my story,
asked questions until he understood the problems thoroughly, and
received my three petitions. In those petitions we asked for the
moon: four-year multiple-entry visas (worth a million dollars apiece
to us) for all our veterans, plus a dozen new hands! He outlined his
plan of action and requested that I phone him at a given number the
following evening.

Twenty-four hours later his progress report sounded encouraging.
He had spoken to the East Pakistan chief secretary in Dacca who
agreed to our receiving the visas. He had called across India to the
director of immigration in Karachi who informed him that all our
files were in the capital city, Rawalpindi. Again he called across
India to the secretary of home affairs in Rawalpindi directing him to
act favorably on our petitions. He asked that I call him again the
following morning.

At the appointed time, twenty-four hours later, I again called
President Ayub's principal secretary to learn of a new development.
The home secretary in Rawalpindi, instead of passing the order in
our favor, had dispatched by plane all the files on every one of our
ABWE members thirteen hundred miles across India to Dacca!

He said, "The files will reach here soon; call me again tomorrow
evening." I had no idea what this development could mean! Jay
Walsh and I had a helpful consultation together before he returned
to Chittagong. We both redoubled our prayer efforts.

At 5:00 P.M. the next day, in my third follow-up telephone conversation with the principal secretary, I learned that the files had
arrived. Something in the files required further consultation with
the governor of East Pakistan (the man our enemy Akand had tried
to poison against us!) As the principal secretary was just leaving
for the governor's mansion, he suggested I call him again in two
and a half hours. The tension in my soul reached a new high. What
had he found in those files? The decision to be made in the next
two hours would have an incalculable influence on the destiny of
ABWE and Memorial Christian Hospital! The success or failure of
our program hinged on that decision! I never prayed more earnestly
or fervently than I did during those two hours.

"Father, touch and mold their minds and hearts to let Your work
continue here."

When the crucial moment arrived, I picked up the telephone with
a slightly trembling hand.

"Mr. Secretary," I asked, "what's the decision?"

"Dr. Olsen," he responded, "I have finished my consultation with the governor and President Ayub has finalized the matter. He has decided to grant your every request! And we know, doctor, that you plan to depart on your home leave within a week so I have notified the East Pakistan chief secretary to expedite your visa through the local immigration office." They had agreed to the whole proposition! How utterly fantastic! "The king's wrath is as the roaring of a lion, but his favor is as dew upon the grass."

"Oh, thank You, Father!"

That evening I became concerned anew that I had nothing in writing from the president's office. Because the principal secretary already had said that a letter would be unnecessary, I was concerned lest a further request annoy him. After an hour of thought and prayer, however, I sensed a green light to go ahead and try to obtain a written order. When I reached the principal secretary by phone he was again warm and friendly. And when I gingerly asked for something positive in writing he agreed quickly without any annoyance whatsoever. I could collect the document, he said, at 8:30 the following morning. I felt the time was ripe to ask another question.

"Is it possible, Mr. Secretary, that the helpful things you have done for us could have any beneficial effect on the visa problems of any other mission group?" He replied that he didn't know, for he was unfamiliar with any problems that other groups might be having. Then I saw my chance!

"You mean, then, that no cabinet decision or presidential order had to be rescinded in helping us?"

He responded, "Why, no, neither the president nor the cabinet has taken any action on visas for mission personnel."

Just that quickly the elusive diagnosis was finally made — the diagnosis I had been working on for nearly two years — the diagnosis the US ambassador had not been able to make! That statement made it clear at once that the visa pressures originated from the secretary of the Home Department, not the cabinet or president, and that the president had overridden that lower decision. This new information might be used to help other mission groups.

That next day was locked forever in my memory. In the morning I picked up the document stating that all our requests had been approved at the very highest level. Later I went to the immigration office. The officials were very respectful! Listening to their Bengali conversation, I learned they were about to stamp two-year multiple-entry visas into the Olsens' and Gurganuses' passports. Now speaking from a position of strength I tackled them on this, pointing out that our approvals were for four-year multiple-entry visas. After another whispered conversation and a whispered telephone call, they stamped into our passports four-year multiple-entry visas!

Then I reported the week's happenings to the American consul-general. Flabbergasted, he found a stub of pencil in his drawer and began to write furiously on a piece of scrap paper the incredible information I was telling him. After two years of steady deterioration, the whole depressing visa situation had changed overnight for us. I mentioned the importance of knowing that the visa problems were not related to a presidential or cabinet decision. Knowing this, the American ambassador could now safely approach the highest level for relief to be given all Americans facing visa problems. (Several months later the American ambassador did just that!)

As I flew back to Chittagong, with the precious visas and letter in my pocket, I remembered Joan's words regarding our unexpected breakfast with the president of Pakistan. In response to my question, "I wonder why God arranged that?" she had replied, "The day will come when we will know for certain." Now that day had come — and it was a great day!

Our guidance factor in solving the visa crisis had been truly phenomenal. I thought of Nehemiah, the ancient who traveled to a distant land to build for God; he, too, "prayed to the God of heaven and spoke to the king." Just as in his case, "the king granted me, according to the good hand of my God upon me." And King Solomon surely knew what he was talking about when he avowed, "The king's heart is in the hand of the Lord, like the rivers of water: He turns it however He wills."

The Gurganuses were ecstatic when I handed them their visas upon arrival in Chittagong for they, also, were poised for furlough. Joan, too, was overjoyed. We completed our packing in two days, with a huge assist from our colleagues, and headed out for furlough in America. As we passed through Chittagong I turned over to the printer the completed manuscript for my Muslim Bengali-to-English dictionary. Our first five-year hitch was history — as for our Commander, there had "not failed one word of all his good promise!"

15

Furlough and Firstfruits

I KNEW if I got up my elbow would begin searing again. But I got up anyway and walked slowly to the window to check my guards. Patrolling the brightly lit roads in our housing area, they looked quite impressive with the shotguns on their shoulders. I wondered how many *dacoits* (armed bandits) were watching them from the dark shadows of the jungle. Sitting down again, gently easing myself into a chair, I thought about furlough. It was time then for our second furlough to begin; but now everything about that furlough was in doubt. No use making any plans now. If the war ended and we survived its challenges, then I could think seriously about that second furlough.

Our first furlough had been hectic. The kids found it exciting to get back to the land of malted milks and hot dogs. To their parents it seemed like the whirlwind year vanished after a few days of greetings, meetings, and pack-it-all-up-again. In East Pakistan, during that year of our first furlough, the team accomplished much. They racked up many new firsts, including some fine new believers. And the drama of a man named Daniel defied the imagination.

*   *   *

Wheaton, Illinois, located exactly on the opposite side of the world from East Pakistan, was to be our 1966-67 furlough home. En route, we stopped first at Bangkok, Thailand. The modern streets and highways there were a far cry from those in East Pakistan. When the airport taxi hurtled along at fifty-five miles an hour, it felt to us like a blastoff into outer space.

Next stop, Hong Kong! We enjoyed a pleasant time with all our Hong Kong colleagues and made some necessary purchases in that free port city. Through an interpreter, I preached to a Chinese congregation in a rooftop church held atop a massive, six-floor apartment building. East Pakistan was never like this!

Flying on to Los Angeles, we were deeply moved to see the first lights of mainland America, the land we had left five years before to carry out our assignment across the seas. There to meet us in Los Angeles were the Paul Goodman family and the Tom McDonalds. Oh, the joyous reunion!

Driving through Los Angeles the kids noticed a brilliant, flashing sign: "Topless! Pizza!" They asked, in bewilderment, "What good is topless pizza, Dad?" Staying with the Goodmans in their lovely home over several days, we shared all our East Pakistan news.

The next stop was a very special one — my parents' home in Big Lake, Missouri. To shake hands with my big, generous Dad and hug my slight, weeping Mom again, taught me in one minute what furloughs are for. My brother Jim and his wife Beverly were also a delightful part of that reunion. Our several days together flashed by like lightning, for there was so much to talk about — and so many old times to remember. Reluctantly, we departed on the last lap of our long journey.

Waiting at Chicago's O'Hare Field were Joan's wonderful parents, Donna Ahlgrim, and four people whose names were included in the visa package from President Ayub: Jesse and Joyce Eaton and school teachers Florence Theaker and Marilyn Malmstrom (whose first visa application had been denied). What a thrill it was to hug Dad and Mom Baur again and to see our colleagues, most of whom would soon depart for East Pakistan!

We drove on to Wheaton, a farwestern suburb of Chicago and home of noted Wheaton College. Our rented house, ready and waiting, was a pleasant, roomy, rambling house, just right for our family, with room for our parents and other friends to visit us.

We arrived in Wheaton the day before school began. The children attended the fine Wheaton Christian Grammar School where the teachers are experienced at absorbing children from overseas settings. All four of the children, accustomed to small classes, had to learn how to hear instructions given to a larger group.

Although we had never before lived near Chicago, we selected that area, central to our supporting churches, as the logical place to locate; even there my travel would have to be very efficiently organized to allow me much time at home with my family.

Soon after our arrival, a local car dealer, a great missionary lover, gave us the best deal of the year on a fine car for my long travels. Joan's brother Jack arranged for her a second car so she could get about town in my absence. Our neighbors helped us greatly to feel at home in Wheaton.

One day, as Joan and I walked along a downtown Wheaton street, pain suddenly exploded in her right eye. With her hands shielding her eyes, I led Joan like a blind person back to the car, then home. Careful examination produced a diagnosis: "iritis — cause unknown." Despite treatment the pain and discomfort continued on and on, month after month. Joan wore sunglasses indoors and out. Our home must have looked like the local haunted house — she always had the shades down to keep out the pain-igniting light.

A well-known and substantial mission board, with offices in Wheaton, faced severe problems in some of its overseas medical missions. Called in as a consultant, I shared with them the thirteen basic principles upon which we had established our medical mission to East Pakistan. Finally, I related the many benefits which had accrued from each of these principles. Later, I learned the meeting was very worthwhile, for important decisions were made which, they felt, greatly improved the agency's medical missions program.

October wedding bells climaxed a lovely story involving Donna Ahlgrim, the co-worker who attended with us the 1959 ABWE candidate classes. New York pastor Willard Benedict, after the death of his wife, was greatly moved by Harry Goehring's death, and determined to take Harry's place working with tribal people in East Pakistan. Willard knew Donna, who also possessed an affinity for Hebron station and the tribal people. Acquaintance became love, and love became a beautiful wedding, with Joan participating as an attendant. One of the visas approved in the president's visa package was that of Willard Benedict.

Thanksgiving was a special delight with my mother and father visiting us in Wheaton. Dad and I took Joan shopping at the supermarket. As he and I rounded a corner, we found her standing behind a stack of cans, tears coursing down her cheeks.

"What's the matter, honey?" I asked.

"Oh, there's so much!" she sobbed. She was remembering our last Thanksgiving in East Pakistan. Because our few remaining food supplies were shipped to Malumghat during the war, it had been very difficult to scrape together something remotely resembling a Thanksgiving dinner. Now, surrounded by every possible frill for a feast, suddenly it was just too much. With Mom and Dad in Wheaton, our scrumptious Thanksgiving feast was a triple treat.

Dad and Mom Baur visited us for several wonderful weeks becoming reacquainted with their grandchildren and reviewing with us the happenings of the previous five years. Many other guests came, including Jeanette Lockerbie. We talked late one night about her suggestion that a book should someday be written covering God's work in our lives and in southern East Pakistan! Someday, perhaps, but not then — we had no time.

My main responsibility during the furlough year involved returning to our supporting churches and individuals to express personally our great appreciation for their interest and generosity. Coupled with that expression I presented what had been accomplished during our first term of service. The presentations involved preaching, lecturing, or showing colored slides.

At first I was fearful that I might stumble over my English tongue, for I usually preached in Bengali in East Pakistan. After one or two addresses, however, that concern receded into the background. Meeting and sharing with hundreds of old friends and acquaintances I found delightful. In doing so I traveled tens of thousands of miles, crisscrossing America from east to west, south to north, and on into Canada. In addition to our supporters, I reached new churches and several colleges and answered calls to appear on talk shows and inspirational radio and television broadcasts. My schedule made it necessary to be away from home many weeks during our furlough year. Sometimes I spoke as many as thirty times in a two-week period. Because God had done much for us in our first term of service, the meetings were well attended and, over the months, many responded to the invitations at the close of the services. "Thank You, Father," was our frequent prayer.

Simultaneously with our furlough, the mission team was piling up numerous firsts in East Pakistan. Donn Ketcham did an admirable job of guiding the organization and development of the hospital that year. He performed the first emergency and elective surgical opera-

Dr. Ketcham removing   "Miss Becky" instructing Bengali nurses
a leg to save a life

tions. The first hospital beds arrived and the first Bengali nurses were hired. The first newspaper article, full of false allegations, appeared against the hospital and its work. The article charged that our doctors forced Muslims to convert to Christianity, compelling them to stand with their feet on the Holy Koran! I learned later that the instigators of such crude slander were Akand and his friends.

Other phases of our mission's work also recorded firsts. The first full family group followed Christ in baptism in Chittagong. Lynn Silvernale and Mrs. Dass completed the first draft of their translation of John's gospel for printing and distribution to key checkers throughout the country. Ralph Ankenman ramrodded the first camping program for Bengali young people. I smiled to myself, remembering his report given in typical Ankenmanese: "Four score and twenty days ago, our field council brought forth upon this field a new notion, conceived in a hurry and dedicated to the preposterous proposition that something could get done around here on time. For five days in January there was a general set-to testing whether any missionaries dedicated to such a cause so conceived could long endure. That battleground was called camp and we are glad to report victory."

Jay Walsh followed up carefully on the president's visa package until all the precious visas were in hand. Nine new hands arrived during the year on the strength of those visas. Four were people I had contacted several years earlier, before going overseas: pastor Jesse and Joyce Eaton, physiotherapy technician Larry Golin (with wife Jane), and Millie Cooley, an experienced operating room nurse from Detroit. The other new arrivals were Willard Benedict (with Donna Ahlgrim Benedict) and three capable, dedicated primary school teachers, Marilyn Malmstrom, Florence Theaker, and Shirley Harkness.

While we were in America on furlough, the first man in the Malamghat area who had decided to follow Christ saw plenty of action. During the construction phase of the hospital, this Muslim workman had approached Tom McDonald's Buddhist cook about reading the cook's Christian Bible. When the cook refused to lend it to him, the workman stole the Bible and pored over it for many hours. Deeply moved by the beauty of its words, he ultimately came to believe that Christ was all He claimed to be. No Bengali or American Christian had talked with him about spiritual matters.

One day, on the roof of an unfinished house, overwhelmed by his new knowledge, he accepted Christ into his life. His act of faith was accompanied by a visionary, mystical experience which rendered him semiconscious. Tom reported this unique development to Jay Walsh who put a Bible in the hands of the new believer and gave him much valuable teaching. The man, who took upon himself the name Daniel, studied his Bible avidly and spoke openly in the Muslim community about his new faith in Christ. Although the sophisticated authorities accept such changes of religious viewpoint quite calmly, villagers and village priests sometimes react violently.

One night local men broke into Daniel's house, stole his Bible, and presented it to a petty local official named Thanda Mia ("Mr. Cold"). The official, who knew little or nothing about Pakistan's constitutional provisions, questioned Daniel, indicted him for wrongdoing, and handed him over to local men who savagely beat him into unconsciousness. Our enemy Akand, again in the area, had harangued these men to provoke the beating. Exiled to an island, Kutubdia, Daniel had not been seen in our area for nearly a year.

A few weeks after our departure for furlough, Daniel one day reappeared at the hospital. When he learned of the tribal Short-Term Bible School in progress at Malumghat he asked if he could join the group. His unusual request was indicative of a loving, humble spirit. Most local Bengalis would not deign to sit for instruction with Tipperas whom they sometimes disparagingly called "monkeys." Daniel not only sat with Tipperas, but day after day he studied with them, ate, and slept with them. At this point Donn Ketcham's parents, Dr. and Mrs. Robert T. Ketcham and their friend, Miss Ruth Ryburn, visited Donn and Kitty in East Pakistan.

Dr. Bob Ketcham, a beloved and gifted minister, gave three messages on the Twenty-third Psalm to the students, with Jay Walsh and Ancharai interpreting. Just before one of these sessions, men came, called Daniel outdoors, and threatened him, viciously demanding that he drop his profession of Christian faith. Included in their intimidation package was the threat that his wife would be taken from him and exiled to Kutubdia Island.

Frightened but firm, Daniel spoke: "I cannot change what I truly believe with my heart." Still breathing out threats, the men left.

Daniel returned trembling to the schoolroom to hear, as he walked through the door, Donn's father expounding on "I will fear no evil." Knowing nothing of Daniel's problem, Dr. Bob Ketcham taught, "When the sheep hears the growl of the bear, he need only look up and be sure his shepherd is there; then he can put his nose back in the grass, secure that the shepherd will dispatch the bear. In the same way, if evil men attack you, be sure you are very near the Lord who is your Shepherd; then put your nose back into the Word of God and let the Great Shepherd deal with the evil men attacking you!" Dr. Bob did not understand until later why those words launched a freshet of tears down Daniel's dark cheeks.

A few days later Daniel providentially avoided an ambush designed to capture and kill him in the forest. A day or two later the violent group of men came to our hospital property twice where Donn confronted them and sent them away. Later, at a time when the mission personnel were in field council meetings at the housing property a half mile away, that group of fifteen to twenty men returned by truck, armed with clubs (and their petty official). Angrily they called Daniel out of the Bible school session to intimidate him with harsh questions. As Daniel saw the angry men surging around him, he feared his end was near; not a single American was present to intervene for him.

Mr. Cold shouted, "You say you are a Christian! But that cannot be! In Pakistan you are not allowed to change from Islam to Christianity. That is the law in Pakistan. You cannot change!"

At that precise instant, every eye was drawn to the strange figure of a man, his white garments flapping in the breeze, pulling up on his bicycle.

The stranger, having heard the petty official's vehement words, declared sternly, "Your statement is quite incorrect! Pakistan law provides for full freedom of religion. This man may believe anything he wishes to. I advise you to trouble him no further!" His message delivered, the white-garbed stranger fluttered off on his cycle never to be seen again.

Mr. Cold, now less certain of himself, asked Daniel to bring his Bible from the schoolroom. At the official's demand, Daniel opened the big black Bengali Bible to read a passage. Stopping him, the official threatened harshly to take him off in the truck that instant to kill him unless he threw the Bible down.

With the Bible clutched firmly to his chest, Daniel responded steadfastly, "Taking my Bible, I am ready to give my life." That type of courage coupled with the words of the white-clad stranger were too much for the murderous group. Fearing that some divine visitation had come their way, they suddenly ceased the harrassment and, one by one, departed — leaving Daniel standing tall and straight, Bible clutched to his heart, weeping noiselessly at his deliverance. Back in America, as I read of Daniel's experience I did not dream that one day in the future I would stand with Daniel in the midst of another murderous mob.

On the American front, the summer months were a mad melee of final visits to supporting churches, purchasing and packing for our second term of service overseas.

In June Wendy graduated from grade school and traveled with another family to her boarding high school in Murree, West Pakistan (in the mountains thirty miles north of Rawalpindi). Despite the busful of school friends who came to see her off, the parting and the step into the unknown were scary. We promised to be there by September 1 to be together a month before going on to East Pakistan.

I flew with Joan to the west coast where a San Francisco super-specialist in iritis problems unraveled the cause of her eye disturbance. Her eyes had been invaded by the *herpes* virus (cause of the common cold sore), an organism which likes to remain indefinitely in the eye once it gains a foothold there. By departure time the virus had become quiescent and her pain subsided.

How do you purchase Christmas and birthday presents for your children four years in advance? Joan possessed an uncanny ability to sense what each of ours would like year by year in their life overseas. Also we packed some useful, nutritious foodstuffs (unavailable in East Pakistan) in the fifty-five-gallon steel drums. Dried goods easily damaged by the tropical climate we sealed into tin cans. Many church friends and neighbors helped us complete the mammoth job of packing personal effects and hospital items. Exhausted, we spent the last few days with our loved ones, then flew to the East coast. Keeping our promise to Wendy, we arrived in Murree on September 1. What a happy reunion!

At Murree, we collapsed for a month to recover from the hectic

Nancy in Murree

Memorial Christian Hospital

year of furlough. We slept, hiked, organized parties for the children, played games, and caught up on a backlog of correspondence. The children took riding lessons, becoming quite proficient in horsemanship. I treasured the opportunity given me to address the student body and counsel with students making spiritual decisions. In early October, we bade Wendy good-by and flew on to East Pakistan.

Our excitement mounted when we began the last lap of our trip from Chittagong to the hospital. Because the monsoon rains had turned the Matamuhari River into a raging monster, the road had been breached and we were forced to cross by ferry. Our wonderful welcome by Bengali and American brothers and sisters made us know we were home. Settling in our house, we hired our "ecumenical team" of household helpers: a Buddhist cook, a Christian washerman, and a Muslim part-time sweeper-gardener.

The hospital looked beautiful to me! During the year of our absence the medical group, led by Donn, had put in the beds, furnishings, and cabinetry. They had moreover established a smooth running system of operation. Jay Walsh was completing construction of a *pukka* four-plex (Pickitt Hall) to house four nurses' families. A number of fine Bengali nurses, some of them husband-and-wife teams (both nurses), had been hired.

I found that our long hours of mind-bending work designing the hospital were now paying off in efficiency. We had based our hospital design around several key ideas:

1. Suitable accommodations for patients of all classes. (Hospital wards and outpatient facilities for the poor, and private or semi-private hospital rooms plus private examining rooms for the affluent.)
2. One nursing station centrally located between the two wards, the private wing, and the recovery room and intensive care unit. (This center system facilitates efficient nursing care of the patients.)
3. A clean inner corridor system in the surgical-obstetrical wing. (This helps keep wound infections to the minimum.)
4. A central supply and sterilizing section. (This unit receives, records, cleans or sterilizes, stores and issues all equipment and supplies.)
5. A laboratory, X-ray, and pharmacy wing convenient to inpatients and outpatients. (These essential facilities are used by both groups of patients.)

Soon after arrival I enjoyed a long chat with Daniel. A simple man, he had gained a remarkable knowledge of the Scriptures from

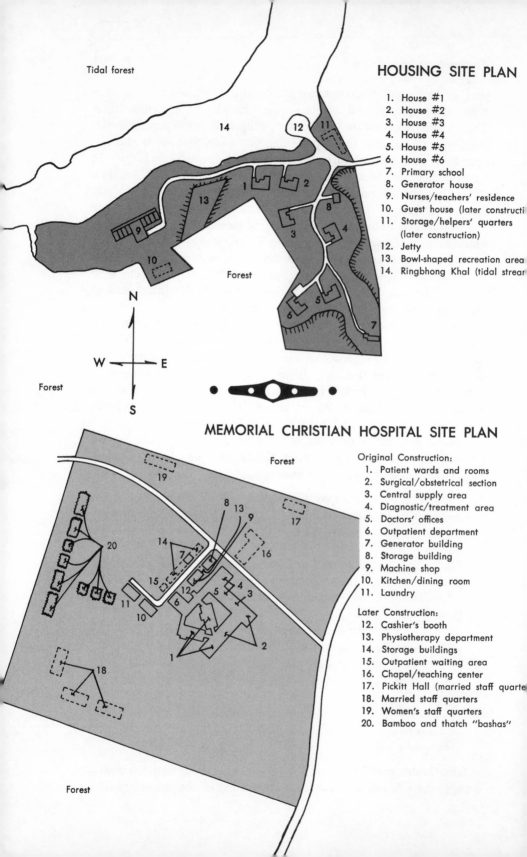

HOUSING SITE PLAN

1. House #1
2. House #2
3. House #3
4. House #4
5. House #5
6. House #6
7. Primary school
8. Generator house
9. Nurses/teachers' residence
10. Guest house (later constructi
11. Storage/helpers' quarters
    (later construction)
12. Jetty
13. Bowl-shaped recreation area
14. Ringbhong Khal (tidal strear

Tidal forest

Forest

Forest

N
W — E
S

MEMORIAL CHRISTIAN HOSPITAL SITE PLAN

Forest

Original Construction:
1. Patient wards and rooms
2. Surgical/obstetrical section
3. Central supply area
4. Diagnostic/treatment area
5. Doctors' offices
6. Outpatient department
7. Generator building
8. Storage building
9. Machine shop
10. Kitchen/dining room
11. Laundry

Later Construction:
12. Cashier's booth
13. Physiotherapy department
14. Storage buildings
15. Outpatient waiting area
16. Chapel/teaching center
17. Pickitt Hall (married staff quarte
18. Married staff quarters
19. Women's staff quarters
20. Bamboo and thatch "bashas"

Forest

his personal study and from Jay
Walsh and others who had taken
time to teach him. How I appreciated his courage and radiant faith!
In recent months, despite rumblings
in the background, he had succeeded
in living in the village with his wife.
A great accomplishment!

Daniel

I found it exciting to be at work again in Memorial Christian
Hospital. I was seeing virtually all the illnesses common to America
plus a number of tropical and otherwise exotic diseases. Malaria,
smallpox, kala-azar (black fever), and tuberculosis were prevalent.
Due to poor sanitation and impure water supplies, typhoid fever,
cholera, bacillary dysentery, amoebic dysentery, hookworm, roundworm, whipworm, and virus hepatitis were common. Other infections, such as pyelonephritis, osteomyelitis, infected wounds, and
tetanus (lockjaw) were fostered by the hot, humid climate which
made East Pakistan a giant incubator for germs. Vitamin deficiency
states, kwashiorkor, and malnutrition plagued many among the populace. We often admitted female patients with complications of child-
birth (hemorrhage, obstructed labor, ruptured uterus, vesico-vaginal
fistula, toxemia, eclampsia, etc.).

Our surgical schedule frequently listed inguinal hernia, hydrocele,
rectal fistula, tumor, bowel obstruction, cleft lip or cleft palate, skin
graft, fracture, osteomyelitis, abscess, etc. The incidence of duodenal
ulcer was amazingly high and, in many cases, only surgery could relieve the sufferer. Often the fact that the patient came late, or after
the application of village treatments, greatly complicated the cases.

Because I had done very little surgery over the last several years,
I felt on edge my first days back in the operating room. Soon, however, my surgical skills returned, making me feel very much at home
again operating. Shortly after our return from America, I examined
a teenage Buddhist boy complaining of nosebleeds. I found a tumor
invading his nasal passages, a kind of tumor dangerous to remove
because of its tendency to bleed fiercely. With the family's coopera-
tion, I obtained four units of blood and scheduled the surgery. We
used every last drop of that blood! The operation was so gory that
one nurse nearly fainted and had to leave the operation. But the
dangerous tumor was successfully excised. When I removed the
nasal packs a week later, unexpectedly the blood again began gush-
ing. Before we got the bleeding stopped, the boy nearly lost his life.
Finally, however, he recovered completely and, with his father, made
a decision to follow Christ. He came very close to death to find life!

Another patient, a Hindu cancer victim, gained eternal life that last month of 1967 — then went on to glory a few weeks later. How satisfying it is to treat the whole man.

In December we held a baptismal service, the first in that area in the history of the world. Eleven, including Daniel, followed in baptism their Lord's example and command — they were the firstfruits! From people such as these the church would be formed in the southernmost regions of East Pakistan.

We finished up the year with a spiritual ministry to a group of fellow missionaries. I had accepted the invitation of another large mission to be their conference speaker. Sharing with them, I illustrated selected passages from the Scriptures with our experiences of seeing God in action. God also spoke to us in those days and some, including teenagers, made important life decisions. I stepped into the new year with a settled and happy conviction: "It's great to be a Christian, and be able to know and carry out God's personal plan!"

16

Epidemics and Effects

Because of our Bangladesh predicament, I had no trouble remembering the predicament which plagued us in 1968. Three epidemics involved us that year! While two of them attacked only the Bengali community, the third particularly played havoc with the Americans. Most of the effects were dismal because disability and death are never pleasant. The last epidemic, however, affected us in unexpected and surprising ways.

The picture of a furiously burning bamboo house appeared suddenly on my mental screen — no doubt a smallpox victim's basha burned because there was no other way to destroy the germ. Or perhaps it was one of the thousands of houses recently burned by the advancing, rampaging West Pakistan army. Or was it the fire that shocked us at the beginning of 1968?

* * *

"Ahgoon! Ahgoon! Hoshpatalay ahgoon!" the watchman shouted as we met together early in 1968 at one of our homes on the housing site. When we heard his cry of "Fire! Fire! Fire at the hospital!" our hearts sank. We raced out of the house to hear the crackling fire a half mile away and to see flames shooting high into the black sky. Were patients trapped and dying? Was it possible that so much work and prayer could be going up in flames? Leaping into Land Rovers, we raced toward the hospital dreading what we might see. Then — what relief! The hospital and its patients were safe. One hundred yards away, a group of bamboo shops were burning furiously to the ground. In an effort to do away with one of the shopkeepers, an enemy had locked him in his shop and ignited its tinder dry roof. The shopkeeper battered his way out of the burning prison, took one look at his flaming inventory, and collapsed in a dead faint at my feet. For him the new year had started badly.

Many others also found the new year distressing, for we were in the grip of a cholera epidemic! Hundreds in our area were contracting the dread disease capable of destroying one's life within

205

Canvas-covered cholera ward

hours. Several weeks earlier, when the epidemic first struck, we analyzed what we would need to handle the serious problem: extra doctors, extra nurses, ambulances, ambulance drivers, special cholera beds, more ward space, hundreds of gallons of intravenous fluids, medicines, and money. Lacking most of these assets, we contacted an excellent organization in Dacca, the American-financed Pakistan-SEATO Cholera Research Laboratory. The perfect timing of our request solved a serious problem they were facing. Dacca was fresh out of cholera that quarter making it impossible to carry out their important research projects. Responding magnificently, they sent all the men and materials we lacked to tackle our cholera epidemic. They had as many as forty American and Bengali doctors, nurses, and other personnel with us at a time.

Cholera, different from ordinary diarrhea, results in the painless passage of pints of pale fluid. The loss of vital body fluids and salts in the copious cholera stools produces shock, then death. The secret of treatment is giving huge quantities of intravenous fluids sufficient to balance the loss, along with antibiotics to kill the cholera germ.

We cleared one of our wards for use by the cholera team. When their ambulances began to ply the highway, overnight the ward was filled by dangerously ill cholera patients with cold clammy skin, sunken eyes, and dropping (or dropped) blood pressures. Over each patient hung a bottle of rapidly dripping intravenous fluids. A plastic collection pail sat under each special cholera bed with its plastic funnel leading into the pail. Within two or three days most patients were cured and returned home to convalesce and gain strength. When the patient census exceeded the ward space, a huge tent was erected to receive the overflow.

"Please give us a consultation on the patient in tent bed nine, will you, Vic? She doesn't act like ordinary cholera and she's sinking fast." I found the young mother feverish, gasping, terminal! I was sure something besides cholera was causing her distended abdomen. Obtaining fluid from her abdomen by needle, we examined it under the microscope. The unusual parasite we identified drove me to the books where I learned it normally inhabited the farthest reaches of the small intestine.

That's it! I've got it! I exulted to myself. Something had perforated her small intestine, and the one disease famous for perforating that particular segment of the intestine was typhoid fever. If only she had come sooner! She was so far gone that the operation she so badly needed would only hasten her death. Although I expected her to die within the hour, I ordered massive doses of antityphoid medicine. She held her own throughout the day. Surprisingly, the next morning she was a bit improved.

"It's now or never," I told my team. "Take her to the operating room." When I opened that tense abdomen, fluid erupted eighteen inches into the air like an artesian spring. One look at that infected lower abdomen, with every surgical landmark obliterated, forced me to pray, "Father, this perforation will be terribly difficult to find and this lady can't tolerate many minutes of surgery. Please help me to find it quickly." After sixty seconds of dissection I found a beautiful long roundworm wiggling through the perforation, marking it perfectly! "Thank You, Father!" Remarkably, the woman survived.

As the month of January ran out, so did the cholera epidemic. Of the five hundred cholera patients who had received treatment at Memorial Christian Hospital, only two had died of cholera! Over three tons of intravenous fluids were dripped into them. Several highly important research projects were also completed during the epidemic, of which one has quite revolutionized the treatment of cholera patients around the world. We treasured our new friendships with various of the Dacca doctors and, in response to their interest, shared our faith with them. The people of the countryside were deeply grateful to us for the treatment provided them at the hospital.

As the cholera epidemic wound down around Malumghat, a smallpox epidemic exploded in Chittagong city. Before the government vaccination program became effective, every section of the city heard the wails and chants of survivors burying hundreds of smallpox victims. The Ketchams' laundryman had taken a bride in Chittagong the month before. The expensive wedding, with all the trimmings, had put him in debt for years to come. Called from Malumghat to the side of his bride of a month, in anguish he watched her die from smallpox. East Pakistan, land of sorrows!

Political disturbance of eipidemic proportions also infected East Pakistan early in 1968. Sheikh Mujibur Rahman, released by the police after eighteen months of imprisonment, walked out of jail into the arms of waiting Pakistan soldiers who ordered him into a jeep. Fearing the worst, Mujib bent down, picked up dust from the road, rubbed it on his forehead, and prayed, "Oh, Allah, I was born in this soil. Allow me to die here."[1]

Taken by the soldiers to the Dacca military cantonment, he languished for five months in solitary confinement without books, newspapers, or visitors. He, along with thirty-four others, was charged with conspiring with Indian citizens to foment an armed revolt aimed at leading East Pakistan into independence from Pakistan.

In February, two of the thirty-four were shot in jail, one fatally; the authorities explained the two men had tried to escape. When the public rioted, concerned for Mujib's safety, the police put them down. At Rajshahi University, in the north, police fired on a procession protesting Sheikh Mujib's imprisonment, killing a favorite chemistry teacher, Dr. Zoha. This news exploded further demonstrations throughout East Pakistan. When the army was called out to help the police quell the disturbances, more crowds were fired on in Dacca, Noakhali, and Kushtia. Thousands demanded that Sheikh Mujib be released.

At Malumghat two new developments early in the new year gave us a sense of accomplishment. First, our Malumghat Christian School (for MKs) opened for business. Until then, the women had taught our children at home using correspondence courses. The opening of the school operated by trained teachers represented an important step forward. Then, the government authorities kindly established a post office in our hospital naming it "P.O. Malumghat Hospital." One of our own Bengali men became the postmaster, thus improving the security of our mail service.

One cool night, in a village twelve miles from the hospital, a householder sent his six-year-old daughter to the bamboo barn to bring some straw for the fire. As she gathered the straw, one of the huge buffalos, annoyed, hooked and impaled the child with a toss of its mighty horn. Unloading her from the boat at Malumghat, they carried the injured girl to our front door. Her ripped abdomen spelled immediate surgery! But we were out of oxygen for anesthesia, and would remain so until Donn returned from Chittagong; the timing of his return was in doubt.

Just as Jesse and I arrived at the hospital with the patient, Donn pulled in from town! "Thank You, Father!" After removing a foot or two of badly damaged intestine, I sewed together the two good ends and treated the little one with powerful antibiotics. Happily, seven days later, the family took her back to their village home healthy and well again.

In quick succession, new pets were added to the scenery. When the Walshes were given a baby monkey, Linda Walsh and Lynne Olsen became its mothers. Promptly dubbed "Linus" (because she sucked her big toe) the little monkey entertained everyone royally. When the children trooped off to school, Linus raced along not far behind. Loving attention, she perched on the schoolroom windowsill clowning incessantly. Joan's amusement changed to indignation, however, when the monkey learned how to swing, with filthy hands, up and down the lines of freshly washed clothes.

One morning I spoke at staff devotions, a brief chapel service with which we begin each day's work. To make my talk meaningful, I mentioned that we have no trouble distinguishing between mango, papaya, and jackfruit trees because we know each one by the fruit it bears.

"We too are trees," I taught, "and people know what we are by the fruit that we bear. We are not only trees, but also we are radios; we are broadcasting, sending out messages, all the time which tell others what we are." Afterwards, Debendra, a tiny washerman not quite five feet tall and one of the world's finest Christians, came up to me with a twinkle in his eye. Stuttering as usual (because of his severe speech impediment) he agreed that he might be a tree, but he

Nurse Millie Cooley with teachers Shirley Harkness, Florence Theaker, and Marilyn Malmstrom in saris

Lynne with Linus

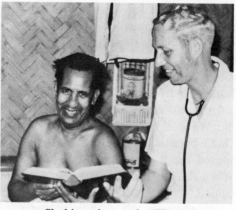

Shuki, at last truly "Happy"

Debendra — maybe a tree but not a radio

was sure he wasn't a very good radio! Despite his stuttering problems, Debendra had become an excellent witness for Christ as the case of Shuki clearly revealed.

Shuki, ("Happy") born into the Hindu community with a chip on his shoulder fifty years earlier, did not match his name. He had been the Walshes' cook when we first arrived in Chittagong, the one who had nearly resigned when he mistook Nancy's mosquito bites for smallpox. Finally, Shuki did leave the employ of our group. Years later, he broke his hip falling from a bus, but it had never been treated. The broken bone had healed in a deformed position. Donn hoped to help Shuki through a complicated operation. Knowing that Shuki's knowledge of Christ and Christianity was marginal, I visited him before his operation. To make it simple, I selected one scripture verse (John 3:16) from a pamphlet he was reading, discussed it with him, and prayed with him in preparation for his surgery.

Unknown to me, a little earlier washerman Debendra had come also to talk to Shuki about Jesus. He gave him a stammering but warm explanation of exactly the same passage (John 3:16) and encouraged him about his operation. A few minutes later Shuki's old employer, Jay Walsh, stepped into his room. Shuki must have been mystified when Jay began to discuss with him John 3:16. By then Shuki had very little resistance or antireligious bias left. When Jay talked to him about believing, there in his hospital room Shuki made the great faith decision. I have never known any new believer who had a more sudden or more marked change of attitude and personality. From a negative, sour character, he became a joyous, radiant Christian; at last he truly matched his name — Happy!

Burns from open fires were common in the cool season. A five-year-old boy came with the skin burned off his face, frontal scalp, and right upper arm. Although his eyes peered hideously from raw, red flesh, his "granny" refused the necessary skin graft treatment — until I showed her two successful graft cases on the ward. After a week of treatment, I took many strips of skin from his thighs and completely resurfaced the child's face, scalp, and upper arm. In one strip I cut holes to fit exactly around the eyes.

During the days before the burned child came to us, infection had entered his system and plagued him throughout his postoperative days. Although his grafts were taking, his thin little body steadily deteriorated. His breathing became shallow and labored, and at last he lapsed into semiconsciousness. As I walked into his room one morning he wheezed, gasped, and stopped breathing. In a second I had my stethoscope over his heart. But there was nothing to hear, for his little heart had ceased beating. He was gone. Impelled by a surgeon's reflexes, I picked up the limp little body and raced toward the operating room, nearly a block away. Then, in a moment, I was breathing pure oxygen into his lungs and rhythmically compressing his skinny chest over his heart. After a long, long time the tired little heart began faintly and fitfully beating again. After another twenty minutes it beat more regularly. After another half hour, he took an occasional gasping breath. After many more minutes his breathing became more regular. Finally, I returned him to his room barely living. I never expected him to survive but, somehow, bit by bit, his breathing and heartbeat strengthened, and he became more alert. After many days of "little-by-little" convalescence, he finally returned home, a shadow of his former self.

Because of an invitation to hold a spiritual life conference at Murree Christian School in West Pakistan, I accompanied Wendy and Lydia Gurganus back across India by air to the school. In the science classes I spoke throughout the week on Christian evidences. Biblical-inspirational subjects captured our attention during the evening meetings. Other hours I rapped and counseled with dozens of students. Day by day, as our meetings and discussions progressed, God's spirit began influencing and directing many. By the end of the week several dozen had responded to God's work in their lives by accepting Christ or dedicating their lives to Him. Some gave themselves for fulltime Christian service. My own heart was thrilled and refreshed to see God work deeply in many young lives.

Within a month of my return to Malumghat, two Mogh men came to inquire about the Christian faith. One had heard something about Christ from a Christian in Burma ten years earlier. He came to us to fulfill his desire of ten years to learn more of that person named Jesus. The men listened intently, asked questions, and took literature with them when they departed. Our later contacts with these two men were of the highest interest.

On Easter Sunday morning I preached in the Bengali service on the glorious resurrection of Christ. In the English service I began using a machine called an overhead projector. A beautifully designed instrument, it allows the speaker to project transparencies on a screen day or night or write his outline as he speaks. I have used it ever since in Bengali and English meetings with increasing appreciation. The Bengalis always are fascinated by the projector.

Pastor and Mrs. Kuhnle from Milwaukee visited us for several days. We greatly enjoyed receiving them and introducing them to many friends including Fazlul Karim Choudhury, Mr. Salam (a noted businessman of Chittagong), and the Ahmeds in Dacca. Pastor Kuhnle's messages and Mrs. Kuhnle's vocal solos pleased and blessed us all.

Prior to their arrival Lynne went down with hepatitis. The day of the Kuhnles' arrival Joan and Jeannie Lockerbie went to bed with the same illness. Millie Cooley had been seriously ill with hepatitis for several months.

Hepatitis is an inflammation of the liver usually caused by a very hardy virus resistant to disinfectants and filtering. Only boiling for many minutes kills it. Of all the illnesses affecting Americans overseas around the world, hepatitis is the most common and pesky. Only rarely fatal, it always causes weeks or months of disability. I thought it strange that none of our three patients developed jaundice (yellowness) as would be expected with a substantial case of hepatitis. Only later did I discover the curious explanation for that discrepancy.

Because our hospital was located in an area where no Christians lived, some of the hired employees were Muslims, Hindus, and Buddhists. I offered to hold a Bible class for the educated non-Christian boys, which became known as the "non-Christian Bible class." Our studies together in the gospel of John provoked many lively, interesting discussions. My knowledge of their religious background and thinking was deepened as they learned about Christ the Lord. Within weeks, a Hindu young man, Kagendro, believed and began to follow Christ. Despite family and village pressures he remained solid as a rock.

A disturbing illness, resistant to treatment, struck Joyce Eaton. When the decision was made that she must return to America, the mission and church again gathered together for a special day of

"Bob Adolph's excellent labora-   Short-termer Helen Carr
tory"

prayer and fasting. As before, the day of faith was a very deep,
heart-reaching, and unifying experience for us all, Bengalis and
Americans alike. God heard our prayers and brought Joyce through
the crisis allowing the evacuation to be canceled. "Thank You, Father."

Bob Adolph's excellent laboratory, perhaps the best in East Pakistan, greatly helped Donn and me as we cared for Joyce Eaton, the
hepatitis patients, and many other complicated cases which came to
us daily. Although some of Bob's medical technician trainees were
becoming increasingly proficient, we urgently needed an experienced
American technologist to take Bob's place during the Adolphs' furlough. Helen Carr, an attractive, cooperative, capable technologist
from Michigan, arrived in June in response to our need and God's
direction. We were delighted.

Surgery was tough during those days! As our electrical generators
were almost constantly out of order, we were forced to operate using
daylight augmented by miners' headlamps. And, since our water
pumps could not operate without electricity, a severe water shortage
also resulted. All water had to be carried by hand. We looked forward with eager anticipation to the day when utility electricity would
come our way.

The children kept thinking up new imaginative ways to keep
Lynne happy. Now out of quarantine, she was still restricted to the
house. They organized a huge play wedding with many children
taking part, and allowed Lynne to be the minister. Each participant
was elaborately dressed for the wedding ceremony. Joan and Kitty
Ketcham, as invited guests, listened quietly until Lynne began to in-
tone the words from the *Star Book for Ministers,* "Dearly Beloved,

we are gathered together for the purpose of uniting these two, Martha Gurganus and Tom Ketcham, in the holy bonds of . . . ah . . . *maternity*." Here the two mothers' sudden "coughing" almost disrupted the solemnity of the occasion.

During the monsoon season, Miss Noela Elvery, an Australian member of Gospel Recordings, Inc., joined us for three months. Jeannie Lockerbie, recognizing the need for new recordings, had made the contact on behalf of our field council. Many of our Pakistani personnel cooperated to produce recordings in Bengali, Muslim Bengali, Chittagonian dialect, Tippera, and Mru. We were stuck, however, for a Mogh believer to produce Mogh recordings. Despite our prayers over many days, we had failed to find a suitable Mogh broadcaster. We prayed again the day before those recordings were to be made — and waited. That evening, one of my Mogh friends who had come a month before for spiritual instruction, appeared at Malumghat. He had forgotten nothing he had learned during his previous visit and, back in his jungle village, he had been poring over the new simplified translation of the gospel of John. Greatly enlightened and prepared by his studies, he was ready to place his faith in Christ. That night, in a bamboo house dimly lit by a feeble oil lamp, he made his decision. The next morning he was ready for the recording assignment for which God had sent him — an assignment which he carried out with considerable finesse. "Thank You, Father."

Mary Lou Brownell, trained in missionary dentistry, ordinarily cleaned, filled, and extracted our teeth when necessary. In her absence Mark developed a painful infected tooth, forcing me to become a dentist overnight. Learning from Mary Lou's books that extraction was required, we gave Mark a brief anesthesia and removed the offending tooth.

Recording session with Ancharai Tippera and the miracle Mogh

Later in the day he reported nonchalantly to a gang of kids surrounding him, "After they gave me that shot I saw double — then I saw triple — then I saw nothin'!" At bedtime, when he put the tooth under his pillow, he feared the tooth fairy might fail to comprehend the spectacular quality of his tooth.

He explained, "Man, after all, I had full dead anesthesia!" Evidently the tooth fairy was duly impressed, for she left three rupees instead of the usual one.

By summertime we knew that Drs. Ralph and Lucy Ankenman would not return from furlough as planned. Circumstances dictated that their furlough be extended another two years. This necessity created a critical emergency for us, because Donn Ketcham was on the verge of leaving for a two-year furlough in America. For one doctor — namely me — to run the hospital alone for two years was unthinkable. Even with two of us working side by side the workload was extremely heavy. We began to pray for some solution to this problem. In early August the Ketchams departed — but not quite soon enough. Four of them had contracted mild cases of hepatitis.

By mid-September nearly thirty ABWE-ers were down with hepatitis! We had a bonafide epidemic on our hands! A week later, when Lynn Silvernale's symptoms appeared, we were forced to close down the outpatient department (Lynn had come from Chittagong to direct the OPD until Jeannie recovered from hepatitis). Several days later I diagnosed my own hepatitis which virtually forced us to close the hospital. Several of our Bengali workers were also infected. A week later our sole remaining nurse, Becky Davey, presented her sore liver for examination. And that completely closed down the hospital!

By this time I had become well aware that I was dealing with a type of hepatitis previously unknown and unnamed. I dubbed it "Chittagong hepatitis." I knew of five types of hepatitis occurring in our area. The disease contracted by our group differed from all of them in several particulars: absence of yellow jaundice, more pronounced liver pain, pain also in the left upper abdomen, and a protracted course lasting months or years. We studied the strange disease with care. MAP (Medical Assistance Programs, Inc.), in America, contacted infectious disease specialists on our behalf. Research doctors came from the Cholera Research Laboratory, Dacca, and the University of Maryland group, West Pakistan, to help me study the disease.

After many tests, reexaminations of the patients, and analyses of my flow sheets of all the cases, we could not match this illness with any known disease. Analyzing the data from the point of view of physiology, I theorized the new disease was caused by a virus which attacked primarily the capsule (covering) of the liver and only slightly the liver cells themselves. Because most of the liver's pain nerves lie in the capsule, this could explain the considerable pain and the absence of jaundice. I wondered whether I would ever be able to prove my theory.

The situation was phenomenal. Practically our whole mission team was bedfast with a new illness unknown to medical science, and our hospital was closed. A certain sequence of events followed with every patient: for the first week or two the patient felt too ill to do anything but rest and sleep; then when the "ickey" feeling passed, each one started working on the pile of projects he had never found time to do.

Jay Walsh, not yet afflicted with hepatitis, one morning stumbled across what looked like mud foundations of a building at the front edge of our property. Inquiry revealed that some local Muslim men had quietly, under cover of darkness, formed the foundations of a mosque! Once the construction of a mosque has reached a certain point, Muslim law decrees that no one can reverse it.

As Jay and I, in my bedroom, consulted about the next move, in walked our Muslim friend Shahabuddin, the son of our influential neighbor Mr. Choudhury. We brought him into the discussion, and he agreed to try to help us relocate the mosque, an anachronism on Christian hospital property.

Later, as he talked with the mosque builders, the local forest officer appeared on the scene. An inspiration struck Shahabuddin. He took the officer and men into the forest on the far side of the road. In a moment he had located a lovely shady spot near a small stream (which would provide water for ritual washing) and announced, "This beautiful spot is the most correct and suitable place for a mosque." When the forest officer quickly agreed to the idea, the men also were carried along in the enthusiasm of the decision and agreed! The knotty problem had been solved in the smoothest possible way.

One fall morning someone reported excitedly to me, "They're attacking Daniel! They're beating Daniel in the village!" From my bed I sent men to rescue and bring back Daniel. They brought him — on a stretcher. After treating battered Daniel, I learned from him that his fellow villagers had increased the pressure upon him steadily over several weeks. Harrassing Daniel's family, the villagers even denied them access to the local water supply. That morning men had come to goad Daniel until a fight erupted. Daniel was choked and beaten;

except for his wife's bravery in stopping the fight, the outcome might have been *finis* for him.

As Shahabuddin was away, I called his cousin Rafique to assist in the adjudication. Our living room became a courtroom packed with twenty men. We heard the charges and countercharges until we were able to recreate the scene of mayhem. We decided there was fault on both sides: the villagers were wrong to harass and provoke Daniel; Daniel was wrong to retort critically against the law and rule of Islam. The villagers agreed to lay off Daniel, and I agreed to deal with Daniel about his offensive statement. I chose to do so from the scriptural viewpoint. We studied together eight passages which taught that we ought to walk wisely, carefully, and graciously in this world, not maligning to a man the beliefs he holds precious. One passage said, to the credit of the apostle Paul, that he never blasphemed the goddess Diana. Daniel was especially moved by the Lord's words, "Behold I send you forth as sheep in the midst of wolves; Be, therefore, wise as serpents and harmless as doves." In humility and earnest repentance Daniel prayed, confessing to God his fault in the matter. He then excused himself to go off and make his apology to the man who so recently had his hands about Daniel's throat, choking his very life away. A great thing, the power of the Word of God in a man's life!

By Christmastime Jay Walsh and I had changed places; he was down with hepatitis, and I was up and about. On Christmas day I conducted in a Bengali church an infant dedication service and preached the Christmas message on "The Birth Certificate of Christ." As we studied from scripture to scripture, line by line we filled in every space of a giant birth certificate. Our Christmas worship was precious to all of us.

As the year drew to a close, we reassessed our situation. With very few susceptibles left, our epidemic was grinding to a halt. The problems created by our sickness and hospital closure were obvious: our ministry of mercy had been inoperative for three months, our people had suffered discomfort and pain, and wild rumors inundated the countryside: "The hospital has been closed down by the government because guns and ammunition were found stored there." "In a gun battle between government forces and the missionaries, some missionaries were injured and later others were deported." "The hospital will never open again because Dr. Olsen has died."

As we looked also on the brighter side, we were amazed at the advantages and positive developments issuing from the Chittagong hepatitis epidemic:

1. We reorganized and streamlined our medical-surgical program.
2. We refined our whole hospital financial and bookkeeping system.
3. We conceived new ways to help inquirers after truth.
4. The national Christians took added spiritual responsibility beautifully, a giant step forward toward organizing their church.
5. We devoted extra time to helping Bengali preachers prepare their messages.
6. We had special opportunities to share our faith with visiting friends.
7. Our spiritual lives prospered with more time for study, prayer, and meditation.
8. Our family life and fellowship were also enhanced by the enforced rest.
9. I completed the Muslim Bengali common language translation of John's gospel, the first such translation in the country.
10. Distribution of the *Muslim Bengali-to-English Dictionary* began.
11. Hundreds of manhours of work were put into compiling the opposite edition (*English-to-Muslim Bengali Dictionary*).
12. We rechecked in depth the standard common language gospel of John translation.
13. I used idle hospital personnel to conduct an important research project on the Bengali language.
14. The Bengali II language syllabus was completely revised.
15. A huge amount of Bengali literature was produced (Sunday school lessons, a simplified doctrine book, tracts, camp lessons, filmstrip scripts, etc.).
16. The first draft of a twenty-five-hundred-word Tippera dictionary was completed.
17. We wrote literally hundreds of letters, getting our correspondence caught up.
18. Several patients devoted large blocks of time to a field council biblical research study.
19. The whole epidemic caused a great upsurge of urgent prayer in America for us and for the work of God in East Pakistan.

Ultimately it dawned on us why God "cranked out" a new disease, unknown to medical science, with a remarkably high attack rate, and symptoms which stopped our normal activities for many weeks, yet allowed us to accomplish huge amounts of sedentary work. Our Father knew that we could not rightfully, in good conscience, close the hospital to accomplish other urgent work even if such a thought had occurred to us. But God took the initiative and *set the priorities*

Joan, when "God . . . set the priorities"

Himself! Apparently some work or works among the nineteen were of such high importance that a drastic rearrangement of our schedule was warranted.

Although we had come to understand our Chittagong hepatitis epidemic, we could not yet comprehend the purpose nor outcome of the political cauldron which bubbled more violently than ever during November and December, boiling over into the New Year. Several months earlier, in June, the court trial of Sheikh Mujib and the thirty-three had begun. Because some of the group were alleged to have met Indian conspirators in Agartala, India, the case became popularly known as the "Agartala conspiracy case." For some weeks the military and police were able to control the simmering agitation against the trial. But in November, when Bengali sentiment blew wide open, control was no longer possible. The pot boiled!

17

Rampage and Revival

BLINKING OUT of my reverie for a minute, I checked my watch —
9:40! Just twenty minutes left before lights out would bring the
blackness of the perilous night upon us. I arose, walked slowly to
the dresser, and took a small .22 caliber revolver from the drawer.
Awkwardly, with my left hand I loaded the six cartridges into the
chamber. The thought of using the steel blue revolver sickened me
momentarily. But quickly another thought came to temper that
feeling: *Shooting a handgun left-handed, I would have a pretty slim
chance of hitting anyone!*

Shooting and tumult had also ushered in 1969 in East Pakistan.
Despite the riots and violence which rampaged throughout the country, 1969 had been a year of progress and spiritual revival at Memorial Christian Hospital.

*   *   *

The political turbulence of the two preceding months spiraled
on into the new year. Newspaper headlines screamed the daily developments of the Agartala conspiracy trial against Sheikh Mujib.
Students and workers took to the streets to riot passionately, erect
barricades, and *gherao* (surround and besiege) various government
offices. The sleeping Bengali giant had awakened to lash out at
the West Pakistan-dominated central government which had so long
controlled East Pakistan.

With the situation completely out of control, the government
clamped curfew on the revolting citizens. Curfew simply meant
that anyone caught on the streets by policemen or soldiers would be
shot dead in his tracks — no questions asked! Sometimes curfew
would be lifted, allowing people to hurry off to the bazaar to purchase provisions for the next few days.

In February, when I traveled to Dacca on business, I found the
city thick with tension. I met with officials of another mission in
the beautiful Dacca Intercontinental Hotel to discuss their stalled hospital project. Fortunately, we had been able to diagnose the road-

block and open up a new initiative for their project. At the end of our meeting, curfew was suddenly clamped on Dacca. *Perfect timing!* I thought. *The Hotel Intercontinental is not a bad place to be stuck overnight!*

The next day, when the curfew was lifted, I returned to the home where I usually stayed in Dacca. The owner, a high government official under my care, had built onto his mansion a beautiful private room and bath for me to use during my periodic trips to Dacca. There I listened to President Ayub Khan's special nationwide radio broadcast. He announced his irrevocable decision not to be a candidate for president during the upcoming election. On the following day President Ayub terminated the Agartala conspiracy trial and released Sheikh Mujib from prison! Joyous pandemonium gripped Dacca and spread like wildfire out into the districts. Thousands of Bengalis escorted Sheikh Mujib in a tumultuous procession from the cantonment down the main streets of Dacca. He stopped at places symbolizing Bengali nationalism: the *Shahid Minar* (monument to students who died to preserve the Bengali language), the graves of three heroes of Bengal, and the grave of Zahirul Haque (the coaccused in the Agartala conspiracy case who was killed by guards). At the last grave, when he lifted his palms to heaven and prayed to Allah for the departed soul of the deceased, he wept. The next day (February 23) he made an impassioned speech to an estimated one million delirious followers at the Dacca race course meeting ground.

In March President Ayub Khan held a round table conference (RTC) with political leaders of East and West Pakistan. Sheikh Mujib and the other politicians agreed on their demand for two essential changes: one, the presidential system of government with an all-powerful president must be relinquished in favor of a parliamentary system of democracy with supremacy of the legislative branch (parliament). Two, the electoral college system of elections must be replaced by direct elections in which each man casts his vote for the candidates he deems worthy. When President Ayub agreed to these two demands, most of the politicians were euphoric — but not Mujib. He wanted more! His demands were embodied in the famous six points he presented to the RTC, and Ayub had agreed only to the demands in point one.

The last five proposals were designed to halt West Pakistan exploitation of the East and give to East Pakistan more autonomy. Sheikh Mujib made no headway in the RTC with his last five points.

When Mujib returned to East Pakistan to report the refusal of the Ayub government to accept the last five points, another groundswell of protest rumbled across East Pakistan. Again law and order broke down. Once more East Pakistan was paralyzed by riots and strikes which the police and military could not wholly contain. Finally, on March 25, 1969, President Ayub stepped down, defeated by Bengali public opinion and the man who had molded it, Sheikh Mujibur Rahman. Yahya Khan, commanding general of the Pakistan army, took control of Pakistan, placing the country under martial law. Yahya, the Muslim name for John the Baptist, was like his namesake, a tough and uncompromising man.

Sickness in the body politic was not the only illness we encountered during the first quarter of 1969. In early January Joan turned yellow. Ordinary viral hepatitis struck her three weeks after her Chittagong hepatitis relented! A few days later Mark turned the same color from the same disease. Without our valuable servant help, we could not have kept functioning.

We enjoyed a profitable visit from Ray Knighton, my friend from Christian Medical Society days. Dodging the curfews, I brought him to Malumghat to meet with our recuperating medical team. Ray had become president of MAP (Medical Assistance Programs, Inc.), the organization which obtained donated medicines from American drug companies, then sent them on to us and other mission hospitals around the world. MAP's service to us had been invaluable.

We brainstormed many matters with Ray. He informed us that he could arrange payment of the ocean freight bills for medical supplies from MAP if we could obtain from the East Pakistan government a written statement that they approved and recognized MAP as a bonafide voluntary aid agency. I began working and praying to that end. (Before the year ended, success — worth thousands of dollars to us — crowned the Dacca negotiations.)

By the beginning of May, after many weeks of closure, we had enough medical people sufficiently recovered from Chittagong hepatitis to reopen Memorial Christian Hospital. I did the doctoring, Becky Davey managed the inpatient and surgical nursing, Jeannie Lockerbie directed the outpatient department, and Mel Beals did the dentistry and supervised hospital maintenance and construction, and Jesse Eaton, who began managing the business administration and bookkeeping, added immeasurably to the stability of our work. Simultaneously a senior medical student, Dave Reid (with wife Becky and infant daughter Julie), arrived to share in the work for two months. They were sponsored by a MAP scholarship program.

The day we reopened the hospital, a prominent Muslim priest who lived some miles away awakened with abdominal pain. Over three days and nights that boring pain, accompanied by fever and vomiting, became excruciating. During a few minutes of fitful, painful, exhausted sleep in the early morning hours of the desperate third night, he dreamed. The first figure to appear in his dream announced himself as the prophet Muhammad. After his message, Muhammad faded from sight to make way for a second prophet dressed in Middle Eastern style. Announcing himself as the prophet Isa (Jesus), he spoke the same message: "Your sickness is unto death. You must go to the young man at the Christian hospital, Dr. Olsen. He is your only hope!"

At daybreak, when he told his relatives to take him to the Christian hospital, they remonstrated with him, "The hospital is still closed."

"Never mind," he croaked hoarsely, "take me to that Christian doctor. The prophets have spoken!"

That morning, the fourth morning since the hospital reopened, we received the critically ill priest. After a moment's examination, I knew I must operate on him that same day (along with four other acute surgical emergencies). At the time of operation I found the priest suffering from a condition unusual in East Pakistan — acute appendicitis! Because his appendix had ruptured, causing abscess and peritonitis, the operation was lifesaving.

Several days later, the priest, an uncommonly fine man, asked for a private interview. We met later in my office where he thanked me for his treatment with deep sincerity. I was grateful for my studies in Muslim Bengali, for his speech was peppered with Islamic words. Explaining that he considered me a *giani* (person with spiritual insight), he told me his dream.

"I understand one meaning or reason for the dream," he continued. "The prophets sent me to the hospital where, under your hand I have been born again. I was dead, but now I am alive again. Can you advise me, Daktar Sahib, of any further purpose of my dream?"

"Perhaps," I responded, "you were sent here so you could be not only physically reborn, but also spiritually born again." I opened the brand new Muslim Bengali Gospel of John (translated during my illness) to the perfectly pertinent chapter three. Just as this noted Muslim priest had come to me, a supposed *giani,* centuries earlier a famous religious leader of Jerusalem (Nicodemus) had come to the true *giani,* the Lord Jesus Christ. We read together Christ's words to the Jerusalem teacher: "Unless a man is born again, he cannot see the kingdom of God."

Tears filled the eyes of the Muslim priest before me as he declared, "That's what I want, to be born again spiritually and someday enter God's kingdom!" I taught him more thereafter from the Scriptures and have reason to believe that his desire was fulfilled.

In mid-March, when the Walshes departed for furlough, their flight from Cox's Bazar was canceled due to riots in Chittagong. In the evening they drove on to Chittagong where they made suitable connections. Later the same month the order was passed that all firearms and ammunition must be turned in to the local police. We complied, but were concerned because the guns were our protection from mad dogs which had entered our housing property several times in the preceding months.

A few weeks earlier Joan and I had heard a strange crying, wailing sound outside. Investigating, I found a black dog mercilessly chewing on a whimpering puppy underneath the Walshes' car. As I poked a stick under the car, the black dog came raging out at me, fangs bared, snarling. I could see it was rabid (mad). Unable to get past my stick, the partially paralyzed animal turned and ran crazily toward other houses. I raced for my 12-gauge shotgun, spotted the dog heading toward the school (filled with children), aimed, and brought it down with a fortunate long shot. After our guns were impounded, we were not sure how we could handle a similar emergency if it should develop. And rabies is nearly 100 percent fatal — only one survivor known to medical science!

In April, a thirty-year-old husband and father entered the hospital with a massive tumor of the skull. First, I removed the eye which had been unseated from its socket by the expanding tumor. When the family produced four units of blood, I decided to attempt the huge neurosurgical operation, despite my paucity of brain surgery instruments. The man's life depended on it.

I prayed in the instrument room, "Heavenly Father, You know I cannot do the operation without that one missing instrument. Please help me manufacture a suitable substitute." In a few minutes I located an old instrument which I broke in two and bent into the shape, more or less, of the missing instrument. I thought it should work.

Because I had two days earlier operated on medical student David Reid's wrist, he could not scrub in on the case. Although Dave was disappointed, he determined to stand by throughout the operation. Millie Coolie and Bengali surgical technician David Bayen assisted me skillfully. Becky Davey, to whom I had given basic anesthesia training, competently put the patient to sleep and conducted a beautiful anesthetic throughout the long, grueling operation.

Through an ear to ear incision, I uncovered the massive tumor and the many blood vessels feeding it. At every stage of the operation blood loss was copious. But the Mickey Mouse instrument I had fashioned worked like a charm. Finally, after completely drilling and sawing around the huge mass, I found it dived deep inside the patient's head, cruelly pressuring the underlying brain. Because the tumor was attached to his brain and its covering, those involved tissues also had to be removed. When I finally handed the great mass of tumor, bone and brain tissue to the nurse, I had to work furiously for many minutes to stop the massive bleeding. In the end I borrowed some tissue from behind the ear to patch up the hole in the brain covering. After ten hours of exhausting surgery I finally inserted the last stitch and stripped off my bloody gown.

Although the patient's condition remained stable throughout the night, I was concerned about what I might find the following morning. Walking apprehensively toward the recovery room, suddenly we heard peals of laughter inside. There our neurosurgical patient was sitting up on his bed cracking jokes like an inebriate! After several days, when the swelling in his brain subsided, his normally quiet, shy personality returned. Wonderfully, he recovered without complications. "Thank You, Father!" News of this neurosurgical operation traveled by the bamboo telegraph throughout the district and the nation.

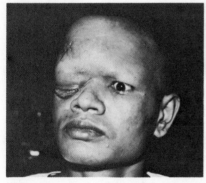
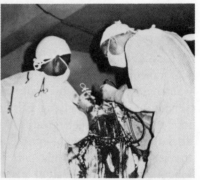
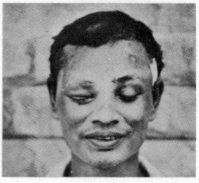

"Ten hours of exhausting surgery"
before
during
after

May 1 marked an important development. The Malumghat hospital branch of the East Pakistan Bible Correspondence School officially opened with principal Mel Beals in charge. Our branch would cover the southern half of Chittagong and Chittagong Hill Tracts districts. Malumghat became, in a new way, a center for putting God's Word into the hands and hearts of thousands of interested Bengali people. Many on our own hospital staff immediately began a race to see who could finish all the courses first.

As I led the prayer meeting one Wednesday night, an unfamiliar young man with tribal features entered. Welcoming him, I asked his name. He introduced himself as Gonijan Tippera, the son of one of our illiterate gardeners. (Later I learned that "Goni," a high school student ranking at the top of his class, was probably the most highly educated and brilliant Tippera in East Pakistan.)

Because his parents were Christians, and because my teaching subject for that night was faith, I asked, "Gonijan, when did you believe in Christ?" His answer was hesitant and a bit vague. Stirred by the biblical teaching on faith that night, before he slept he restudied all the verses I had presented.

On Sunday morning I preached on two kinds of faith — receiving faith and recognizing faith. Newly aware that he was a professing Christian but not a possessing one, this brilliant boy came Sunday afternoon for help. On our verandah, with deep sincerity, he placed his faith in Christ.

Then Goni said, "I feel happy! Is there any objection to my telling someone else about my new faith?" I assured him that God wanted him to share his light with others. He began the following Sunday morning by giving his testimony of faith and conversion before the entire church group. Joan, out of bed at last and able to attend her first Bengali service in thirteen months, was thrilled with the service and Gonijan's part in it. He returned to his boarding school to become a spiritual leader there.

The children developed a great interest in the hospital, patients, operations, and medical work. They helped out, doing odd jobs around the hospital, and kept close track of the progress of interesting patients to report to their mothers at home. We allowed them, two at a time, after proper instruction to watch operations in progress.

The smaller children initiated their own hospital in our back bedroom. In the "operating room" they put doll Raggedy Ann to sleep with an injection and gave her artificial respiration with a rigged-up balloon. After sewing up the doll's incision with black thread, they stuck intravenous fluids in her arm and taped the stomach tube to her nose. After the first dozen operations, Raggedy Ann was more black thread than doll.

Three months after we handed over our hunting arms to the police, the political chaos had eased sufficiently under martial law for the firearms to be returned to us. Fortunately, not a single mad dog had set paw on our property during that three months! Only three or four days after the guns were returned, however, a vicious mad dog entered the property and, with fangs dripping, headed for Mark. He pushed an umbrella at its gaping jaws, turned, and fell flat on his face. Fortunately, the dog snapped at the umbrella long enough to allow Mark time to get up and sprint home.

Mark, greenish-white around the mouth and trembling, shouted, "Quick, there's a mad dog — and Lynne and Jimmy are coming from young people's meeting." As I raced in the Land Rover to give the warning, the mad dog attacked Sandy, teacher Shirley Harkness' dog, then ran toward the other houses. I tried, but just failed to run down the deadly animal with the Land Rover. Mel then stepped out of the house with his recently reclaimed shotgun and killed the rabid dog. But — our three months without guns had been three months without rabid dogs. "Thank You, Father!"

During the monsoon season we welcomed the Adolphs, Jean Weld, and Mary Lou Brownell back from furlough. In early August further wonderful relief came in the form of Dr. John ("Jake") Jaquis with his family. When Jake and his wife Rosie had learned that I would be the only doctor at MCH and badly needed assistance, they decided to give a year of their lives to help us out. Amazingly, within two weeks they sold their home in a very tight market and obtained in six days their visa to East Pakistan!

Dr. "Jake" Jaquis, nurse Jean Weld, and patient

Jake's coming gave me time to work on a serious problem in our church life. Two groups of "Christians" attended our Christian services. One group were natives of Chittagong District and had come to Christ out of non-Christian backgrounds. Those in the second group were born into the Christian community in other districts of East Pakistan. Despite their long contact with Christianity, most in the second group had limited knowledge of the Christian faith and were merely nominal, professing "Christians." They were, however, good workers, loyal to the hospital, more highly educated than the others, and felt a certain pride of being born into the Christian community.

Tension existed between the two groups which would be cured only when the nominal "Christians" truly found Christ. Just before hepatitis struck us down, I held some get-togethers with these friends and had them fill out a questionnaire which confirmed my suspicions. They did not possess or understand the way of salvation and eternal life. We began praying and working with increased intensity to help this group really come to know Christ.

The first break came when a male nurse and his wife requested infant dedication for their new son. When they admitted that neither of them had been spiritually reborn, I demurred about the dedication. Two nights later the husband came with many questions. We sat together on the roof of my house studying the biblical answers to each question. He truly found Christ that night.

Two days later his wife also keenly felt her need and, sari flying in the breeze, raced to the hospital for spiritual help — but we were in the operating room. Back in her house she paced restlessly another hour, then again ran to the hospital — we were still in the operating room. Then, back in her house, suddenly the thought came to her, *I don't need that doctor or those nurses to place my faith in Christ. There is nothing to keep me from talking to God directly.* In her bamboo house she did talk to God and accepted His Son.

On Saturday night when I visited their bamboo home and heard her story, we rejoiced together — and made plans for the dedication of their son the following morning. At the lovely service not only was the son dedicated, but at the end of the service a number of adults dedicated their lives to Christ. The revival at Memorial Christian Hospital had begun!

Eager to share their faith with family members, the couple traveled to the opposite end of East Pakistan. There the wife led three of her relatives to Christ and brought two younger brothers back to the hospital where we helped them gain eternal life. Simultaneously, Debendra, stutteringly sharing his faith with a fellow washerman, helped him to find the Saviour. A Hindu cancer victim believed before she died, and another Hindu from 150 miles away decided at Malumghat to follow Christ.

Several days later two male nurses became involved in a fistfight, something practically unheard of in the Christian community. My judgment fell hard on Ajit, the guilty party.

"Ajit," I said sternly, "you know we have come halfway around

Ajit, after the fistfight

the world to help people in Christ's name and tell them of Him. You, the son of a minister, by your fight have hurt the reputation of the Lord and the hospital. You should be very ashamed."

Literally overcome by misery and regret, Ajit suddenly became stiff, his eyes rolled back in his head, and he fell to the floor unconscious. After he came to, he confessed his fault to God and man and made everything right.

Later in the afternoon I returned to find him considerably recovered. When we probed the causes of his fault, he freely admitted he had never made a personal decision for Christ. But the teaching and preaching he had heard and the Bible correspondence courses he studied had partially melted his aggressive heart. His resistance blown wide open by the day's experiences, he accepted Christ into his life. That same afternoon, his wife also settled her relationship with the Saviour once and for all. A few weeks later another fine couple (husband and wife, both nurses) made the great faith decision after our final study together in their home. Jesse Eaton and Becky Davey had a powerful spiritual influence on the lives of another couple (both nurses). They, too, decided for Christ. Because God's Spirit was working dynamically at Malumghat, revival had crested!

One night a patient in severe pain came from Cox's Bazar. After examination, I took him immediately to the operating room to relieve his obstructed intestine. The following morning the police intelligence officer from Cox's Bazar arrived, found me, and anxiously said, "I have come for two reasons: first, to know whether or not you require a Dr. DeCook who is applying for a visa to come to your hospital. Secondly, my best friend was brought to your hospital in serious condition last night. I must know if he is alive."

Explaining about the midnight surgery on his friend, I replied, "You can go talk with your friend now; he's doing well." Then, extolling Dr. DeCook and his professional ability, I explained how very much we needed him and how we were depending on the officer to write the strongest possible positive statement to his superiors about our need for Dr. DeCook. His letter must have been a humdinger, because the DeCooks' visas were issued in record time despite our listing them as new hands and not replacements for previous workers.

We learned that, including the DeCooks, twelve out of twenty-three members of the 1969 candidate class were appointed to East Pakistan. We were delighted!

Because Jake had come, the Olsens were able to take a vacation (our first in two years) to spend September in West Pakistan with Wendy. Our month together was full of good things, including a trip by road through the historic and ruggedly beautiful Khyber Pass into Afghanistan. After a week in Kabul, the capital city, we returned to Murree, West Pakistan, to send out nearly one thousand letters (in answer to twenty pounds of accumulated mail).

Returning to the hospital, we reached Dacca to find a special surprise awaiting us. A high government official, my patient and friend, had arranged for us an enchanting trip by ship from Dacca to Chittagong. We were driven in a shiny black Mercedes Benz limousine to the handsome, freshly painted ship, a craft capable of handling three hundred people. Upon arrival we learned that we would be the only passengers! Freshly refurbished, the ship would not begin its regular passenger run until the return trip from Chittagong. As we stepped on board, the crew stood at rigid attention while we

The ship of our "fairy tale journey"

shook hands with the captain and first mate. When they asked if we were ready to depart, I requested the captain to hold a few minutes while we took some pictures.

Back on board, we were shown our quarters: the royal suite which had been constructed some months earlier expressly for the state visit of the king of Nepal! The steward explained that his only work was to serve us and that we might call him at any time. He showed Lynne and Nancy to their attractive room and Mark to the prince's suite. As Mark looked inside, a "royal" cockroach flew out of the darkness, landing on the princely pillow. Mark selected a less regal room for the journey! The royal suite (by then renamed the President's Suite), air-conditioned, contained a seven-foot-square bed with a floor-length deep purple velvet curtain which could be drawn across the open side. Adjacent to our suite was a private lounge deck covered with thick red carpet.

Throughout the fairy tale journey, we were treated as though I were a king or president of a great nation. Proceeding majestically down the mighty river, we reveled in the beauty of the countryside, the white-sailed boats, and the occasion itself. When darkness crept over the land we weighed anchor for the night. Mark's eyes were as wide as saucers as he watched the huge anchor splash into the water and the mighty chain rattle deafeningly until its anchor rested in the river mud. In the morning we passed out into the ocean (Bay of Bengal) and steamed on to Chittagong, the end of our twenty-four-hour journey. We used the ship as a floating hotel for forty-eight hours while we completed business in Chittagong before proceeding on to Malumghat. The lovely trip seemed a heaven-sent benediction to our vacation. "Thank You, Father."

At Malumghat we found that several more of our colleagues, recent arrivals from America, had succumbed to a second wave of Chittagong hepatitis. Mercifully, Dr. Jake was spared. Several weeks later we put Joan back to bed: her ordinary hepatitis had relapsed.

Our medical group made a substantial contribution to the tribal short-term Bible school in November. The new gospel recordings and hand-crank phonettes arrived, fascinating the tribal people. The Bengalis of southern Chittagong District were equally entranced. In fact, the total stock of phonettes was exhausted in two days!

Keeping our generators functioning and electricity flowing continued to be a never-ending battle with spare parts twelve thousand miles away. So we were thrilled when a sophisticated, new electricity-generating plant was established at Cox's Bazar. High voltage lines (thirty-three thousand volts) now passed our hospital, some of the pylons actually resting on our hospital property. But three installations were necessary to make that electricity flow into our hospital and homes:

1. A step-down transformer located between the hospital and housing properties (to convert the high voltage into usable voltage electricity).
2. A high voltage feeder line from the main line to the transformer.
3. Normal voltage lines from the transformer to the hospital and housing sites.

The cost of the triple installation would be sixteen thousand dollars! Because we lacked the funds, we prayed for favor in the sight of the pertinent official in WAPDA (Water and Power Development Authority). Perhaps he would install the units at WAPDA expense on the grounds that we were a charitable institution. I flew to Dacca several times to approach the head of WAPDA with zero success. He was adamant that we must pay the bill to obtain the installations, despite our humanitarian service to the multitudes. Stymied, we intensified our prayer efforts. When the guidance factor came, it seemed foolish to return to the official one more time. Having learned, however, not to argue with the sense of guidance, I flew to Dacca again to meet with the official.

Apologetically he said, "Please forgive me, but I simply can't talk with you today. I am trying to deal with a terrible, crippling strike of our Dacca workers. But you have come a long way, so I want you to talk to my officer in charge of line development."

When I told the second officer my story, he looked at me squarely and said, "I like what you're doing, doctor, and I'll do everything in my power to help you. If I can find my way around one knotty problem, I will be able to make the installation for you; and your cost will be only two or three thousand dollars."

When I asked about the nature of the knotty problem, he replied, "Our rules say that if the high voltage branch line passes across your property you must pay for the installation."

The solution came to me in an instant!

"I can solve your problem," I responded, "if you take the feeder line off the pylon in the forest beyond our hospital property, it will reach the transformer without touching our land. Besides, this arrangement will be much safer, for the thirty-three thousand volt line will then pass over the uninhabited forest rather than over our nurses' quarters."

His face lit by a broad smile, the officer declared, "That's it! I can do it for you!" The guidance factor had paid off again — because the Guide Himself had our affairs well in hand. "Thank You, Father!"

18

Whigs and Whirlwind

MY HEAD NODDED for a minute, in that Bangladesh bedroom, as weariness momentarily overcame the double stimuli of pain and adrenalin.

I might as well go to bed, I thought. *The attack might not come immediately after the electricity goes off.* I would need all the sleep I could get. I remembered that our Bengali people had been far from sleepy the year before (1970). They were wide awake to the impassioned political campaigning for the December elections when, for the first time, they would vote directly for the candidates. Several political parties actively campaigned. Like their political ancestors, the British Whigs, Sheikh Mujib and his Awami Leaguers toured the country preaching parliamentary democracy and the need to discard powerful one-man rule, the rule of President Yahya Khan.

As a macabre prelude to the elections, a whirlwind of unprecedented proportions came dancing, like a whirling dervish, up the Bay of Bengal to burst furiously upon unsuspecting East Pakistan. Other storms of fresh visa problems and exceptional persecution battered our mission, our hospital, and our flock.

* * *

Reinforcements arrived to help us in the new year of 1970: Dr. Joe and Joyce DeCook (with four children) and Linda Short, a bright, vivacious girl no taller than her name implied. Retiree Dr. Paul Adolph, our friend and father of Bob and Barb, came to share in the work for two months (and used every free moment to enjoy his grandchildren).

Millie Cooley, after recovery from a year-long rather severe illness (perhaps the first and most virulent case of Chittagong hepatitis) and with language study completed, began her valuable work on the wards and in the operating room of the hospital.

We admitted one morning a young husband and father with a broken femur (thigh bone). The X ray revealed a fracture suitable for treatment with an intramedullary rod (steel rod driven down the

233

marrow cavity of the bone). Among our surgical supplies, I found one such rod which, although used, was nearly the correct length. Although I lacked some of the proper instruments for the operation, I decided to inaugurate this type of treatment in our hospital. As usual, I prayed with my patient before he was anesthetized — this time a maximum intensity prayer! Through appropriate incisions, I drove the intramedullary rod into the bone with a sterile hatchet (instead of a surgical mallet) and seated the rod finally with hatchet and ordinary pliers (instead of an orthopedic driver).

Despite the primitive equipment, the result was perfect. "Thank You, Father!" When a fellow physician, Dr. Robert Keys, visited us for two weeks, he brought me the necessary instruments to carry on this type of surgery "the way the doctor ordered."

With Drs. Jaquis and Adolph on deck, I was freed for nearly a month to share the teaching load in two short-term Bible schools for Bengalis. Jay Walsh and Gene Gurganus had pioneered such an effort the year before with good success. This year Gene and I would give a ten-night series in Chittagong, then repeat the series at Malumghat. Gene Gurganus' subject was "New Testament Survey" while I taught *"Shikka O Shakkho — Probhu Jishu Khristo, Amader Nomuna* [Teaching and Witness — the Lord Jesus Christ, Our Example]." We studied together the methods of Christ, the master teacher and the matchless witness; then I taught how we can apply His principles in teaching others and giving witness to our faith.

For his final messages Gene used a giant wall chart ten feet long to show the plan of the ages. The overhead projector allowed me to use many visual pictures of spiritual truth which I supplemented with object lessons. The crowd of ninety roared their approval when my helper smashed a clay pot full of water, dousing us both. They readily understood that a second waterpot with only a nail hole in it was equally useless, for neither pot could hold water. Then I ex-

Gene Gurganus with chart of the plan of the ages

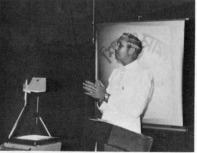
Vic Olsen with "visual pictures of spiritual truth"

plained that the pots represented God's law. Whether we have committed major crimes or only "ordinary" sins, we are guilty in either case of breaking God's law and are held accountable. The Bible put it this way: "Whoever shall keep the whole law, but offend in one point, he is guilty of all."

Although the Bible school was designed primarily for believers, others attended, too, and several of them made the great faith decision which opens the door to life everlasting. A carpenter came from a distant place to attend the Bible school. He had possessed a desire to learn more of Christ since age ten, when his father had pointed to an airplane flying overhead and told him that the men who drive the planes through the skies "are white men who follow, not the prophet Muhammad, but the prophet Jesus." On the ninth day of the meetings he came to me to report, with tear-marked cheeks, that he had believed.

On the third night of the meetings, our last purely nominal Christian nurse (the man who had been attacked in the fistfight between two male nurses) listened enraptured.

He later explained, "My spirit was so lifted by the meetings I felt I was walking a foot above the ground. At home, I finally fell off to sleep only to dream that I was standing before the whole church. In my dream I was praying in the highest, most poetically beautiful form of our Bengali language, 'Oh God, I have come to confess my sin and ask your forgiveness. I know that Christ died for my sins according to the Scriptures, and at this moment I open my heart to Him and accept Him as my Saviour!' Suddenly I awakened from my dream and the thought struck me, *That's the prayer I really should pray so that I might have eternal life.* So, sitting in my bed under the mosquito net I prayed that beautiful prayer from my heart."

One afternoon a beautiful Hindu mother of six entered the hospital, at death's door from hemorrhage. I dared not operate until we replaced some of the lost blood. I sat beside her in the operating room until we had pumped a unit and a half of blood into her system, then surgically stopped the bleeding. On the ward we gave her more blood over several days. She asked questions about Christ and seemed entranced with all she heard. Mary Lou looked at the plastic bottle of blood dripping into her system and pointed out that someone had given that blood that she might live. Then, when she explained that Christ gave His life's blood so that men might live eternally, the patient was deeply moved. She became a follower of Christ. Her husband, a village doctor and pillar of his community, made a similar decision in my office several days later. Unknown to me, he had attended several sessions of the short-term Bible school, and his quick mind had soaked up the teaching. I developed a great affection for this family and sometimes on Sundays would visit their home, teach them from the Scriptures, and help them share their faith with the many neighbors who crowded in.

One day, Mark and our friend Momin tangled with a mad dog. Momin, a member of the local leading family and nephew of Shahabuddin, was my friend and Muslim informant for Muslim Bengali translation work, and a hospital employee. Momin and Mark, on a bird-hunting trip, had stopped at the Dulahazara bazaar two miles south of the hospital.

Seeing a rabid dog running toward the bazaar, Mark and some Bengali boys ran to tell Momin, who hurried to load one of the guns; but the cartridge would not fit properly. He succeeded in loading the second .22 caliber rifle just as the huge brown angry dog careened around the corner fifteen feet away! As Mark and others in the crowd stumbled back into the store behind Momin, sending cans and fresh fruit flying in every direction, he fired. The snarling dog flinched — but kept charging! In one lightninglike blur of movement Momin ejected the cartridge, pulled a new one from his pocket, inserted it, slammed home the bolt, and fired from the hip at the furious animal less than six feet away.

The attacking animal fell dead at Momin's feet with a neat, round hole between his eyes. Still shaky, Momin and Mark arrived home to tell their wild story. Momin could not conceive how he had reloaded the rifle in that split second. He refused to stay for tea, insisting instead on hurrying off to the mosque to thank God for His care and protection. We did some thanking ourselves.

For the first several months of the year I functioned as field council chairman, which increased my administrative workload. In our March annual meeting, Joan was reelected field council secretary for the third consecutive year, keeping her administratively involved as well. The night school training in secretarial work, which Joan had taken years ago, was paying off. Her minutes were detailed and lucid. She distilled the nuggets from *Robert's Rules of Order* and other such books to produce a practical parliamentary rule book which was at once understandable, workable, and geared to our field council approach. She culled the field council minutes from day one and produced a booklet with an organized listing of all the field council's official actions and home board regulations. She greatly assisted the constitution committee, capably headed by Jesse Eaton, to finalize our field council constitution. In addition, she taught school, visited on the women's ward, kept our home functioning, and helped me in a hundred different ways. What a wife and helpmate! "Thank You, Father!"

On a red-letter day in April, Willard and Donna Benedict left Malumghat to reopen Hebron station — after four years of closure! Although Malumghat had become the center for helping our tribal people, that was a second-best arrangement. Now that function would revert to Hebron station, much better situated to help the tribal people.

In May our Lynne completed eighth grade to become the first graduate of Malumghat Christian School. Looking sweet in white, she gave a brief talk about her own spiritual experience.

She concluded, "Some people dedicate their lives to the Lord before huge crowds or at the front of churches — but I made that decision in a shoe closet." One day when she had carried a handful of shoes to a closet, she explained, the shoes reminded her of a familiar chorus, "Do you know, O Christian, you're a sermon in shoes?" Sensing that she would never succeed spiritually unless she dedicated her life to Christ, she dropped the shoes to pray and offer herself to the Lord for His use.

Lynne and Mel Beals at graduation

Christian leader Shudhir baptizing Bengali style

May also marked the climax of the revival occurring in our midst. After I finished teaching prebaptismal classes for six weeks, seventeen followed Christ in baptism, the largest single group to that time. We walked to a suitable pond a mile away where a Bengali leader preached an impassioned message to the large crowd. Then, one by one, each candidate declared his faith in Christ and was baptized in the name of the Father, the Son, and the Holy Spirit. The beautiful service thrilled us all.

On our way back, we were denied passage through a village which had allowed us to pass to the baptism an hour before! This was only the beginning of sorrows, for heavy persecution fell on some who had declared their faith openly through baptism.

With the new government of General Yahya Khan in power, Ayub Khan's previous promises to us regarding visas were no longer recognized. Fortunately, we had brought in a number of new members before visas again became tight. In East Pakistan, at that time, we had thirty adults and thirty-one children; in Murree Christian School, West Pakistan, we had seven teenagers and one adult (Mrs. Helen Miller, wife of deceased Paul Miller, who had returned to Pakistan to be a housemother at the school). Furthermore, the seventeen appointees in America who were preparing to join us would need visas. The new government had stopped giving us four-year multiple-entry visas and instituted a system of four-year single-entry visas, then changed to one-year single-entry visas — for those who could get them. The long delays of many months in granting visas also made it clear that the government again was putting severe pressure on us.

In June the Ketchams and Walshes returned from furlough and we bade Dr. Jake, Rosie, and their family goodby. By giving us time for teaching and sharing, the Jaquises had played an important part in the revival we had seen. And that revival brought the church a giant step forward toward actual, official formation.

Of all the pets the children enjoyed, a spider-armed black gibbon named Gibby pleased them the most. Although intelligent, she could not quite understand that swinging along the electric wires with the generator operating was dangerous. Two or three times she was hit by a jolt of electricity and knocked to the ground; but most of the time the wires were innocuous. That was what made it so confusing. Lynne and Joan designed a system for getting her out of the tree before the generator started up each evening. Seeing Lynne hugging and patting her mother under the tree made Gibby jealous.

Because her little anthropoid heart could not tolerate Lynne's loving-up anyone else, immediately she would come swinging out of the tree into Lynne's arms.

I admitted to the hospital, one day, a girl with unusual but obviously serious symptoms. When the father admitted she had been bitten by a "crazy dog" some weeks earlier, I feared the worst. Because drinking

Gibby, the children's favorite pet

water is painful and difficult for rabies patients, the water test helps confirm the diagnosis. So I handed the child a glass of water and asked her to drink. Eyes wide with panic, she took just a sip. The spasm that gripped her throat extended to stiffen her whole body. The test was positive! A few hours later she died.

We frequently admitted to the hospital patients with tetanus (lockjaw). The tetanus germ usually entered the body through neglected cuts, infected ears, or an umbilical cord cut with a dirty piece of tin or bamboo. Called in Bengali the "bow disease," the violent spasms and convulsions of tetanus bend the afflicted body back in the form of a hunter's bow. In all my years of training and experience in America I had seen just one case of tetanus — now our hospital contained at least one case most of the time. In addition to medication, we often were forced to do a tracheotomy (making an opening into the windpipe) to keep the patient alive. Because of our vigorous treatment and the devotion of our nursing staff, well over half of our tetanus patients survived.

We allowed the children to see cases of tetanus, diphtheria, smallpox, and cholera, so they could understand the importance of their immunizations and accept them gratefully.

When our own brothers and sisters required surgery, we were thankful for our fine staff and facilities. During that period I operated on David Bayen (our capable Bengali surgical technician), Joyce DeCook, and little ten-year-old Philip Walsh. While operating on Philip, I was able to take a small piece of liver to help us in our study of Chittagong hepatitis, for Phil had suffered from that illness some months before. The microscope kindly confirmed my theory that the illness affected mainly the liver capsule! Our jungle medical science had inched a step forward — and the three surgical patients recovered well.

The May baptismal service marked the beginning of pressure and persecution, not only of some who were baptized, but also of others and the hospital itself. Unexpectedly, two vitriolic articles against the hospital were released through PPI (Pakistan Press International), an indigenous news agency. The articles were then picked up and printed in several newspapers. It was alleged that most of our patients died, and that we were making Muslims become Christians by force. Akand was not involved this time, for he had moved to West Pakistan. Our detective work uncovered a coalition between some local Muslim priests and their friend, a reporter for PPI. When I traveled to Dacca to tackle the problem, I found the reporter to be a tough, vindictive man. His superior, however, proved to be more mature and reasonable and, after hearing my story, talked about making amends.

Our friend, Momin, incensed about the articles, traveled about the countryside setting the record straight and encouraging people to protest the articles. Hearteningly, many did write to the newspapers on our behalf. Simultaneously, the police intelligence branch began a secret investigation of our hospital and its activities. Some of their men attended the hospital as "patients" while others quietly asked questions throughout the area. The director of this secret investigation was the Cox's Bazar officer whose friend's life we had saved by midnight surgery.

With the sense of oppression lying heavy in the area we continued our daily work of caring for the sick and injured. One day, Daniel walked two miles to the Dulahazara bazaar for a haircut and shopping. Unexpectedly, two sneering young men approached him in the barber chair and questioned him harshly, mentioning the newspaper articles. Daniel responded calmly.

"Let me see inside your bag," rasped one of them as he dumped Daniel's Bible and religious booklets on the ground in front of the barbershop.

"He's preaching, he's preaching!" shouted the men as they threw the booklets into the air. In a moment the crowd had dragged Daniel across the street and presented him to the Muslim priest waiting in the tea stall. The whole affair was a well-planned trap to do away with Daniel!

"He's preaching, eh?" snarled the priest. "You know what to do with him — give it to him!" They dragged Daniel over the rough ground to the schoolyard where they stoned him and beat him with umbrellas and canes. The blood began to pour. As men did to Daniel's Master centuries before, so they did to Daniel, pushing him on a high place and shouting, "Preach to us, your highness! Preach to us!" Only Pontius Pilate and the crown of thorns were missing.

Seeing a bus coming, they seized him again and threw him in the road in front of the bus. With screaming brakes and tires the bus swerved just in time to miss Daniel. Grabbing him again, they dragged Daniel across the road and threw him into the gutter. Our ambulance driver, Shukhendu, passing through the bazaar, glimpsed what was happening and burned up the road to the hospital.

Bursting into my office, he shouted, "They're killing Daniel! They're killing Daniel in the bazaar!" Leaping over the legs of two startled private patients, I raced to the ambulance with Shukhendu and Momin in tow. Within three minutes our ambulance squealed to a stop in a cloud of dust. Even before we stopped I dived out the door into the agitated crowd of seven or eight hundred people. As a whisper passed over the crowd ("The daktar sahib is here"), a way opened through the surging mass of people. As I exploded into the center, I just glimpsed two men, their faces contorted with hate, fading back into the crowd. There in the middle lay Daniel, semi-conscious, dirty, battered, and bruised, with blood, perspiration, and urine covering his face. As I glared at the circle of men, many of them my patients, they backed away.

Gently, we picked Daniel up and took him by ambulance back to the hospital where we ensconced him in our most pleasant private room. There he told us the story, including its finale. Just as we had arrived in a cloud of dust, a man with a sharp dagger in hand was reaching for his tongue and a second man, Daniel's executioner, stood by with a larger blade to cut his throat. Another man had been sent to bring gasoline to pour over him and ignite, thus ending the "Daniel problem" forever. But God ruled otherwise.

A few nights later, men armed with large *daos* (machetes) began to roam the area around our housing site. In the darkness, one of them quietly slipped into the Walshes' home. When Eleanor awakened to see a man standing in the back bedroom, urgently she shook Jay awake. As Jay bellowed like a wild bull, the intruder sprinted off into the surrounding forest.

To compound the pressures, a second investigation of the hospital was launched, this time by the civil government. Other problems bore in upon us too. For two months we had found it exceptionally difficult to balance the budget. And the patient load was unusually heavy, making it difficult to carry out our total assignment. Finally, when our backs were against the wall, we knew it was time to act. We called our other activities to a halt and devoted ourselves to a day of prayer! Bengali and American Christians spent hours together praying through all the complicated problems.

The fallout from the day of prayer began to appear immediately. Almost overnight the workload lightened and the budgetary pressures began to ease off. My contact with the leading local Hindu influenced him to call off the persecution of several of our people. The police intelligence branch investigation of the hospital worked out to our great advantage when the official report denied the false allegations and upheld our integrity and good intent. And the local legend was strengthened — the legend that any effort to hurt or damage the hospital work always fails because "Allah hears their prayers and protects them."

The second investigation also completely exonerated us; the SDO challenged the Muslim priest responsible for much of the trouble, saying, "You son of a chicken, I warn you to leave the hospital people alone, for they have done more good for the people of this area in a few years than you have ever done!"

And, best of all, our witness was fruitful. In the month following our day of prayer, at least ten people found new life in Christ.

One of the ten, the Buddhist headmaster of a primary school near Hebron station was carried into the hospital in serious trouble. Tuberculosis, which had attacked his spine, caused a crooked back and paralyzed legs. He could not move his legs, feet, or toes. Among surgeons around the world, there is a difference of opinion about whether or not to operate on such cases.

After much prayerful and thoughtful consideration, I decided not to operate. Instead I gave him strong doses of antituberculosis medicine and ordered physiotherapy (exercise and other treatments of muscles and joints). Larry Golin, who had completed his language study and settled in at Malumghat, had initiated our physiotherapy department. Daily Larry manipulated and massaged those motionless legs, and daily we gave the injections and tablets. But there was no response. I began to reconsider operating on the headmaster's spine. But, before another day passed, the patient could move his left big toe. The medicine had begun to bring the disease under control! From that point there was steady progress all the way. After some weeks, with a body cast in place, Larry taught him to walk again, first with crutches, then without.

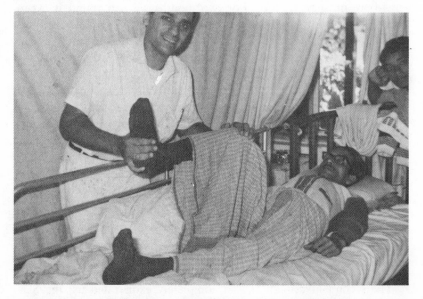

Larry Golin giving physiotherapy to the headmaster

During the second week of the patient's stay, I learned that two years earlier he had developed an interest in the Christian Bible and the Christian faith. I answered his many questions and taught him from the Scriptures. Soon he accepted the Saviour, and a few days later his bright and precocious teenage son followed suit. Nobody in his village ever expected to see him walk again. But the day came when he arrived home, handed his canes to another, and walked laboriously from the boat up the slippery bank to his house.

During the last quarter of 1970 the church groups of Malumghat and Chittagong formed Bengali-American steering committees to finalize the church documents in a culturally relevant way, and officially organize the churches. Recurrent problems and crises had delayed and interrupted that work many times; other problems and unimagined crises would further frustrate that work in the days ahead.

In mid-October we celebrated at last the arrival of WAPDA utility electricity at Malumghat! As the officer had promised, WAPDA installed at their own expense the huge steel pylons, heavy gauge wiring, and the expensive transformer. Our maintenance and construction crew under Jay Walsh and Mel Beals had poured the concrete posts to carry the standard voltage wires from the transformer to our two sites (hospital and housing sites). Our costs, minimal compared to WAPDA's, were subsidized by a fine, Chicago-based Christian foundation to which Bob Adolph had applied successfully. The blazing outside lights helped our night watchmen protect equipment from theft. And when our own generators operated properly again they could be used as an ideal emergency electrical supply.

In November, the charismatic Mujib moved about the East Pakistan countryside like a whirlwind, in preparation for the December elections. His Awami League symbol, the boat, was plastered all over the cities and villages of East Pakistan. His slogan *Joi Bangla* (Victory to Bengal) reverberated throughout the land.

Sheikh Mujib, a middle-of-the-road candidate, seemed much more highly visible than the communist-oriented parties on his left or the more orthodox Muslim religious parties on the right. Mujib drew huge crowds in nearby Cheringa and Cox's Bazar. His political speeches centered on the six points he felt just and necessary. Like the British Whigs three hundred years earlier, he demanded lessened authority for the ruler in power, establishment of true parliamentary democracy, freedom for all religious groups and social betterment of the masses. He did not go so far as American Whigs of two centuries ago, however, by opting for revolution against a distant central government. Rather, he fought for more East Pakistan autonomy within the overall framework of Pakistan.

Also in November, another whirlwind germinated in some southern sea to begin its powerful circular motion moving toward East Pakistan. Far more colossal than its predecessors, the storm gained in intensity and fury as it screamed northward up the Bay of Bengal. On November 12, when the juggernaut cyclone with its massive wall of water smashed head-on into the vulnerable delta area of East Pakistan, the results were cataclysmic. Nearly half a million people died in an hour! The survivors spent weeks burying the dead finally to eradicate the stench of decaying flesh. Billed as the greatest single natural calamity of the century, the November cyclone caused incredible damage. The animals, housing, and food supplies of hundreds of thousands of people were destroyed in a few moments' time.

I was in Chittagong when the killer cyclone pounced. Although only its edge struck our area, sleep was impossible throughout the night. The frightful wind screamed, shutters banged, glass shattered, branches cracked, and even resilient palm trees snapped like matchsticks. I marveled at the ferocity and power of the wind.

The storm spawned many unique stories. A grandfather, hearing the onrushing wall of water in the distance, stuffed his five grandchildren into a trunk and closed the lid. The grandfather died but the children survived. A small child, semiconscious, was hurled into a treetop where a python coiled around it to hold the child safely in the tree until rescued. The rushing water snatched her baby from the arms of a young mother clutching a tree; in a moment a wave deposited another living infant into her waiting arms. That those children were the rare exceptions, a newspaper headline made clear: "Do Not Send Children's Clothing to Cyclone-Affected Area. No Children Remain."

Although the devastation and need were phenomenal, the Pakistan central government responded in a most desultory and disinterested way. The nations of the world rallied more to the East Pakistan crisis than did the government of Pakistan itself. This development turned the windstorm into a windfall for Sheikh Mujib! In the three weeks remaining before the election Sheikh Mujib traveled about the country decrying the "criminal neglect," as he termed it, of the Pakistan central government in East Pakistan's hour of need. Convincingly, he thundered that this neglect proved the need for East Pakistan's greater autonomy.

Election day (December 7) in East Pakistan was remarkably peaceful. Multitudes in both wings went to the polls to cast their vote for the boat, the umbrella, or the bicycle. When the ballots were counted, the nation was stunned to learn the landslide extent of the victory of the boat, the Sheikh, and his Awami League. For the National Assembly (senate) the Awami League had gained 167 seats of the 169 alloted to East Pakistan! Because the total National Assembly seats numbered only 313, these 167 seats gave the Awami League an absolute majority. This meant that Sheikh Mujib needed no coalition with other parties and would *become the prime minister of all of Pakistan!* Because the vote was split in West Pakistan, no other party remotely approached gaining the power voted to the Awami League. In the East Pakistan Provincial Assembly (state legislature) the Awami League gained 288 out of 300 seats, another smashing majority. The latter-day Whig and the whirlwind had combined to change the face of Pakistan politics — and set the stage for hell on earth.

19

RApE ANd REpREssioN

THE IDEA OF AN ATTACK *on Malumghat tonight seems so incredible, so unreal,* I mused as I waited for the inevitable "lights out" and the climax to follow. Similarly, when the West Pakistan army had launched its surprise attack on East Pakistan, it seemed like an hallucination or some impossible fantasy.

The year started so well, I remembered. *The elections were fair and orderly. The unity of the Bengali people behind their new leader was inspiring to see. And, at last, they would have a chance to begin relieving the hated disparity between East and West Pakistan.* Our mission team, too, started out the year right — on a strong spiritual note.

*   *   *

In the first week of January we enjoyed several days of spiritual retreat at Cox's Bazar. Our speaker, Rev. Aslam Khan, who had come from a Muslim background, came to us from Lahore, West Pakistan. His messages, his spritual wisdom, and radiant Christian life meant much to us. He seemed greatly interested when he learned that we were looking for a capable, high level Bengali Christian to be our mission administrative officer.

"I know just the man for you," he said, "I have a Bengali friend who has been a Christian two or three years; he holds a highly responsible job in Lahore. I think he would like to return to East Pakistan and would be happy in the Lord's work. I will put him in touch with you."

During their three months with us, we offered our high school MKs an opportunity to work at the hospital for the same number of rupees we paid any employee who held their jobs. Each one received training for his or her work. Wendy served as a nurse's assistant in the outpatient department. Lynne helped in the pharmacy and studied to be a nurse's aide. Tom Ketcham and Doug Walsh learned the work of surgical technicians to help Donn and me in the operating room. Sharon Miller kept records and otherwise assisted matron Becky Davey. The kids did excellent work that winter and played an important part in our medical-surgical mission.

The first three months of East Pakistan's 1971 were dominated by three strong-willed men: Sheikh Mujibur Rahman, General Yahya Khan, and Zulfikar Ali Bhutto. Sheikh Mujibur Rahman, the charismatic Bengali elected by his fellow Bengalis to be their leader and the prime minister of all of Pakistan, was determined to make his six points stick and gain more autonomy for East Pakistan. General Yahya Khan was president of Pakistan and its martial law government. Although reconciled to some increased autonomy for East Pakistan, he was prepared to go to any lengths to keep the east wing from declaring independence and breaking away from the Islamic republic of Pakistan. Zulfikar Ali Bhutto was the flamboyant, leftist head of the Pakistan People's Party (PPP) which won nearly 60 percent of the National Assembly (NA) seats allocated to West Pakistan. He vainly hoped to share power with Sheikh Mujib in the new government despite Mujib's absolute majority in the NA. It soon became clear that Bhutto and Yahya were working together against Mujib.

In mid-January Mujib and Yahya met. The president learned that Mujib considered the six points unalterable; any negotiations would have to start from that base. Yahya did not criticize the six points, but suggested that Mujib's party should strive for an agreement with Mr. Bhutto and his leftist party.[1] Yahya, in public, referred to Mujib as the next prime minister of Pakistan.

At the end of January Bhutto came to Dacca for talks with Mujib. When Bhutto refused to accept two of the six points and Mujib rightfully declined to share power with Bhutto, a deadlock ensued. Simultaneously, Pakistanis hijacked an Indian passenger plane to West Pakistan. When the plane was destroyed, India angrily banned all Pakistani planes from flying over Indian soil. From that day all Pakistani flights had to be routed far south around the tip of India. Our children returning to high school would have to fly four thousand miles from Dacca to Rawalpindi instead of the usual fourteen hundred miles. The plane would refuel at Ceylon, an island nation located at the tip of India.

In late January President Yahya called for the NA to meet in Dacca on March 3. That was the day the Bengalis were waiting for! With an absolute majority in that parliament, they could frame a new constitution, based on the six points, to gain greatly increased autonomy for East Pakistan.

Our visa problems continued to be serious. The Pakistan government, under President Yahya Khan, had granted no visas to our staff

for a long time. Some of our team had been in application for many
months. Only with great difficulty did I arrange single-entry short-
term visas for three of us to take an important trip. As project director
for the Muslim Bengali Bible translation and chairman of the
translation committee, I needed to attend the Bible Translators' Institute to be held in Thailand in February. Of course, Lynn Silvernale and Mrs. Dass, our chief translators, went; Joan also accompanied
the group.

On our way out of the country a friendly police official warned,
"Our immigration authorities have made a mistake. According
to the rules, the type of visa they have given you is canceled the
minute you leave the country. They cannot legally allow you back
into East Pakistan on this visa."

I was delighted! This meant we could make a strong attempt for
fresh visas in the Pakistan embassy in Thailand. Maybe, if the
Pakistan authorities had failed to pass on to their Thailand embassy
the strict rules regarding missionary visas, we might even obtain
four-year multiple-entry visas, for us the acme of all visas.

At the Pakistan Embassy in Bangkok, Thailand, I found the officer in charge of visa matters was a Bengali, not a West Pakistani.
Chatting away in Bengali, we found that we had some mutual
acquaintances. He seemed delighted to have a visitor from East Pakistan who could converse with him in his own heart language. Quickly
our brief acquaintance developed a warm and friendly quality.

Finally, when I requested a four-year multiple-entry visa to be
granted the same day, he replied, "We do not ordinarily supply visas
so quickly, but I think I can help you. Please come back in four
hours." At the appointed time I returned to pick up beautiful four-
year, multiple-entry visas! Incredible! "Thank You, Father!"

We traveled south for two hours to reach the Translators' Institute
located at a beautiful site on the shores of the Gulf of Siam. We
learned much from some of the world's greatest experts on the subject.
We were impressed that many translators were giving years to provide the Scriptures to tribes of ten, thirty, or fifty thousand, while
we were translating for the Bengali race, numbering 125 million
people!

Fellow translators from Malaysia and Indonesia had studied and
struggled for a year trying to solve a particular problem: how to
translate for a mixed population of Muslims and non-Muslims.
Facing a similar situation in East Pakistan, we had conducted research
which revealed the best solution to such an enigma — two separate
translations, one for each group. Our research and experience not

only solved our difficulty, but also the problem faced by these other translators.

While Lynn and Mrs. Dass remained on throughout February, Joan and I returned to East Pakistan (with our coveted visas in hand) on February 12 in order to be home for Wendy's birthday the next day.

Two days after our arrival at Malumghat, Mr. Bhutto, back in West Pakistan, dropped his bombshell! He announced that members of his party elected to the NA would not attend the first NA meeting to be held on March 3! Then, fantastically, he threatened West Pakistani MNAs (senators) of other political parties with physical harm if they flew to Dacca to attend the NA meeting.[2] However, these crude tactics of intimidation failed, and most of the MNAs of other parties booked their seats for Dacca. Even some of Mr. Bhutto's own PPP members began agitating to proceed to Dacca. But, at the last minute, President Yahya saved the day for Bhutto.

On March 1, shortly after lunch, we listened to Yahya speak to the nation on a nationwide hookup. In his speech,[3] given in English, he made one of the most colossal blunders in the history of Pakistan. He canceled the March 3 meeting of the NA in which power was to be turned over to Sheikh Mujib and his Awami League! The NA session was postponed indefinitely!

Convinced that President Yahya had no intention of turning over the government to legally elected Sheikh Mujib and his Awami League, multitudes of Bengalis poured out into the streets of cities and towns throughout the country to protest this speech. Dacca University students burned the Pakistan flag. March 1 marked the beginning of the end of East Pakistan.

During the first three days of March, massive crowds of unarmed demonstrators filled the streets protesting the cancellation of the NA meeting. Shockingly, Pakistan soldiers fired hundreds of rounds of ammunition into the emotional, defenseless masses of people. We learned that over a thousand Bengalis died at the hands of their West Pakistani "brothers" during those two and a half days. The people cried out for justice; and many, thoroughly disillusioned, screamed for Bengali independence from Pakistan.

Simultaneously PIA passenger planes, which could have been bringing MNAs from West Pakistan to a peaceful and democratic sitting of the National Assembly in Dacca, began ferrying hundreds of Pakistani soldiers in civilian clothes to build up the army in East Pakistan. The same planes carried back to West Pakistan the dependents of West Pakistani military officers and businessmen. At the same time, tanks deployed in border areas began to rumble back toward Dacca. The governor, a man liked by the Bengalis because he was sympathetic with their aspirations, was recalled to West Pakistan and replaced by a tough general. While unarmed civilians were being killed by Pakistan soldiers, Radio Pakistan announced President Yahya's invitation to all political leaders to attend a meeting in Dacca on March 10.

During the third day of March everyone waited with bated breath for Mujib's speech in which he would respond both to the strange, impersonal invitation to the March tenth political talks and to the bloody attacks of the preceding forty-eight hours. Millions expected him to announce that since autonomy within Pakistan was a lost cause, independence now would be their goal. That announcement he did not make. Instead, he declined to participate in the March 10 meeting because "the blood of the martyrs on the streets is hardly dry, many of the dead are still lying unburied, and hundreds are fighting death in hospitals."[4]

Furthermore, he called for a nonviolent, noncooperation movement against the government of Pakistan. He demanded that the government withdraw the army to the barracks. He called on the Bengali people to maintain peace and discipline and avoid lawlessness. We appreciated his admonition that "all who live in Bangladesh are Bengalis, and it is our sacred duty to afford protection to the life and property of every citizen whether Bengali or non-Bengali, Hindu or Muslim." He promised to address a rally on March 7 to give the people their next instructions.[5]

Virtually all of East Pakistan's 75 million cooperated completely with Sheikh Mujib's call to nonviolent noncooperation: rural peasants, urban laborers, small and large businessmen, intellectuals, students and their professors. They observed the rest of March 3 as a day of national mourning, as Mujib had commanded, for that was the date of the blasted NA meeting. The whole country came to a standstill as the people refused to work or pay further taxes.

On March 6, faced with the remarkable success of the noncooperation movement and another speech by Mujib the next day, President Yahya made a stern radio address to the nation. Yahya criticized Mujib, set a new day for the inaugural session of the NA (March 25), and ended with a strong warning:

> As long as I am in command of the Pakistan Armed Forces and Head of the State, I will ensure complete and absolute integrity of Pakistan. Let there be no doubt or mistake on this point . . . . It is the duty of the Pakistan Armed Forces to ensure the integrity, solidarity, and security of Pakistan.[6]

We could not fathom the total meaning of Yahya's warning speech on that day, but one point was clear — he would meet with armed force any attempt to make East Pakistan independent of Pakistan! Sheikh Mujib had twenty-four hours to prepare his response to Yahya's tough speech.

The next day an incredible mass of humanity (estimated at one million) crowded the Dacca race track grounds to hear Mujib's fateful address. Hundreds of thousands waited expectantly for him to declare independence and hoist the flag of free Bangladesh, already sewn by some Bengali Betsy Ross. But the flag was not raised, and independence was not declared. Rather, he said:

> There is still a possibility of our living like brothers with the people of West Pakistan, if there is a peaceful settlement. Otherwise there is none. If the Pakistan Army commits any more excesses, we may never look at one another's faces again.

Further, he declared:

> The bloodstains of those killed have not yet dried, and I cannot step on the blood of the martyrs to attend the National Assembly on March 25. Yahya Khan has convened the assembly. But my demands are:
> 1. Lift martial law.
> 2. Take the soldiers back to the barracks.
> 3. Investigate the mass killings.
> 4. Transfer power to the elected representatives.
> After these we will consider whether we could sit in the National Assembly or not.

He closed his impassioned speech with his familiar rallying cry "*Joi Bangla!* [Victory to Bengal!]."[7]

On the same day, an even tougher military officer arrived in Dacca to become the new governor of East Pakistan. Because of his brutal tactics in smashing a resistance movement in the West Pakistani province of Baluchistan, Lt. General Tikka (red hot) Khan was known as the Bomber of Baluchistan. His coming was a signal that the government of Pakistan and the Pakistan army were going to get tougher. The noncooperation movement was adhered to so faithfully, however, that the high court justice even refused to administer the oath of office to Tikka Khan!

Throughout the first week in March, ABWE publicity expert and film maker Bob Burns was living out his personal adventure in Dacca. After three weeks of filming our mission's East Pakistan work, Bob was escorted by Jesse Eaton to the capital city where they found the heavily guarded airport jammed with hundreds of terrified West

Pakistanis and other foreigners wanting out of East Pakistan. Because the Pakistan air force had taken over the airport, Bob's PIA reservations were useless. He was stuck in the turbulent, blood-stained city, tossed about by the onrushing tides of history in the making. After six days of dodging curfews (and riding a borrowed ambulance to the airport during curfews), my harried friend finally got a seat and flew off to a saner part of the world.

The Pakistani ship, *M. V. Swat,* arrived at Chittagong port on March 8 full of arms and ammunition. Chittagong dock workers refused to unload the vessel. Because PIA flights to Dacca were canceled and trains jammed to overflowing, Jay Walsh drove our high schoolers, including Wendy and Lynne, to Dacca. With considerable difficulty he arranged seats on the flight to West Pakistan, and they started on the long journey around the tip of India. British, German, and Japanese dependents and nonessential workers were evacuating rapidly out of East Pakistan. The Dacca airport was jammed with terrified West Pakistanis, especially dependents, fleeing from East Pakistan.

On March 15 the Malumghat countryside was peaceful. We began our three days of annual field council meetings with nearly all our members in attendance (the Gurganuses remained in Chittagong because of the unsettled conditions there). In Dacca Sheikh Mujib announced he was taking over the civil administration, and issued thirty-five directives containing the guidelines for this new administration.

On the same day *Time* magazine printed a lucid article on the deteriorating situation in East Pakistan;[8] the article closed with the observation that a declaration of independence would be little more than an anticlimax. But Mujib, showing impressive restraint, was willing to negotiate further — and on March 15 President Yahya arrived from West Pakistan for just that purpose. The senior East Pakistan civil servants for the first time failed to appear at the airport to welcome their president.

During the ten days of talks (March 16 to 25) there seemed to be substantial progress. According to official Awami League sources[9] Yahya expressed his sincere desire for a political settlement. He agreed to institute an inquiry into the army firing which had killed Bengalis. Broad agreement was soon reached on Mujib's four demands. The experts and technicians on both sides went to work to thrash out the details. Mr. M. M. Ahmad, the economic adviser to the president, was flown in from West Pakistan to help work out the fine points of the agreement. After studying an Awami League document concerning transfer of power to the elected representatives, he suggested three amendments.

During those ten days, however, other more disturbing developments were taking place. The daily PIA flights continued to ferry to Dacca soldiers dressed in civilian clothes. Military transport planes arrived full of arms, ammunition and provisions. Ironically, Yahya shipped soldiers and arms to East Pakistan more quickly than he had sent aid after the devastating cyclone. The military took control of the airport, turning it into a fortress complete with machine gun nests and artillery. Commando groups, specialists in assassination, sabotage, and undercover operations, were deployed in various cities. One by one, six shiploads of troops departed Karachi, West Pakistan, for Chittagong in the East. Bengali soldiers and policemen noticed, moreover, that their stocks of reserve ammunition were being reduced, on one pretext or another, and that senior Bengali officers were being dispatched on various useless or insignificant missions.

The Bengali people, during the ten days of negotiations, maintained their disciplined noncooperation and the onrushing momentum of their movement. Because of continued army firing on Bengali crowds, thousands more began to speak of *"shadheen Bangla* [independent Bengal]." In Dacca, Bengali activists burned more Pakistan flags and pictures of Jinnah, the founder of Pakistan. Surreptitiously, they hoisted a new flag said to be the banner of the forthcoming independent Bangladesh. Even in nearby Cox's Bazar, a Hindu student named Shubash publicly trampled and burned the Pakistan flag. But Mujib refused to bow to the cries and pressure of such activists. He had determined to complete his negotiations with President Yahya Khan.

The Mujib-Yahya talks began in Dacca on March 16. But in Chittagong, Bengalis died on the streets when the Pakistan army fired heavily on unarmed demonstrators. Two days later, a man with friends in high places flew from Karachi to Dacca. There he shocked newsmen when he told them that two army generals had confided to him that the army planned to tranquilize the Bengali leaders into thinking the talks were succeeding, then attack East Pakistan without warning.[10] Of course, no one wanted to believe that ghastly possibility.

By March 21 President Yahya had accepted, in principle, the demands of Sheikh Mujib. Their respective delegations were working over the wording of the documents. That day a frightened but determined Bhutto arrived in Dacca with his own personal bodyguard armed with machine guns. He promptly established himself on the eleventh floor of the plush Hotel Intercontinental where his armed guards patrolled the hall. Then he rejected the tentative agreement reached by Yahya and Mujib.

On March 24 Mujib and his advisers accepted, with only minor changes in wording, the three amendments to the transfer of power document suggested by the president's economic adviser. That night a military helicopter flew from Dacca to Chittagong where the army garrison was commanded by a Bengali officer, Brigadier Mazumdar. Unexpectedly relieved of his command, the high-ranking Bengali officer was flown in the same helicopter, under armed guard, back to Dacca where he disappeared.

On the second anniversary of Yahya Khan's presidency of Pakistan, March 25, Mujib waited for Yahya's advisers to set the time for the final meeting. Mujib's suspicions were aroused, however, when he learned that the president's economic adviser had hurriedly boarded a PIA plane that morning and flown back to West Pakistan. In Chittagong, the new military commander suddenly ordered his soldiers to unload the munitions from the *M. V. Swat*, still nestled at a Chittagong dock. Tens of thousands of Chittagonians came out in the streets, and thousands menacingly surrounded the soldiers who were unloading the munitions ship. The army shot its way through the mob, leaving at least thirty-five Bengalis dead on the docks.

In the afternoon, Bhutto held a news conference in Dacca to report he still was opposed to two of Mujib's six points. Thereafter, Bhutto's and Yahya's advisers met together. At 5:45 P.M. Yahya departed the heavily fortified presidential house, the very house where we had negotiated for visas with former President Ayub Khan and his principal secretary. Secretly, Yahya boarded an airplane and flew back to West Pakistan. That night a Sheikh Mujib statement was read to the press. He called for a general strike on March 27 to protest the continued killing of unarmed civilians by Pakistan troops. Later, the instant a message was flashed from Karachi to Dacca that President Yahya had landed safely, the Pakistan army generals in Dacca gave the fateful order.[11]

Some thirty-five foreign correspondents were headquartered in Dacca at the modern Hotel Intercontinental. By 10:00 P.M. they observed that the hotel military guard had doubled in number and new faces replaced familiar ones. Every other soldier faced inward toward the hotel rather than outward toward the street. At 11:00 P.M. the soldiers herded the correspondents back into the hotel.

A captain informed them, "My orders for tonight are that if anyone tries to leave the hotel after 11:00 P.M. we are to shoot him." Before midnight the chatter of machine guns sounded throughout the city, notifying Dacca (and the world) that the carnage had begun! *The Pakistan government had unleashed its army to smash East Pakistan!* While negotiations were still in progress, without warning, ultimatum, or curfew order, the surprise attack was launched.

Throughout that long night three battalions of soldiers (one infantry, one artillery, one armored) killed defenseless Dacca Bengalis with bayonets, rifles, machine guns, mortars, artillery pieces, rockets, flame throwers, and tanks. With military precision they tackled seven main targets: Dacca University, the police barracks, the East Pakistan Rifles (EPR) cantonment, Sheikh Mujib's home, the Radio Pakistan transmitter, offices of a pro-Mujib newspaper, and Hindu homes.

Tank cannons and machine guns opened up on two male student dormitories at Dacca University. Several hundred young men, the cream of Bengali youth, died that night from Pakistani bullets, shells, and raging flames. Later, when an art student was found sprawled across his easel, it became apparent that dozens never knew what hit them. At the Hindu students' dormitory, the students who survived the attack were forced to dig graves for their slaughtered fellow students. Then they, too, were shot and stuffed into the graves dug with their own hands.

Simultaneously, tanks opened fire on the barracks where over a thousand policemen slept, an area I knew well. Troops moved in to ignite the quarters with incendiary rounds of ammunition. In another section of town a similar attack smashed the cantonment of the East Pakistan Rifles (a Bengali paramilitary force). The whole section became a seething mass of flames where many officers' families were roasted alive.[12]

About 1:00 A.M. army vehicles filled with soldiers arrived at Sheikh Mujib's modest home. They shot dozens of rounds indiscriminately at the house from rifles and machine guns; when bullets slammed into the room of Mujib's six-year-old son, Russell, a splinter struck the child's leg. From his second-floor bedroom, Mujib shouted at the soldiers to stop firing — the firing continued.

Pushing his wife and children into the bathroom for safekeeping, Mujib shouted again, loudly, "Stop firing!"

When the shooting eased off, he admonished the colonel in charge, "Why didn't you telephone me and come? I am always here." Ransacking his books, diaries and life history notes, the soldiers struck him on the back and pushed him out of the house.

An officer barked, "Don't kill him."

After a week's incarceration in the Dacca cantonment, Mujib was flown to West Pakistan where he was imprisoned in Mianwali Prison.

He was kept in solitary confinement without books, newspaper, or radio.[13]

Hundreds of Hindus (some casteless laborers, others businessmen, even a famous philanthropist and a college professor) died that night. From the tenth floor of the Hotel Intercontinental foreign correspondents watched an army contingent machine-gun and burn the offices of a noted pro-Mujib newspaper, *The People*. (The motto of this newspaper: "You cannot fool all the people all the time.") Another military unit captured Radio Pakistan's Dacca transmitter which became the center for their broadcasts throughout the country.

In addition to the seven prime targets, the Pakistan soldiers, during the first eight hours of March 26, also attacked industrial areas, railway stations, ferry terminals, roadside slums, and main food bazaars. Sleeping butchers, wrapped in their blankets and lying in their bazaar stalls, were riddled without warning as they slept.

At 8:00 A.M. the radio announced that President Yahya had returned to West Pakistan and would broadcast to the nation at 8:00 P.M. At 8:30 A.M. a worried-looking, heavily guarded Mr. Bhutto left the hotel for the airport. At 9:00 A.M. the radio declared that curfew was in effect and anyone seen on the streets would be shot at sight. At 10:00 A.M. Pakistan radio in Dacca announced a series of stiff martial law orders to the people of East Pakistan.

Another radio (the Radio Pakistan Chittagong transmitter), obviously in the hands of the Bengalis, proclaimed the independence of the new nation of Bangladesh. We heard all these broadcasts at Malumghat.

Then, from midday to midnight, the old city section of Dacca felt the fury and the flame of the Pakistan army. The leading contingents of soldiers poured machine gun fire into the houses; the second contingents doused the houses with gasoline and ignited them. From noon until 2:00 P.M. seven hundred men, women, and children bled or burned to death in Old Dacca. The carnage continued in section after section of the old city until midnight.

When the army reached the Hindu area of the old town, the merciless massacre increased in intensity. Then, with glee, the soldiers attacked the offices of the pro-Mujib daily newspaper *Ittefaq*. Four tanks poured their fire into the building, producing a raging inferno which not only destroyed the building, but also the four hundred people who had taken shelter inside it. While the people of Dacca absorbed these horrors, throughout the province units of Pakistani soldiers machine gunned in their barracks sleeping Bengali soldiers of the East Bengal Regiment. The massacre included Bengali officers, their wives and children.

At about 5:00 P.M. more than three hundred troops attacked the girl students of Rockey Hall, Dacca University.[14] Stripping them naked, the troops raped, bayoneted, and murdered lovely Bengali girls. Dozens of the girls jumped to their death from the roof of Rockey Hall rather than suffer the fate of their sisters.

At 8:00 P.M. Yahya Khan broadcasted to the nation from West Pakistan.[15] He did not mention the thousands of unarmed Bengalis who had perished in the preceding twenty-one hours, but he branded Sheikh Mujib and the Awami League as enemies of Pakistan guilty of treason.

A few minutes later the thirty-five foreign correspondents at Dacca's Intercontinental Hotel were bundled into four waiting Dodge army trucks and taken to the airport. Soldiers carefully searched every correspondent and confiscated all film, tapes, diaries, notebooks, and notes. At three hours after midnight the reporters took off for West Pakistan.

Simultaneously with the attack in Dacca, other units of the Pakistan army smashed into cities and towns across the land. They followed the same scenario of kill, rape, loot, and burn! They disarmed and killed hundreds of Bengali policemen and militiamen. Quickly they controlled strategic points — airfields, radio transmitting stations, telephone exchanges, telegraph stations, police stations, tall buildings, and commanding hilltops. The Pakistan army clearly hoped so to smash the country and its leadership in the first forty-eight hours that no resistance could develop in this "country of clerks."[16]

But this diabolical plan turned out to be a colossal blunder. Overcome by rage, the Bengalis' bravery — and foolhardiness — was fantastic. Arming themselves with staves, spears, *daos,* and a few ancient firearms, they launched human wave attacks at the pockets of soldiers holding strategic positions. Thousands of Bengalis died in hails of machine gun and rifle bullets — but, when the Pakistani ammunition was exhausted, the remaining Bengalis hacked the soldiers to death.

Confronted with this unexpected uprising, the Pakistan army withdrew to the cantonments, airports, and a few other strategic spots. There they were surrounded by thousands of Bengalis who hoped to starve them out. Then many crazed Bengalis retaliated, killing and committing atrocities upon hated West Pakistani civilians and collaborators. During this period, which lasted about two weeks, planes and helicopters from Dacca strengthened every garrison with fresh troops, arms, ammunition, and supplies. When their deliberate preparations were complete, the Pakistan army units burst out of their cantonments and, in another cold-blooded orgy of killing, rape, plunder, and burning, they smashed the country's main population centers. During the first week in April the Pakistan forces established a foothold in Chittagong. By mid-April they controlled not only Chittagong, but most of the cities and towns of Bangladesh.

Determined to cripple the Bengali cause for decades, the army continued its systematic massacre. Working from carefully prepared lists, special commando units of the Pakistan army hunted down and exterminated Awami League leaders, intellectuals, professors, students, doctors, lawyers, journalists, and Hindus. The stories of the butchery and brutality meted out to these men and their families were endless.

Although thousands of young women were killed, the most attractive among them were captured to become sex slaves in the military cantonments. When the girls tried to hang themselves with their clothing, their garments were taken from them. Then, when they tried to strangle themselves with their long black hair, they were shaved bald. When they became five or six months pregnant, they were released with the taunt: "When my son is born, you must bring him back to me." Many such infants were strangled at birth.

As the killing continued steadily in the cities and towns, Pakistani Sabre jets strafed and rocketed defenseless villages and bazaars. Then strong mechanized units began moving out to raid the villages. Guided by their ever-present intelligence lists, the army extended the killing-raping-looting-burning operation to the countryside and struck terror to the hearts of the simple village people. "Golden Bengal" had become orange with fire, black with smoke, and red with the blood of Bengalis.

20

Bloody Birth

TIME FOR FINAL PREPARATIONS, I thought to myself, *it is nearly 10:00!* I stood, walked to my bed, and gave the dummy under the sheets a final punch in the interests of realism. Before turning off my light, I reread the meaningful Scripture passages I had studied during morning quiet time in my hospital bed.

Flipping out my bedroom light, I opened the curtain and looked outside. Shotguns over their shoulders, my guards were patrolling their beats according to instruction. Then I lay down gingerly on the thin mattress behind the door, checked my revolver, and placed it beside my head. There was no lack of sincerity in my prayer! Despite an immense exhaustion, my mind remained alert enough to pick up my train of thought at March 26, 1971 — just four weeks before.

*   *   *

The world thought that the holocaust was happening in East Pakistan — but the world was wrong! The Bengalis knew that East Pakistan had died in the early morning hours of March 26 when the troops fanned out to kill and burn and to capture their guiding spirit, Sheikh Mujib. As we worked in the hospital on Friday morning, March 26, the Chittagong station of Radio Pakistan crackled to life. In an instant we learned that the Chittagong station was under the control of the Bangladesh liberation army, not the West Pakistanis. Passionately a voice broadcasted in Bengali a declaration of independence:

> *Today Bangladesh is a sovereign and independent state.* On Thursday night West Pakistani armed forces suddenly attacked the police barracks at Rajarbagh and EPR headquarters at Peelkhana in Dacca. Many innocent and unarmed people have been killed in Dacca city and other places of Bangladesh. Violent clashes between the East Pakistan Rifles and police on the one hand and the armed forces of

Pindi on the other, are going on. The Bengalis are fighting the
enemy with great courage for an *independent Bangladesh.* Resist
the treacherous enemy in every corner of Bangladesh. May God aid
us in our fight for freedom. Joi Bangla![1]

Huddled around a transistor radio, our Bengali staff went wild!

Two weeks later this informal radio declaration was confirmed
by a written Proclamation of Independence.[2] Elected leaders left
their safe haven in India and crossed the border to a village they
renamed Mujibnagar (Mujib city), Bangladesh, for a day of ceremonies and speeches. There they presented the Proclamation of
Independence, formed a Bangladesh constituent assembly (to function *in absentia*), appointed the first cabinet of the Bangladesh
government (to act *in absentia*), and declared Sheikh Mujibur Rahman the first president of Bangladesh (*in absentia.*)

In Chittagong the Bengali freedom fighters were able to prevail
longer than did the Bengalis in Dacca. On March 28, as the battle
raged around our Chittagong chapel/headquarters building, thirty-
four Bengali Christians huddled inside. Rifle fire hit the buildings
while shells and rockets smashed into other buildings nearby, badly
damaging a nearby Hindu temple. Heroically the Gurganuses, Reid
Minich, Lynn Silvernale, and Jeannie Lockerbie remained in Chittagong several harrowing days and nights, comforting the Christian
flock and bandaging bloody Bengalis.

During this period the Bengali liberation army made frequent
broadcasts from Radio Pakistan's Chittagong station, which they
called Radio Free Bengal. Their impassioned messages were highly
effective in keeping Bengali morale high. On March 30 the Pakistan
army generals decided that Radio Free Bengal must go! Two Sabre
jets lifted off a Dacca runway and streaked toward Chittagong.
Banking in off the Bay of Bengal they roared over Chittagong,
sighted their target, and each fell into a screaming dive. When
their strafing and rocketing runs were complete, Radio Free Bengal
was dead! Our hospital staff listened in vain for further word from
the Bangladesh liberation army.

On the same afternoon, when the Pakistan army gained control of
the DC's hill and erected a machine gun which pointed directly down
at the girls' house, Jeannie and Lynn decided it was time for a
change of scenery — the danger had become acute. Reid departed
Chittagong temporarily to drive the girls and a group of endangered
Bengali friends to us at Malumghat. Later the girls' house was
struck with flying bullets. The Gurganuses holed up in Chittagong
with other American and Canadian families in a house flying large

American and Canadian flags to await some means of evacuation so they could proceed on their furlough.

The war came last to our Malumghat-Cox's Bazar area, situated in the southern finger of the country. For weeks before the Pakistan army arrived, we were under the control of the *Mukti Fouj* (liberation army), later renamed *Mukti Bahini* (freedom brothers or freedom fighters).

In the Malumghat area, during the first week of warfare, the local police handed over to the freedom fighters rifles from the police station arsenal. Two truckloads of local Bengalis, some of them our friends, bravely headed for Chittagong to help fight the Pakistan army. Over the next several days local Bengali freedom fighters came to us with three separate demands. Although we had promised to care for their injured and were sympathetic to their aspirations, we could not agree to all their demands.

They first insisted that we hand over to them the two West Pakistani watchmen who had been our employees for several years. Because our Bengali friends would have hacked them to death before the sun set, we refused to hand over the two Pathans. Jay Walsh, responsible for the watchmen, after nightfall dressed them in Bengali clothes and hid them away in a room in our servants' quarters. There, surrounded by tens of thousands of Bengalis who wanted to kill them, they quaked in terror night after night.

When the freedom fighters returned, this time demanding our hunting arms and ammunition, we gave much thought and prayer to how we should respond. If we refused to turn over the arms, they might take them by force and some among us might be hurt. If we gave up the guns, however, they would use them to ambush and kill men; and we wanted no part in the killing. Furthermore, we would be left incapable of defending ourselves against any mad dogs (or mad men) who might attack us. The "guidance factor" moved us to refuse to hand over the firearms! *If we had decided otherwise,* I reflected, *the guards patrolling their beat outside my house would have only daos or bamboo staves over their shoulders!* "Thank You, Father!"

Then the freedom fighters came asking for vehicles to help them move about the countryside. In this, we felt we could legitimately help them. If we gave them a vehicle, however, the Pakistan army might someday call us on the carpet for doing so. So we put Jay Walsh's International Scout in a convenient spot, keys in the ignition, and notified our freedom fighter friends that we would not object to their "stealing" the vehicle.

On Palm Sunday afternoon, April 4, we picked up a British Broadcasting Company (BBC) broadcast which made an electrifying announcement: "A British ship will leave the port of Chittagong tomorrow morning carrying any foreigners who wish to evacuate from East Pakistan."

The Eatons, Benedicts, Millie Cooley, and Florence Theaker, due for furlough, decided in a few minutes that they should try to reach the ship despite the potential danger of the trip. With American flags streaming, they and Reid Minich headed north. The convoy made forty-five miles before sundown. They stayed overnight in a rest house and, shortly after sunrise next morning, headed for Chittagong. The "no-man's land" between the two opposing forces began at the blasted Chittagong radio station on the outskirts of the city and extended three hundred yards to the first Pakistan army emplacement; that was the touchiest part of the trip, but no bullets flew. They arrived in Chittagong just in time to catch the *Clan MacNair* which the Gurganus family already had boarded. The ship, containing thirty-seven Americans and eighty-two other foreigners, covered the three hundred miles across the bay to Calcutta in two days. To protect those of us who had remained behind, our people said as little as possible to waiting reporters. God had seen them safely through the dangers.

On the same Palm Sunday that our colleagues departed from Memorial Christian Hospital, Pakistani troops entered another mission hospital two hundred fifty miles away in the town of Jessore. At the harsh call of the Pakistani soldiers, the Italian missionary in charge stepped out of his room into the hospital courtyard. Despite his raised hands and the bright red cross he wore, a Pakistani submachinegun chattered; the Roman Catholic priest jerked convulsively and died in a pool of blood. A fellow priest reporting the brutal killing continued: "The Bengalis (all Christians) had taken refuge with women and children in the garden. The soldiers killed them with machine guns. The massacre lasted twenty minutes."[3] During the war two other foreign missionary priests were killed, one of whom was William Evans, an American. Pakistani soldiers bayoneted him, shot him, and threw his body in a river.

By April 9 our American men were taking turns sleeping up front at the hospital property to provide support for our night watchmen. Everyone in the area was quite jittery. That night Larry Golin had the duty. About 3:00 A.M. a Bengali watchman awakened him excitedly, saying, "Two jeeploads of men have just driven through the hospital property back to the housing site." Hurrying to the back property, Larry found fifteen men systematically prowling our housing property; some of them were moving around the nurses'/teachers' residence. Unable to learn what they were up to, he knocked on my bedroom window and quickly explained the problem.

As I leaped out of bed and hurried over to find the group commander, Larry awakened our other men. The commander turned out to be a man well known to me, a Bengali physician — strange things these doctors get themselves mixed up in! Asking him for an explanation, I insisted that his men immediately stop snooping around the women's sleeping quarters.

Sending a man to call them back, he said mysteriously, "I am here on a very special mission. I need one of your houses immediately." When we found out the purpose of this strange request, we were dumbfounded! The Mukti Fouj high command had ordered him *to install the new transmitter for Radio Free Bengal in one of our houses!* With visions of Sabre jets diving in to smash our patients and us, we remonstrated with him. Knowing that agreement would be suicidal, because the well-equipped Pakistan army would quickly locate that radio beam, we argued until the sun came up. Finally, wearily, reluctantly, the commander agreed to take his men and the transmitter away until we had opportunity for a group meeting; we set a time when they would return.

In the meeting, after prayer and analysis, we were doubly sure we must try to prevent the installation of the radio in our buildings, for our patients, our hospital, our homes, and our lives would be jeopardized. Suddenly, before the appointed time, during a period of earnest group prayer, the freedom fighters returned — with transmitter. As I slipped out the door to meet them, I could think of no words which would have the slightest effect on those hard-faced men. But somehow, by the time I walked the fifty feet to the end of the driveway, I had something to say.

"We've come to install the radio!" the commander said.

"But there are two things we must first discuss," I replied.

"What two things?" he snapped.

"First, you know the Pakistan army has captured Chittagong and is headed this way. They will arrive here before many days. And, second, you know that the Sabre jets will, very soon after any broadcast from here, bomb, strafe, and rocket our hospital and houses. If our hospital is damaged and we are killed or injured, what are you going to do when the Pakistan army bullets hit you, or your old father, or your strong son? Without our hospital and doctors, you will die. The hospital is even more important than the radio. You need them both, so put the radio someplace else so that the hospital is not jeopardized!"

By some kind of divine alchemy, the points struck home and the hard faces softened. They accepted the proposition! Joined by some of our other men from the prayer meeting, we agreed to loan them a small generator to use if they could find no other suitable place with electricity. As they quietly drove away, we marveled at the change which had come over these tough Mukti Fouj officers whose word was law. "Thank You, Father!"

We had a number of new believers awaiting baptism. Eager to teach one last baptismal class before our upcoming furlough, I made arrangements for the class to begin the second week in April. Meanwhile, we were meeting almost daily to analyze, prayerfully, whether or not to evacuate. Almost all foreign nationals had long since left the country. Although none of our group had peace of mind at that point about leaving our work, we felt obliged to make certain contingency plans and preparations — just in case the situation suddenly deteriorated. One contingency plan involved heading north, another moving south across the border into Burma.

But there were two big gaps in our information. We did not know how the military had treated other mission hospitals. And knowing that tense soldiers sometimes do foolish things when they come upon an unexpected situation, we wondered whether the Pakistan military knew that we Americans were located at Malumghat. To learn the answer to the first point, we decided to send a spy to another mission hospital far to the north in the Chittagong Hill Tracts to learn what happened when the Pakistan military had reached that point.

On the morning of April 16 I selected the spy, a tribal man who worked in the hospital as a laboratory technician, and sent him off on his bicycle into the unknown. Shortly thereafter, a jeep crammed full of waving, shouting men screeched to a stop in front of the hospital for just a moment, then raced off to the south.

They had shouted, "Take cover! Take cover! The jet planes are coming! They are bombing and strafing!"

The Pakistan air force Sabre jets were attacking Patiya (forty miles north) and Amirabad (twenty-five miles north). Would we be next? After sending Lynn and Jeannie to the roof as plane-spotters, we decided immediately to paint huge red crosses and red USAs on the roofs of our hospital and homes. But we had one problem — we could locate only one can of red paint. Mixing it with gallons of white, we had pink crosses and pink USAs, a very anemic warning to any murderous jet pilot who might pass that way.

We hurried to our homes to warn and advise our wives and children what to do in case of attack. I explained to the kids, "You just need to know two things. First, God did not evacuate; He is still around to love you and take care of you. And second, at the sound of any jet plane you must go immediately to the middle bathroom or the hall outside it; there you have more brick walls around you than anyplace else in the house. OK?"

"Yeah, Dad," the children said, wide-eyed.

As I prepared to go dig a trench in the forest (which would be safer than the house under some circumstances), I learned the value of having a junior high son in the family.

"Dad," Mark said eagerly, "You don't have to dig a trench! I can show you a neat trench out there left over from World War II."

"Come on, Mark, let's see it," I responded. Sure enough, Mark took me unerringly to one of the "neatest" trenches I had ever seen. It took us twenty-five minutes to clear out twenty-five years accumulation of leaves, weeds, and crumbling dirt. Now we were ready for anything!

Later, in the hospital, I visited a patient known as Mr. Amin the banker (really Captain Haroon, a Bengali military hero). When the captain was seriously wounded in a battle near Chittagong a week before, we sent blood transfusions so his Bengali doctor could do an emergency abdominal operation. He had recovered sufficiently to be brought to our hospital. Two days later I diagnosed his incision's dehiscence (coming apart) and I called for Donn, who repaired his patient's separated incision.

In the evening of April 16, Reid Minich and three American officers from the US consulate appeared unexpectedly at Malumghat. They were visibly shaken, for they had passed through Patiya and Amirabad where a little earlier, the Sabre jet machine gun bullets and rockets had killed a number of unarmed village people. They brought word from the US ambassador and US consul general recommending evacuation.

After introductions and a bite to eat, we debriefed them carefully, especially on the points about which we lacked information. They had word that the mission hospital to the north of us had been well treated by the Pakistan army. And, furthermore, the Pak army top brass in Chittagong and Dacca were well aware that a large contingent of Americans was located at Memorial Christian Hospital. They came to

Reid Minich, *left,* with men from US consulate

advise us to go, but the information they brought encouraged us all the more to stay.

In our prayerful and thoughtful meeting, the majority were led to remain at Malumghat. The American officials advised us, "Listen to the Voice of America (VOA) news broadcasts. If any exceptional danger develops, we will try to notify you over the 7:00 A.M. or 7:00 P.M. newscasts." Several of our team, overdue for their annual vacations, decided to take advantage of the opportunity offered them by the American officers to fly to West Pakistan. The next day the three officers and Reid Minich returned to Chittagong to arrange a temporary ceasefire on April 19 to allow our group to pass safely by road. The Adolphs, Mary Lou, Jean, Shirley, Linda, and Gwen made it, according to plan, all the way to West Pakistan or America. The next morning the Beals family evacuated by road to the Burma border, crossed the river, and entered Burma. The rest of the team settled in for the long haul — or so we thought. I spent the rest of April 20 making final arrangements for the baptismal class and casing a nearby village as a place of possible temporary retreat should there by any active fighting when the Pakistan army arrived. Joan and I made further progress on our packing for furlough.

In the evening an emergency case required surgery. Returning to her room after the late operation, Becky Davey prepared to retire. Although she seldom listened to the radio, Becky flipped it on to the VOA station. At the conclusion of the 11:15 news summary came a startling announcement: "This is a special announcement from Washington to American citizens at Malumghat! All nonessential personnel proceed immediately via motor vehicle to the Burma border. The route to Chittagong is no longer available. I repeat —"

The meaning was instantly obvious — something had happened in the last twenty-four hours to greatly increase our "danger factor," and a major battle north of us was raging across the highway to Chittagong making the road impassable!

Becky knocked on everyone's bedroom window repeating the gist of what she had just heard. Within minutes we gathered for our fateful midnight meeting. Becky presented the announcement. Then someone shared a rumor that the Mukti Fouj might be digging in for action near the hospital. It was the strangest meeting we ever held! Although we had sat in many meetings, recently as well as during the 1965 war, no one in the room ever before had felt guided to evacuate from the war zone. God, however, simply seemed to remove His restraining hand and quietly say to every heart,

"It's time for the group to go." At first we fought against the idea, but that was useless — it *was* time for the group to go.

Donn and I desired to remain at Malumghat to help our Bengali brothers and sisters, care for the wounded, and protect our property and investment. After I was elected chairman of the remaining miniscule field council (including Reid Minich in Chittagong), someone observed that the lights were still on at 1:00 A.M. Strange — they had been going off promptly at 10:00 for many nights.

As Joan and I returned home, we decided not to awaken Mark and Nancy until sunrise. We packed their clothes, a few of their treasures, and Joan's clothes. We succeeded in finding roughly half the important papers (never there when you really need them) and packed them along with the passports and cash. As we worked together shoulder to shoulder, many of the precious experiences and special times together flashed through my mind. It was a very poignant night — we weren't at all sure we would meet again this side of glory. Wonderfully, the electricity remained on until 4:00 A.M., allowing each family to complete the packing. We tumbled into bed exhausted.

Up at dawn, I awakened our hospital staff with the loud bell which pealed out across our hospital property in the still morning air. Sleepy-eyed, they came stumbling out of their houses to find out what was happening. When I told them of the radio message,

Packing up for evacuation

Off to the Burma border!

the midnight decision, and that most of their American friends were evacuating into Burma, they came wide awake instantly. I consoled them as best I could. The final good-byes were shattering to all, Americans and Bengalis alike. Even the two Muslim West Pakistani guards, disregarding the risk, pulled aside the window curtain in their secret hideout to give the Christian farewell sign to the departing Americans. Knowing that their chances of survival decreased as our team left, the two Pathans wept like small children.

Then the four Land Rovers full of twenty-nine departing Americans headed south with US flags flying. The sullen sky spit a few drops of rain as my loved ones passed from sight. Because Donn drove one of the Rovers, I was left alone with our staff that morning of April 21.

Immediately I called everyone together into the chapel. They were jittery and upset. From the Bengali Bible, I read those marvelous words at the end of Matthew's gospel where our Lord said: "All power is given to me in heaven and in earth . . . And listen, I am with you always, even to the end of the age." As I said a few words about the passage, I saw the strain beginning to ease. Then, suddenly, a gigantic explosion split the air!

I thought, *it's too late for contingency plans. The Pakistan military has arrived!* Simultaneously, I saw a blur of moving people in front of me; some dived under the benches, others headed for the doors.

Then, as I heard a distant rumbling sound, I shouted, "Stop, come back! It's all right!" The explosion was not a shell blast — just a freak crack of thunder! We laughed — and laughed — and laughed. And that helped. Finally we were ready to think and pray seriously about the important decisions facing us.

Explaining to the Bengali staff that the radio message spelled danger, and that they too must evacuate, I wrote out four possible plans of action on the blackboard. After discussing together the pros and cons of each plan, I explained that each family must make its individual decision, and then Dr. Ketcham and I would help to carry it out. Most tentatively decided they would like to move into our back-property houses or to a nearby village until the army passed by and the bullets stopped flying.

After the meeting I made ward rounds, examined patients, and discharged most of them. I had lunch with Momin Choudhury who would be our righthand man throughout the difficult days ahead. He brought definite news that the Bangladesh liberation army was digging in strongly just two miles to the north of us in the Fashiakhali forest. This meant that the Mukti Fouj intended to tackle

Momin Choudhury

the Pakistan army at that point! To get around those positions, the Pakistan army would likely flank them and drive south through the forest, possibly reaching our houses and hospital buildings simultaneously. This intelligence promptly nullified any plan for staff members to stay at our homes or villages near them. Furthermore, when the liberation army would fall back from the superior fire power of the Pakistan army, they would retreat directly to our hospital. They might easily take shelter in our brick buildings and, to save their lives, use them as a fort.

"We will need another meeting tonight," I told Momin, "to help the staff make plans to evacuate to more distant places."

Donn returned by suppertime to report, "We had no flat tires or any other real problems. It rained all the way, but stopped just as we arrived at noon. A storekeeper loaned us his verandah to be our headquarters and the ladies cranked out some cold baked beans and Vienna sausages. While I took care of currency exchange in the bazaar, Jay made arrangements for a huge sampan big enough to carry everybody. They were already loaded in by the time I returned from the bazaar. So I missed the chance to give Kit and the kids a last kiss. Kit, bless her, was as brave as could be and never flinched. David and Marty were torn between the pain of leaving Daddy and the excitement of a boat trip across the three-mile-wide river. My Becky cried. Noah's ark pulled slowly out into the stream, and I stood alone on the shore with a heavy heart."

At 7:00 P.M. Kaitha Phrue, the spy, returned with his report on the mission hospital north of us. Contrary to the US officials' information, local Bengalis had killed the hospital's four West Pakistani watchmen (like the two we were trying to save). Then the Pakistan army had fired on the hospital; one artillery shell had torn into the leprosarium, killing a leper. The Pakistani soldiers had searched the hospital for Bengali Mukti Bahini patients to kill. When these soldiers killed townspeople on the road beside the hospital, they forced hospital employees to come and throw their bodies into the river. The remaining Britishers were tightly restricted to their homes and hospital, and the whole situation was "very tense." After hearing his report, I was doubly sure we had to evacuate our staff to safer points far from the hospital.

At 9:30 P.M. we called our staff together for another meeting. Kaitha Phrue gave his report and I explained the liberation army military preparations taking place just two miles to the north of us. Finally, the majority decided to depart the following morning for our Hebron station. A few, with friends in interior villages, decided to stay with them and a few others elected to evacuate to Burma. We were exhausted when we hit the hay.

The next day was April 22. *That was just yesterday,* I reflected, lying drowsily on my pallet behind the door. *It seems like a month ago.*

We were up at 6:00 that morning and meeting with our staff at 7:00 to make the final count of who was going where and to calculate how many boats were needed for Hebron. After the meeting Donn mounted a motorbike and rode off to Cheringa to arrange twelve boats for our Hebron contingent of evacuees.

Outside our hospital entrance, I also jumped on a motorbike and took off for our dock to organize the loading of their supplies on other boats. Then it happened! As I accelerated sharply and reached cruising speed, suddenly the motorbike fell apart beneath me! The main bar cracked in two, the cycle collapsed, and I smashed into the brick road. Dazed, bruised, battered, I vaguely saw people running toward me from all directions. Only then did I feel the waves of deep, sickening pain in my right elbow. I knew the X ray would reveal bad news. Staggering like a drunken man, I somehow negotiated the one hundred yards to the hospital, called for the X ray technician, and ordered the correct anteroposterior and lateral views of my own elbow.

Within four minutes he had taken the picture, developed it, and placed the dripping film before the viewbox. There I saw with surgeon's eyes my elbow shattered into four main pieces. *Badly comminuted fracture involving the elbow joint itself,* I diagnosed silently. *An operation will be necessary to reduce the fragments perfectly and insert some steel hardware to hold the reduction.*

At that precise moment, Donn Ketcham, back from Cheringa, walked in. With one look at me holding my elbow and the terrible X ray, he groaned, "Oh, no — not that!"

We put our heads together and quickly made the plan for the day. We scheduled the operation for that night. Then Donn went to work paying salaries to those evacuating and doing a dozen other jobs. After application of a sling, an hour's rest, and some aspirin, I went back to work problem-solving, counseling with staff members, and dispatching them by Land Rover to their waiting boats. By sundown we had finished evacuating all those going to Hebron and to interior villages. Early the next morning we would send off the Burma contingent.

By 8:00 P.M. we were in the operating room. The circumstances were less than ideal! The murderous West Pakistan army advancing toward us could arrive any time. Our anesthetists were gone. Only one of the three Bengali male nurses who remained behind to help knew anything about the operating room.

But we had some things going for us. The four-inch steel pin essential for the operation had arrived unexpectedly several weeks before when MAP, Wheaton, on their own initiative, obtained US government funds amounting to $16,500 to send our instruments and medicines on order by air. And my wonderful buddy Donn was there, probably the only other surgeon in Bangladesh capable of performing the operation. And there were my three Bengali brothers who had evacuated their families, but remained behind to help put my elbow back together. Looking at them hazily through morphia, I remembered how each one of them had come to faith in Christ and become my brothers. (Bhanu, for example, had been the man who sat for hours with me in our roofhouse, a few months before, asking his questions about God and the Bible, then making the great faith decision.)

Conscious that my surgical career was hanging in the balance, I found myself perfectly calm and relaxed as we prayed together in Bengali. I marveled at how stabilizing it is to know you are at the right place doing the right thing at the right time in God's personal plan. Then the pentothal injection. The many eyes of the operating room lights peering down at me began to swim and dance — then oblivion.

I knew nothing for the next two hours, then awakened to a burning, boring pain in the operated elbow and Donn saying, "Your

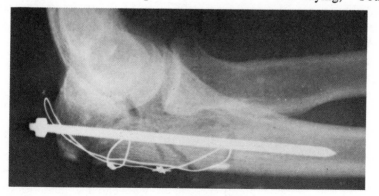

X ray of elbow with pin inserted

operation is over. I am putting on the splint now. From the looks
of the X ray, the Lord was with us." Lapsing into unconsciousness
for another moment, I awakened again to laughter. Unknown to me,
emerging from oblivion, I had made some joke in Bengali.

The X ray was beautiful! When I saw the perfect placement of
the steel pin and the steel stitches and the completely accurate re-
alignment of the fragmented bone, I did not doubt Donn's implication that there had been six of us in the operating room — the great
Physician had been there, too, to guide as only He can do.

Sleep and pain alternated throughout the night, but I hoped to
avoid an injection which would leave me fuzzyheaded. By 5:00
A.M., however, the pain was raging and I took my Demerol. The
morning of April 23 had arrived.

That was this very morning, I marveled, lying there nearly asleep
behind the door. Just seventeen hours ago I had been in the hospital
getting that shot of Demerol. By 9:00 A.M. I had been awake and
fairly clear-headed, able to function. The Burma contingent of
evacuees, including our capable translator Mrs. Dass, her husband,
four Bengali doctors we had sheltered, and others, had gathered
about my hospital bed to say good-bye. I had prayed with them
before a tearful farewell.

Hearing that the Pakistan army had established a main camp
thirty-five miles north of us and were daily raiding further and
further from that point, I had left my bed to make arrangements for
Captain Haroon to be removed from the hospital. If the Pakistan
army caught him in the hospital, he surely would never leave his
bed alive. Then Donn finally had gotten the local Mukti Bahini to
evacuate two other injured soldiers, the last patients in the hospital.

Unexpectedly Reid and a British clergyman had arrived with a
station wagon full of valuable and essential medical supplies. Reid
had contacted a Chittagong-based Pakistan army officer who ordered
the medical college hospital to give him what we lacked. Reid
confirmed that Pakistan army troops had established themselves in
Dohazari thirty-five miles to the north. They had encountered no
firing from either army. After a bite to eat and a few moments of
fellowship, they had departed to reach Chittagong before sundown.

In one way, it had been a very heartwarming day. Hearing of my
injury and operation through the ever-efficient "bamboo telegraph,"
many people had come to express their sorrow, pay their respects
and present some gift — even a Burmese cigar. Some were rich, others poor, but all had come by foot, for no buses were running at the
time. I felt deeply grateful for friends who cared enough to walk
fifteen miles during wartime for such a purpose.

Our man Leslie also had walked miles, arriving in the evening to bring the unsettling news: "The armed bandits are coming tonight to attack you and the hospital." In our strategy session, Donn and I decided to move the two West Pakistani watchmen from the servants' quarters; with everyone evacuated they were alone and would be in extreme jeopardy at night. Sending our Bengali watchmen on a ten-minute wild-goose chase, we had sneaked the two petrified men into our house and tucked them away in Tom Ketcham's bedroom.

Then, Donn, with loaded shotguns in hand, had headed off for night duty at the hospital. Less than two hours ago I had called my five watchmen together, promoted them to guards, armed them, explained how to load and fire the weapons, put a dummy in my bed, loaded my revolver, and reread the Scripture passages (out of a daily devotional book) which had so impressed me in the morning:

> The Lord is my rock and my fortress and my deliverer, my God, my strength in whom I will trust . . . the angel of the Lord encamps round about them that fear him and delivers them . . . The Lord is my helper; I will not fear what man shall do to me.

Just a few minutes ago, I had turned out the light, lain down on my pallet behind the door, placed the loaded revolver by my head, and remembered the cascading series of events of the last four weeks. Numb with fatigue, I thought, *The lights are still on, but it must be after 10:00.* Then, despite the danger, my exhausted mind closed down and I fell into a deep anesthesialike sleep.

I awakened suddenly at the sound of voices outside my window, every sense vibrantly alert. *But wait, it is light — the sun has cleared the horizon. The night is over and not a shot was fired.* I hurried to the door to call my guards.

"What happened?" I asked.

"Nothing," they responded with glowing faces. "The lights stayed on all night long. No one dared to come out of the jungle to attack us. Allah heard your prayers, Daktar Sahib. Allah kept the lights on all night long and saved us! It was a miracle from Allah."

I had no quarrel with their diagnosis, for I could not remember how many weeks had passed since the lights had last remained on the whole night through. A fragment of a psalm came to me: "He that keeps Israel shall neither slumber nor sleep."

The same God who watched over Israel so many centuries ago, I thought, *is also the God of Malumghat.* How tremendous! "Thank You, Father!"

On April 24, Malumghat — usually such a busy, active, noisy place — was like a tomb with staff and patients gone. In the morning,

Shantosh, a highly educated Hindu who had worked with us as language teacher and translator for several years, arrived trembling and out of breath. Posing as non-Hindus, he and his parents had passed through a Pakistan army checkpoint and barely avoided detection. Because he had so narrowly escaped death, hours passed before he regained full control of himself. Donn spent the morning making entries in the books for the thousands of rupees he had doled out. Moving slowly, I supervised the packing and storing of three drumfuls of valuables my colleagues had left behind when they evacuated.

Late in the afternoon a notorious dacoit with a prison record walked the forest road at the edge of our property, casing the location of our buildings. He terrorized the watchman at the firewood loading area a hundred yards away. Later the word reached us that he had boasted that his gang would attack us without fail that night and "the two doctors will not be around much longer." The picture was very clear. Only Donn and I remained to keep the looters from the loot. It sounded like the dacoits would have no compunctions about doing away with us to get their hands on the spoils.

Still concerned that all of our guards were Muslims from the same village who might be subverted by the bandits, I called in four Hindu employees from their jungle hideouts to increase the night guard — and keep the others honest. Donn took six guards and four shotguns to the hospital. Again, I remained at the houses with four shotguns and seven guards.

Then I had a brainstorm! Of all the men we had at our disposal, two particular men knew their lives absolutely depended upon us and would do anything asked of them to keep us alive — the two West Pakistani watchmen. However, in the last weeks they had become frightened, weeping, pathetic creatures. Only if they could pull themselves together would they be of any value to me. That evening, when I walked down the hall and entered their bedroom, they fell to clutch me by the feet. Using simple Bengali and a few words of their Urdu language, I explained the danger and my need for them to help protect us and our property. Then I shoved a shotgun at one man and my revolver toward the other. Somehow, my speech and the firearms strengthened them; suddenly they shaped up.

I placed the Pathan with the semiautomatic shotgun on the roof. The one with the revolver I placed near my bed with the instructions, "You must keep wide awake and see that no one kills me while I sleep." Still weak from my injury and operation, I knew I had to get some sleep every night. Selecting a different bedroom, I lay down. The pain was still there — but less. I fell off to sleep.

At midnight one of Donn's guards observed the notorious dacoit and several henchmen entering the forest fifty feet north of our property, then walking back toward our housing site. Immediately, Donn walked the half-mile to our back property to alert our guards. At 2:30 A.M. one of my night guards, excited, awakened me. They had seen lights in the forest around us near our boundary line. Wonderfully, our lights were still on! I advised and encouraged the guards, then went back to sleep. At 3:30 A.M. the guards again saw lights in the forest but did not disturb me. I awakened at 6:00 A.M. to learn that again the lights had remained on all night long to discourage the bandits surrounding us from attacking. "Thank You, Father!"

On Sunday, April 25, a messenger arrived from Hebron with the shocking news that a hospital staff member, Shudhir, had died suddenly from a longstanding illness. He had died in his village home beside Hebron, the place where he had gained everlasting life. We sent a letter back to Hebron and hospital badges for everyone to identify them as hospital staff members.

Several of our brothers came from their jungle hideout to worship with us. X-ray technician Sharno Dewari chose a hymn, the Bengali version of "Oh, the Deep, Deep Love of Jesus." The minor key matched our feelings about the carnage going on around us. Male nurse Bhanu Malakar read the Twenty-third Psalm which we discussed together a few minutes. Sharno closed in prayer.

That afternoon, Donn caused a minor crisis on the countryside when he shot two stray dogs skulking about the property. Villagers down the road, positive the West Pakistani army had arrived, fled from two villages and began to empty out a third. Someone who knew the facts arrived just in time to call them back to their homes. The incident served to assure the dacoits that our guns were loaded.

At nightfall we again armed our Malumghat militia. Again the West Pakistani guard sat with loaded revolver at the head of my bed while I slept. Again the lights remained on all night long!

By the next day, the Pakistan army raiding parties, penetrating further each day, had reached a point fifteen miles north of us. They would soon reach Malumghat. Reluctantly, we took down the Bangladesh flag which had graced our flagpole and vehicles for a month, then hoisted the Pakistan flag which the Pakistan army insisted must fly on every building. Donn questioned whether or not we should follow the lead of some local leaders and drive north to meet the West Pakistan military command before they reached us.

We decided against it for the time being because we did not wish to appear to be against our Bengali friends and their cause, nor did we wish to answer any questions about the freedom fighter's military preparations two miles north of us. At bedtime we again armed the Malumghat militia; again the lights remained on throughout the night; again the bandits feared to attack.

The April 27 Scripture reading sounded good to me:

> Brothers, the time is short . . . whether we live, we live to the Lord; whether we die, we die to the Lord; whether we live, therefore, or die, we are the Lord's.

A Pakistan army raiding column reached Cheringa, only six miles north of us. They brutally killed several people and began burning the houses of Hindus and Awami League leaders. We could see the columns of smoke from Malumghat.

It won't be long now, I thought to myself. I drove left-handed to the Hindu villages near us to warn the people to flee. Because they trusted us, some of them gave their total worldly wealth into our hands for safekeeping. A passion was burning in our souls that, somehow, we had to save the lives of these Hindu friends and neighbors who were in serious jeopardy.

When we learned that a column of troops would be heading toward Lama, a mile from our Hebron jungle station, we feared for our hospital staff there and reconsidered the matter of driving north to meet the Pakistan military. If we were to do so, we could notify them that the people at Hebron were our hospital staff. Also we could make sure that the soldiers approaching us, as well as the generals in Chittagong, actually knew two American doctors were at the Malumghat hospital. And we could appeal for the lives of our Hindu neighbors. We decided to try meeting the military at Cheringa where they were expected the next day. Wonderfully, the all-night electricity continued until the dacoits left the area to find greener pastures.

On the afternoon of April 28 we took our peace offering (the two West Pakistani watchmen) to meet the Pakistan army officers at Cheringa. We drove quickly past the area where the Mukti Bahini were digging in, hoping they would not fire at the two West Pakistanis in our Land Rover. Our trip was fruitless, for the military failed to keep their appointment with the leaders of Cheringa. Because we had exposed the two Pathan watchmen to public scrutiny, we hid them both on the roof of our house for the night.

In next morning's Bible reading Moses told the Israelis that God had directed them into the wilderness for forty years "to humble you, and to prove you, to know what was in your heart, whether you would keep His commandments or not." *God has directed us into this wilderness of blood and fire,* I thought as I read. *May we keep His commandments, prove ourselves trustworthy, and learn the necessary lessons of humility.*

Donn and Momin found a celebrity in Cheringa and brought him back to Malumghat for discussions. Major Zaman, a West Pakistani, had migrated to East Pakistan long before we had come. Retired from the Pakistan army, he had come, established a huge farm, and made his life among the Bengali people. When the war flared, however, many Bengalis wanted to kill him because of his nationality. He took refuge in a jail, but had reentered public life the day before when the Pakistan army reached Cheringa. He became the liaison man between the Pakistan army and the local Bengali population. We decided to go together to the Pakistan army camp thirty-five miles to the north at Dohazari. His introduction to the Pakistan commander might help our cause.

On the way to Dohazari we came upon a platoon of Pakistani soldiers burning a Hindu village. The burning houses roared like a blast furnace and belched out huge, black billows of smoke which became a monstrous black pillar defacing the sun-washed sky. *What a horrible, sickening sight!* I thought as we passed the laughing troops.

Major Zaman gave us a glowing introduction to the major in charge of the Pakistan army camp. We then presented to him the two West Pakistani watchmen whose lives we had preserved since the beginning of the war. When the two Pathans spontaneously sang our praises, we were off to a good start. We requested that all our staff members and their families be exempted from any military action. When the major agreed to this request, we gave him samples of the badges our staff members would wear for identification.

Then, gingerly, we appealed for the lives and property of our Hindu neighbors, offering reasons why they should be spared. The major would make no guarantees on this point. He mentioned that practically all Hindus were bad people for they loved India and were in cahoots with India to tear East Pakistan away from Pakistan. He claimed that Indian soldiers were fighting on the Bengali side in the war and that he had captured many of them. "I had all those bloody prisoners and spies shot dead!"

A few moments later, he gave an emotional diatribe against a former Pakistan army officer, a Bengali captain, who had learned about the army crackdown on Bengalis before his two West Pakistani fellow officers. When the Bengali captain killed the two fellow officers, he became a marked man. Their intelligence reports indicated that the Bengali captain had been killed in battle. But we knew that intelligence to be wrong; the Bengali officer was Captain Haroon. He had been treated by Donn and then shipped off by me to Burma!

Back at Malumghat, I went to sleep remembering the words of my evening Bible reading, "The whole creation groans and travails in pain up to the present time." What a perfect description of Bangladesh!

Expecting the Pakistan army to arrive any moment, the last of our Hindu neighbors had left their homes and fled to the jungle on April 29. Their Muslim neighbors promptly looted their houses that night (despite the previous admonitions of Sheikh Mujib that Muslims and Hindus should live together in peace). Our hearts bled for the Hindu people — everyone seemed against them. For political reasons, the Pakistan army wanted to kill them and burn their houses. Because of religious differences and a centuries-old rivalry, many Bengali Muslim neighbors were willing to persecute them. And their myriad gods and goddesses were powerless to assist them. Donn, Momin, and I were their only earthly hope.

Our hospital staff already had been at Hebron and in the jungle villages for ten days. As those in the jungle ate a meager meal and tried to sleep, the nearby call of a leopard or the trumpeting of wild elephants often startled them; shivering with fear, they drew their sleeping children closer.

On May 1 Momin arrived to tell a touching story. Hindus had taken him to their jungle hideout during the night to tell him to bring to us their words of gratitude and homage.

On the next day, Sunday, several of our men came from their jungle hideouts to visit us during daylight hours and to worship with us. I had asked Sharno to lead the service and give the message. He did so beautifully from the great Romans 8 passage on Christian liberty. He pointed out that although Bengalis had worked, fought, and died for *shadheen Bangla* (free Bengal), that freedom had not been attained. We Christians, however, have obtained already full freedom — from sin, spiritual death, and hell — through our Lord Jesus Christ. After the service Sharno returned to his family in the jungle, for we had decided our people must remain away from the hospital until the Pakistan army reached us and passed on. Only then would we know whether or not a dangerous battle would explode around us.

By May 3 I felt better than I had for four days; the antibiotic I was taking for low-grade wound infection in my elbow was working.

Momin reported on his trip of the night before to the Hindu hide-outs in the jungle. We had sent by him powdered milk for the babies and small children. They had wept in gratitude. Because many of them were stricken with illness, we packed up some simple medicines for Momin to deliver. Momin learned that some local Muslims had tracked them down in the jungle to harrass them. There the marauders threatened a Hindu doctor that they would abduct his two attractive daughters unless he paid them two thousand rupees the following morning. Lacking the money, the doctor's group retreated deeper into the jungle and settled in with another group of refugees who possessed a shotgun.

Donn saw six patients in the morning. His work as doctor, nurse, scribe, pharmacist, cashier, and bookkeeper, began to consume hours each day. There was little I could do to help him with my arm in a sling. I spent hours on problem solving and trying to save the Hindus. One of our hospital staff men came from the jungle to report that the danger of robbery was increasing nightly; the people had to remain awake all night to protect themselves. *When, oh when, will that Pakistan army come,* I wondered anxiously. *Our people will not be able to remain in the jungle and at Hebron forever.*

At 8:30 A.M. on May 5 the Pakistan army arrived in force! The convoy of seventy-four trucks, jeeps, and other vehicles carried hundreds of Pakistani soldiers. They had run the gauntlet at the point two miles north of us without incident. The freedom fighters had decided it was useless to tackle such a powerful force and had faded into the jungle. As jeeploads of heavily armed officers turned into the hospital, the rest of the convoy stopped and waited. Donn quickly sent a messenger to me at the house, and I drove immediately to the hospital. In the group talking to Donn were the major we had met at Dohazari and a navy commander, both with machine guns in hand. The commander of the column was a tough colonel who looked as though a smile would fracture his face, so he never risked it. They were tense, for they had just passed the dangerous area where they had feared a possible ambush.

As I arrived, the colonel was speaking sharply to Donn who had hesitated an instant before replying to some of the colonel's questions. They were tough, taut, and strictly business. We answered several questions as fully as possible without incriminating any Bengali friends. Then, when they pressured us about the freedom fighters we had treated, Donn made an excellent point.

"You men are soldiers and have your military code. You must understand that we are doctors and we, too, have a code. And our code is very simple: When someone is sick or injured or in pain, our code says we treat him and help him regardless of his religion or race or politics."

We pressed our initiative and asked it he would confirm his major's declaration that our hospital staff and their family members would be safe from army action.

"Certainly," he replied, "your hospital staff will be safe. We want your hospital operating. Bring your staff back and put them to work."

"Even the Hindus who work for us?" I asked. He didn't like that question.

But after a moment's consultation with the other officers, he replied sharply, "Yes, we will even guarantee the safety of the Hindus on your staff as long as they are not Awami League political leaders."

"How about our Christian community?" we inquired.

Without a second's hesitation he replied, "Of course we'll guarantee the safety of your Christians — we have nothing against Christians."

Although the situation was delicate, the appeal that was vibrating in my heart had to burst out. I appealed for the lives of our Hindu neighbors! Considering the appeal an impudent intrusion into army affairs, his black eyes blazed.

Before he could speak, however, I quickly detailed four reasons for the appeal: "You have guaranteed the safety of our Hindu staff, but if the local Hindu villages are attacked, that promise is meaningless. Also, you kindly guaranteed the safety of our Christian community. Some of our Christians live in those same villages. If the local Hindu villages are attacked, then, your second guarantee also is meaningless. Furthermore, these local Hindus helped us to save the two West Pakistani watchmen we returned safely to your major. Finally, the Hindus in this area are ordinary people, not freedom fighters or Awami League leaders. For these four reasons we appeal for the safety of our Hindu neighbors."

With a barely controlled fury, the colonel ground out, "We'll see," then turned on his heel and roared off to Cox's Bazar. The tense moment we had long dreaded was over.

As we talked with these officers, one of the Bengali collaborators in their convoy slipped into a village one-half mile away and raped a village woman. Simultaneously a Pakistan naval force was landing at Cox's Bazar. The Pakistan forces savagely killed Hindus in Cox's Bazar that day and burned Hindu temples and houses. They beat to death Shubash, the student who had kicked and burned the Pakistan flag weeks before.

We doubted that our appeal for Hindu lives would succeed. But

God apparently added to our entreaty some divine imperative in the hearts of those hard men, for in our twenty-seven-mile stretch from Cheringa in the north to Ramu in the south, the Pakistan army did not kill a single Hindu! "Thank You, Father!" (Later we learned that General Niazi, the commanding general of the whole West Pakistan army in Bangladesh, complained to a foreign diplomat, "Although our work is progressing well, I am facing some difficulty in the southern end of the country where two American doctors are obstructing my works." Because his "works" consisted of ruthlessly killing innocent and unarmed Bengalis, we appreciated the compliment!)

Within five minutes after the military convoy disappeared, a messenger arrived from Hebron with disturbing news. Our hospital staff at Hebron faced imminent danger of armed robbery — that night they would be hit! What perfect timing! Because the danger of army action at the hospital had just passed and because we had gained guarantees of their safety, we could take immediate steps to bring our staff back to Malumghat. Donn drove to Cheringa, sent sixteen boats up the river, and arranged for police protection at Hebron that one night until our staff could return the following day. That night armed bandits did surround the Hebron contingent, but the police guard prevented attack. "Thank You, Father!"

Simultaneously, we received reports that our staff members in the jungle also faced greatly increased jeopardy of armed robbery. I sent the word back to them, "Come back to Malumghat immediately. The Pakistan army has passed, and now it is safe for you to come!"

We decided to keep on the hospital property our Hindu and other staff members and their families who ordinarily lived in the nearby villages. To work out their accommodations from our housing map was more complicated than a game of chess. We could not supply beds for everyone, but purchased dozens of bamboo mats; at least we could give each person a mat to sleep on. By sundown our families who had lived for two weeks in the jungle returned to us. What joy to have them back!

At 7:30 A.M. on May 6 four jeeps roared up and disgorged a star-studded cast: a Pakistan army brigadier general (the sector commander), a colonel (martial-law administrator of Chittagong District), a naval commander, four captains, one bushy-haired television producer with his cameramen, two bedraggled Frenchmen (lighthouse builders from a tiny offshore island), and assorted heavily armed dogfaces who promptly surrounded our house. As we greeted the officers, two soldiers ordered our gardener quickly to shift the

Pakistan flag from our Land Rover and fly it from the housetop. Simultaneously, another officer with submachine gun ready, kicked open our front door and searched every room in the house to be sure no assassins lurked there. Only then did the general and other officers enter the house. As our cook prepared to serve tea to the visitors, an officer forced our gardener to taste a spoonful from every cup to make sure our Bengali cook was not poisoning the Pakistan army top brass.

The officers, although coolly courteous, had not come just to pass the time of day. When they quizzed us sharply, we gave them information we were sure they already possessed. Then they wanted to shoot a TV interview with us making anti-Bangladesh and anti-Awami League statements. Somehow, we were able to dodge out of the television interview by diverting the discussion in various directions, telling them the detailed history of the establishment of Memorial Christian Hospital and explaining our own conversion experiences. At the end of our recital, the TV producer, shaking his head, rasped, "They've said nothing of any value to us."

The martial-law administrator (colonel) did us one favor; he endorsed our list of guns, saying we were allowed to keep them despite the general orders that all firearms were to be handed in. Simultaneously, outside, a captain was grilling Momin on all the same points. Finally, cautioning us that we must always give army officers complete and truthful answers, they departed. In retrospect, we were astounded that we had succeeded in ducking out of the television interview. "Thank You, Father!"

That night we received seventeen boatloads of 120 people, dozens of chickens, several goats, and mountains of baggage. Our Hebron contingent had returned! What a joyous reunion it was! Receiving the wife of our dead brother Shudhir, however, was painful. Disregarding strict Bengali custom, she put her head on my shoulder and sobbed and sobbed. After comforting and consoling her as best I could, we took her to their home, where a group of friends gathered. There we prayed together.

In my May 7 morning Bible reading I noted, "You shall hear of wars and rumors of wars. See that you are not troubled . . . God is our refuge and strength, a very present help in trouble. Therefore we will not fear."

In our morning staff meeting, we told the group what God had done for us and instructed them about how to conduct themselves. Some of them wept when they learned we had received no news of our families. Later I headed for Chittagong to send cables. Seeing Reid again was great! I noted that he looked tired and much thinner;

simultaneously, he was noting the same about me. I learned from various sources that he had done a superb job moving about Chittagong, helping many people, counseling and encouraging them. He, too, had faced tense moments with Pakistan army officers.

Reid had received word that our thirty-four Burma evacuees were well in Bangkok, Thailand! I fired off cables to them and the home board that all of us were alive and well, and that our property had been saved from damage and looting. When I called the United States consul general in Dacca, he seemed overjoyed to hear my voice. He drank in all the information I could give him about Chittagong-Malumghat matters and asked me to come to see him. I agreed to try to come within two or three weeks.

The next day, while I was busily involved in Chittagong writing letters, sending cables, checking up on friends, etc., Pakistan soldiers jeeped from their new base camp in Cox's Bazar to the Malumghat-Dulahazara area where a major had a long talk with our elderly neighbor Fazlul Karim Choudhury. Wonderfully, they killed no Hindus and burned no Hindu houses except one, the house of the *mohajan* (wealthy moneylender). Because the mohajan was influential and his sons educated, and because they had to take some anti-Hindu action for their military records, they ignited the mohajan's house.

When the soldiers departed, Donn drove to the spot. Incensed to see dozens of Bengali Muslims looting the mohajan's belongings, Donn grabbed a couple by the "seat of the sarong" and scruff of the neck and threw them out. After a stern lecture, he hurried back to the hospital, stuffed my revolver in his belt, and returned with a carload of hospital staff men. They rescued three carloads of the mohajan's trunks, boxes, etc.

On the following day, May 9, Thanda Mia ("Mr. Cold"), the petty official who had terrorized Daniel and the most evil man I have ever met, began publicly attacking Donn's character in the bazaar. He claimed that Donn, intimidating Muslims with a huge knife and taking photographs, "looted" the mohajan's house. Soon the local Muslims were talking about the "Christian looters" and warning our hospital staff members to stay away from the bazaar or they would be beaten.

Fearing the Pakistan military would react badly when they heard this distorted story, Donn drove to Cox's Bazar to explain the facts and make his peace with the stone-faced colonel. The colonel asked Donn and Momin many questions and observed that the Awami League had caused much suffering among the people.

"The people, therefore," he said, "will naturally retaliate and loot Awami League houses — it can't be stopped." He advised Donn to remain at the hospital property and not move about the country-side.

As I waited for Donn to return from Cox's Bazar, an old friend, a son of the Hindu mohajan, came out of the jungle to make a strange proposition. He asked, "If I convert to Christianity, would you allow me to bring my family out of the jungle to live at the hospital?" That was a shocker! He hurried on to explain that, although we might consider his Christian interest insincere, in fact it was very sincere. He offered as proof of this contention his perfect attendance at a short-term Bible school, a written statement he had given at that time that he considered the Christian message true, and his numerous visits to the hospital to discuss the Bible with some of his Christian friends on the staff.

I told him, "Friend, I will have to give thought and prayer to your idea and discuss it with my brothers." Arranging bed and food for him, I asked him to return the following morning.

That night eleven of us met to deal with the request. We decided that whether the mohajan's son called himself Christian or Hindu, the Pakistan army was after his skin and his family. The hospital, therefore, located beside the main road, would be the most dangerous possible place for them. I advised the young man to take his family to India and to accept Christ.

On May 10 we learned that Mr. Cold and his devilish band looted and burned to the ground eighty-seven empty Hindu houses during the night! We were sick at heart! After taking risks to save these people and their property from the Pakistan army, Bengali Muslim neighbors of these poor people set the torch to their houses. When the morning sun rose, these same men began cutting ripe Hindu rice and placing it in their own storehouses. We had to stop Mr. Cold.

Hindu homes in flames

Deciding to enlist Major Zaman in our crusade against him, Momin and I jumped in the car to head for Cheringa. As the engine idled, we prayed asking God to help us, somehow, stop this human Satan. Major Zaman was not at home. As we drove about looking for him, we stopped at the police station to inquire if he was there. At the police station we happened upon a meeting of the Peace Committee, a group of Bengali leaders set up by the Pakistan army to help them pacify the countryside. We gave this powerful group the pitch about Mr. Cold and how he was preventing peace from coming to our area. We struck some responsive chord! Furious with Mr. Cold, they sent messengers to bring him immediately so they could judge him and stop him from burning any more houses!

Back on the main highway we met Major Zaman and took him with us to Malumghat. There, I talked with hospital employees who were still being threatened for their "looting" and prevented from visiting the bazaar. We recruited Major Zaman to help. Cooperatively, he went directly to the bazaar and made a public announcement that no hospital staff person could be touched. It worked! "Thank You, Father!"

New misery stories began pouring in:

"The Hindus living in the jungle were drenched with rain last night."

"Many Hindu women can't bathe — they have no second sari."

"Mr. Cold's men raped a Hindu woman in the jungle two miles away."

"Nearby, the educated wife of a Hindu schoolteacher was stripped naked in broad daylight and 'searched for gold.' "

Donn came back from the outpatient department blazing with rage after treating two old Hindu widows, a young mother, and an eight-year-old girl who were beaten and stabbed by Mr. Cold's men when the women protested the stealing of their rice. He also admitted to the hospital a Hindu who had been stabbed in the abdomen by a Muslim priest! The country had gone stark, raving mad!

I drove to Chittagong to make further efforts to gain entrance permits for our American staff. In my absence the Pakistan military forced the Cheringa Peace Committee and police to burn the homes of numerous Hindus and Muslims who were Awami League leaders. They were setting more Bengalis against Bengalis.

People kept coming with problems — problems — problems. Decisions — decisions — decisions. As we tried to help our Christians, the harried Hindus and various Muslims under pressure, every decision had to balance the possible reactions of the Pakistan army, Mr. Cold, the Peace Committee, the police, and the Bangladesh freedom fighters who were someplace off in the jungle or across the border in Burma making plans for the future. While Donn spent most of his time caring for increasing numbers of patients, handling payroll, etc., my time was consumed with the complex decisions and negotiations. Although ferocious action against Hindu villages continued to the north and to the south of us, we succeeded in bringing our local Hindus out of the jungle back into their homes. But they lacked both food to eat and money to purchase it.

By May 15 we decided we must somehow mount a relief operation for Hindus and poor Muslims. Momin and I recruited Major Zaman to help gain permission for the relief program. That day we accepted a beautiful seventeen-year-old Hindu girl to protect her from the rapaciousness of soldiers and unfriendly Bengali Muslims; one of our Christian families took her in.

Knowing that Donn could not manage the increasing patient load and all the complex daily negotiations necessary to keep our neighbors alive, Momin begged me not to go on furlough until another of our mission men returned, preferably Jay Walsh who was most experienced. He was right, of course. I also needed Joan to properly finalize certain aspects of the packing known only to her.

Remembering that I had an important date with a blonde in two and a half weeks on June 3, I thought to myself, *Looks like I'll be missing Wendy's graduation from high school; the chances of getting Joan and Jay or one of our other men back this month are close to zero.* It was a painful thought, for I very greatly longed to see Lynne and Wendy and attend Wendy's graduation.

The next day Donn drove to town, cared for some business, and sent off the cable I had drafted, asking for Jay or one of the other fellows to come as soon as possible. Because a one-armed surgeon can't manage surgical emergencies, Donn hurried back the same evening and told me his adventures: "As I approached Patiya (twenty miles before Chittagong) I saw a huge smudge of smoke on the horizon like a giant fingerprint spoiling a beautiful painting. The base of the column of smoke was a sheet of flame at least one mile wide." We had known the Patiya area would be a prime target for military action because of many Hindu villages in the area.

"On my way back this afternoon," Donn continued, "near Patiya I noticed a man lying in the ditch beside the road, so I stopped to investigate. Get the scene now! The day is peaceful and beautiful. The flame trees are a riot of color. There are purple flowering trees and the creamy frangipani blossoms are in full bloom. The sky is clear blue, and heaped up over the hills are whipped cream clouds. And the road is full of people peacefully walking to the local bazaar about a mile away. Farmers are plowing in their fields. The people walking down the road seem afraid to look at the man lying in the ditch. When I examine this Hindu, I find he has been shot in the back, right through the spine, and the bullet has torn a huge hole in his abdomen. The grass is soaked with his blood. Although he is still alive, his pulse is gone and there is nothing in the world I can do to help him. How a soldier could shoot an absolutely defenseless man in the back, I can't comprehend."

On May 17 Major Zaman, taking Momin, traveled to Cox's Bazar on our behalf. He raised the question of Mr. Cold and our interest in mounting a relief operation for the Hindus. The army officer agreed to further squelch Mr. Cold and, wonder of wonders, breezily agreed to our launching a relief operation so long as it was not too showy or ostentatious. (This in spite of the fact that his commander-in-chief, President Yahya Khan, had sent loaded Red Cross planes back to Geneva saying, "There is no need for any relief in East Pakistan.") "Thank You, Father!"

The next day four jeeploads of Pakistan army officers and soldiers pulled in at midmorning. After a long, useless conversation in which a new colonel advised us about how to carry on missionary work, they departed. The last officer in the group, hanging behind a second, quietly said, "God bless you!" on the way out. We wondered what he meant by that. Perhaps he was a Pakistani Christian — or a pious Muslim who appreciated our care for the people.

We were delighted to see Reid and the British clergyman drive in with a friend from Dacca, Rev. Phil Parshall. He was able to tell us much that had happened in Dacca and points north. When the guard found a highly posionous snake (banded krait) at the Olsen house, we were happy we had established our headquarters at the Ketcham house. Another "snake," one of Mr. Cold's men, raped a young Hindu woman two miles down the road that day.

When Major Zaman came in the morning of May 19, I found his heart open to hear what I had to tell him about Christ. As I shared my faith with him, he seemed to take it in as never before. *Who knows what will happen to him,* I thought. *Maybe some dark night the Bangladesh freedom fighters will sneak out of the jungle and slit his throat.* I hoped he would ponder the way of eternal life. I learned the name of the scoundrel who raped the Hindu woman and helped set the torch to the eighty-seven Hindu houses. Discovering that a powerful friend in the community had some hold over this man, I recruited the gentleman to put some pressure on the rogue and turn off his evil deeds.

One of our Christian washermen came bringing a fellow washerman with a strange name, Panchkuri ("Twenty-five"). The Christian had been giving his witness to the Hindu for months and "Mr. Twenty-five" was ready for the great faith decision in Christ.

Two days later we began our food and clothing relief program for our Hindu neighbors! It was, perhaps, the first relief operation in Bangladesh — certainly the first approved program. "Thank You, Father!"

The Peace Committee had stopped Mr. Cold only temporarily, and the military had so far failed to throttle his activities. His men began rounding up Hindu livestock, molesting more Hindu women, and threatening to burn additional Hindu houses. He announced to the Hindu community that they must convert to Islam in the next three days or leave the area. Several Hindus came to us begging us to make them instantaneous Christians, for they would never in the world agree to Mr. Cold's proposition. We had to explain that becoming a Christian means understanding something about Christ and His teaching and making a free moral decision to accept and follow Him. We said we would try to think of some other way to help them immediately, and provide Bible teaching for them as soon as possible.

In the afternoon I headed for Chittagong hoping to find some way to gain entrance permits for our mission team. Sadly, I could see no way for it to work out in time to make Wendy's graduation.

In Chittagong Reid had received a cable from Jay dispatched in Bangkok, Thailand. Everyone without Pakistan visas had received four-year multiple-entry visas! How thrilling! They still lacked, however, the special permit required to enter war-torn East Pakistan; and the highest Pakistan army officer in Chittagong said he had insufficient authority to grant the approval. That meant a trip to Dacca.

In Dacca on May 23 I learned that permission was not yet being granted for foreigners to enter East Pakistan. I learned also that the first plane from Bangkok, Thailand, to Dacca would arrive that very evening. Although I knew it was foolish to think any of our people could be on that flight (they had no permit) I felt an inner compulsion that I should go to the airport.

The Bangkok flight landed on time. "I'm afraid we have come on a wild-goose chase, Phil," I said apologetically to Phil Parshall as we waited for passengers to disembark. When the airport door opened, the first passenger to enter was a bright-eyed, blond-haired boy — my son Mark! Then came Joan, Nancy, Donn's family, Jay Walsh and his family! "Oh, thank You, Father!"

As I kissed Joan and the kids and welcomed everyone, Jay said, "Don't get too excited, buddy. We'll be here only forty minutes to clear customs, refuel, and head on for West Pakistan. When we couldn't get special permits to enter East Pakistan, we decided to go to the high school kids in Murree. Unless you can do something fantastic, we'll be leaving here in thirty to forty minutes."

I was ready to try for something fantastic — Joan and Jay, the two people I desperately needed, were there. If I could get them admitted to East Pakistan, we might just barely be able to make that date with our blond daughters in Murree, West Pakistan. Sending my friend Phil Parshall to contact a friend who was a high government officer (a patient of mine), I phoned the American consul general.

After hearing my story, he said, "I would do anything in the world I could to help you in this, Vic, but my hands are tied. They are not listening to anything I say regarding matters like this. I am terribly sorry." Phil returned with bad news — the government officer had just left his home and would not be available for hours.

With ideas exhausted and only a few minutes remaining before departure, I was whipped. The time was gone. Standing under the high-domed roof of that soldier-studded airport, my soul crying out within me, I agonized, "Oh, Father, what can I do? Help me! Help me!"

In an instant a thought struck — a very simple, elementary idea: *The time is gone. It is too late to get help from anywhere out in the city. Anything that is done must be done here in this airport.* Turning, I stopped a man to ask, "Who is in charge of this airport?"

"Wing Commander Khaja," he replied.

"Where's Khaja's office?" As he pointed a bony finger, I raced for the office. Elbowing my way through surprised submachine-gun-toting West Pakistani soldiers, I pounded on the wing commander's door. In a moment, the door opened, a man stuck his head out and asked, "Who are you?"

"My name is Olsen," I responded. "Who are you?"

"My name is Khaja; what do you want?"

"Wing Commander, I want you. You're the most important man in the world to me just now!"

Stepping out of the room, he said, "What can I do for you?"

When I blurted out my story, he replied, "I'm afraid there's nothing I can do for you."

"But Wing Commander, if you can't do anything for me, then no one can help me. Please think it through from every angle and see if there is not some action you can take that might allow my family and colleagues to remain in Dacca."

Rubbing his chin thoughtfully, he decided on a telephone call to a general. I understood only a few of the words in their three-minute Urdu conversation — and every one of them sounded bad. Hanging up the receiver, he shook his head, saying, "I'm afraid I can't solve your problem."

My last hope just died was the thought that pierced my soul that moment.

"But there is one thing I can do for you," the wing commander continued. "I can get your family off the flight for this one night, but they'll have to continue on to West Pakistan tomorrow unless you can gain special permission from the martial law authorities downtown."

"Thank you, Wing Commander. Pass the order for them to remain tonight. I'll take it from there."

As I ecstatically returned to the Olsens, Ketchams, and Walshes, my heart sang, *Thank You, Father!* When we left the airport, the wing commander handed me a slip of paper with the name of the colonel whom I must see the next morning.

At the Parshall's house, Mark and Nancy told me breathless little squibs of what happened during the evacuation and their stops in Rangoon, Bangkok, and Penang. Joan gave me a more connected story:

"As we drove away from the hospital, that day in April, I didn't know whether or not I would ever see you again on earth. But, deep down, I had peace of mind knowing that we were each carrying out our part in God's plan for us — and that it was right. At Teknaf Jay arranged for a huge, leaky, old sampan with a tattered sail to float us and backpacks of food and suitcases across the Naf River six miles to the unknown — Maungdaw, Burma.

"Wall-to-wall people"

"Arriving at 7 P.M. we found the Beals still at Maungdaw. With them our group numbered thirty-four (four men, nine women, and twenty-one kids). The shocked Burmese officials finally checked our luggage and settled us in a rest house with a floor and a few tape-strung bed frames to sleep on — no sheets, no pillow cases, no pillows, no mattresses! With men and boys sleeping in one room, mothers with small children in another, and older girls and the rest of us in a third, we really had wall-to-wall people. Mark used his muddy tennis shoes for a pillow. Phew! Joe DeCook cradled his head on a roll of toilet paper — and didn't worry about squeezing the Charmin! That night, in a conference with Burmese intelligence officers, Jay and Mel learned that the West Pakistan troops had that day reached a point seven miles north of the hospital. It seemed likely, then, that they would arrive at the hospital the next day — so we had plenty to worry about right away. I didn't sleep much that night.

"About 10:30 the next morning ancient army trucks came to bounce us sixteen miles to a little port on the Mayu River called Buthidaung; there we would board an old tub to take us the eight-hour trip to civilization (the town of Akyab). Soldiers with automatic rifles rode herd on us to protect us from the communist guerrillas infesting the northern Burma jungles. We boarded the battered, World War II vintage launch at 1 P.M. But ten hours later we did not appear to be near any port. The sharp wind was whipping the waves — and us — with increasing force as we neared the open sea at the mouth of the river. When the launch struck and shuddered on several sand bars, we knew the pilot was lost! The sea was rough, the rudder had broken, the night was dark, and we were traveling without lights to avoid guerrilla attack. Giving up hope of finding the channel in the dark, the pilot somehow limped back up the river a little and dropped anchor for the night.

"Sleeping on a pile of suitcases of various sizes and shapes (and corners), wrapped against the cold wind in a mosquito net, and rolling with the waves, suddenly the hard floor of the night before seemed to me like pure luxury. As I lay there the questions I couldn't answer kept gnawing at my heart: What had happened to you and Donn at Malumghat when the army arrived? Did a major battle smash the hospital? Theoretically, the crisis had come that day, and, oh, how I longed to know!

"The night was long, but dawn came at last. The rudder was repaired and the anchor lifted — but the battery was dead! Finally, the incoming tide beached us on the sandy shore of an island. Up to this point our backpacks had provided sufficient food, but now it was time for breakfast and, except for some tins of C-rations, 'the

Bounced in ancient army
trucks

Beached on an island shore
— *left to right,* Joan, Joyce
and Joe DeCook, Jeannie
Lockerbie, and Lynn Silvernale

backpacks were bare.' So Jay left with two Burmese to look for a
village to buy food. Meanwhile, two of our armed guards left in
search of help, and the children swam and played on the beach as
the tide went out leaving our launch high and dry on the sand.

"At last, Jay returned with plenty of bananas and local pastries for
us all. In the early afternoon a Burmese Navy P.T. boat came to
rescue us and take us on to Akyab. There we were met by worried
American embassy officials from Rangoon who had expected to meet
us the night before. They could only wonder if we had been killed
by guerrillas, for foreigners are not allowed to enter the dangerous
jungles north of Akyab. They told us afterward that they could
scarcely believe their ears as they heard across the water the children's voices singing happy choruses from sampans ferrying us from
the P.T. boat to the river bank at Akyab. They helped us through
customs and, in turn, surprised us with ice cold American soft drinks,
brought from Rangoon.

"After a shower, a change of clothes, and a hot meal at a nearby
Catholic mission school, we were flown by chartered plane to Rangoon and taken to a large modern hotel. We felt like David when
he wrote, 'You [God] brought us into the net; you laid affliction
upon us . . . we went through fire and water; but you brought us
out into a wealthy place!' There Embassy officials sent cables for us

— including a long one to the Walsh, Ketcham, and Olsen children at Murree, explaining our evacuation and reassuring them as best we could about you and Donn.

"Next morning at 9 A.M. the telephone rang in my room at the hotel. The operator said, "I have a call for Mrs. Olsen from Dr. Olsen in Maryland, USA. My first thought was, *He can't be in Maryland — he's at the hospital!* — but then I knew it would be your brother Charles. He had learned of our arrival in Rangoon from the State Department in Washington. When he asked what he could do for us, I suggested, 'Please call the girls in Murree and tell them . . .' and then I repeated to him the message we had sent in the cable. What a comfort! I thought surely the cable or Charles' call would get through to them. But I learned later that neither reached them, and the teenagers in Murree were going through days of terrific anxiety, knowing only that we had been told by our government to leave Malumghat.

"The Americans in Rangoon showered us with kindness and the American ambassador invited us to tea."

"Yeah, Dad," Mark interrupted, "and we got to watch the ambassador feed his two pet tigers. It was really neat!"

"After a couple of days in Rangoon" Joan continued, "we flew on to Bangkok. We figured that as soon as the Pakistan army passed the hospital and took the area, order would be restored and we could safely return. But we couldn't just go back. In addition to needing permits to reenter East Pakistan, many in our group, as you know, had expired Pakistan visas.

"We had learned in Rangoon, and the news was confirmed by the American ambassador in Bangkok, that the Pakistan government was taking a dim view of our backdoor exit from East Pakistan where there was no customs checkpoint. Angry editorials had appeared in the Pakistan newspapers. On the basis of this and other information, our ambassadors, both in Rangoon and Bangkok, strongly advised us to return to America and not to expect reentry visas for some months — if ever. But an approach to the Pakistan embassy in Bangkok (the friendly visa officer who had granted us those wonderful visas in February) brought the answer, "I will do what I can to help you, but I must first refer the matter of permission to reenter to my government in West Pakistan. The reply probably will not come for a couple of weeks." About this time our two-week tourist visas for Thailand were running out; to qualify for two more weeks we would be required to leave the country and return. So we decided to fly to Penang in Malaysia for a few days' rest.

"The night before we left, I awakened in the night and, feeling

uneasy about you and restless, couldn't go back to sleep. So I took my Bible from the bedside table, asking the Lord to give me some word — something from Him. I opened the Bible and my eyes fell on the story in Jeremiah 24 about the two baskets of figs; I read until verses 5 and 6 almost leaped from the page:

> Thus says the Lord, the God of Israel; Like these good figs, so will I acknowledge them that are carried away captive from Judah, whom I have sent out of this place into the land of the Chaldeans for their good. For I will set my eyes upon them for good, and I will bring them again to this land.

'I have sent out . . . for their good . . . will bring them again to this land.' With a new peace and quiet assurance I dropped off to sleep.

"The next day we flew to Penang and checked into a hotel. That night at 10:30, I was awakened by an urgent rapping on my door. It was Kitty Ketcham and Joe DeCook with a telegram from you saying that you, Reid, and Donn were safe and the hospital intact! After they left, overwhelmed by relief, the tears came — but they were tears of joy, for you were safe! ! Of course, I didn't know then about your smashed elbow or the nights of danger and the miracle that saved you and Donn at the hospital.

"The next three days I spent sending out a newsletter to friends and loved ones in America, telling about our evacuation and that you three were safe. In Penang, we received news that word had come from West Pakistan that we would be allowed to reenter West Pakistan and visas would be granted. So we returned to Bangkok where all fourteen who lacked visas received four-year multiple-entry visas! Then we understood God's purpose for sending us out the back door of East Pakistan through dangerous territory to Bangkok — in that city we were able to get the million-dollar visas! In addition to the visas we needed special permits to return to the war-torn east wing. Most felt they would rather wait for that permission in Bangkok in order to fly directly to Dacca. But those of us with children in Murree elected to fly to West Pakistan and spend that time with our children. So this afternoon the Walsh family, and Kitty and I and our children, boarded the first plane to resume flights between Bangkok and Dacca, and took off for Karachi, expecting just a forty-minute layover in Dacca to clear customs. I had no idea that *you* would be here — or that we might be able to stay. Oh, honey — who would have thought we would be back together this very night?"

As Joan finished thrilling me with her glowing recital, I suddenly remembered that I had a patient/friend in town who was said to have some contact in martial-law headquarters, Dacca. It came to me strongly that I must see my friend despite the lateness of the hour. Reluctantly excusing myself, I drove to his house.

After our greetings and family talk were finished, I said to him, "I have heard that you have some connections with the martial law authorities downtown."

Then, showing him the slip of paper with the colonel's name on it, I asked, "You wouldn't happen to know this colonel, would you?"

His face lighting up with a broad smile, he replied, "Of course! He's a very good friend of mine. As a matter of fact, I just happen to have an appointment with him at nine tomorrow morning! Would you like to come along?"

Jay and I did go along with the friend and, through his intercession, the colonel broke every martial-law regulation on the books regarding the return of foreigners into the country. The special permit was granted! "Thank You, Father!"

It required a day or two to get reservations to fly to Chittagong. In the interim I briefed Jay on the full background of all our negotiations to save the people in our area and launch the relief operation. As soon as he arrived at Malumghat, a day or two behind us, he would free me from my duties, and allow me to finish packing so we could try to make the date with Wendy and Lynne.

After reaching Chittagong in the evening, the Olsen and Ketcham families headed immediately for Malumghat. Although under the circumstances it was not desirable to travel at night, we did so anyway, for every moment was precious. And Kitty was not willing to lose a minute in seeing Donn. Stopped by Pakistani soldiers at the main bridge on the outskirts of Chittagong, we joshed them, talked our way through, and sped onwards. The night sky was glowing red-orange from villages blazing on both sides of the highway. The Pakistan army, day after day, just kept burning and burning and burning.

We stopped, halfway to the hospital, at Dohazari to get gas. The proprietor, an old man, asked nervously, "What time is it?" "Four minutes until 10:00 P.M.," I replied. Because it was not yet 10:00 (curfew time) he agreed to give us the gas. But, the old gentleman moved very slowly, and at 10:04 he still was draining gasoline from a drum to finish filling our second car. Sauntering thirty steps toward the road, I suddenly saw the bright moonlight glinting off the bayonet of a Pakistani soldier!

As I walked up to him, the moonlight glinted also from his eyes and he raised his rifle and bayonet saying grimly, "Stop. Who are you?" I stopped with the tip of his bayonet an inch from my abdomen. I doubt if he understood much of my reply, but perhaps he picked up the words doctor, hospital, Malumghat.

"You go car!" he snapped.

As I retreated to the car I saw his fellow soldier, with fixed bayonet, approaching the station from the other side. The two of them executed a perfect flanking maneuver and advanced quietly on the old man as he squatted to finish draining gasoline from the drum. Mark, unexpectedly, came upon one of the soldiers who waved a bayonet at him to send him scampering wide-eyed back to the car.

Sensing their presence, the old man looked up, terror written on his face. As the old gentleman stood slowly to his feet, a soldier smashed him across the face with his open hand to send him reeling against the building. Fearing for his life, the proprietor ran inside his station.

The two soldiers then approached us, brandished their bayonets toward the south and said, "Go!"

Angry, I answered, "I'm not going until I pay my bill."

As I opened the door into the station, the old man groaned, "Forget about the money. Just go. Just go." I shoved sixty rupees into his hand and we drove off, dreading what might happen to the old man.

Arriving at Malumghat at 11:00 P.M., Kitty knocked on Donn's bedroom window and called, "Donn! Donn! Let me in! It's Kit."

"Kit who?" Donn murmured foggily — then he came wide awake! Incredulous, he unlocked the door and hugged them all.

Later he confessed, "The Lord knew just the right night to send them! That was the very night I had sat and bawled out of sheer loneliness."

On our last morning at Malumghat (May 30), I took an hour from our frantic packing to talk with a high-caste Hindu friend whom I had known for eight years. Many of our mission team had talked with him about spiritual matters over the years, but he stumbled over the idea that every single human being was a person who had broken at least part of God's law and needed a Saviour. His war experiences, however, removed this psychological block. He now thoroughly understood the blackness of the human heart. I asked him if he were ready to place his faith in Christ. He was ready, after eight long years of consideration! Beautifully, sincerely, he prayed, asking Christ to be his Saviour and to enter into his life. He was the "firstfruits" at Malumghat of the agony and bitterness of the horrible war.

That afternoon, on the way to Chittagong, we wondered if Reid had succeeded in getting reservations for West Pakistan. Arriving, we learned that with great difficulty he had arranged the seats. We flew on through to Dacca, Karachi, and Rawalpindi. At twilight a taxi took us the last forty miles up the mountain to hug our daughters, Lynne and Wendy, the night before Wendy's graduation! "Thank You, Father!"

After the lovely graduation ceremonies, we spent the week recovering and sharing our various experiences with each other. For weeks our family had been scattered in three separate points in Asia, but now at last we were together again. We enjoyed a leisurely, delightful trip through Europe to arrive in America in July.

*   *   *

During the last half of 1971, while we Olsens were in America, a dramatic series of events engulfed our mission team and changed the anatomy of the Indo-Pakistan subcontinent. (A colleague has written in detail about the activities of the ABWE Chittagong contingent during this period and the preceding several months.[4])

By the first week in June, the Pakistan government had decided to admit foreigners to East Pakistan, and the rest of our Bangkok contingent had returned to Dacca and traveled to their stations.

The traffic leaving East Pakistan, however, was much heavier than the incoming traffic. By then four million Bengalis had walked, stumbled, or dragged across the border into India to escape the rapacious Pakistan troops. From them, foreign journalists and then the world had learned more of the massacre going on inside the country. As our mission team members were returning to their stations in Bangladesh, India was temporarily closing her borders because cholera had struck many of the refugees fleeing to Indian camps. Hundreds were lying dead beside the highways, roads, and trails which led to India. The vultures, crows, and village dogs fought over the human carrion.

Later in June at Malumghat, Mr. Cold was finally brought to bay. Jay followed up our original request to the army commandant who finally took action. A Pakistan army officer publicly dressed down Mr. Cold, humiliated him, and ordered him to cease oppressing the local Hindus. At last his pressures eased off our Hindu neighbors.

Dozens of Hindus, moved by Christian love and sacrifice, inquired about the Christian faith. Our Americans and Bengalis organized classes and interviews to tell their Hindu neighbors about Jesus. Many, convinced by what they learned, accepted Christ as their Saviour and Lord, determining to be His followers in baptism and in life.

In July President Nixon sent his presidential adviser, Henry Kissinger, to West Pakistan. There, feigning illness in a town very near the high school our teenagers attend, he was spirited away secretly to China by the West Pakistanis. In Peking he began negotiating President Nixon's summit meeting with the Chinese leaders. Our Bengali friends were angry that America and China were supporting their hated enemy, West Pakistan.

Meanwhile, in India, thousands of young Bengalis were being trained to become guerrilla fighters for Bangladesh. Because most of them were students from some school or college, the Mukti Fouj was one of the most highly educated guerrilla forces in military history. They learned their lessons quickly and well. In early July their activities were very limited. But by the end of the month, the intensity of their operations began to increase. In Dacca and Chittagong freedom fighters successfully blew up electric transformers, plunging large areas into darkness. In our Chittagong District they sent to union council

Newsweek cover picturing Bengali guerrillas

FREDERIC OHRINGER

chairmen money and letters suggesting that the chairmen use the money to purchase cloth for their burial. They successfully exterminated at least eight union council chairmen in Chittagong District.

By August the Mukti Fouj was more than a *fouj* (army), for it had boats, sailors, and frogmen. Therefore the name Mukti Fouj was superceded by Mukti Bahini (liberation brothers or liberation forces). During August the frogmen succeeded in sinking a number of Pakistan army supply ships in Chittagong and Chalna harbors.

Sheikh Mujib was transferred to jail in the West Pakistani town of Lyallpur. There he was placed on trial before a secret military court, charged with treason. Although he refused to take a defense lawyer, one was imposed upon him, as Mujib later said, "to obtain a certificate to hang me."[5]

On August 9, Prime Minister Indira Ghandi of India signed a sensational treaty with Russia. Article nine "provided for consultations between the two countries in case of war or threat of war to either of them, with a view to removing that threat."[6] Bengalis, as well as Indians, were pleased with this article. The freedom fighters

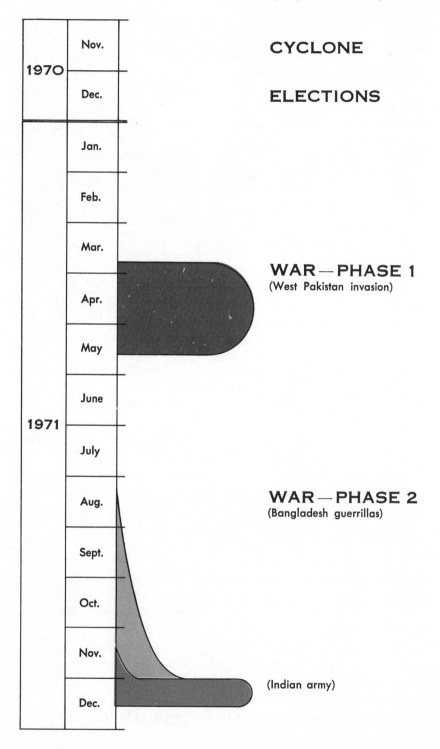

continued to damage roads, bridges, railway lines, and telephone communications. They were becoming skillful in ambushing smaller groups of Pakistan troops. In a few areas they successfully fought pitched battles with sizable Pakistan army contingents.

In September injured *rajakars* were admitted to our hospital. These men, Bengali and non-Bengali collaborators with the Pakistan army, were hired and armed by the army for semimilitary duties. When the freedom fighters caught them, they killed some and cut off the hands, ears, or noses of others.

In October, the freedom fighters became increasingly active. As they killed more and more West Pakistani soldiers, they captured additional highly useful guns and ammunition. Phase 2 of the war had begun. (See chart.) Nine million Bengalis had crossed into India to become refugees in the numerous camps. Our food relief operation at Malumghat continued and increased in scope. The Pakistan government was not granting visas to our new appointees or for our few veterans who had not been part of the fortunate group who obtained visas in Bangkok.

On October 23, Indian Prime Minister Indira Ghandi began a three-week tour of western capitals. She aimed to stimulate world opinion to bring pressure to bear on Pakistan's Yahya Khan, stop the senseless killings in Bangladesh, release Sheikh Mujib, and provide a government which would receive the overwhelming number of refugees back into Bangladesh. She was not successful.

November was marked by increasingly potent border skirmishes between the Indian army and the Pakistan army across the Bangladesh border. On November 22 a particularly sharp encounter involving troops, tanks, and aircraft occurred at Boyra, India.[7]

On December 1, India's prime minister demanded the withdrawal of the Pakistan army from Bangladesh. On December 3 the Pakistan army responded with a surprise, "preemptive" air attack on eight Indian airfields! Modeled after the highly successful preemptive Israeli air strike against Egypt in the 1967 Israeli-Egyptian war, the copy was a dismal failure. Relatively little damage was done, but the Indians then had sufficient excuse to order their poised army to smash across the borders of Bangladesh and attack the West Pakistan occupation army.

The Indian generals knew in advance that they would be fighting a battle of many obstacles. With most of the country's large and small bridges sabotaged, they would have to use other means to cross substantial rivers and dozens of streams. The Engineer Corps worked wonders for the Indian military machine.

The Indian generals launched a five-pronged offensive into Bangladesh. Instead of tackling heavily fortified Pakistani positions, they skirted them to drive quickly on towards the nerve-center city of Dacca. This "lightning concept" was designed to prevent Pakistani troops from pulling back to make an all-out final defense of the "Dacca bowl."[8] The Mukti Bahini, knowing perfectly the people and the terrain, gave the Indian army immeasurable help.

On December 5, the Indian navy scored. Attacking the West Pakistani part of Karachi, they sank four Pakistani warships and bombarded the harbor. On the eastern front, the Indian navy already had sunk the Pakistan navy's prize submarine, the *Ghazi*.

On December 6, India recognized diplomatically the independent nation of Bangladesh. The Pakistan government, in quick retaliation, snapped all diplomatic ties with India.

On December 8 the Indian advance continued closing in on Dacca. When the Indians cracked the Pakistani code, Indian electronic warfare specialists sent confusing radio messages to the Pakistani fighting units. Indian psychological warfare began with a radio announcement and leaflets dropped to the Pakistani forces. The message said,

> The Indian forces have reached all around you. Your air force is destroyed. You have no hope of any help from them. Chittagong, Chalna, and Mangla ports are blocked. Nobody can reach you from the sea. Your fate is sealed. The Mukti Bahini and the people are all prepared to take revenge for the actrocities and cruelities you have committed . . . why waste lives? Do you want to go home and be with your children? Do not lose time; there is no disgrace in laying down your arms to a soldier. We will give you the treatment befitting a soldier.[9]

On December 11, five hundred Indian paratroopers, commanded by General Nagra, were dropped sixty miles north of Dacca — they were the first prong to reach the beleaguered city.

Eleven hundred miles away also, the two armies were fighting ferociously across the border separating India from West Pakistan. As President Yahya Khan was trying to decide whether or not to execute Sheikh Mujib, a grave was dug outside Mujib's cell. Danger arose that other prisoners in the jail might attack and kill him. When that danger became acute, a jailer brought him out of his prison and, just as we had brought men into our house to save them from angry people, the jailer took Mujib into his own house and held him for two days, saving his life.

On December 13, General Niazi, who had complained that Donn and I were hampering his "works" in southern Bangladesh, stated

Joyful flag-raising at the hospital

that the Pakistan army would "fight to the last man." Soon thereafter, when the defeat of West Pakistan forces was inevitable, Pakistani soldiers and their collaborators snatched dozens of Bengali
intellectuals from their jail cells and brutally executed them. Bangladesh could ill-afford to lose these brilliant, talented men.

On December 16 the Indian paratroopers were knocking on the
door of Dacca. Indian General Nagra, acquainted with Pakistani
General Niazi, sent him a personal note: "My dear Abdullah, I am
here. The game is up. I suggest you give yourself up to me and I
will look after you."[10]

On December 16, 1971, at Malumghat, our staff and many visitors, conscious that Bangladesh was about to be born, gathered at
the hospital to raise the new flag of independent Bangladesh. After
a Bengali pastor offered prayer for the new nation, the flag was
raised briskly to the top of the pole. As the crowd shouted *"Joi
Bangla!"* barefooted Mukti Bahini fired volleys of shots into the air.

At 5:01 P.M. that same day, General Niazi signed a document
of surrender! Then he jerked the epaulet off his shoulder, unloaded
his revolver, and handed over his cartridges to the commanding general of the Indian forces. The signing ceremony took place, fittingly,
at the Dacca race course where, nine months before, Sheikh Mujib
had given his impassioned speech. My friend Rev. Phil Parshall,
writing from Bangladesh, graphically summarized the birth of Bangladesh:

March 25, 1971 to December 16, 1971 — A nine month full-term waiting period which included fourteen days of agonizing labor followed by the bloody Cesarean birth of the world's eighth largest nation.

Name: Bangladesh
Size: 75 million people
Disposition: Extremely jubilant
Prognosis: Democratic, socialistic and secularistic.

December 17 — Bhutto took over the reins of government from disgraced President Yahya Khan in West Pakistan. Reportedly, Yahya wanted to execute Mujib and predate the execution, but Bhutto refused and brought Mujib to Pakistan's capital city.

The people of Bangladesh were intoxicated with joy that their leader still lived and that their dream of independent Bangladesh had come true. Simultaneously our mission team drafted a letter to President Nixon. The letter passionately and eloquently detailed some of the agony and atrocities seen by our medical staff. It pointed out that the Bengalis had acted in a way consonant with American ideals as expressed in the American Declaration of Independence:

> That whenever any form of government becomes destructive to these ends [the rights of life, liberty and the pursuit of happiness], it is the right of the people to alter or abolish it, and to institute new government.

The letter closed with an appeal for humanitarian aid to the shattered nation and diplomatic recognition of Bangladesh.

Pakistani General Niazi signing surrender document, Indian General Aurora at left
WIDE WORLD PHOTOS

Birth of a Nation

© 1971 Chicago Sun-Times

During the last quarter of 1971 God showed His hand often to our mission team. Forty-six Bengalis followed Christ the Lord in baptism at Malumghat. None of our mission property was looted or damaged. Several survived potentially dangerous moments: Mary Lou, Linda, and teacher Jewl Spoelhof were shopping in Cox's Bazar on December 4 when the first Indian planes attacked, bombing and strafing the town. Mel Beals was captured by the Mukti Bahini. (Non-Bengali collaborators with the Pakistan army captured the same day were executed the following morning while Mel was released to return to Malumghat.) On December 14 a building one-half mile from our hospital was bombed and rocketed by Indian air force jet planes. At the height of the Indian air force bombing of Chittagong, a whole shipload of supplies lying on the docks was blasted — except for thirty-seven cases of MAP medical supplies for our hospital! Captain Haroon, his incision well healed, returned from Burma to be the military commander over our whole Malumghat-Cox's Bazar area.

On January 3, in a mammoth public meeting in Karachi, Pakistan, the new president, Bhutto, like a Pakistani Pontius Pilate, cried out to the crowd, "Do you want Mujib freed?" When the crowd shouted, "Yea!", Bhutto answered: "You have relieved me of a great burden."[11]

Secretly, in the early morning hours of January 8, Mujib was flown to London. The announcement of his London arrival electrified the world, especially lovers of Bangladesh like us. After a brief twenty-four hours in London, he was flown by RAF jet to New Delhi.

On January 10 at 1:20 P.M., Sheikh Mujib returned to the victorious Bengalis and his beloved Bangladesh! In an incredible, ecstatic, tumultuous moment he stepped from an RAF plane and greeted a multitude of his followers. Jay Walsh was present at the Dacca airport to observe that climactic occasion. The infant nation, with its guiding spirit back, took its first brave but tottering steps into the future.

21

Meeting "Mujib"

When the Olsens departed for America in June, 1971, for our second furlough, we did not foresee the onset of phase two of the war which culminated in an independent Bangladesh.

To meet us at Chicago's O'Hare airport were Joan's family and MAP friends — our reunion was particularly joyous as a finale to the uncertainties of the previous months. (Not until Christmas did we enjoy a delightful repeat performance at the Olsen family reunion at my parents' home.) With a big assist from MAP, we settled our family in Wheaton, Illinois. While searching for a suitable house, we stayed in the vacation-empty homes of old friends from our Milwaukee Bible class (Roger and Alice Dauchy) and new friends (the Taylors, Margaret and Ken, author of *The Living Bible*). Because churches and other groups were hungry to hear about Bangladesh, I entered quickly into a heavy round of deputation.

In August newspapers reported the sensational walkout of Bengali diplomats in Washington. Protesting the killing of Bengalis in Bangladesh, they pulled out of the Pakistan embassy, leaving it to the West Pakistanis, and requested asylum from the US government. The Chicago newspapers never reported the final outcome; I made a mental note that I would have to track down the "missing diplomats" on my first trip to Washington.

In October I finally took time, after ten years, to be inducted into the American College of Surgeons during that august body's annual meeting in Atlantic City, New Jersey. Although I gained benefit and much pleasure attending the scientific sessions and being once again in the academic atmosphere, I did not regret for a minute the watershed decision twelve years earlier which had put academic matters on the sidelines and launched us into frontline action in East Pakistan.

In November I received an invitation to attend a private consultation in Washington, D.C., on the East Pakistan situation; I felt constrained to readjust my deputation schedule in order to attend. Staying with my brother Charles and his wife Jan, who lived in the

ABWE president, the Reverend Wendell Kempton, congratulating
Dr. Olsen on induction into American College of Surgeons

area, made the Washington visit doubly pleasant. Those who addressed the consultation on East Pakistan were a diverse group:
US Senator Edward Kennedy, a congressman, a US State Department official, an American professor, and representatives of the Indian embassy and the Bangladesh Mission ("shadow embassy").
Representatives from the Pakistan embassy came, took one look at
the other participants and departed, refusing to speak.

As soon as the Bengali representative, Mr. Enayet Karim, finished his excellent address, I met him and we talked together. I
learned that the Bengali diplomats who had walked out of the Pakistan embassy in August had set up offices elsewhere in Washington to
become the "shadow embassy" of Bangladesh. Here were the missing diplomats.

"I want to go there!" I exclaimed.

"One of my men can take you now," he replied.

Within a minute after my arrival at the Bangladesh Mission, I
spotted an old friend from Chittagong! An author and educator,
Abu Rust Matinuddin was formerly principal of Chittagong College; he had consulted with me on my dictionary project and had
become my patient. More recently, he had been a senior counselor
in the Pakistan embassy, then defected to the Bangladesh Mission.
Embracing joyously, we talked of many things. I inquired about his
health and advised him about his further treatment.

Finally my friend observed, "You know, you have another friend here."

"No, who is that?" I asked.

"Come along," he said, "I will show you." Taking me down a long hall, he escorted me into the office of the Bangladesh ambassador! There, sitting behind his desk, was Mr. M. R. Siddiqi, a very prominent businessman and long-time friend from Chittagong! Leaping to his feet, he greeted me warmly and we began to talk. Our talk continued five hours nonstop! He wanted to learn everything that had happened to me and to our hospital during the war, and then he shared his many war experiences. In the process of our marathon discussion we completely forgot the noon meal, and our friendship and mutual respect deepened. Finally, taking my leave, I flew back to Chicago and Wheaton.

During the first half of December we were glued to the newspaper headlines and the television news broadcasts as the Indian army crashed across Bangladesh borders to close in upon Dacca. And then on December 16 our joy was complete when we learned that Pakistan's General Niazi had surrendered, that independent Bangladesh was born, and that our Bengali friends and brothers were free. Within hours after receiving the thrilling news, I phoned Ambassador Siddiqi at his home in Washington. Although a thousand miles apart, we rejoiced together at the stunning development; he seemed deeply moved by my call.

When I asked when I might get my visa for Bangladesh, he responded, "I cannot say, for neither Bangladesh nor America has issued me authority, yet, to grant visas. But don't worry, there will certainly be a visa for you."

In January I called Washington again, this time to talk to Ambassador Siddiqi specifically about visas. He explained, "Although I have received authority from Bangladesh to grant visas, your American government has not yet approved my doing so. Because America has not recognized our country diplomatically, it cannot give approval for us to grant visas."

Then, as I heard the ambassadorial pen scratching on paper, he continued, "Dr. Olsen, don't worry about your visa. I am making an official notation that we will reserve Bangladesh visa number one for you in recognition of service to our country! We deeply appreciate your love for Bangladesh and our people."

My heart leaped, for this could mean that after years of crushing visa problems in Pakistan, mission personnel would be freely granted visas to Bangladesh!

The ambassador continued; "Tomorrow will be my last day here.

Mr. Enayet Karim, whom you have met, will be taking my place. I am leaving because Sheikh Mujib, within hours after his release, called me from London saying I must return to Bangladesh for my next assignment. So I will look forward to seeing you in Bangladesh when you return there."

In mid-January I traveled again to Washington, D.C., this time to confer with State Department officials. With me were Mr. Pierson of our ABWE office and Rev. Wendell Kempton, the new ABWE president, a capable, astute, and well-connected leader. Through his contacts we reached into a high level of the State Department. The leader of the three men who met with us was the pertinent deputy assistant secretary of state. When we expressed amazement that these officers could recite from memory many of the names of our mission members, they explained that during the war and evacuation many cables containing those names had crossed their desks. They seemed well aware that ABWE was the largest American organization in Bangladesh.

Because we greatly appreciated all the interest and care they had shown for our people during the critical days of the war, we first expressed our gratitude to them. Then, when we shared our hope that the United States government would provide prompt and generous humanitarian aid to the people of Bangladesh, the officials assured us that the American Congress would soon pass legislation granting funds for aid to the new nation.

The officers shared with us nonclassified information which they had received concerning Bangladesh. Inevitably, they mentioned the matter of US recognition of the new nation. When we asked them their views on recognition, they mentioned various obstructions to speedy recognition (presence of Indian soldiers in the country, etc.). Then they asked for our ideas on the subject. That was the moment we were waiting for. We spoke strongly for recognizing Bangladesh as soon as possible. Several points which I advanced in favor of early recognition apparently made little impact. But one argument seemed to strike home: the fact that we, as American citizens living in Bangladesh, would be hampered in our work and rapport with the people if America delayed recognition.

The chief officer responded with obvious sincerity, "That point is very important to us and will be carefully considered during our future discussions on the subject." We were grateful for the interview.

In January I participated in the Wheaton College Missions Emphasis Week, addressing the faculty on one occasion and the student body twice. God spoke to young men and women, and I learned later that many were deeply stirred by the needs of the people of Bangladesh.

Also in January the ABWE Executive Committee acted on a request from MAP that I be allowed to serve as MAP's first acting medical director while continuing my ABWE duties. ABWE agreed to this proposal and President Kempton, in Wheaton five days later, visited MAP President Raymond Knighton to notify him personally of this approval. At the close of that meeting Ray said, "Vic, I think maybe you and I should go to Bangladesh to see what we American Christians can do to help in this year of their great need." His suggestion jolted me! The thought of returning before our furlough was completed had not occurred to me. I told Ray I would think it over gladly!

Within four days, I was sure that we should act on Ray's suggestion. Calling from Detroit, I finally tracked him down in Oklahoma City. He wanted another day for final prayerful consideration and decision. The next day he called back with an enthusiastic, "Let's go! I'm sold that it's the right move!" We decided to depart in three weeks.

Unknown to me, on February 2 a fascinating meeting was proceeding in Washington, D.C. Senator Edward Kennedy, chairman of the Judicial Subcommittee on Refugees and Escapees, was holding hearings in Washington in Room 1114 of the new Senate office building. Among others giving testimony that day was the deputy assistant secretary of state for Near Eastern and South Asian affairs — the very officer we had met in Washington and with whom we had shared our views on early recognition of Bangladesh.

Senator Kennedy, strongly in favor of immediate recognition, pressed the point forcefully. He then asked what limitations our lack of recognition placed on our American consul general in Dacca. The State Department official replied that lack of recognition prevented the American consul general from discussing "matters of a political character with government officials."[1]

In "diplomatese" that meant the American consul general was absolutely prohibited from discussing with the leaders of the new nation all the vital and pressing matters affecting Bangladesh, America, India, Pakistan, and the international community.

Within a week of those hearings I called the State Department official, as a courtesy measure, to tell him I would be traveling to Bangladesh to view the situation and consult with the prime minister, Sheikh Mujibur Rahman. Although I was unaware that our Dacca consul general was so seriously hindered, I felt constrained to say, "If there is anything I can do to be of help to you in Dacca or Chittagong or in my meeting with the prime minister, I would be glad to do so."

Two days before our departure to Bangladesh, the State Department called from Washington.

"We have decided," the spokesman said, "that we would like you to do something for us in Dacca — convey a message to the Bangladesh prime minister." As he continued I listened intently, taking careful notes on a piece of scratch paper by the phone. When I learned the content of the message, I readily agreed to convey it to Mujib — with pleasure!

In lieu of the visa which he still was not allowed to grant, Mr. Karim of the Bangladesh Mission provided me with a helpful letter to present to the Bangladesh High Commission in Calcutta, India; there our Bangladesh visa would be granted.

Exhausted by meetings in various cities right up to the day of departure, I slept overnight in the plane from Chicago to London where I was to meet colleague Ray Knighton. Taking advantage of the long haul together from London to Calcutta, we spent hours planning our Bangladesh program. We stretched and breathed fresh air at three refueling stops at Frankfurt, Damascus, and Bahrain.

At the Bangladesh High Commission in Calcutta, our letter produced instantaneous results, VIP treatment, and the necessary visas. I was thrilled as we finally skimmed in for a landing at Dacca airport on February 17. We were doubly happy when we spotted Jay Walsh and Bob Adolph at the airport to meet us. Jay brought us up to date on the finale of the war and some profitable contacts they had enjoyed with various officials in the new government. Then Jay astounded me by saying he had known for nearly three months that I would be coming — I had known it myself for only three weeks!

Drs. Olsen and Knighton with Mr. M. R. Siddiqi in Dacca

"I had two vivid dreams around Thanksgiving time," he recounted, "in which you returned to Bangladesh. I was expecting you."

The following morning we entered the office of my friend, former Ambassador Siddiqi, now minister of trade and commerce, a key member of Sheikh Mujib's cabinet, one of the top six or eight men in the country. It was a delight for both of us to meet again, this time in *shadheen Bangla!* As we had much to discuss, the time passed quickly. In short order he granted numerous petitions and concessions which gave us greater facility than we had ever before enjoyed. Moreover, he arranged for us appointments with Prime Minister Sheikh Mujib and the minister of health and family planning. How grateful we were for such a friend to expedite so efficiently our urgent work.

The minister of health and family planning, a native of Chittagong, was also a great help to us. He and his secretary promptly granted several important petitions and produced the necessary approval letters on the spot. Never in Pakistan days had we accomplished so much so quickly!

As we looked around Dacca, we saw much devastation not yet repaired: shell-pocked buildings, burned-out village and slum areas, blasted vehicles, a fortified mosque (a desecration according to Islamic law). On a visit to the Mukti Bahini ward of the Dacca Medical College Hospital, we saw dozens of freedom fighters with serious war injuries; many had legs blasted off from stepping on land mines. The mood of the people was a strange mixture of jubilation, pain, shock, and anger.

At 5:15 P.M. on February 19 we met with the Prime Minister himself — Sheikh Mujibur Rahman, the architect and father of Bangladesh! As I introduced our party of four (Ray, Jay, Bob, and myself), he received us graciously and seated us around him. Despite the heavy weight of responsibility and his long, nerve-wracking solitary confinement imprisonment when the threat of execution weighed constantly upon him, he looked strong and vigorous. He appeared younger than I had expected. From the introductions he understood that we were Christians, Americans, and medical people who wanted to help through medicine and other ways.

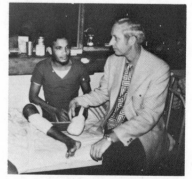

Visiting amputee in Mukti Bahini ward

Drs. Olsen and Knighton with Prime Minister Rahman

He spoke explosively, emotionally, about what had happened: "The barbarous Pakistan army destroyed my economy; they destroyed my hospitals; they destroyed my schools; they destroyed my communications systems; they destroyed my food *godowns* (storehouses); they destroyed about three million people; they burned about thirty million houses. Although I was away then, you were present here. You know everything! Now we need all kinds of help. We need medicines. There are no medicines left in my country."

When I explained we were preparing a shipment of vitamins worth hundreds of thousands of dollars, although grateful, the prime minister responded, "But my people have no food. What will my people do with vitamin tablets? If they don't get food twice a day, a hundred medicines won't help them. And, also, the monsoon is coming. My people require shelter." Thus, at the outset of our meeting we had learned three great priorities — medicine, food, housing!

At that point I presented to the prime minister a copy of the *Muslim Bengali-English Dictionary,* and Ray presented a beautiful copy of the Bible (provided by Dr. Ken Taylor) with "Sheikh Mujibur Rahman" inscribed in gold upon it. He received both books with obvious interest and gratitude, thanking us warmly.

Mujib then expressed his appreciation of the American people, but his disenchantment with the American government who supported his enemies, the West Pakistanis. At the peak of his harsh diatribe against our government, he said Washington's policy "has blackened the face of America!" Obviously the time had come to give him the new message from the United States government! I explained the telephone call from the State Department, detailing the facts they wished me to convey.

"First, Your Excellency," I said, "the US State Department sends to you its warm regards and best wishes! Secondly, they want you to know that the United States government will do its utmost to provide maximum humanitarian relief and rehabilitation to the war-affected people of Bangladesh! Thirdly, I am to tell you that the matter of diplomatic recognition of Bangladesh is now under very active consideration by the United States government and the question will be settled as soon as possible!"

How I enjoyed bringing that message of good will and conciliation from the American government — and bearing to Bangladesh the first word that diplomatic recognition was under active consideration. Prior to the Washington telephone call, all official pronouncements had stated that the matter of recognition was not even under consideration. The warm message I conveyed to Sheikh Mujib clearly defused on the spot much of his anger and stabilized the rocky relations between the two nations over the next weeks until America officially recognized Bangladesh.

Jay mentioned the letter sent by our mission team on the field to President Nixon regarding the brutal war we had seen; that letter also had urged early recognition and generous humanitarian assistance. Later Jay spoke about meeting Mujib's wife in Dacca two days before her husband's release from prison in West Pakistan.

The prime minister expostulated more about the genocide which had been inflicted upon the Bengali race. "My people have been killed! Three million people have been killed — innocent women, innocent girls, old men of ninety. Their houses were burned, and when they came running out they were shot. Now my people keep bringing me the bones of the victims." Later, he spoke hopefully about the future, feeling that his government could build a sound economy because of the natural resources of the country. Finally, he asked us to do everything and anything we could to help the nation of Bangladesh. The interview was explosive, emotional, and heartrending. Our talk with Mujib had made us all the more eager to do everything in our power to help this newest nation of the world.

On February 20 we traveled by road to Chittagong. Even on the countryside we saw devastation on every hand: burned villages, tank tracks beside the road, blackened hulks of blasted tanks, many sabotaged bridges, a Hindu shrine defaced by a large shellhole, smashed Hindu temples. Because we had to cross four rivers by car ferries, the trip was time-consuming. On arrival in Chittagong we saw signs of shelling, bombing, and burning. Although the people rejoiced over their liberation, many looked dazed and shocked; others appeared thin and gaunt, while some still nursed their war wounds. It was a genuine thrill to see Reid, Jeannie, Lynn, Mrs. Dass (back from Burma), and many other Chittagong friends. I was feeling more at home with each step of the journey toward Malumghat.

Disabled tank in paddy field

Blasted bridge

Upended ship in Chittagong harbor

Then Reid introduced me to a new member of the Chittagong team. The mission had hired the friend recommended by spiritual retreat speaker Rev. Aslam Khan to be our high-level Bengali administrative officer.

Reid said, "Vic, meet Mr. Andrew Akand."

His dark eyes dancing impishly, Andrew Akand asked, "Do you remember the time that you and I were fighting in the commissioner's office?"

"No," I replied thoughtfully, "when was that?"

Then, for the first time, I heard his story, the story of Akand, the vitriolic, anti-Christian young Muslim. As he recounted the tale of his hatred for Christians, his effort to turn the governor against us, his anti-Christian center in Chittagong, and his agitations in the Malumghat area against our hospital, I did remember the confrontation in the commissioner's office with an angry young man who stalked out of the office before our conversation finished.

"Also," Andrew continued, "I was the man behind Daniel's beating and exile to Kutubdia Island. In those days I was your most bitter enemy."

Still trying to make all the pieces fit, I reasoned out loud, "But now you are our mission's administrative officer, and you call yourself Andrew, certainly not a Muslim name. What happened?"

Then Andrew glowingly recounted his trip to West Pakistan, the patient teaching and explanations of a Christian there, and his ultimate faith decision for Christ. Like a latterday apostle Paul, he had been a great enemy of Christians and Christianity; then Christ touched his life, changing him into a strong, fruitful Christian. "Thank You, Father!"

Although we arrived at the hospital after dark, someone spotted us; and Bengali brothers and sisters came running from all directions. I was nearly incoherent with joy and excitement. With those greetings concluded, we drove the last half mile through the forest to the housing site for another thrilling reunion with American brothers and sisters. I was home at last.

We heard many of the exciting experiences of our colleagues during the last days of the war. When we visited the nearby villages, crowds of Hindus whose lives had been saved came to meet us, clutch us by the feet, and express their gratitude. We talked with Momin and Shantosh and many other old friends. Momin proudly showed us the food relief operation which had grown immensely since we began it in the early days of the war.

Then we met with our field council to discuss, analyze, brainstorm, and pray about what should be done to help the shattered infant nation. And, further, how it could be done. We soon established the top priorities: medicine, food, utensils — and houses before the monsoon rains would come slashing down.

Since our existing mission staff was already greatly overworked, any significant relief operation in the area would require many new hands and hundreds of thousands of dollars. The mission group, although mentally and physically exhausted, were magnificent during those meetings. With a disciplined effort they intelligently analyzed the many problems involved.

Ray and I departed, the richer for our experience of being together with the ABWE team. When the plane ride we had been offered, from Chittagong to Dacca, canceled out (someone had put water instead of gasoline into the fuel tank), apparently we were stuck in Chittagong. As we mulled over the bad news, a speck appeared in the sky and became a plane that landed at Chittagong. This unscheduled small emergency plane happened to have just two available seats and exactly enough room for our luggage. "Thank You, Father!"

In Dacca we had a last round of discussions with Mr. Siddiqi. I presented to him also a beautiful Bible with his name inscribed upon it as a token of our esteem; he received it warmly with thanks. When I detailed for him the message from the United States government which I had delivered to the prime minister, I learned he had received already from Mujib the gist of the communication.

Handing me a sheet of paper, the minister said, "Now we would like you to carry word from our government to the US government; first please read this cablegram from the Bangladesh Association in Canada about what is going on in Pakistan."

Taking the cable, I read its ominous message:

PAKISTAN RIOT IMMINENT. MESSAGE RECEIVED BENGALIS HATING SLAUGHTER. PLEASE ARRANGE IMMEDIATE EXCHANGE AT ALL COST. GIVE TOP PRIORITY. STOP BENGALIS BEING SENT TO CONCENTRATION CAMPS.

"We are receiving many cables like this from Bengalis all over the world," Minister Siddiqi continued. "The Pakistanis have begun harassing the quarter-million Bengalis who are stuck over there in Pakistan. Belongings have been confiscated, husbands and wives are being separated, some Bengalis have been killed, and others sent to concentration camps. Please tell the US government that we appeal to them to use their good offices to force Pakistan to stop harassing the Bengalis and release them to return to Bangladesh —

we want every single one back. We will gladly send to Pakistan all the non-Bengalis stuck here in Bangladesh."

Writing furiously on a piece of Calcutta hotel stationary which I had snatched out of my briefcase, I noted down the details of the message. I promised to deliver the message immediately upon my arrival in America.

As soon as our business in Dacca and India was finished, Ray and I packed our exhausted frames into the jet which would take us to New York City. Our minds were full of questions: How could we possibly put together a program in the short time available to us before the monsoon rains would lash Bangladesh? Where could we get the hundreds of thousands of dollars necessary to provide significant help? Where would we find fifteen or twenty men free from mid-March to mid-June?

"Well, time will tell," Ray declared.

Time had better start talking in a hurry, I mused.

22

Bangladesh Brigade

MARCH, 1972, was a whopping big month! On March 1 we had only a deep desire to help the stricken people of Bangladesh — but no method, no manpower, and no money! On March 31 I reached Dacca with twenty-one colleagues, more manpower to follow, and a grant of hundreds of thousands of dollars. "Thank You, Father!"

During the first week of March Ray Knighton and I spent long hours together planning, organizing, budgeting, and putting on paper an actual proposal. Our plan included the supply of medicines, food, utensils, and four thousand houses. Because Congress was allocating millions of dollars of foreign aid money for relief in Bangladesh, and because MAP was registered as a voluntary aid agency with the United States Agency for International Development (AID), we decided to apply to AID for the necessary funds. We needed nearly a million dollars from them.

While I met deputation commitments, Ray flew to Washington to present the application in person, answer any question, and emphasize the need for a speedy decision — the monsoon rains would not wait for anyone, not even the world's most rich and powerful government.

Where would we find fifteen or twenty strong young men, available from mid-March to mid-June, willing to work for subsistence wages, and who cared enough about hurt and starving people to be willing to help? We decided that students from Christian colleges would be our best bet. The timing, however, would be wrong for students on the semester system. Only students attending a college with a full four-quarter system could give that quarter, then make up their school loss during the summer quarter.

Even as we began contacting colleges, word about a possible Bangladesh project flashed from student to student at nearby Wheaton College. Like wildfire the news spread through the student body. The Bangladesh emphasis in the missions conference had opened the hearts of many young men and women to the needs of the

319

shattered people of the infant nation. And Wheaton College had just begun operating on a full four-quarter system! Within a few days students began phoning me and knocking on my door in Wheaton. Soon we had nearly fifty applications! Others came or called from Iowa, Minnesota, and New Jersey. "Thank You, Father!"

Overwhelmed by the abundance of applications, we entered the selection phase. MAP vice-president Beth Knighton, skilled in personnel management, conducted individual interviews. We sought young men and women who were not only physically healthy and mentally alert, but also Christians deeply motivated and deeply dedicated to Christ. The Bangladesh Brigade, so named by the Wheaton Travel Agency which arranged the flights, consisted of two dozen men and women:

DIRECTOR: Dr. V. B. Olsen

ASSISTANT DIRECTOR: Edward Meyer   PHYSICIAN: Dr. John Jaquis
BUILDER: Kenneth Goldsmith   MECHANIC: LaVern Witt
NURSES: Diane Thompson, Joan Voss
STUDENTS: Constance Edwards, Deanna Lawrence, Chris Ellerman, Kenneth Enlow, David Gotaas, John Huffman, Douglas Jacobsen, Thomas Kraakevik, Donald Lemon, Barton McMains, Stephen Morgan, Timothy Omley, C. Robert Purdy, Mark Sakowski, Gary Sloan, David Winston, Dan York

Wheaton College produced sixteen of the students and Waterloo, Iowa's Walnut Ridge Baptist Church provided the doctor, mechanic, and two nurses. At our first team meeting on March 10 we faced the "agony factor" — the agony of wondering whether or not the money would be granted. AID in Washington could not decide the matter until President Nixon signed the foreign aid bill.

I could only say to the group, "There's no guarantee the project is on. But we must proceed as though it were approved or we will never build any houses in Bangladesh before the monsoon rains. That means you must immediately get passport photos taken, apply for your passports, and begin the long series of immunizations for overseas travel to Asia — on faith! Please let me know, individually, on your way out today whether you're 'in' or not." No one backed out.

On March 16, brigade members met again at the Olsen home. Although President Nixon had signed the foreign aid bill, we still had received no positive decision from Washington. There seemed to be some problem or hangup in the AID deliberations. But all brigade members continued getting their unpleasant immunizations. In my deputation meetings in churches I began asking congrega-

Bangladesh Brigade at Kennedy Airport

tions to pray that Christians would give for spiritual work in Bangladesh twenty thousand dollars (one-fiftieth the amount we were asking from the government for humanitarian aid).

After more days without confirmation from Washington, we began making daily telephone calls to AID. The obstruction in Washington had something to do with word received from their contacts in Dacca. Finally, a definite clear-cut yes from Washington erased the agony factor; AID officials promised that the written contract soon would be forthcoming.

On March 27 twenty-two of us arrived at O'Hare Field, Chicago, for takeoff. With flash bulbs popping, television cameras grinding, and reporters grilling different members of the brigade, prayer was offered and we boarded for the long flight to the other side of the world.

At a two-hour stop in New York I gave the first "do and don't" cultural briefing and handed over language lists, carefully prepared by Joan, containing a hundred common Bengali words. I gave everyone a smile button, our team insignia. We aimed to put smiles on the faces of devastated, homeless Bengalis. During a priceless forty-five minutes of sharing and prayer, I could feel we were merging together as a team.

In Frankfurt, Germany, we transferred to a Pan Am 747 jumbo jet which pleased my youthful confreres — and me. After refueling stops in Istanbul, Beirut, and Teheran, we arrived in New Delhi, the capital of India. A tour of New Delhi, a trip to the Taj Mahal, and their first curry dinner occupied the team until our departure for Bangladesh.

We arrived in Dacca in the middle of the night of March 31. Clearing customs was simple, but only with great difficulty did I find enough transportation at that hour of the night to move the team and all the baggage to a hotel. By then some of my companions were suffering from a well-known Asian malady called "Delhi belly."

On April first I felt like an April fool when I met with the head of AID Dacca, and learned that he was against our project! He feared we would be called a brigade of CIA agents and that the group might be in danger; an Indian army camp was located adjacent to our hospital at Malumghat. When I explained that the presence of the Indian army made the Malumghat area an exceptionally safe place to be, and that we would be very sensitive to the total situation, he seemed only slightly mollified. Finally, after consultation with a US consular officer, it was decided that we could, after all, "go ahead with the project."

I decided to begin reading, in my personal daily devotions, the Old Testament books by Ezra and Nehemiah, two men who also traveled to a distant land to do some building. Before departing Dacca, we invited the AID officials for lunch with the brigade members who promptly planted a smile button on each of them and began to win their confidence.

Reid, Jeannie, and Lynn greeted us at Chittagong airport, fed us, and provided accommodations for the night — quite a feat! The next morning, April 4, we headed downcountry by bus, arriving at Malumghat about noon — the very day that the American government officially granted diplomatic recognition to Bangladesh!

At Malumghat our four girls moved into the nurses'/teachers' residence, eight of us were billeted at empty house number two, and the rest moved in with ABWE families. Nurses Joan and Diane went to work at the hospital while Connie and Deanna became my secretaries and postal clerks for the brigade.

After a day and a half of getting acquainted, settling in, and meeting with the ABWE team, the Bangladesh Brigade hit the villages and started to work. At the end of the first day's work I could see that we would need fifteen or twenty trucks to move the massive amounts of housebuilding materials. I also needed to open a project bank account in the city, crack loose some diesel fuel, and locate some cement to build two brick and mortar storehouses. The next morning, April 7, I headed for Chittagong by jeep.

In my four days in Chittagong I met the new DC of Chittagong District to explain our project to him. Fortunately, the Cox's Bazar

SDO happened to be in the DC's office; this allowed me to brief him without a separate trip to Cox's Bazar. They invited me to attend a special meeting on relief matters to be held two days later.

At the meeting, a very important one, an announcement was made that all relief projects would henceforth require two approvals: a high-level written approval in principle from the Dacca-based Ministry of Relief and Rehabilitation and an approval of the project details at the DC level. Because I needed the relief ministry approval and because I could find no available trucks in Chittagong, I flew to Dacca on April 10.

Having finished the book of Ezra in my morning Bible reading, I began the book of Nehemiah. I spent every spare moment thinking through how to organize the brigade's work in such a way that we actually could complete the four thousand houses. The organizational problems were complex. During my four days in Dacca I was fortunate to obtain a beautiful approval letter which instructed the Chittagong DC to provide me some trucks. Wonderfully, a high level United Nations official agreed to loan me six UN trucks! Then a CARE official loaned me cement and in the AID office I learned that their Washington headquarters had granted us nine hundred thousand dollars for our Bangladesh Brigade project! "Thank You, Father!" And the previously hostile Dacca AID officials gave me a private office, telephone, secretary, etc., for my Dacca visits! On April 14 I returned to Chittagong.

Early on the morning of April 15, as I read the tedious third chapter of Nehemiah, two principles suddenly leaped out of those pages at me — principles which showed me how the work of the Bangladesh Brigade should be organized. "Thank You, Father!"

That day I arranged drivers for our six new trucks and sent the first shipment of cement to Malumghat. I presented the written high-level approval to the DC who in turn granted his approval and agreed to provide more trucks from his stock! Then I enjoyed the experience of a lifetime: when I wrote a check for thirty thousand dollars, I broke the bank! The American Express bank officials had to bring in *taka* (worth fourteen cents apiece) from the Bangladesh State Bank to cash the check; I walked out of the bank with 200,000 *taka* in my suitcase. On the way out of town I picked up thirty loaves of bread and twenty-five pounds of butter for the ravenous horde.

I arrived after dark to find the brigade men tired, frustrated, and discouraged. Although they had worked very hard for ten days, they had not found a system that would begin to achieve the goal of constructing four thousand houses in the allotted time; and only seven weeks remained. I remembered instantly the points from Nehemiah three which had struck me so forcefully that morning.

I joyfully greeted Dr. "Jake" Jaquis who had just arrived with builder Ken Goldsmith and his wife Dorothy. She became house-mother to our gang of eight staying in house number two; her motherly touch brightened our days immeasurably. Ken went to work building the brick and mortar storehouses and Jake stepped into his old slot in the hospital.

The next two days, April 16 and 17, were crucial to the success of the project. In our meeting on April 16 Jay summarized the progress to date and made some useful observations. The students ventilated the many problems they were facing in the field and the slowness of progress. I could see they were having a crisis of confidence in themselves. They were not at all sure we could succeed. Nehemiah three even had an antidote for the poison of discouragement. The chapter, ordinarily considered one of the least interesting chapters in the Bible, merely listed the groups of people working together, side by side, rebuilding the wall of the holy city of Jerusalem. I was struck, however, that no expert builders were listed in the "Holy Land brigade"; there were priests, priests' helpers, goldsmiths, perfume makers, and women, but no expert builders or carpenters were named. If those amateurs could complete the wall of Jerusalem in fifty-two days, then we also, despite our lack of expertise, should be able to complete our work in fifty-two days, almost exactly the time we had left to work.

I explained further, in the meeting, that Nehemiah three had strengthened my impression that instead of concentrating our men to work together in one or two villages, we must send out multiple teams to work simultaneously in many villages. The Nehemiah passage also imparted another principle: instead of each team doing the same small phase of the work, assembly-line style, in village after village, each team must, instead, manage and supervise the total operation in its target villages from initial survey to final inspection of completed houses.

With these principles as our guidelines and valuable suggestions from Jay and the men who had worked ten days in the field, we put together our housebuilding system:

1. Twelve teams, each consisting of one student and his interpreter, would work in the field at all times. (Assigned to this field work were Chris, Doug, Tom, Don, Bart, Steve, Tim, Bob, Mark, Gary, Dan, and Dave Gotaas.)

2. Each team would manage and supervise the whole work from beginning to end in the villages assigned to it.

3. A supply department, headed by Jay Walsh, would procure the three basic materials — bamboo, giant bamboo, and sungrass — for distribution to the teams in the field. (Assigned to this department were Ed, Ken, John, and Dave Winston.)

4. We would promote the construction of standard village homes, such as villagers have been erecting for centuries, which required no carpenters or other skilled workers.

5. We would provide labor money to the villager so that he could buy food to eat while he constructed his house and hire several fellow villagers to help him erect the home speedily.

6. Our men would not spend time in the harsh, time-consuming work of on-the-spot supervision of house building (they had already learned that an American trying to "hurry the East" by the force of his own personality creates a bad impression upon the people — and headaches in the American).

7. We would appoint responsible village leaders as supervisors and pay them a small bonus for every house completed in time under their supervision.

8. As an incentive to speedy work we would grant a bonus, also, to every villager completing his house on schedule.

9. We would apply further positive reinforcement by giving house

Shahabuddin Choudhury advising Brigaders Doug Jacobsen and Bart McMains

builders only half the building materials at first; then, if they used the materials well, we would distribute the remainder of their materials.

As the meeting continued and the pieces of the puzzle fell into place, the table of organization was shaping up in my mind. But we had no one to do the important work of visiting, helping, supervising, and troubleshooting for our young men working in the villages north and south from the hospital; the table of organization had two big gaps in it.

At that moment two Bengali men entered the room, our friends Shahabuddin and Bahadur (Momin's brother), both members of the leading family of the area. Then it clicked! If I could hire these two capable, intelligent men, with perfect knowledge of the area plus friendships and acquaintances galore in the villages, our personnel problem would be solved! As we approached the two men that very night, Jay mentioned the need in his supply department for a capable Bengali contractor who could organize dozens of subcontractors and suppliers of building materials. Shahabuddin suggested Abbas, a friend of the hospital and a patient of mine. The next day we came to terms with these men, hired them, and our table of organization was complete!

During the last two weeks of April we worked and refined the new system; it worked slicker than greased lightning! When the accountants we were expecting did not come, I called the team together to find out whether or not any of our men had accounting skills. Dave Gotaas had studied the subject, so he became our accountant — and kept an excellent set of books. On a trip to Chittagong I broke the bank again with a check of forty-five thousand dollars; the three hundred thousand *taka* filled my large suitcase.

I obtained four trucks from the Cox's Bazar SDO and another four from the Chittagong DC. These eight with the six UN trucks, plus four locally hired trucks, brought our fleet to eighteen. Mechanic LaVern Witt did a marvelous job keeping those monsters functioning.

On a Sunday, the last day of April, the Bangladesh Brigade conducted our mission's English church service. Ed Meyer and Ken Enlow sang a duet, then Gary Sloan played a piano solo and did the preaching. Reciting some of the difficult and heartbreaking problems the men were facing in the field, Gary mentioned the passage in Matthew 25 in which Christ spoke about helping hungry, thirsty, naked, and homeless people: "Inasmuch as you have done it to one of the least of these my brothers, you have done it to me."

Then Gary pointed out, "The passage goes on to say that those who fail to help the hungry, thirsty, naked, and homeless have failed Christ, for He said, 'Inasmuch as you did it not to one of the least of these, you did it not to me.'"

Then he read a poem which he had written on a bouncing bus returning after dark from a tough day's work. Particularly powerful was a section of the poem in which Gary wrote as if the Lord were speaking directly to him about his reaction to the crowd:

> For I have confronted you with an impossible task and problem to solve, filled with countless widows, never-ending need, and a pleading so often it soon becomes a duplicate of the one before—
>
> You tried, did you then turn away frustrated,
>> turn away broken or hardened,
>> turn away?
>
> I too saw the crowd, left the crowd, felt the crowd, and met their inner loneliness. I too felt their greedy tug, their impatient loudness, and their shallow submission.
>
> and I too reacted
> . . . I too decided . . .
>> for I too was human.
>
> Feel them, touch them, my son — for as they touch you, they touch me. As you touch them — so too — it is I that you touch.
>
> I am hungry—
>> I am homeless—
>>> I am thirsty—
>>>> I am a stranger—
>>>>> I am naked—
>>>>>> I am the one more.

Gary's message speared Shahabuddin's heart; I talked with him for a long time that morning about Christ and His way of eternal life.

During the month of May the housebuilding continued unabated under the blistering sun. The Bangladesh hot season, like a gigantic steam bath, sapped the men's strength, and melted the pounds from them. Various ones lost five pounds, ten pounds, twenty pounds, even thirty pounds during their days of serving the Bengali people. They became hard and brown — and sometimes emotionally ragged because the emotional-spiritual trauma was the greatest. As they awakened in the morning, their hands groped for Bibles; they knew they needed something from God each day to face the noisy, grasping crowds.

Weekend trips and soccer games provided welcome release. Some of the brigade men were members of the championship Wheaton College soccer team; consequently, they succeeded in beating both our quite good hospital team and the strong Indian army team.

Meanwhile, MAP in Wheaton was also under pressure. Because they did not receive cash from Washington throughout the whole first month of our work, they were forced to borrow from a helpful Wheaton bank to keep us functioning at top speed in Bangladesh. Bless them! They packed for shipment hundreds of thousands of dollars worth of medicines already in their warehouse plus generous donations to Bangladesh from many fine American pharmaceutical houses. Ultimately they dispatched three huge chartered jet planes filled with medical supplies. MAP headquarters gave us tremendous support in our difficult work in the field.

At the hospital one day, a child's shout rang out. I looked up to see a sturdy boy running toward me and wearing a broad smile on his skin-grafted face. As he hugged my legs, I recognized the tyke whose burned face I had resurfaced, who had "died" one day before my eyes, whose lifeless body I had rushed to the operating room, and whose little heart finally began beating again after cardiac massage and lengthy artificial respiration! Gripped by rising emotion, I stooped to hug him back and thought, *How great it is to be a surgeon working hand in hand with God in Bangladesh!*

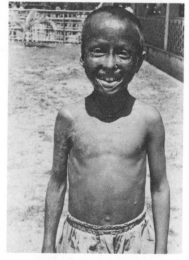

"I stooped to hug him back"

To stay on top of the project, direct the progress of the work, receive thousands of petitions for houses, decide the correct locations for building, and dispatch the teams in ever-widening circles from our Malumghat headquarters forced me to work sixteen-hour days. In May I had more "break the bank" fun, bringing back, on my last trip, a huge trunk full of eight hundred thousand *taka* (worth over $110,000).

Ours was a complex, mammoth undertaking! We put to work over fifty thousand people cutting bamboo and sungrass in the jungles of the Chittagong Hill Tracts, floating the materials down the long winding rivers, lugging them to the homesites, and building the houses. The villagers used the giant bamboo for uprights; much of the regular bamboo was split and woven into walls. The rest of the bamboo was formed into a latticework support for the roof. Finally, the sungrass was fixed in place over the latticework to make a fine, rainproof roof.

Our satisfaction was immense as we saw houses sprouting all over the countryside from Teknaf in the southernmost tip of Bangladesh to Dohazari, thirty-five miles north of the hospital. We also built hundreds of houses in Chittagong city. Our ambitious (some said impossible) goal was the construction of four thousand houses in the few weeks we had at our disposal. The final count amazed — and gratified — us. We had constructed or repaired over ten thousand houses! We had spent a portion of our nine hundred thousand dollar grant for needed utensils for several thousand families. And MAP was in the process of sending nearly two million dollars worth of medicines, two hundred thousand dollars worth of garden seeds, thirty-five thousand dollars worth of foodstuffs, and twenty thousand dollars cash for incountry rice purchase. Somehow, we had put together a three-million-dollar project for Bangladesh! And we had the full twenty thousand dollars I had hoped to gain for spiritual work in the new nation. "Thank You, Father!"

On ethical grounds, we decided that the mission and the church should not carry out village preaching and teaching while our housebuilding project was going on. Because we believe in the principle of separation of church and state, we felt it would be inappropriate to carry out those religious activities in conjunction with a government-funded aid project. Furthermore, we wanted to avoid giving anyone the slightest impression that we were buying Christians with houses. The mission and church found, however, that the compassionate, loving help given to the local people in their hour of need greatly stimulated their interest in the Christian faith.

Individuals came to inquire, "What made those educated boys come all the way from America to sweat and work in our village to help our poor people?" Requests came from villages for church members to come and explain the faith which motivated these young men.

On their own time, the brigade members also had fine opportunities, through their interpreters, to share their faith with interested individuals. And, in the wake of housebuilding, church and mission members were busy for weeks telling newly interested Bengalis about Christ. A number found eternal life during those days, including many members of a village of the Mogh tribe. For the first time, a sizable group of Moghs made the great faith decision! "Thank You, Father!"

Bamboo floating
downriver

Dr. Olsen checking
size of bamboo
poles

Weaving latticework
roof

Finishing a new house

Because these Mogh people had Burmese antecedents and thus understood the Burmese language, we had a great need for Burmese New Testaments. The new Mogh believers had a deep desire to study God's Word and distribute it to hundreds of other Mogh families.

At that point a ship, the *MV Logos,* staffed by a Christian crew and sponsored by a Christian organization (Operation Mobilization — OM), eased up to a dock in Chittagong port. While many Chittagong citizens visited an educational book exhibit on the ship, teams of OM workers from the ship distributed Christian literature in Chittagong and on the countryside as far south as Malumghat.

Because our ABWE literature division, under Jeannie Lockerbie's direction, had provided most of the Bengali books for the exhibit, the *Logos* directors kindly said, "Look around the ship; if you can use any of our books, we'd be glad to donate them to you." Jeannie industriously searched that ship from stem to stern and top to bottom. Deep in the bowels of the ship, in the corner of a musty hold, she found a huge stack of books. Taking one into the light she opened it to discover she was holding a Burmese New Testament! She had come upon a thousand Burmese New Testaments! The OM leaders gladly donated them for the spiritual nourishment of our Mogh people. "Thank You, Father!"

In early June most of the Bangladesh Brigade dispersed to return to America. Three men — Ed, Tim, and Dave Gotaas — remained behind several weeks to finish winding down the project. As a dozen of us traveled together on our way out of the country, in Dacca we were pleasantly surprised to receive an invitation from the American ambassador (termed the *chargé d'affaires* at that point) to a reception in our honor! We attended with pleasure. While refreshments were being distributed, our team members draped themselves on the ambassador's attractive leather furniture. Then he spoke.

Eying the youthful group (some of them still teenagers), he asserted, "They say that confession is good for the soul — and I have a confession to make to you."

Then, fantastically, this leading representative of the world's most powerful nation confessed to us that he had been antagonistic to our project! Not only that, he further explained, "I did everything in my power to block your project. I was in Washington at the time and made a maximum effort to stop you."

Oh, oh, I thought, *that was the obstruction in Washington that prevented the final yes decision for so many days.* Despite the ambassadorial pressure, the approval was finally given.

"Let me explain to you why I was against your project," the ambassador continued. "Despite the fact that you were dedicated 'peace corps' types, I knew you would fail, for you had set an impossible goal for yourselves. Not only is this a very difficult country in which to work, but also your time was very limited and you were young and inexperienced at such work. I feared that the failure, the culture shock, and the local illnesses would be hurtful to you. Knowing that the Indian army was located near the hospital, I also feared for your safety." (At that point I thought of the friendships that had developed between brigade members and Indian army officers, and the red-hot soccer game between the Bangladesh Brigade and the Indian army team.)

"Furthermore," the ambassador explained, "I knew certain elements in the country surely would claim that you were all CIA agents, causing me no end of trouble. And I was sure, because of your lack of knowledge of the customs here, I would no doubt receive outraged reports about miniskirts in mosques, etc.

"Now I have made my confession to you — but I want to say one thing more. I also owe you an apology! You have confounded me. None of the things that I feared have actually happened. And not only did you achieve your goal, but you far surpassed it. I cannot conceive how you did it, but what you have done is a remarkable victory for America and our foreign aid program in Bangladesh. I not only offer you my apology, but I want to congratulate you on your marvelous work. Every report I have heard of you and your work has been outstanding. I am proud of you — and your country is proud of you."

Humbled by his comments we thanked him, enjoyed the refreshments, and headed for the airport. Waiting for our flight I contemplated the ambassador's analysis and his fears; he was an intelligent, capable man, experienced in the country. Why did his dire predictions fail? As I pondered the question, the answer came to me clearly: Our team was not composed of ordinary "peace corps" types. Rather, our success was due to the *double dedication* of the Bangladesh Brigade. Because our young men and women were deeply dedicated to Christ they gained an outstanding dedication to the task to which their Lord had called them. The ambassador had no way to know that our group possessed this extra spiritual dimension which so powerfully reinforced their dedication to the work. But on the front lines it spelled the difference between failure and success.

23

"Mr. Music"

During April-May, 1972, while the Bangladesh Brigade was rebuilding villages, a parallel and interweaving drama unfolded. Shomar Dass, a central figure in the drama, was the director of music for Bangladesh government radio and television. Although I had never met him, I knew him by reputation as "Mr. Music" of Bangladesh. He had written the music to many of the patriotic songs which lifted the spirits and voices of millions of Bengalis during those dark days of massacre and oppression. Shomar Dass and his songs were a living legend in Bangladesh. To him was given the responsibility of writing the full orchestration of the country's national anthem, "My Golden Bengal." Not only did he write music, but as a skilled performer, he also sang beautifully and played an instrument called the harmonium. He was, perhaps, the most highly placed nominal Christian in Bangladesh.

On April 13, 1972, the door flew open to the private chamber of the prime minister of Bangladesh. He and several cabinet members looked up in astonishment to see an agitated man burst into the room. The sudden intrusion shocked the handful of ministers, the elite of Bangladesh leadership. The prime minister himself had ordered that no one should be admitted until the urgent special meeting concluded; and Sheikh Mujibur Rahman was accustomed to obedience.

The trespasser, Shomar Dass, stood uncertainly inside the door. In his forties, with greying sideburns, he was a stately figure, taller than most Bengalis. But now his handsome, tear-marked face was contorted with grief.

"What is the matter with you, Shomar?" Sheikh Mujib called out. "Why do you look so sad?"

At his prime minister's words, all of the famous performer's carefully prepared phrases deserted him. Afflicted with his first case of stage fright, he stood there — speechless, miserable, pitiful.

"Shomar Dass," said the prime minister patiently, "come here and tell me what is making you unhappy, so I can try to help you."

As Shomar Dass approached and embraced his leader, the very act seemed to loosen his tongue. "I come asking not for myself," he blurted out, "but for my son who is dying. He must go to another hospital and the road is too bad. If we take him by road he will die."

Then summoning up "all his strengths and all his hopes," as he later put it, the distraught father made his plea to the prime minister: "I have come to request the use of your private helicopter."

Shomar Dass buried his head in his hands, recalling to himself the hectic events that had finally brought me into the picture. Even before our first meeting, a mutual friend (Dacca missionary Calvin Olson) had brought me to examine Shomar's critically ill son. Lying unconscious in a long dark ward of a Dacca hospital, eleven-year-old Albert Dass had remained in a deep coma for thirteen days. When I arrived, I noted instantly the dripping intravenous fluids and the feeding tube issuing from a nostril. In the dim light the wasted child looked waxen, ghastly. He lay very still. I could see no movement except the rhythmic, shallow motion of his respiratory muscles. Women of the family, weeping soundlessly, kept their vigil near the dying boy. I saw no sign of the father.

Taking the medical history in detail before his father arrived, I talked at length with Albert's mother. She spoke rapidly but clearly in Bengali. I felt thankful for my years in the country, which made it possible for me to comprehend the strangely beautiful cadences of her speech. Her motherly recital, full of meaning to medical ears, suggested several possible diagnoses.

An equally methodical and detailed physical examination of the child supplied more missing pieces to the diagnostic puzzle. Albert was not only unconscious, but his left arm, left leg, and a portion of his face were completely paralyzed. I felt sure he had an "intracranial space-occupying lesion," a medical euphemism for a mass or lump inside the skull involving or pressing on his brain. The most common cause of such a lump is a brain tumor. At this point, Shomar Dass arrived at the bedside and introduced himself.

"You're here!" he said with deep feeling. "I'm not a very religious man, Dr. Olsen, but we have been praying for two days that we might find some way to contact you. We heard you had returned to Bangladesh. Now, suddenly, here you are at my son's bedside!"

Shomar then explained his brief absence from the hospital. "I knew no way to contact you, Dr. Olsen, and I was becoming desperate. Thirteen days, and my son shows no improvement; rather, he is getting worse day by day. In my despair I said, 'anywhere —

anything; I will do anything, no matter what, or what the cost, to get help for my son!' So I went to ask our foreign minister to help make arrangements for travel to some foreign country — any country — so my son would get help and not die. When I returned to the hospital just now to find you — the experienced surgeon I had heard about — bending over my son, I knew it was a miracle from God!"

Strange talk for a "not very religious" man, I thought.

The father immediately wanted to know what could be done for his son. Medical ethics forbade a response before discussion with the professor of medicine who was attending Albert. An old friend, the professor cooperated fully. The test I suggested to the family involved drilling holes through the patient's skull and injecting air into his brain. The procedure was dangerous, but Albert had nothing to lose; his little life would soon be gone. The test is usually followed, often within hours, by a full-scale brain operation to attempt to remove the mass. The professor promised to investigate whether or not a neurosurgeon and the necessary instruments were available in Dacca.

Later, far into the night, I answered all the questions that anguished parents naturally ask. I learned further that four years earlier a lovely daughter had died in a tragic fall. Some of the questions had a spiritual flavor, indicating that Shomar Dass and his wife were thinking deeply. I learned that they were unacquainted with the Bible's teaching about salvation and eternal life. I shared my faith with them, and we prayed together that God would heal their dying boy — and draw them to Himself.

The next day the professor reported that the test and operation could not be done in postwar Dacca. I advised the family that the most sophisticated treatment could be obtained at the hands of a neurosurgeon in a foreign country. Failing this, I could undertake the case at Memorial Christian Hospital for, although we are general surgeons, we tackle neurosurgical cases when necessary. Shomar responded decisively. "My wife and I believe God sent you here in answer to our prayers. Take Albert to your hospital." More strange talk for a "not very religious man."

But how would we get this critically sick child to our hospital so far from Dacca? Obviously, we must travel by air, as Albert could not tolerate the trip over 250 miles of rutted, damaged roads. Since the regular commercial flight landed over seventy miles from the hospital, a special flight would be needed.

At the airport I asked to see the commander-in-chief of the Bangladesh air force. An officer took me to a carefully camouflaged emplacement, past guards, to his office deep within the massive con-

crete structure. The air chief, who knew all the available aircraft
at Dacca airport, was not reassuring. One small UN plane might
possibly land at an abandoned World War II airfield six miles from
the hospital — *if* the strip's surface was intact. I did not feel happy
about the risk involved. "The only other possibility," said the commander-in-chief, "would be the prime minister's personal helicopter
— but I'm afraid it wouldn't be available. You see, an important
minister recently requested use of the helicopter and even he was
denied."

I sent Calvin Olson to tell Shomar Dass he must somehow make
contact with his prime minister (this alone a tall order!) and ask
for the needed helicopter. In the meantime, I would finish the urgent
business which originally brought me from the hospital to Dacca —
obtaining trucks and vital approvals for our three-million-dollar
MAP/ABWE project.

They went immediately, Shomar and Calvin, to the office of the
chief executive. Despite Shomar's acquaintance with Sheikh Mujib's
private secretary, he was told the prime minister could not be disturbed by anyone, no matter how urgent his business. Thirty minutes — sixty minutes — ninety minutes — a father's heart breaking! Suddenly, unable any longer to tolerate the grief and suspense,
Shomar leaped from his seat, brushed past the guard, thrust open
the forbidden door, and burst into the prime minister's presence,
only to find himself speechless.

Finally able to blurt out his story, Shomar Dass submitted his
last-hope request for the use of Sheikh Mujibur Rahman's personal helicopter. Eying the distraught man and listening to his plea,
Sheikh Mujib stopped the special cabinet meeting, swung around,
and picked up the telephone. Calling the air chief, he issued the
directive to prepare his helicopter for a flight to Memorial Christian
Hospital.

Dr. Olsen with the
prime minister's per-
sonal helicopter

From ambulance to
helicopter

"Before I left that day," Shomar Dass later recalled, "Prime Minister 'Mujib' said, 'I promise I will pray for your son. Your son is like my son.' "

That afternoon, as frequently happens in the premonsoon season, all aircraft were grounded by the threat of a tropical storm. The following morning we lifted the frail body of the unconscious boy from the ambulance, lashed his stretcher to the floor of the helicopter, and wired his intravenous fluid bag to a ceiling strut. Albert's father, mother, sister, aunt, and surgeon piled in. (The mother was nine months and two days pregnant!) The motor roared, the rotor whined, the cabin vibrated, and we were airborne. Throughout the long journey, as we skimmed over charming villages and sinuous rivers, I checked Albert frequently. He did not stir except for a few involuntary twitches in his unparalyzed leg. But his little heart kept beating. After landing within a mile of the hospital, we completed our journey by ambulance.

I planned to arrange immediately the complicated pneumo-encephalogram test. But something clicked in my mind, an idea I could not shake. I decided to delay the test and give the patient strong doses of antituberculous medicine on the one-in-fifty chance that the brain mass might be a "tuberculoma" caused by the tuberculosis germ.

Dr. Donn Ketcham and I proceeded with this treatment. Thirty-six hours after initiating the medication, we thought we detected possible very slight improvement.

Hospital staff members, by now deeply identified with little Albert in his struggle for life, prayed for him as though he were their own son. The nearby church held special prayer times for the child.

We continued the treatment another thirty-six hours. Unquestionably, now, we could see improvement. "Thank You, Father!"

The dangerous brain test and operation were never done. Little by little, day by day, in response to the medication Albert emerged from oblivion.

On the day his new baby brother was born, Albert became restless and agitated in his stupor. Donn suggested that the lad sensed his mother's absence and was making a monumental effort to break out of his fog. A few days later Albert said his first words. From that point it was steady progress all the way. Happy parents! Exuberant hospital staff! All were overjoyed!

Shomar Dass told me with deep emotion, "A stone has come out of his mother and me. When you asked us for our permission to make the tests and to perform the dangerous operation, we thought, *How can a father and mother give such permission when the doctor cannot guarantee he will give us our son back again?* But God enabled us to give the permission. And now — it is a miracle. Albert does not need surgery! My son was dead and now he is alive."

Albert's father had purchased a painting for that hospital room, the beautiful picture of Jesus knocking at a door. We studied together the words of Christ which had originally inspired the artist, Holman Hunt: "Behold, I stand at the door, and knock: If any man hear my voice, and open the door, I will come in to him." Shomar understood perfectly that this was the answer to his need for eternal life and forgiveness; he needed to open his heart's door and accept Christ into his life. Early in the morning hours of Albert's twelfth day in the hospital, Shomar Dass — unable to sleep, conscious of his need, and thankful to God for his son's improvement — made

Shomar Dass   Steady progress for Albert

the great faith decision and opened his heart's door to the great Physician!

"I told you, doctor, that you would be the first to know," my new brother told me later, his eyes brimming over with tears of joy and relief.

One day Albert struggled to the sitting position. Soon movement returned to the paralyzed left leg. His left arm responded last, but physiotherapy kept it supple until it, too, began to move. His first steps were awkward and labored. But soon Albert could be seen lurching about the hospital, cheering the other patients with his broad, infectious smile. I remember a day Donn and I walked into our little patient's room. Hobbling to the dresser drawer, where he kept his cache of treasures, Albert produced candy bars and insisted on sharing them with us. And Albert loved chocolate!

Thrilled by his son's recovery and his newfound faith, Shomar wanted to serve God with his music. We arranged at Malumghat the first concert he gave as a true follower of Christ. His performance was spellbinding and stirred our hearts deeply.

When Albert's walking improved sufficiently, we wrote the discharge order. On that joyous day, the hospital staff waved goodbye to the Dass family as they departed for their home in Dacca.

Shortly after his return to Dacca, Shomar Dass arranged an appointment with the prime minister. More orderly than the previous one, the meeting was nevertheless equally emotional. This time the tears were tears of happiness, however, and Shomar Dass suffered no stage fright. He related rapid-fire details about the life-saving helicopter trip, the difficult decision to delay surgery, initiation of the medical treatment, the breathless wait for signs of improvement, and finally, the indescribable joy of Albert's first word, first step, first chocolate bar.

"Sir," Shomar said to Sheikh Mujib, "at that hospital everything is mixed with prayers. The church people helped us in every way — and they prayed. The nurses worked long hours lovingly caring for Albert — then they prayed. Dr. Olsen and Dr. Ketcham treated Albert skillfully — and they prayed, as well. God answered and guided the doctors to delay the operation and give the correct medicine. God heard all our prayers and made the treatment work. And now, how can I give you enough thanks for your personal helicopter which made it all possible?"

His Excellency Sheikh Mujibur Rahman, architect of Bangladesh, father of the nation, leader of 75 million people, beamed his delight at the recovery of the little boy.

"Shomar," he said, "that's good, very good. I'm happy I could give you the helicopter to take Albert to the hospital."

Then, softly the prime minister said, "Remember my promise, Shomar? I, too, prayed for your son."

When Shomar related to me Mujib's words, I was very moved. Daily the prime minister worked to bring order out of the incredible chaos of his war-shattered country, the world's eighth most populous nation. *Yet amid all the complicated affairs of state,* I reflected, *his heart is open to the needs of individuals. That's the kind of man he is.*

Jeanette Lockerbie with Dr. Olsen in Bangladesh

During this period a friend came to visit me, her daughter Jeannie, and the rest of the ABWE team — Mrs. Jeanette Lockerbie! When she heard of Albert's remarkable progress, she visited the Dass family in their hospital room. Delighted by reports of the Bangladesh Brigade's progress, she rode in the high cabs of huge, lumbering M-35 trucks and accompanied me on bone-jarring jeep rides to see the men in action at the building sites. Her visit was a bright spot for us all.

*   *   *

The ashes of war had barely cooled in Bangladesh in April of 1972, when I journeyed there. Ships were still upended in the strategic harbor of Chittagong. Bullet holes in buildings and burned out ruins told a grim story. Bones picked clean by vultures and publicly visible skulls were evidence of the recent horror. But everywhere there was a feeling of new beginnings for the long-exploited Bengali people.

My daughter had come part way to meet me, but it was impossible for me to travel from Dacca to Chittagong with her and her companion. Bangladesh Airlines (Bangladesh Biman) boasted only two commercial aircraft and long lines of waiting passengers. But with seventy-five million people in Bangladesh, I unexpectedly encountered Dr. Donn Ketcham in the airport. He waited with me and undoubtedly was an influence in my getting a plane bound for Chittagong that same day.

I was driven by Dr. Ketcham from Chittagong to the hospital at Malumghat. The sixty-five miles was almost a four-hour trip, jarring my orientation to the Los Angeles freeways where the same distance takes barely one hour. Goats, cows, chickens, a wedding procession carrying the groom in a decorated carriage, army vehicles, buses that dare anything to hit them, bicycle rickshas, village markets along the edges, and milling crowds kept us inching the sixty-five miles.

It was dusk when we pulled under the arch that proclaims Memorial Christian Hospital and drove into the staff housing area. From among the many — some of them old and beloved friends — who came to meet the car, a tall figure stepped toward me. My glib "Dr. Livingstone, I presume?" and the quick "No — Dr. Olsen" spanned the years as we greeted each other warmly.

My visit to Memorial Christian Hospital was an unforgettable experience. I learned much about the role the hospital had played in the recent war. I saw a unique ministry, in which four major religions could be found in a single hospital ward.

My tour began in the men's ward. On the right, as we entered, we saw a patient with a crippling disease. Through my interpreter, he shared something about himself.

"I am Hindu," he told us. "I have been here for twenty-five days, and everyone is most kind. I have been in this fine hospital twice before, and I am soon going home to my village which is forty miles away."

A partly curious, partly inviting glance drew us to the bedside of Mr. Hafez. Through my interpreter he was quick to explain that he was of the Muslim faith, but that in this Christian hospital, the Christians treated everyone alike.

"All care has already been given," he stated, "and today traction will be removed. Slowly I will walk on crutches. My great cause for anxiety is all gone." He looked thoughtful as he added, "The doctors and nurses treat me not only with themselves, but with prayer. There is something very nice about everyone here."

At the far end of the ward a patient sitting on the edge of the bed beckoned us. He had a treasure to display! This patient, Mr. Pha Phrue, waxed eloquent over the expertise of Dr. Donn Ketcham; then he reached under his pillow to produce proof — a meticulously wrapped item which he described as a bladder stone. When this had been duly commented upon, he rewrapped it in cotton and then in waxed paper and buried it under his pillow, assuring us, "I will preserve this carefully."

As had the others, this patient expressed his satisfaction with the "behaviors" of all the staff.

"I am Buddhist," he explained, "and some here are Muslim and many are Hindu. In this Christian hospital all peoples are treated like brothers. Not me only," he emphasized, "but all patients are treated by doctors like a son by his father."

And then we came to Mr. Shuki in his corner bed.

Shuki *means* "happy," we were told. And that he appeared to be! He had been in Memorial Christian Hospital for a year and four months for a series of operations on his right thigh and left knee.

Quite on his own he eagerly shared his philosophy and his faith.

"It is the willingness of God that I am here, that I have suffering. I have been long time a true believer, since 1967. God put me here to get more in touch with Him, and I have accepted His will."

The mention of Dr. Olsen's name brought a glow to his face.

"It was 1967, and I was a patient in this hospital. Someone from the staff had given me a tract to read. I was reading it at the place of John 3:16 when Dr. Olsen came on regular rounds of the patients. He sat down and talked with me for fifteen minutes. He showed me what John 3:16 means and taught me how I could become a true believer." Shuki quoted his favorite Bible verse in Bengali, then listened intrigued as I quoted it in English.

Outside the hospital on the hillside was a scene reminiscent of the gospel accounts — a multitude of hungry people. From dusk the evening before, they had been converging from villages around, trudging many miles in order to get their weekly supply of relief food.

Sitting with my interpreter in the shade of the bamboo shelter from which supplies were being distributed, I heard stories of heartache and tragedy. Homes burned down, men hunted and hounded into the jungle. One man, the leading Hindu of the district, described the aid given by Drs. Olsen and Ketcham during the blackest days, in these words, "What they did for us was oxygen to suffocating men."

Some Bengalis who fill important positions in ABWE's ministry in Bangladesh can trace their involvement to a desire to find reading material in English. Shantosh, translator and language teacher, first came to sit and read the books and magazines at the bookroom in Chittagong. When the young Hindu learned the missionaries needed a language teacher, he took the job. He helped translate the gospels and other material for evangelism.

"During the disturbance in this country," Shantosh says, "I worked very closely with Dr. Olsen and he helped me a great deal with my family. In fact, but for Dr. Olsen they would have been killed."

"Dr. Olsen also helped me when the military was killing Hindu boys and men like me; he personally went to the military and informed them that we had not taken part in any political or military activity. So they believed his word and promised they would not hurt any of us Hindu people. This is just one of the things he has done for my people."

Since my primary purpose in visiting this new land of Bangladesh at that time was to work with Dr. Olsen on this book, it was vital that I spend time with him. Yet his tightly packed schedule in supervising his brigade of college students ruled out all but a few strictly literary sessions. But we licked the problem; I rode along in the jeep as the doctor went from place to place. Sometimes we met up with a team of students and listened to their eager reports and their requests for building materials. Frequently he went to the bamboo markets along the river banks. I stood on a sandy beach under a sun that shot the thermometer up to 128 degrees one day. Taller by far than anyone else, Vic bargained in native style for the mammoth supplies of bamboo poles and sun grass for the thatched-roof homes.

Our jeep frequently was stopped and surrounded as people spotted the daktar sahib. Broad smiles lit up the faces, and hands stretched out eagerly to shake the doctor's hand.

Later in the home of the leading Muslim of the district, Mr. Fazlul Karim Choudhury, his son Shahabuddin named one after another of the hospital staff, speaking of them in glowing terms.

"Not only do I say these things," he assured me, "but also all over Bangladesh it is said."

Mr. Choudhury, himself a much decorated man for his compassionate service to his people, said with quiet intensity, "I have met many great people in my lifetime; presidents, governors, and other high officials. But in all my eighty-eight years I have never met such a good man as Dr. Olsen."

24

Visa # 001

THE MONUMENT before me was stark, powerful. Acres of grassy parkland surrounded it, and in the distance I could see the great stone Indian parliament buildings, two of New Delhi's grandest structures. Overshadowed by the massive, brooding Arch of India, the monument itself was strikingly simple — a rifle with fixed bayonet stuck downward in a block of granite and an empty steel helmet atop the rifle butt. A military honor guard and flickering eternal flames to the right and left of the monument kept their constant vigil.

War memorial in New Delhi

I asked the relief guard, who was at ease, "What does this rifle mean?"

He answered in broken English, "It means that our people are able to remember the *jawans* who died in Bangladesh."

His explanation made clear that I was viewing the war memorial to the Indian young men in uniform who had given their life's blood on Bangladesh soil to save and liberate my Bengali brothers. Deeply moved, I thought instantly of another young man who had come from His celestial home nineteen centuries ago to pour out His life's blood on the alien soil of planet earth, not just for Bengalis, but for me and for every other member of the human race.

As I surveyed the steel helmet, steel rifle barrel, and steel bayonet, I remembered the cruel military oppression and slavery of the Bengali people — the dying and running away of multiplied millions of them — their impotence to save or liberate themselves — India, stepping in to defeat the enemy and liberate the Bengalis — finally, the bloody birth of Bangladesh.

I saw that this series of events remarkably portrayed my own spiritual development. I, too, had been oppressed and enslaved, not by a barbarous army, but by selfish, hurtful instincts and forces of spiritual darkness. I, too, was impotent to liberate myself from those oppressive impulses and forces. Like the Bengalis I was dead and running — spiritually dead and running from reality. Then, just as India launched her army into Bangladesh to liberate the nation, so God had invaded my life to save and liberate me. And, as Bangladesh gladly accepted the proffered help, I, too, had accepted God's help by receiving His Son. The birth of Bangladesh by a stroke of the pen on the surrender document portrayed that deep, inner spiritual rebirth that I had experienced the instant I believed some two decades earlier. "Thank You, Father!"

On June 13, 1972, the day after my arrival in America following the Bangladesh Brigade project, I returned to the familiar building on Connecticut Avenue in Washington, D.C. The old nameplate reading "Bangladesh Mission" was gone. In its place I saw inscribed upon a new nameplate the words "Bangladesh Embassy." Inside, my friend, Ambassador Enayet Karim, graciously presented to me the visa promised me by his predecessor — Bangladesh visa number 001! As he handed me the visa, he again expressed his appreciation for our work in Bangladesh. The ceremony was simple, but warm and meaningful to both of us. I conveyed a verbal message to him from Minister Siddiqi and shared my impressions of the progress in Bangladesh, then took my leave.

Three months later on Sunday, September 17, 1972, ten months after the birth of Bangladesh, a church was born — the first church in the history of the world to be established in southern Chittagong District! Although Malumghat Christians had worshiped together

Ambassador Enayet Karim presents visa 001 to Dr. Olsen

and functioned as a church group since the inception of the hospital project, it took time for the national Christian group to grow and prepare its constitution and other church documents in Bengali. I remember now the many hours I spent working on those documents and the months I devoted to leading the church group. Although all of our mission team members played significant roles in the development and establishment of the church, Mel Beals and Jay Walsh were especially involved; Mel guided the final stages of development.

The newly constituted, independent, indigenous church promptly selected its Bengali leaders and conducted the first communion service. Other groups of Christians, nuclei of future churches, now meet regularly at several other points in southern Chittagong District. Christians, Christianity, and Christian truth have come into the great "Christian vacuum" area between the circles of influence of William Carey and Adoniram Judson!

The new church and the new nation will face myriad problems as they press forward to gain maturity, stability, and stature. Those who make up the church are exuberant that their Bangladesh has achieved freedom and nationhood — for they are Bengalis. Also as Christians, they — and we American Christians — hail many steps taken by Sheikh Mujib and his government. The Bangladesh government —

1. is granting us visas freely;
2. has added, to the daily radio reading of the Koran, readings from the Bible and other holy books;
3. has replaced Friday (the day of Muslim worship) with Sunday as the weekly business holiday;
4. has discarded the previous Islamic republic system of government in favor of a modern secular nation in which separation of mosque and state prevail;
5. has established a parliamentary democracy which allows the people to change an unwanted government through the ballot box;
6. has instituted a constitution providing full freedom of religion (including the right of. the individual "to profess, practice, or propagate any religion" and the right of every religious community or denomination "to establish, maintain and manage its religious institutions."[1]

As I contemplate now the possibilities for the future, in light of the life-revolutionizing events of the past years, the thought returns, *it's great to be a Christian!*

It's great to be a Christian caught up in the joy of God's personal plan!

It's great to be a Christian called to serve in Bangladesh!

Appendix A

FINDING GOD'S WILL AND HIS PERSONAL PLAN

The fact that God, the Creator of this immense universe, cares about each of us, wants to guide us along life's pathway, and has a personal plan for each of our lives is one of the most inspiring ideas the human mind could contemplate. The Christian Scriptures make clear that the idea is factual. Those who write or speak about this concept use various terms to express it: understanding God's will, discovering God's direction, detecting God's desire, learning God's leading, gaining God's guidance, perceiving God's plan.

"That sounds great! I want it," you say, "but how do I find it?" First prepare yourself! There are four preparatory steps or prerequisites stated or implied in a classical New Testament passage, Romans 12:1, 2 (Berkeley, italics added):

> I beg you, therefore, *brothers,* in view of God's mercies, that you *present your bodies* a living sacrifice, holy and acceptable to God, which is your reasonable service. And *do not conform* to the present world system, but *be transformed* by the renewing of your mind, so as to sense for yourselves what is that good and acceptable and perfect will of God.

The four prerequisites for perceiving God's plan are:

1. *Salvation.* Make the great faith decision, accepting Christ into your own life as the Saviour He came to be.
2. *Dedication.* Present (give, yield, dedicate) yourself completely to God, telling Him that you are fully His, that you will do anything He asks and go anywhere He sends you.
3. *Separation.* Clean up your life. Separate yourself from the wrong and evil things in this world. They will obstruct your ability to gain God's guidance.
4. *Transformation.* Daily study the Scriptures and talk to God to keep yourself growing, maturing, and changing for the better.

Divine guidance is essentially a matter of God applying inner impressions on your mind. He gives you peace of mind when you decide correctly and remain on the track. When you decide wrongly, get off the track, or when it is time for the next step in your program, He withholds or withdraws this peace of mind. The Father's plan is not like a blueprint laid out on a drawing board with every detail visible at one glance. God's plan for you, rather, is like a scroll which reveals His will bit by bit as the scroll is unrolled. Unrolling your scroll completely will take a lifetime.

The four steps in discovering God's will are: 1) erase and pray, 2) read and remember, 3) consider and think, 4) decide and check.

1. *Erase and pray.* Make a conscious mental effort to erase your own desire as though you were erasing a blackboard clean, so that God can imprint upon your mental chalkboard His will and plan for you. Then pray, asking God to finish the erasing process (especially in the subconscious part of your mind which is so hard to reach), guide you, reveal His plan to you, and give you wisdom to decide correctly.

2. *Read and remember.* Read pertinent portions of the Scripture, for God already has revealed His will about hundreds of subjects. Obtain a topical concordance so that you can quickly and easily find Bible passages which deal with the subject at hand. Even if the Scripture does not speak directly to the decision before you, remember the great principles of God's Word which apply to many decisions, and ask yourself these questions:

   A. Could I do this in Christ's name? (Col 3:17).
   B. Can I imagine Jesus doing this or deciding this way? (1 Jn 2:6).
   C. Will this action bring any glory to God? (1 Co 10:31).
   D. Would I want to be found doing this when the Lord returns? (1 Jn 2:28).
   E. Will this action bring impurity or useless harm to my body, which is the temple of God's Spirit? (1 Co 6:19, 20).
   F. Will this activity be a hindrance which will hamper my spiritual progress? (Heb 12:1).
   G. Will my following this decision offend another Christian, cause him to stumble, or make him weak? (Ro 14:21).
   H. Will this action be a help or a hindrance to non-Christians around me? (Mt 5:16).

3. *Consider and think.* Consider the ways that are open before you, the available options. Write them down, then consider them more carefully one by one. Consider, too, the circumstances surrounding you and your decision; the circumstances sometimes point

clearly in a certain direction. Do not hesitate to consider also the advice of mature Christian friends or parents (they know you so well). Think and meditate over all aspects of the question at hand. If many factors are involved, draw a line down a piece of paper and list the factors pro and con. Prayerfully meditate over your list until the decisive factors become clear.

4. *Decide and check.* Don't let the matter ride indefinitely and miss God's guidance by default. Decide! Check for peace of mind. If you decide correctly regarding God's will or plan for you, He signals you, "Correct decision there," by a wonderful sense of inner peace. If you have decided wrongly, the peace of mind will not come. And what if peace does not come? Then you must return to step number one and start all over again. The trouble usually lies right there — you never really erased your own will in the first place.

In matters large and small I have found this approach to knowing God's will and finding His personal plan practical and successful.

Appendix B

BASIC PRINCIPLES OF MEDICAL MISSIONS

1. Only high caliber, compassionate medical work is worthy to represent the Lord.
2. Because "black bag" and clinic treatments fail to heal many patients, a hospital is a desirable beginning.
3. The site for a new hospital must be chosen with great care.
4. Two or more doctors are necessary to provide continuity of medical care.
5. The doctors should study tropical diseases before beginning a practice in the tropics.
6. The doctors and nurses must have adequate time for protected and uninterrupted language study.
7. At least one of the Home Board members should be a Christian physician.
8. Nonmedical missionaries should be appointed to the hospital to share in the administrative and spiritual work.
9. Nationals should receive training in medical-spiritual work.
10. A hospital in a poor area cannot be expected to be completely self-supporting, or charges will be excessive and the poor neglected in favor of the wealthy.
11. The medical work must be geared to spiritual sharing and spiritual healing.
12. Christian believers must be helped, baptized, loved, strengthened, and incorporated into an indigenous church.
13. The medical staff must have spiritual strength and stamina, plus an intimate walk with God so that the highest spiritual standards are maintained.

(Adapted from Dr. V. B. Olsen's policy statement
presented April 15, 1959)

NOTES

CHAPTER 6

1. American Scientific Affiliation, *Modern Science and Christian Faith* (Wheaton, Ill.: Van Kampen, 1948).
2. Henry M. Morris, *The Bible and Modern Science* (Chicago: Moody, 1951, 1968).
3. Irwin H. Linton, *A Lawyer Examines the Bible* (Grand Rapids: Baker Bk., 1943).
4. Linton, p. 36.
5. Simon Greenleaf, *The Testimony of the Evangelists* (Grand Rapids: Baker Bk., 1965).
6. Ibid., pp. 47, 50, 51, 52.
7. Ibid., pp. 28-29.
8. Morris, p. 95.
9. Blaise Pascal, "Of the Necessity of the Wager," *Great Books of the Western World,* 54 vols. (Chicago: Encyclopaedia Britannica, 1952), Vol. 33, p. 217.

CHAPTER 12

1. "The Peaceful Mrus of Bangladesh," *National Geographic,* Vol. 143, no. 2, Feb., 1973, pp. 267-86.

CHAPTER 13

1. Mohammed Ayub Khan, *Friends Not Masters: A Political Autobiography* (New York: Oxford U. Pr., 1967), p. 1.

CHAPTER 16

1. K. A. Kamal, *Sheikh Mujibur Rahman and Birth of Bangladesh* (Dacca: Shainpukur Art Press, 1972), p. 109.

CHAPTER 17

1. *Bangladesh: Contemporary Events and Documents* (Bangladesh: Ministry of Foreign Affairs, External Publicity Division, 1971), pp. 37-41.

CHAPTER 19

1. Prabodh Chandra, *Bloodbath in Bangladesh* (New Delhi, India: Adarsh Publ., 1971), p. 120.
2. Ibid., p. 122.
3. *Bangladesh: Contemporary Events and Documents,* pp. 84-86.
4. Chandra, p. 123.
5. Ibid., pp. 124-25; *Bangladesh: . . . Documents,* pp. 88-90.
6. *Bangladesh: . . . Documents,* pp. 90-93.
7. Ibid., pp. 93-99.
8. "Jinnah's Fading Dream," *Time,* March 15, 1971, p. 31.
9. *Bangladesh: . . . Documents,* pp. 99-102.
10. Ajit Bhattacharjea, *Dateline Bangladesh* (Bombay, India: Jaico Pub. House, 1971), p. 218.
11. Anthony Mascarenhas, *The Rape of Bangladesh* (London: Vikas Publ., 1971), pp. 4-5.
12. Chandra, p. 5.
13. Kamal, *Sheikh Mujibur Rahman and the Birth of Bangladesh,* pp. 193-94.
14. Chandra, pp. 133, 135.
15. *Bangladesh: . . . Documents,* pp. 107-111.
16. Pran Chopra, *The Challenge of Bangladesh* (Bombay, India: Popular Prakashan Press, 1971), pp. 61-62.

CHAPTER 20

1. *Bangladesh: Contemporary Events and Documents,* p. 107.
2. Ibid., pp. 114-19.
3. Bhattacharjea, *Dateline Bangladesh,* pp. 13, 179.
4. Jeannie Lockerbie, *On Duty in Bangladesh* (Grand Rapids: Zondervan, 1973).
5. Kamal, *Sheikh Mujibur Rahman and the Birth of Bangladesh,* p. 195.
6. D. R. Mankekar, *Pakistan Cut to Size* (New Delhi, India: Indian Bk. Co. 1972), p. 32.
7. Ibid., p. 36.
8. D. K. Palit, *The Lightning Campaign — Indo-Pakistan War 1971* (New Delhi, India: Thompson Press, 1972), pp. 101-102.
9. Mankekar, p. 36.
10. Palit, p. 134.
11. Fazlul Quader Quaderi, *Bangladesh Genocide and the World Press* (Dacca, Bangladesh: Alexandra Press, 1972), p. 296.

CHAPTER 21

1. *Relief Problems in Bangladesh, Hearing Before the Subcommittee to Investigate Problems Connected with Refugees and Escapees of the Committee on the Judiciary, United States Senate, Ninety-second Congress, February 2, 1972* (Washington: Government Printing Office, 1972).

CHAPTER 24

1. *The Constitution of the People's Republic of Bangladesh* (Dacca: Gov. of Bangladesh, 1972), p. 13.

ACKNOWLEDGEMENTS

I owe a particular debt of gratitude to my wife, Joan, who spent hundreds of hours wisely advising and helping me; my collaborator, Jeanette Lockerbie, who first suggested that this book be written, traveled to Bangladesh to further the effort, and gave valuable counsel during the writing; and my typist, Lillian Smith, who, despite her busy life as wife and mother, sacrificially devoted huge blocks of time promptly.

How I have enjoyed working with Moody Press! The editorial, production, advertising, and sales staffs have advised well and shown every courtesy.

I am thankful for my ABWE colleagues in Bangladesh who encouraged me in the writing of this book and made valuable suggestions.

I am grateful, too, for encouragement by the Reverend Wendell Kempton, President of ABWE, and Dr. Raymond Knighton, President of MAP.

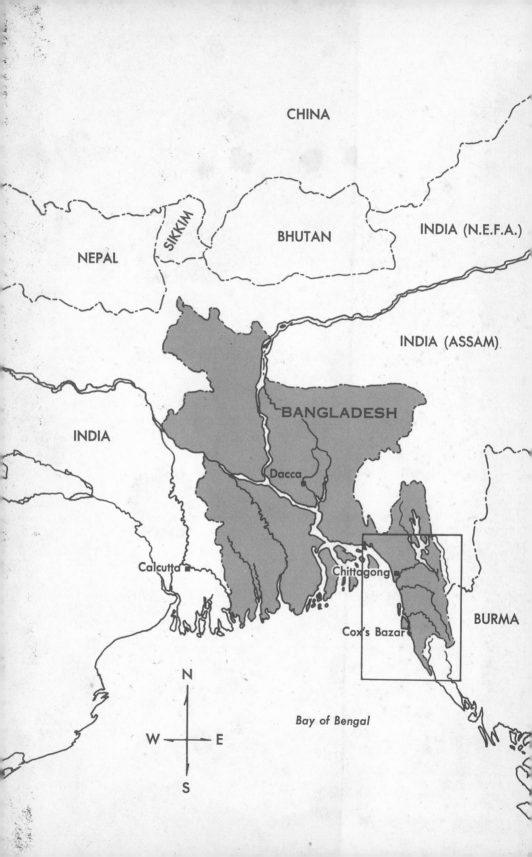